INTRODUCTION

HE SCARCITY OF MARRIAGE RECORDS for South Carolina has been a real stumblingblock for genealogists. The current marriage license law did not go into effect until 1911. Marriage records prior to that year are difficult to locate. In the colonial period marriages could be performed by license, issued by the Ordinary of the Province, or by the publication of banns in the parish church. This system worked fairly well for the coastal parishes of South Carolina. Unfortunately, there was no systematic procedure for recording the licenses issued. For consistent documentation we must rely on the seven extant parish registers. The percentage of those extant is not great, considering that there were twenty-one parishes in South Carolina in the colonial period. Marriage bonds were also issued, but only two volumes of these have been found. One solitary record of marriage licenses issued is extant, and although it is very spotty it is included here.

For areas other than coastal South Carolina marriage records are practically non-existent. People in these areas were likely married by the local minister or a minor official. However, records of churches other than the Church of England have been located in a few instances, along with some ministers' journals. Marriage settlements, pre-marital or occasionally post-marital agreements, do exist from a very early date, but for the period before 1800 they are largely for the coastal area of South Carolina. Before an act was passed specifically requiring the recording of marriage settlements in a separate series, such records are found in the Miscellaneous Records of South Carolina. The scant sources we have for marriages in upper South Carolina consist of a few legal records in the counties and a small number of church records.

Newspapers have not been used for this compilation, as marriage notices recorded there are largely published and easily accessible. Marriage references found in deeds, wills, or court cases have not been included either. The records included here are those which indicate at least an approximate date or definite time period. For some marriages more than one record is extant, as in the case of a marriage settlement and a church record. The researcher should not be confused by conflicting dates, remembering that settlements were pre- or post-marital agreements.

The Church of England was *supposed* to record marriages as well as other vital data for all residents of the parish, whether they were members of that faith or not. While this was not done consistently, it was done often enough to make note of here. Also, the same marriage might be recorded in more than one parish register, indicating that the parties were from different parishes. The researcher should note that many of the sources used here also contain records of marriages performed after 1799, and some contain other records on the same families, particularly church records. The abbreviations of the sources used, and their locations, are given below.

Bush R QM	Bush River Monthly Meeting Minutes. Originals in the Quaker Collection, Guilford College, Greensboro, North Carolina. Published in Hinshaw's *Encyclopedia of American Quaker Genealogy*.
Camden Dist WB	Camden District Will Book. Also known as Kershaw County Will Book A-1. Original in Kershaw County Court House, Camden, S. C. Microfilm copy available at S. C. Archives.
Cane Cr MM	Cane Creek Monthly Meeting Minutes. Originals in the Quaker Collection, as above. Published in Hinshaw as above.
Ch Ch PR	Christ Church Parish Register. Published in *The South Carolina Historical and Genealogical Magazine (SCH&G)*.
Charleston MM	Charleston Monthly Meeting Minutes. Originals in the Quaker Collection as above. Published in Hinshaw as above.
Chest Ct Min	Chester County, Minutes of the County Court. Originals in Chester County Court House, Chester, S. C. Film copy available at S. C. Archives. Published in *Chester County, South Carolina, Minutes of the County Court 1785-1799*, by Holcomb & Parker.
Circ Cong	Records of the Circular Congregational Church, Charleston, S. C. Published in *SCH&G*.
Fairf Pres Ch	Minutes of the Session of Fairforest Presbyterian Church, Union County, S. C. Originals in the Historical Foundation of the Presbyterian and Reformed Churches, Montreat, N. C.

Hist Oburg	Giessendanner records, published in *The History of Orangeburg County, South Carolina*, by A. S. Salley.
Lanc DB	Lancaster Deed Book. Original in Lancaster County Court House, Lancaster, S. C. Microfilm at S. C. Archives.
Mar Set	Marriage Settlements (followed by volume and page number). A series in S. C. Archives.
Marlboro Co.	Marriage licenses issued by the probate judge of Marlboro County, S. C., found in various probate books. Originals in Marlboro County Court House, Bennettsville, S. C. Microfilm copy at S. C. Archives. Published in the *National Genealogical Society Quarterly*.
MB Chas	Marriage Bonds. An original volume in the Charleston Library Society, Charleston, S. C. Published in *SCH&G*.
MB NY	Marriage Bonds. An original volume in The New-York Historical Society. Published in the *National Genealogical Society Quarterly*.
Misc Rec	Miscellaneous Records (followed by volume and page numbers). A series in the S. C. Archives.
Moses Waddell	Register of Marriages performed by Rev. Moses Waddell, a Presbyterian minister in the Pendleton County area of S. C. Original at the Historical Foundation of the Presbyterian and Reformed Churches, Montreat, North Carolina.
96 OJ	Ninety Six District, Journal of the Ordinary. Also referred to as Pat Calhoun's Surrogate Court book. Original in Abbeville County Court House, Abbeville, S. C. Published by Southern Historical Press as a separate volume.
OJ 1764-1771	Journal of the Ordinary of the Province of South Carolina 1764-1771. Original in S. C. Archives. Published in *Probate Records of South Carolina*, Volume 3, by Brent H. Holcomb.
Pr Fred PR	Prince Frederick Parish Register. Published as a separate volume.

Pugh diary	Marriages from the diary of Evan Pugh, a Baptist minister in the Pee Dee section of S. C. Photostatic copies of the original in the Manuscript Division, South Caroliniana Library, University of South Carolina, Columbia, S. C.
Pvt Papers	Private papers of the Governor. At S. C. Archives.
Reg Prov	Books of the Register of the Province. A series at S. C. Archives.
Sec Prov	Books of the Secretary of the Province. A series at S. C. Archives.
SPG	Papers of the Society for the Propagation of the Gospel in Foreign Parts. Microfilm at S. C. Archives.
St And PR	St. Andrews Parish Register. Published in *SCH&G.*
St Hel PR	St. Helenas Parish Register. Published in *SCH&G.*
St Jas PR	St. James Santee Parish Register. Published in *SCH&G.*
St John Luth Ch	Records of St. John's Lutheran Church, Charleston, S. C. Microfilm at S. C. Archives.
St Math Luth Ch	Records of St. Matthew's Lutheran Church, St. Matthew's, S. C. Originals at South Caroliniana Library, University of South Carolina, Columbia, S. C. Published in *The South Carolina Magazine of Ancestral Research.*
St Michaels Luth Ch	Records of St. Michaels Lutheran Church, Irmo, S. C. Published in *The South Carolina Magazine of Ancestral Research.*
St Phil PR	St. Philip's Parish Register. Published separately (two volumes).
Stoney Creek Pres Ch	Records of Stoney Creek Independent or Presbyterian Church, Beaufort District, S. C. Originals at the Historical Foundation of the Presbyterian and Reformed Churches, Montreat, N. C. Microfilm at S. C. Archives.

T & D PR	Parish Register of St. Thomas and St. Denis. Published by the Genealogical Publishing Company, Baltimore.
Trin Meth Ch	Records of Trinity Methodist Church, Charleston, S. C. Originals at the church.
York Pro	York County, S. C., Probate Records. Originals in the York County Court House, York, S. C. (followed by box and file number).

My thanks to Mr. Charles W. Nicholson for translating the records of St. John's Lutheran Church from the German. The inclusion of the Marriage Bonds in The New-York Historical Society are courtesy of The New-York Historical Society, New York City. My thanks also to Rev. J. Richard McAlister and Trinity Methodist Church, Charleston, for permission to include marriages from their records. My thanks as well to the owners of the Evan Pugh diary for permission to include marriages found therein: Kathryn Willcox Patterson, John M. Willcox, and T. L. Willcox.

BRENT H. HOLCOMB, C. A. L. S.
Columbia, South Carolina

_____ & Mary Dargan, 27 July 1784.   Pugh diary

_____, Christian & Margaret Meysterin(?), widow, 27 June 1773. St. John Luth Ch

_____, Johann & Anna Maria Nunneman(?), 15 Feb. 1782. St. John Luth Ch

_____, Johann & Christian Kaufmann(in), widow, 2 July 1771. St. John Luth Ch

_____, Philipp & Maria Braun(in), 11 May 1769. St. John Luth Ch

_____, Reinhard, baker & Magdalena, daughter of Matthes Rose, 24 Sept. 1771.   St. John Luth Ch

_____ & Mary Lanson, 11 Dec. 1771. St. John Luth Ch

_____ & Elisabetha Diefenbach(in), 5 July 1772. St. John Luth Ch

_____ & Amy Walker, 31 Jan 1748/9.   Pr Fred PR

_____ John & Miss Nessa Wolf, 1738[?].   Hist Oburg

Abbot, David & Katherine Hall, 3 February 1722/23. St Phil PR

Abbot, John & Elizabeth Houce, P Licence, 1 February 1744/5. St Phil PR

Abbot, William & Catherine Hope, P Licence by the Revd. Mr. Alexr. Garden, 16 October 1747. St. Phil PR

Abecklin, Kilian & Maria Schwartz, 12 Jan. 1741; Hans Freydigs, Christian Schwartz, wit.   Hist Oburg

Abercrombie, John & Sarah Mitchell, widow, 4 Jan. 1777. St. Phil PR

Aberle, Fridrich, Carpenter & Christian Schwintrigsheim, 28 March 1776.   St. John Luth Ch

Abraham, James & Sally Allgent, 14 Feb. 1773. St. John Luth Ch

Ackarman, Albert & Sarah Walker, 30 Apr. 1752. St. Hel PR

Acorn, Thomas of Charleston, shopkeeper & Eleanor Frazier of same, widow, 15 Nov. 1785; Thomas Roper, trustee. Mar Set 1: 307-310

Actkin, John & Elizabeth Wilson, 22 Jan. 1770. St. Phil PR

Adair, William & Hannah Black, widow, 22 Aug. 1761. St. Phil PR

Adams, David & Anne Jenkins, P Licence, 6 December 1739. St. Phil PR

1

Adams, David, widower & Catharine Grimball, 1 Feb. 1753.
   St. Hel PR

Adams, David & Elizabeth Ellis, (before 1784).   St. Hel PR

Adams, James S. Revd. & Eliza Ann Smith at Beechhill, 26 Feb.
   1799.   Circ Cong

Adams, John & Mary Wilkinson, 6 Dec. 1787.   St. Hel PR

Adams, John & Mary You, 25 Sept. 1793.   Circ Cong

Adams, Nathaniel & Mary Capers, 14 Aug. 1740.   St. Hel PR

Adams, Nathaniel of Parish of St. Helena, planter & Margret
   Ellis, spinster, 30 Aug. 1774; license to Rev. Lewis Jones,
   Christopher Poor, planter, bondsman.   MB Chas

Adams, Nathaniel, widower & Margaret Ellis, 6 Sept. 1744.
   St. Hel PR

Adams, William & Elizabeth Fendin, 29 Dec. 1739.   St. Hel PR

Addenton, John, son of Henry & Sarah and Elizabeth Heaton,
   3 May 1775.   Bush R QM

Addis, George & Bethia Beesley, P Licence, 21 May 1745.
   St. Phil PR

Addison, Joseph & Elizth. Smith, 13 May 1793.   Circ Cong

Adinger, Johannes & Sarah Grossman, 13 July 1779.
   St. John Luth Ch

Adler, Stolbert & Ann Rodgamon, 3 May 1778.   St. Phil PR

Agelton, John & Ann Parker, widow, 3 Apr. 1765.   St. Phil PR

Aggnew, Andrew & Mary Albergotti, 17 Dec. 1752.   St. Hel PR

Aggnew, Andrew, widower & Mary Williams, 8 Nov. 1762.
   St. Hel PR

Aggnew, Andrew, widower & Mary Nelson, 2 Nov. 1777.   St. Hel PR

Air, Charles James & Amarintha Walters Gibbs, daughter of John
   Walters Gibbs, decd. & Amarintha Gibbs, 7 Dec. 1795; Thomas
   Corbett, Daniel Jenkins, Thomas Screven, trustees; Charles
   O. Screven, Thomas Screven Junr., wit.   Mar set 2: 465-472

Air, James & Elizabeth Legare, 8 Apr. 1777.   St. Phil PR

Akerman, Richard & Mary Brown, P Licence, 9 November 1743.
   St. Phil PR

Akin, James & Sarah Bremar, P Licence, 10 Dec. 1741.   St Phil PR

Akin, Thomas & Ann Christie, 18 Feb. 1768.   St. Phil PR

Akins, James & Ann DeVeaux, 2 June 1764.   T & D PR

Akins, James & Ann Deveaux, 2 June 1764.   St. Phil PR

2

SOUTH CAROLINA MARRIAGES 1688-1799

Akles, John & Margery Jordan, P Licence, 3 Nov. 1741.
St. Phil PR

Akon, Thomas & Mary Cameron, widow, 19 Sept. 1779. St. Phil PR

Albergotti, Anthony & Amy Reynolds, 28 Mar. 1757. St. Hel PR

Albergotti, Anthony Junr. & Rebecca Iten, 5 Aug. 1764.
St. Hel PR

Alder, Conrad & Mrs. Anna Burgin, widow of Henry Rickenbaker,
1 Jan. 1740. Hist Oburg

Aldridge, John & Rachel Laywood, P Licence, 16 Feb. 1733.
St. Phil PR

Aldridge, Robert & Jane Hadding, 12 Mar. 1758. St. Phil PR

Alexander, Alexander & Rachel Anderson, 22 Oct. 1767.
St. Phil PR

Alexander, Alexander & Elizabeth Murray, 6 Feb. 1774.
St. Phil PR

Alexander, Andrew & Susannah McKallope, widow, 14 Sept. 1786.
St. Hel PR

Alexander, David of Charles Town, cordwainer, & Mary Wood of
Parish of St. James Goose Creek, spinster, 12 June 1756;
John Wood, planter & Joseph Black, Bricklayer, trustees;
Rachel Wood, Nancy Boswood, wit. Misc. Rec. LL: 511-513

Alexander, David & Mary White, 10 Apr. 1792. St. Phil PR

Alexander, George & Mary Hannah, 1 Mar. 1798. Trin Meth Ch

Alexander, Nathaniel & Rebecca Elmes, widow, 3 Mar. 1746
[1746/7]. St. And PR

Alexander, William & Deborah Mariner, P Banns, 2 Feb. 1741.
St. Phil PR

Alison, Jacob H. & Margaret Lockwood, 17 Feb. 1795. Circ Cong

Allen, ___ & Miss Elizth Rechon, 13 June 1799. Trin Meth Ch

Allen, David & Mary Mitchel, 14 Feb. 1721. St. Phil PR

Allen, Eleazer & Sarah Rhett, 1 Sept. 1721. St. Phil PR

Allen, George & Mary Balu, 17 Nov. 1735. Circ Cong

Allen, Henry & ___, P Licence, 28 July 1744. St. Phil PR

Allen, Henry of Charles Town, taylor, & Jane Linter, spinster,
28 July 1744; license to Rev. Alex Garden; James Porter,
taylor, bondsman. MB Chas

Allen, Hugh, now of Charleston, mariner & Margaret Hennessy,
relict of Garret Hennessy, 15 Oct. 1771; Denham Fearis,
Patrick Fleming, wit. Misc Rec PP: p. 40-41

Allen, James, of Christ Church Parish, & Susannah Currant,
widow, 18 July 1753. St. Phil PR

3

SOUTH CAROLINA MARRIAGES 1688-1799

Allen, John & Mary Bellamy, P Licence, 6 March 1734.
St. Phil PR

Allen, John & Anne Scott by Licence, 29 April 1740. St Phil PR

Allen, John & Mary Cunningham, 24 Dec. 1770; Dennham Fearis,
Ann Roper, wit.   Misc. Rec. PP: 176-177

Allen, John & Mary Cunningham, 24 Dec. 1770.   St. Phil PR

Allen, Joseph & Mary Akerman, widow, P Licence by A. Garden,
28 April 1747.   St. Phil PR

Allen, Joseph & Mary-Anne Taylor, 18 July 1747. Pr Fred PR

Allen, Thomas & Rebekah Barlow, 31 Jan. 1797.   Circ Cong

Allen, William & Mary Finn, 7 July 1728.   St. Hel PR

Alliems, Thomas & Hannah Smith, widow, 7 Oct. 1758.
St. Phil PR

Allisson, James & Elizabeth Eggerter, 23 March 1785.
St. John Luth Ch

Allston, John Senr., widower, & Sarah Belin, widow, 10 Nov.
1748; Alexr. Keith, Saml. Dupree, wit.   Misc. Rec. HH:
222-223

Allston, Jonas & Esther Browne, 12 March 1775. St. Phil PR

Allston, Josias & Esther Brown, 9 March 1776; William Allston,
Junr. & Hugh Swinton, trustees; Mary Ann Brown, Anthy
Mitchell, wit.   Mar Set I: 213-216

Allston, Thomas of Parish of All Saints, bachelor & Mary
Allston, of Parish of George-town, spinster, in the house
of Capt. John Allston, 21 July 1785; Jnt. Waties, Benjn.
Allston, wit.   St. Jas PR

Allston, William & Mary Motte, 24 Feb. 1791.   St. Phil PR

Alston, Joseph & Margaret Cameron, P Banns, 1 Nov. 1741.
St. Phil PR

Alston, Josias & Hester Simons, 26 May 1752.   T & D PR

Alston, Josias & Anne Proctor, 1 May 1755.   T & D PR

Alston, William & Ann Simons, 21 July 1763.   T & D PR

Alston, William & Rachel Moore, 19 Jan. 1775.   T & D PR

Amos, James & Jane Dobson, widow, 24 June 1759.   St. Phil PR

Amy, Willm. & Rebekah Wainwright, per Licence, 26 Sept. 1745.
St. Phil PR

Ancrum, George & Cath Porcher, 26 Nov. 1769.   St. Phil PR

Anderson, Daniel & Martha Esth'r Dubois, 6 May 1794.   T & D PR

Anderson, David & Mary Judon, 25 Nov. 1756.   T & D PR

4

SOUTH CAROLINA MARRIAGES 1688-1799

Anderson, Hugh & Anne Robinson, P Licence, 28 Mar. 1745.
   St. Phil PR

Anderson, James, bachelor & Anne Lewis, widow, 26 Juen 1783;
   Henry Hughes, Samuel Warren, wit.   St. Jas PR

Anderson, John & Rebecca June, widow, 10 Jan. 1793.   St Phil PR

Anderson, Joseph, bachelor & Elizabeth Fitch, spinster, in the
   house of James Anderson, 21 Feb. 1760; Edward Jerman, Thos
   Spencer, Junr., wit.   St. Jas PR

Anderson, William & Catharine Lane, P Licence, 6 Nov. 1733.
   St. Phil PR

Anding, John & Francis Hirsh, P Licence, 22 June 1749.
   St. Phil PR

Anding, John & Margaret, widow of Rudolph Brunner, both living
   below Orangeburgh Township in Berkly Co., 2 Feb. 1756.
   Hist Oburg

Andley, Erasmus & Martha Gunter, widow, 27 May 1779.
   St. John Luth Ch

Andrews, Israel, widower & Mary Robertson, 28 Apr. 1787.
   St. Hel PR

Andrews, John Revd. & Mary Rothmahler, 16 May 1756. St. Phil PR

Andrews, Robert of SaxaGotha Township, & Mary Carney of Amelia
   Township, 11 July 1750.   Hist Oburg

Andrews, Samuel & Sarah Cellar, widow, 8 May 1772.   St. Phil PR

Anger, Joseph & Annie Miles, 26 July 1764.   St. And PR

Anslett, John & Benedicta Banell, 8 Apr. 1769.   St. Phil PR

Ansley, John & Mary Childs, 18 Jan. 1749.   St. And PR

Antony, Abraham & Margaret Cook, 19 June 1779.   St. Phil PR

Appling, Col. John & Eleanor D. Naylor, 1797.   Moses Waddel

Archer, David & Ann Kolb, 26 Sept. 1793.   Pugh diary

Arden, Edward & Eleanor Forth, P Licence, June 1734.
   St. Phil PR

Ardens, Peter & Susanna Kautzman, 25 Apr. 1785.   St. John Luth
   Ch

Arnold, John & Martha Bee, 28 Feb. 1726.   St. Phil PR

Arnold, John & Mary Haskett, P Licence, 18 July 1729.
   St. Phil PR

Arnold, Philip & Margaret Gardenor, P Licence, 30 Nov. 1729.
   St. Phil PR

Arnoll, John & Lidia Reynolds, 18 Nov. 1723.   St. Phil PR

5

Arnott, John & Hanah Gull, 17 July 1728.   St. Phil PR

Arnymüller, Albrecht, powder maker, & Johanna Magdalena
    Elisabetha Martin(in), 17 Feb. 1778.   St. John Luth Ch

Arrino, John & Mary McDaniel, 3 Sept. 1749.   Pr Fred PR

Arthur, George & Sarah Whitesides, 30 Oct. 1772.   T & D PR

Arthur, George & Sarah Whitesides, 30 Oct. 1772.   Ch Ch PR

Arthur, Nathaniel of Parish of Christ Church, bachelor, & Mary
    Simmons, spinster, at the plantation of George Simmons,
    3 Dec. 1772; George Arthur, Mary Simmons, wit.   St. Jas PR

Ash, John & Elizabeth Levingstone, 14 Apr. 1757.   St. Phil PR

Ash, John & Grace Codner, 22 Dec. 1763.   St. And. PR

Ash, John of New Hanover County, NC., & Elizabeth Legare, of
    Christ Church Parish, widow, 22 Oct. 1783; George Barksdale
    & Jno Burwick, trustees; John Ash of Togodo, Nathan Legare,
    wit.   Mar Set 1:   12-19

Ash, John of St. Pauls Parish, & Catharine Lechmere, widow of
    Nicholas Lechmere, late of Beaufort, 11 Mar. 1785; Andrew
    Deveaux of Beaufort Dist., trustee; Archd Campbell, Stephen
    Deveaux, William Deveaux, wit.   Mar Set 1:   241-242

Ash, John & Catherine Lechmere, widow, 10 Mar. 1785.
    St. Hel PR

Ash, Marmaduke & Elizabeth Bordon, P Licence, 9 Nov. 1741.
    St. Phil PR

Ash, Richard Cockran & Ann Daniel, widow, 12 Dec. 1757.
    St. Phil PR

Ash, Samuel & Katherine Clements both of Christ Church Parish
    by the Revd. Mr. Alexr. Garden, 24 Feb. 1726.   St. Phil PR

Ash, Samuel & Hannah Deveaux, 14 July 1785.   St. Hel PR

Ash, Samll. & Elizabeth Burt, 15 July 1731.   Ch Ch PR

Ashby, John & Elizabeth Ball, 8 Nov. 1726.   T & D PR

Ashby, John & Mary Bonneau, 10 June 1755.   T & D PR

Ash, Richard Cochran & Margaret Ash, 18 Apr. 1797.   Circ Cong

Ashby, Thomas & Elizabeth LeJeau, 16 Aug. 1720.   T & D PR

Ashby, Thomas & Margaret Henrietta Bonneau, 18 Dec. 1750.
    T & D PR

Ashby, Thomas & Ann Peyre, 15 July 1772.   T & D PR

Ashton, John & Catharine Preston, 7 Jan. 1779.   St. Phil PR

Askew, Leonard & Catharine Dunning, 19 May 1782.   St. Phil PR

Askew, Thomas & Ann Hogg, 13 Nov. 1752.   St. Hel PR

Askew, Thomas & Hannah McKee, 5 Jan. 1786.   St. Hel PR

Atkin, Edmund & Anne McKenzy, 1 May 1760.   St. Phil PR

Atkins, James & Mary Gray, P Licence, 29 April 1732.
   St. Phil PR

Atkinson, George & Mary Stuart, 14 Mar. 1748/9.   Pr Fred PR

Atkinson, John & Sarah Carter, 6 Sept. 1742; Joseph Lyons,
   Miles Jackson, Lewis York, Chris. Stean, wit.   Hist Oburg

Atkinson, William & Ann Whitfield, 5 Dec. 1784.   St. John Luth
   Ch.

Atkinson, William-Anthony, of Parish of Prince George, &
   Elizabeth Sarah Huggins, of Parish of Prince George, widow
   16 Nov. 1786; Thos. Boone, Jno Jonah Murrell, wit.
   St. Jas PR

Atkinson, Wm. & Lydia Richardson, 8 Oct. 1797.   Trin Meth Ch.

Atmar, Ralph & Elizth Arnold, 4 June 1792.   Circ Cong

Atwell, Thomas & Martha Cox, P Licence, 5 July 1740.
   St. Phil PR

Audibert, Moses & Susanna Tozer, P Licence, 3 July 1743.
   St. Phil PR

Aumoner, James & Susanah Durtatree, ___ Dec. 1709.   Reg Prov
   1711-15, p. 449(41)

Austen, John & Elisabetha China, in House No. 199 King Street,
   28 Sept. 1786.   St. John Luth Ch

Austin, George & Ann Dawes, P Licence by Mr. Garden, 17 Nov.
   1736.   St. Phil PR

Austin, Robert & Catharine Frazer, 26 May 1776.   St. Phil PR

Auston, David & Mary Manson, 19 June 1785.   St. John Luth Ch

Avant, Benjamin of Prince George Parish and Ann Brunston of
   this parish 3 June 1741.   Pr Fred PR

Avant, Francis and Sarah Wigfal Thompson, 6 Jan 1743/4.
   Pr Fred PR

Avenson, Mathias & Martha Ferguson, widow; 7 April 1766.
   OJ 1764-1771

Avery, George & Mary Savy, P Licence, 31 May 1741. St Phil PR

Axe, Thos. & Susana Watt, ___ Dec. 1709.   Reg Prov 1711-15,
   p. 449(41)

Axon, Jacob & Ruth Glazbrook, P Licence by Mr. Garden, 27 April
   1736.   St. Phil PR

Axon, Samuel Jacob, M.D. of St. Paul's Parish & Eliza You, of
   Charleston, 1 March 1787.   St. Phil PR

Axson, Jacob & Elizabeth Tookerman, 9 Nov. 1758.   St. Phil PR

Axson, James, Bachelor, & Esther Champanare, spinster, in the
    house of S. F. Warren, 3 June 1760; Thos Wilson, Andrew
    Rembert, wit.   St. Jas PR

Axson, Thomas & Sussana Dar, 10 Sept. 1794.   Circ Cong

Axson, William & Elizabeth Susannah Mouzon, 8 Oct. 1761.
    T & D PR

Baas, Johann Christian & Jenny French, 15 May 1786.
    St. John Luth Ch

Baas, John & Frances Rosalie Smith, widow, 26 Jan. 1788.
    St. Phil PR

Bacon, Berrisford & Sarah Montgomrie, P Licence, 26 June 1738.
    St. Phil PR

Bacot, Peter & Elizabeth Harramond, 11 Nov. 1764.   St. Phil PR

Bacot, Samuel & Rebecca Foissin, 14 Apr. 1741.   Ch Ch PR

Bacot, Thomas Wright & Jane Desaussure, the younger, eldest
    daughter of Henry & Jane Desaussure, 5 March 1788; Hon Daniel
    Desaussure, Henry Wm. Desaussure, trustees; Sarah DeSaussure,
    Tim Ford, wit.   Mar Set 1:   339-346

Bacot, Thomas Wright & Jane Dessaussure, 6 March 1788.
    St. Phil PR

Badger, Daniel & Christian Eagle, 24 June 1736.   Circ Cong

Bagshaw, Thomas & Bridget Fardoe, widow, 8 May 1772.
    St. Phil PR

Bainbridge, Peter Rev. of Charleston & Ellenor his wife, late
    Eleanor McIntosh, youngest daughter of Alexander McIntosh,
    Brig. Gen., formerly of Dist., of Cheraw, 10 May 1787;
    Thomas Screven, trustee; E. H. Bay, wit.   Mar Set 1: 609-612

Baker, Elihu of Berkley County, S.C., & Elizabeth Ambrose,
    spinster, daughter of John Ambrose, of Prov. of Georgia,
    Gent., 6 March 1733; Eliz. Pinckney, Charles Pinckney, wit.
    Misc. Rec. HH: 248-249

Baker, Elihu & Sarah Hundley, 31 ___ 1745; Isaac Chandler
    trustee; David Russ, wit.   Misc. Rec. GG: 261-265

Baker, Francis & Mary Shepherd, P Licence, 1728.   St. Phil PR

Baker, John & Sarah Evins, 22 March 1729/30.   Ch Ch PR

Baker, John & Eunis Mary Breed, 26 Jan. 1762.   St. Phil PR

Baker, Josiah and Rebecca Buttler, spinster; minister Lewis
    Jones; bondsmen Josiah Baker and John Sheppard of St. Georges
    Dorchester; wit. J. Hammerton, 9 March 1732.   MB NY

Baker, Josiah & Rebecca Butler, 12 March 1732/3.   St. And PR

Baker, Michael & Mary Threadcroft, 7 Sept. 1727. T & D PR

Baker, Richard & Sarah Glaze, P Licence, 13 Sept. 1731.
   St. Phil PR

Baker, Richard and Mary Anne Young(?), spinster; minister
   Lewis Jones; bondsmen Richard Baker of Port Royal, vintner
   and Joseph Murray of Charles Town; wit. James Michie, 27 Apr.
   1733. MB NY

Baker, Richard & Elizabeth Elliott, 6 May 1756. St. Phil PR

Baker, Richard Bohun, of St. George Parish, Dorchester, &
   Elizabeth Miles of St. Bartholomews Parish, widow of Joseph
   Miles, 16 July 1774; Thomas Ladson, brother of st. Elizabeth
   & Isaac McPherson, of St. Pauls Parish, trustees; Eliza
   McPherson, Emily Ladson, wit. Mar Set 1: 177-180

Baker, William & Ann Sanders, 10 Jan. 1766. OJ 1764-1771

Balderkin, George & Hellina Clarivendike or Vandike, 18 Feb.
   1768. St. Phil PR

Balentine, James & Sarah Hirst, 12 Feb. 1761. St. Phil PR

Baley, Richard & Rachel Ladson, 17 Oct. 1754. St. And PR

Ball, Bartholomew and Elizabeth Henlen, spinster; minister
   Thomas Morritt; bondsmen Bartholomew Ball of St. Johns
   parish, planter, and Daniel Bourgett of Charleston Town,
   brewer; wit. James Michie, 4 Apr. 1733. MB NY

Ball, Elias & Mary Dellamare, 1721. St. Phil PR

Ball, Elias of Parish of St. Johns, bachelor & Catherine
   Gaillard, spinster, in the house of Theodore Gaillard, 14
   May 1765; Floride Peyre, Samuel Gaillard, wit. St. Jas PR

Ball, John of Charleston & Elizabeth St. John, daughter of the
   late James St. John, of John's Island, 2 Nov. 1797; Lambert
   Lance, Archibald Ball, of Charleston, trustees; Maryann
   Jefferys, Mary Gough St. John, Lambert Gough Lance, wit.
   Mar Set 3: 159-162

Ball, Joseph Junr. & Ann Scott, 20 Dec. 1764. St. Phil PR

Ball, Stephen and Lydia Sanders, 1 Jan. 1744/5. Pr Fred PR

Ball, William & Catherine Burrows, per Licence, 27 Feb. 1744.
   St. Phil PR

Ballard, Edward & Mrs. Mary Sola, 13 Sept. 1795. Trin Meth Ch

Ballew, Thomas & Ann Cox, 10 Apr. 1753, in Amelia. Hist Oburg

Ballon, Andrew & Miss Hester Suany, 15 Dec. 1799. Trin Meth Ch

Baltezar, Joachim & Elizabeth Matthews, 3 June 1753. T & D PR

Balz, Gottlieb, baker & Barbara Kögel(in), widow, 3 April 1764.
   St. John Luth Ch

9

Bampfield, George & Elizabeth Delamere, P Order of the Deputy
Governor. by the Reverend Mr. Jones, 17 Feb. 1725/6.
St. Phil PR

Bampfield, George, butcher & Barbara Maria Cole, 16 Nov. 1791;
Ruth Cole, widow & William Cole, mariner, trustees; Emanuel
Abrahams, Magdalin Cole, wit.   Mar Set 1: 646-648

Bampfield, George, Gent., & Sarah Amelia Tart, daughter of
Nathan Tart of St. Thomas Parish, 26 Feb. 1794; Thomas H.
McCalla, wit.   Mar Set 2: 241-242

Bampfield, George & Sarah Amelia Tart, 27 Feb. 1794. T & D PR

Bampfield, Geo, a free Mulatto & Barbary Maria Cole, 12 Nov.
1791. Trin Meth Ch

Bampfield, William & Rebecca Cook, 11 Oct. 1761.   St. Phil PR

Banbury, Peter & Charlotte Hutchinson, 9 Apr. 1752.   T & D PR

Banbury, William & Jane Bonnetheau, P Licence, 30 Dec. 1750.
St. Phil PR

Baptist, Bartholomew & Hanah Wilkins, P Banns, 24 June 1741
St. Phil PR

Baptist, Bartholomew & Hanah Wilkins, P Banns, 24 June 1741.
St. Phil PR

Barber, Thomas & Sarah Elder, 23 Apr. 1786.   St. John Luth Ch

Barefield, William of Charlestown & Catherine Houch, widow,
10 Apr. 1765; Michael Munckenfus, Christopher Sheets, of
Charlestown, trustees; Jas Heny. Butler, George Cuhun, wit.
Misc. Rec. MM. 261-265

Barkadale, Charles & Mary Wingood, widow, 7 May 1741.
Ch Ch PR

Barker, John & Isabella Chambers, 14 June 1763. St. Phil PR

Barker, Thomas & Vertue Mardoh, 19 Feb. 1721.   St. Phil PR

Barker, Thos. & Eliza Maxwel, widow, 28 April 1766.
OJ 1764-1771

Barker, Thomas & Elizabeth Maxwell, widow, 28 Apr. 1766.
St. Phil PR

Barksdale, George & Susanna Stone, 14 Mar. 1757.   Stoney
Creek Pres Ch.

Barksdale, George & Elizabeth Patterson, 31 Oct. 1765.
St. Phil PR

Barksdale, John & Anne Hepworth, 12 Dec. 1736. St. And PR

Barlow, Thomas & Catherine Ledbette, 29 Mar. 1764. St. Phil PR

Barlow, Thos & Susannah Godfrey, widow, 29 July 1731.
St. And. PR

10

Barnard, James, bachelor & Esther Jaudon, spinster, in the
house of Paul Jaudon, 3 Dec. 1761; Elizabeth Robert, Esther
Chovin, wit.   St. Jas PR

Barnard, John of Province of Georgia, & Jane Bradley, spinster,
10 Dec. 1743; license to Rev. William Orr; John Johnson, of
Charles Town, merchant, bondsman.   MC Chas

Barnes, Thomas & Susannah Prockter, P Licence by the Revd. Mr.
Alexr. Garden, 17 November 1747.   St. Phil PR

Barnes, William & Ann Minott, 24 July 1761.   St. Phil PR

Barnet, Allen & Ann Purle, P Licence by the Revd. Mr. Alexr.
Garden, 18 March 1747.   St. Phil PR

Barnett, John, bachelor, & Ann Bochett, spinster, in the house
of Henry Bochett, 2 Dec. 1762; John Jennes, Judith Rembert,
wit.   St. Jas PR

Barnett, William & Catharine Smith, 20 Aug. 1789.   St. Phil PR

Barns, Henry & Massy Gowens, a black woman, 1 May 1796.
St. Phil PR

Barns, William, widower, & Martha McKee, 20 Sept. 1773.
St. Hel PR

Barnwell, Edward & Mary Bower Williamson, 8 Jan. 1783.
St. Hel PR

Barnwell, Edward & Mary Wigg, 29 July 1790.   St. Hel PR

Barnwell, John & Martha Chaplin, 31 Oct. 1737.   St. Hel PR

Barnwell, John & Ann Hutson, 8 May 1777.   St. Hel PR

Barnwell, Jno Jur. & Eliza. Fenwick, 28 Jan. 1766.
OJ 1764-1771

Barnwell, John Berners, & Miss Jean Cuthbert, __ Apr. 1776.
St. Hel PR

Barnwell, Nathaniel & Mary Gibbes, 7 Apr. 1738.   St. And PR

Barnwell, Nathaniel & Elizabeth Waight, 1 Dec. 1768.
St. Hel PR

Barnwell, Nath'l, Coll. & Mary Gibbes, 7 Apr. 1738.
St. Hel PR

Baron, Alexander & Sarah Cleiland, 31 Dec. 1772.   St. Phil PR

Barrat, John & Alice Williams, P Licence, 9 Sept. 1732.
St. Phil PR

Barrett, John, son of Benjamin decd., m. Rhoda Taylor, 31 Dec.
1789.   Bush R QM

Barron, Thomas of Georgetown, merchant, & Charlotte Keith, of
same, spinster, 15 Dec. 1791; John Keith, attorney, Mathew
Frisbe, physician, trustees; Norman Singelton, Susanna Keith,
wit.   Mar Set 1: 648-650

SOUTH CAROLINA MARRIAGES 1688-1799

Barry, John & Martha Barry, 25 March 1762.   St. Phil PR

Barry, Robert & Agnes Lovekin, widow, 13 June 1754.   St Hel PR

Bartenfeld, Christof Friedrich, baker, & Maria Margretha Spera,
    27 Jan. 1778.   St. John Luth Ch

Barth, Johannes & Margaretha Katharine Ribert(in), widow,
    26 March 1765.   St. John Luth Ch

Bartlett, Thomas & Anne Waterman, 13 May 1733.   St. Hel PR

Barton, Isaac & Eliz: Wilkinson, 6 Oct. 1752.   St. Hel PR

Barton, John & Jane Perryman, P Licence, 2 Aug. 1733.
    St. Phil PR

Barton, John & Elizabeth Burdell, 16 Oct. 1733.   Ch Ch PR

Barton, John & widow Hale, 23 June 1743.   Ch Ch PR

Barton, John and Honora Bonnell, 4 June 1741.   Pr Fred PR

Barton, John, Bachelor & Elizabeth Pearcey, spinster, at the
    plantation of Benjamin Webb, 9 July 1778; Benjamin Webb,
    Sarah Hannah Webb, wit.   St. Jas PR

Barton, Thos. Junr. & Mary Eleanor Cuck (Cook), 9 July 1730.
    Ch Ch PR

Barton, William & Mary Baker, widow, 10 Apr. 1735.   Ch Ch PR

Barton, William & Eliz: Gibbons, widow, 11 June 1757. St Hel PR

Barton, William of Parish of Prince Frederick, Bachelor, &
    Jane Thomson, of Parish of Prince Frederick, spinster, at
    the plantation of Capt. Anthony White, 24 Sept. 1773;
    Catherine McIver, Anthoy. White, wit.   St. Jas PR

Bashford, Will'm. & Susanna Stevens, 1 March 1753. St. Hel PR

Baskins, James & Prudence Crawford. Ninety Six Dist. Dec.
    1781.   Alexrd. Noble, sec.   Ninety Six Dist OJ

Bastenot, benjamin & Mary Beard, 20 Feb. 1719/20.   St. And PR

Batchelor, David & Sarah Ruberry, 6 May 1713.   T & D PR

Batchelor, David & Sarah Murrell, 16 July 1754.   T & D PR

Batchelor, John & Eliza. Batterson, P Licence, 6 January 1732.
    St. Phil PR

Bates, John & Mary Hall, widow, 16 Jan. 1761.   St. Phil PR

Batey, ___, of PonPon, & Harriott Desausure, 8 Sept. 1756.
    St. Hel PR

Bath, William & Elizabeth Baker, widow, 2 Nov. 1771. St Phil PR

Bathan, Frederick & Margaret King, P Banns by Mr. Garden,
    29 Dec. 1736.   St. Phil PR

12

Baton, Isaac, surgeon, & Eliz: Wilkinson, 6 Oct. 1752.
St. Hel PR

Batsford, Joseph & Bridget Hughes, P Licence, 23 May 1738.
St. Phil PR

Battoon, John & Ann Guy, widow, 25 May 1776.   St. Phil PR

Battson, Thomas & Jemimah Crofts of this parish, 4 Nov. 1747.
Stoney Creek Pres. Ch

Baudrop, Joseph of Charleston, gentleman, & Matilda Benson,
1 Oct. 1797.   St. Phil PR

Baxter, John & Sarah Desurrency, widow of Samuel Desurrency,
decd., 1 Sept. 1791; John Gruber, Joseph Smith, of St.
Bartholomews Parish, trustees; George Kling Jr., Frederick
Sting, wit.   Mar Set 1: 589-590

Baxter, Robert & Eliz. Richmd. Bates, 6 Sept. 1764.   St. Phil PR

Bay, Elihu Hall & Margaret Holmes, 19 Sept. 1781.   St. Phil PR

Bayley, Ralph & ___ Fripps, 30 Dec. 1709.   Reg Prov 1711-15,
p. 449(41)

Bayley, William & Katherine Cameron, 27 March 1763.   St. Phil PR

Baynard, William & Eliz: Grimball, 1 Feb 1753.   St. Hel PR

Bayne, Daniel & Mary Heywood, 5 July 1755.   St. Phil PR

Beacon, Nathaniel & Anne Holman, 17 July 1735.   St. And. PR

Beadon, Stephen & Ruth Rivers, 16 Sept. 1735.   St. And PR

Beaird, John & Catharina Schingler, widow, 1 June 1762.
St. Phil PR

Beaird, Matthew of Parish of St. James Goose Creek & Elizabeth
Beaird, spinster, 30 Apr. 1744; license to Rev. Daniel Dwight;
Anthony Gracia, bondsman.   MB Chas

Beale, John & Mary Ross, 18 March 1762.   St. And PR

Beale, Joseph of Charleston, merchant & Mary Bagnell, widow,
29 Dec. 1798.   St. Phil PR

Beale, Othniel & Katharine Gale, 25 March 1722.   St. Phil PR

Beale, William & Jeane Roach, by permission of Major Finley,
Virginia Line, 24 Dec. 1782.   St. John Luth Ch

Beamore, John & Judith Stewart, 29 Nov. 1719.   St. And PR

Bear, George, widower & Anne England, spinster, at the plantation of Mrs. Tidyman, 27 April 1784; John Wirosdick, Andw
Mills, wit.   St. Jas PR

Beard, Robert of Charleston, Tin plate worker & Elizabeth
Higgins, widow, 17 July 1796.   St. Phil PR

Bearley, Thomas & Martha Atwell, P Licence, 8 July 1742.
St. Phil PR

Bearman, James, bachelor, & Anne Neal, spinster, 8 April 1788;
Daniel Joulee, S. Warren, wit.   St. Jas PR

Beauchamp, Adam & Joannah Corbet, P Licence, 3 July 1730.
St. Phil PR

Beauchamp, Adam & Jane Mackqueen, P Licence, 4 March 1737.
St. Phil PR

Beauchamp, Adam & Elizabeth Nichols, per Licence, 19 Nov. 1745.
St. Phil PR

Beay, Daniel & Miss Jachanan Reschor(?), 3 Nov. 1799.
Trin Meth Ch

Beazley, Thomas & Susannah Appleby, per Licence by the Revd.
Mr. R. Betham; Assist to the Rector of St. Philips, 27 Feb.
1745.   St. Phil PR

Beck, Jacob & Brigitta Smith, both of Amelia Township, 19 Feb.
1754.   Hist Oburg

Beckman, Samuel & Ann Lee, 11 Oct. 1793.   St. Phil PR

Bedgegood, Malachi Nicholas to Chaterine Murfee, 1 Feb. 1795,
Rev. Joshua Lewis.   Marlboro Co

Bedon, John & Elizabeth Massey, widow, 4 Aug. 1736.   Circ Cong

Bedon, John Raven & Elizabeth Baker, P Licence, 18 April 1752.
St. Phil PR

Bedon, Richard & Martha Fuller, widow, 17 Oct. 1745.   St. And PR

Bee, John S. & Mary Warnock, 21 May 1796.   Circ Cong

Bedon, Richard of Colleton County & Martha Fuller, widow of
William Fuller, 15 Oct. 1745; Sarah Ferguson, Sarah Elliott,
Elihu Baker, wit.   Benjamin Cattell of Berkley Co., trustee.
Misc. Rec. MM: 448-454

Bedon, Stephen & Ruth Nicholas, P Licence, 25 August 1743.
St. Phil PR

Bee, John & Martha Miller, P Licence, 7 June 1731.   St. Phil PR

Bee, Matthew & Mary Markee, 23 Aug. 1692; George Franklin,
John Smith, bondsmen.   Sec Prov 1675-95, p. 491

Bee, Peter Smith, gentleman & Frances Ward, 16 March 1798.
St. Phil PR

Bee, Peter Smith of Charleston & Frances Caroline Ward,
spinster, 20 March 1798; Thomas Tunno, Thomas Mathews &
James McCall Ward, trustees; R. Means, Peter Ward, wit.
Mar Set 3: 281-283

Bee, Thomas of Charlestown, Gent., & Susanna Holmes, daughter
of Isaac Holmes decd., spinster; 5 May 1761; Isaac Holmes &
Samuel Brailsford, trustees; Thomas Stanyarne, Jno Champney,
wit.   Mar Set 2: 167-173

Bee, Thomas & Sarah McKinsey, widow, 16 March 1773.   St. Phil PR

Bee, Thomas & Susanna Shubrick, widow, 26 May 1786; Thomas
Heyward, trustee; Maria Heyward, E. Ferguson, wit.
Mar Set 1:   258-260

Bee, Thomas of Charlestown, attorney, & Sarah McKenzie, widow,
sister of Roger & Peter Smith, 16 March 1773; Daniel Grattan,
Henry Harvey, wit.   Mar Set 1:   393-395

Bee, William & Rachael Swan, widow, 6 May 1756.   St. Phil PR

Bee, Willm. & Elizabeth Witter, 20 Aug. 1741.   St. And PR

Beek, Richard & Margaret Haly, 14 Aug. 1743.   Ch Ch PR

Beekman, Barnard & Susannah Duval, spinster, P Licence by the
Revd. Mr. Alexr. Garden, 9 July 1748.   St. Phil PR

Beekman, Barnard & Eliz. Scott, widow, 14 Dec. 1769.   St Phil PR

Beekman, Charles & Mary Courtonne, 26 May 1762.   St. Phil PR

Beekman, John & Ruth Watson, P Licence, 16 Feb. 1737.
St. Phil PR

Beekman, John & Ann Mienson, widow, P Licence by the Revd. Mr.
Alexr. Garden, 3 Nov. 1750.   St. Phil PR

Beerd, Timothy of Beaufort Galley, marriner, & Sarah Hodges,
spinster, 26 Dec. 1743; license to Rev. Lewis Jones;
Daniel Moloy of CharlesTown, bondsman.   MB Chas

Beil, Georg & Maria Eckstein(in), 8 Nov. 1778.   St. John Luth
Ch

Belin, Allard of Parish of Prince George Winyah, & Margaret
Robert, 10 Aug. 1744; license to Rev. John Fordyce; Elias
Horrey, bondsman.   MB Chas

Belin, James & Mary Jermain, 28 Oct. 1750, at Santee.   Ch Ch
PR

Bell, Andrew & Elizabeth Dunlap, widow, 8 Sept. 1739.   St Hel PR

Bell, Daniel & Margery Higgeson, P Licence, 27 July 1742.
St. Phil PR

Bell, David & Sarah Lenneau, 31 Dec. 1795.   St. Phil PR

Bell, Elijah & Elizabeth O'Quin, 17 Mar. 1788.   St. Phil PR

Bell, Geo & Mary Bee, P Licence, 8 Aug. 1744.   St. Phil PR

Bell, George of Charles Town, bricklayer, & Mary Bee, spinster,
8 Aug. 1744; license to Rev. Alexander Garden; Joseph Bee,
carpenter, bondsman.   MB Chas

Bell, James, Bachelor & Jean Anderson, spinster, at the house
of Jean-Elizabeth Dumay, widow, 14 Feb. 1764; Jonah Atchinson,
Joseph Bell, wit.   St. Jas PR.

Bell, James, widower, & Esther Chovin, spinster, in the house
of William Bell, 23 May 1768; Wm. Mathews, Wm. Bell, wit.
St. Jas PR

SOUTH CAROLINA MARRIAGES 1688-1799

Bell, Marmaduke, & Mary Guerin, 21 May 1746.   Pr Fred PR

Bell, William, widower, & Elizabeth Anderson, widow, 8 May
    1765; Alex. Miot, Wm. Roberts, wit.   St. Jas PR

Bellamy, William, wheelwright, & Esther Baker, of Charles Town,
    widow, 8 Aug. 1776; Frances Baker, trustee; Alexr. Marshall,
    Susanna Green, Mary Ann Campbell, wit.   Mar Set 1: 137-141

Bellamy, William & Esther Baker, widow, 8 Aug. 1776.
    St. Phil PR

Bellin, James & Sarah Turkitt, 19 Sept. 1713.   T & D PR

Bellin, James of P. G. Parish & Mercy Hendlin of P. F. Parish,
    23 Apr. 1747.   This was the brides birthday.   Pr Fred PR

Bellingall, Robert of St. Bartholomews Parish, Gentl., &
    Elizabeth Aberson, of same widow of William Everson, and
    daughter of William Nash, decd. 22 Aug. 1767; Tobias Ford,
    trustee; E. Eberson, James Reid, wit.   Mis. Rec OO: 224-227

Bellinger, George & Elizabeth Elliott, widow, 7 Nov. 1751.
    St. And. PR

Bellinger, John & Rebecca Evans, 21 Feb. 1779.   St. Phil PR

Belton, James & Agnes Johnson, 18 March 1758.   St. Phil PR

Beltzer, Christian, butcher, & Maria Müller(in), in Mr. Jacob
    Werner's house, 27 Jan. 1778.   St. John Luth Ch

Benedict, John & Catharine Reder, widow, 15 Aug. 1774.
    St. John Luth Ch

Benet, William & Mary Benet, 14 Jan. 1760.   St. Phil PR

Benfield, John & Ann Colcock, 7 Oct. 1759.   St. Phil PR

Benison, George & Hannah Screven, widow, 18 Mar. 1734/5.
    Ch Ch PR

Benison, William & Ann Brown, 9 Aug. 1750.   Ch Ch PR

Benison, William & Joanna Walker, 12 March 1768.   St. Phil PR

Bennet, John & Elizabeth Hartman, 20 Apr. 1756.   T & D PR

Bennet, Thomas & Mary Methringham, 2 Dec. 1765.   T & D PR

Bennet, Thomas & Anna Warnock, 9 June 1774.   T & D PR

Bennet, Wm. & Miss ___ Dewitt, 12 Feb. 1795.   Trin Meth Ch

Bennett, Henry & Rebecca Nelmes, 10 June 1735.   Ch Ch PR

Bennett, John & Margaret Swinton, 11 Apr. 1751.   Ch Ch PR

Bennett, William & Mary Bennett, 15 Jan. 1761.   Ch Ch PR

Bennis, William & Rebecca Mace, 23 Nov. 1776.   St. Phil PR

Benoist, John of St. Johns Berkley Co., & Sarah Birch, spinster,
    14 March 1743/4; license to Rev. Daniel Dwight; Peter

16

Benoist, bondsman.   MB Chas

Benoist, Peter & Abigail Townsend, P Licence, 16 Dec. 1731.
St. Phil PR

Bentham, James & Eleanor Phillips, 4 May 1772.   St. Phil PR

Bentham, Jas. & Mary Hardy, 4 June 1775.   St. Phil PR

Bentley, Edmund & Mary Wells, 15 Sept. 1741.   Pr Fred PR

Beresford, Richard Esq., & Sarah Cooke, 4 Jan. 1711-12.
T & D PR

Beresford, Richd. & Madam Sarah Cook, 4 Jan. 1711/12.   SPG

Beresford, Richard Esqr., & Ann Elliott, widow, 25 Sept. 1782;
Thomas Ferguson, Roger Parker Saunders, trustees; John Lewis,
Abraham Motte, wit.   Mar Set 1: 31-35

Bernard, Paul, of Parish of Prince Frederick, bachelor, &
Martha Atkinson, of Parish of Prince George, spinster, at
the plantation of Robert Daniel, 8 Nov. 1785; Thomas Ballon,
Peter ___, wit.   St. Jas PR

Berney, Abm & Abl. Creighton (free negroes), 6 Dec. 1792.
Circ Cong

Berney, John & Mary Martin, 23 Nov. 1790.   Circ Cong

Bernviel, Willhelm & Katharina Hanz(in), widow, 10 Apr. 1765.
St. John Luth Ch

Beronow, John, saddler & Maria Honorow, 16 Sept. 1786.
St. John Luth Ch

Berresford, Michael & Susannah Boone, 4 March 1739/40.   Ch Ch PR

Berry, William & Mary King, widow, both in SaxaGotha Township,
21 May 1750.   Hist Oburg

Bertoin, Joseph & Elizabeth Rambert, 23 April 1721.   St Phil PR

Bertran, Thomas & Mary Hancock, P Licence, 2 Apr. 1730.
St. Phil PR

Berwick, John & Sarah Johnson, widow, 20 July 1779.   St Phil PR

Besseliau, Mark Anthony & Martha Chichet, P Licence, 8 Oct.
1745.   St. Phil PR

Besselleu, Louis & Susannah Wood, 27 Aug. 1775.   T & D PR

Besseleu, Philip & Susanna Mason, 10 Apr. 1771.   St. Phil PR

Bessileu, Lewis & Elizabeth Young, 19 Aug. 1790.   St. Phil PR

Beswicke, John & Mary Hill, 17 Nov. 1742.   St. And PR

Beswicke, Thomas & Deborah Haines, widow, 23 Apr. 1734.
St. Hel PR

Beswicke, Thomas & Anne Wigg, widow, 12 Sept. 1749.   St Hel PR

17

Betsch, Adam, a doctor, & Catharina Miller(in), 14 Oct. 1777.
St. John Luth Ch

Betson, William & Mary Pinckney als Evans, by the Revd. Mr.
Garden, by Licence of Governr. Johnson, 1721. St Phil PR

Bety, ___ & Herriot Saussure, 8 Sept. 1756. St. Hel PR

Bilby, John & Mary Haddock, 31 July 1745. St. Phil PR

Billiald, John & Mary Robinson, 25 Nov. 1736. St. And PR

Bingil, Daniel & Catherina Kigleman, P Licence by Mr. Garden,
10 April 1736. St. Phil PR

Binseky, Martin & Mary Stongeon, P Licence, 9 Feb. 1748.
St. Phil PR

Bint, Thomas & Anne Dixon, P Licence, 11 March 1744/5. St Phil
PR

Bird, Thomas & Anne Rivers, 19 Apr. 1753. T & D PR

Birkmeier, J. Daniel & Anna Margaretha Lebert(in), 8 Apr. 1766.
St. John Luth Ch

Birot, Peter & Sarah Leste, P Licence by Mr. Garden, 8 Feb.
1736. St. Phil PR

Birkmeier, Konrad, saddler, & Anna Maria Backer (in), 28 Feb.
1764. St. John Luth Ch

Bishaw, Charles & Anne Hazel, P Licence, 8 March 1744/5.
St. Phil PR

Bishop, Francis & Jane Goodin, P Licence, 20 March 1737.
St. Phil PR

Bishop, John & Anna Shäfer, widow, 8 July 1780. St. John
Luth Ch

Bisset, William & Mary Smith, per Licence, 20 Oct. 1745.
St. Phil PR

Bissett, William & Mary Sutherland, widow, 1 Aug. 1743.
Ch Ch PR

Bissett, William & Catherine Loyer, 30 Oct. 1755. St Phil PR

Bisson, Charles & Anne Sanson, P Licence by Mr. Garden,
___ 1725. St. Phil PR

Black, George & Sarah Brown, widow, 5 Jan. 1786. St. John Luth
Ch

Black, James & Elizabeth Clark Saltus, 6 March 1797. St Hel PR

Black, Nathaniel & Joanah Shepperd, 19 May 1771. St And PR

Blackburn, James & Elizabeth Backstill, widow, 23 May 1777.
St. Phil PR

Blair, David & widow Page, 15 Apr. 1745. Ch Ch PR

Blair, James & Eliza Todd, 13 Nov. 1791.   Circ Cong

Blair, Patrick & Mary Stathams, P Licence, 17 May 1739.
St. Phil PR

Blake, John & Frances Squeal, 28 Dec. 1771.   St. Phil PR

Blake, John, bachelor, & Mary Jeanneret, spinster, in the
house of Jacob Jeanneret Senr., 28 April 1784; James Boone,
Ann Dutart, wit.   St. Jas PR

Blake, John, of Charleston, Storekeeper, & Mrs. Charlotte
Antonie, widow of Manuel Antonie, decd; 15 Dec. 1792;
Nathaniel Russell Esqr. & Stephen Thomas, trustee; Charl.
Troy, Christian Gruber, wit.   Mar Set 2:   37-40

Blake, John & Sarah Enocks, 18 Jan. 1787.   Pugh diary

Blake, Joseph & Sarah Lyndrey, P Licence of G. Johnson,
16 June 1720.   St. Phil PR

Blake, Richard, and Elizabeth Staples, 25 Dec. 1739.   Pr Fred PR

Blake, Richard Jr., widower, & Anne Bearman, widow, in the house
of James Bell, 23 July 1772; James Bell, John Blake, wit.
St. Jas PR

Blakely, Luke, scrivener of Ewhaw, & Mary Ann Murphy, widow,
20 March 1754.   St. Hel PR

Blalock, Lewis & ___, 18 Oct. 1787.   Pugh diary

Blamyer, John of Berkley Co., & Elizabeth Waring, sister of
Samuel Postell, 1 June 1764; Rob: Dymes, W. Skene, wit.
Misc. Rec. MM: 270-273

Bland, George & Mary Douglas, 27 Jan. 1752.   St. Hel PR

Bland, George, widower, & Mary Bowman, 2 July 1761.   St Hel PR

Bland, Richard of St. Lukes Parish, Granville Co., planter, &
Elizabeth Fendin, spinster, 6 March 1769; John Chaney &
Benjamin Parmenter, trustees; John Parmenter Junr., Jas
Hogg, wit.   Misc. Rec. OO: 81-82

Blazdell, Charles & Susannah Wemyss, widow, 22 July 1761.
St. Phil PR

Bliston, Charles & Elizabeth Vine, 8 July 1773.   St. Phil PR

Blott, John & Ann Parks, widow, 27 Jan. 1770.   St. Phil PR

Blundell, Thomas & Martha Clews, P Licence, 2 Aug. 1730.
St. Phil PR

Blunt, John & Jane Jones, 25 Feb. 1722/23.   St. Phil PR

Blyth, Joseph of Georgetown, Physician, & Elizabeth Allston,
spinster, 1 Feb. 1791; Mr. John Pyatt, trustee; R. Brownfield, W. James, wit.   Mar Set 1:   553-555

Blyth, Thomas and Jean Stead, widow; minister Alexander Garden;
bondsmen Thomas Blyth and David Christian of Charles Town,
carpenter, 4 Apr. 1733.   MB NY

Boaree, Stephen and Elizabeth Headwit, widow, 27 Feb. 1738.
Pr Fred PR

Boaund, Samuel, of Charleston, factor, & Mary Gibson, 27 Apr.
1796.   St. Phil PR

Bobby, James & Catherine Smith, P Licence, 5 June 1739.
St. Phil PR

Bochet, Nicholas, of Parish of Prince George, Craven Co.,
carpenter, & Jane Bonhost, spinster, ___ June 1787; Mark
Huggins, Senr., trustee; Jno Shackelford, Mark Huggins Junr.,
wit. Mar Set 1: 319-320

Bochett, Anthony & Hester Mouzon, 9 May 1754.   T & D PR

Bochett, Anthony & Mary Scott, 7 Nov. 1759.   T & D PR

Bochet, Henry, Gent., & Charlotte Walker, 17 Sept. 1793;
Stephen Boineau, trustee; C. Vanvelsen, Thos. Palmer, wit.
Mar Set 2: 202-205

Bochet, Lewis, of Parish of Prince George, widower, & Rebecca
Watts, of Parish of Prince Frederick, widow, 9 Dec. 1784;
Benj. Duke, Joseph Boutwell, wit. St. Jas. PR

Bochett, Henry & Ann Jennens, 13 Aug. 1746.   T & D PR

Bochet, Henry & Judith Boineau, spinster, at the house of
Michael Boineau Senr., 14 May 1772; Jonah Robert, James Ware,
wit. St. Jas PR

Bochett, Lewis & Mary Ashby, 3 May 1764.   T & D PR

Bochett, Peter & Frances DuBois, ___ June 1751.   T & D PR

Bocquet, Peter & Martha Oliver, widow, 23 Feb. 1760. St Phil PR

Bocquet, Peter & Martha Smith, 23 Jan. 1766.   OJ 1764-1771

Boden, Joseph & Mary Mayfield, 31 July 1782.   St. Phil PR

Bodington, George & Sarah Crubin, 13 Oct. 1745.   St. And PR

Bohr, Jacob, widower, & Magdalena, widow of George Schraden,
15 Aug. 1769.   St. John Luth Ch

Boisseau, John & Mrs. Mary Laurens (sister to John Potell?),
5 March 1688/9; Josias Dupre, P. Lassale, John Shelton, wit.
Reg Prov A 1682-90; 338

Bollaugh, William & Mary Britten, P Licence, 18 Apr. 1722.
St. Phil PR

Bolton, Allen & Martha Baker, 27 June 1765; Francis Gaultier,
& John Rutledge of Charlestown, trustees; Elizabeth Hutch-
ings, Alexander Harvey, wit. Mar Set 1: 110-113

Bolton, William & Mary Lunch, 29 Dec. 1779.   St. Phil PR

Bona, Lewis Sn. & Sarah Parmenter, 16 June 1774.   St. Hel PR

Bonar, William of Charles Town, Gent. & Jane Hanson, of same,

spinster, 25 Sept. 1758; William Boone of Johns Island,
trustee; Saml Boone, James Boone, wit. Misc. Rec. LL: 98-100

Bonar, William & Jane Hinson, 25 Sept. 1758. St. Phil PR

Bond, George of Columbia in the Dist. of Camden, planter, &
Rachel Duke of same, widow, 17 Dec. 1790; Joseph Bee, of
Charleston, trustee; John O Cain, wit. Mar Set 1: 559-560

Bond, George Padon of Charles Town, & Constantia Paget, widow
of John Paget, of Berkley Co., 12 Nov. 1747; Nath. Bulline,
wit. Misc. Rec. II: 491-493

Bond, Geo. Padon, & Constantia Padgett, 11 June 1752. T & D PR

Bone, John, of Parish of Prince George, bachelor & Elizabeth
Jordan of Parish of Prince George, spinster, in the house of
Christopher Jordan, 19 Jan. 1762; Cht. Jordan, Jno Jordan,
wit. St. Jas PR

Boneau, William & Hanah-Rebecca Heap, 10 Apr. 1748. St And PR

Boneau, William & Mary Anger, 5 March 1753. St. And PR

Bonetheau, John & Mary Banbury, 25 Feb. 1741/2. St. And PR

Bonetheau, Peter & Elizabeth Weyman, 14 Jan. 1777. St. Phil PR

Bonham, James, bachelor, & Hannah Lewis, widow, in the house
of Mr. James Anderson, 29 March 1787; James Anderson, Elizabeth Barton, wit. St. Jas PR

Bonhost, Jonah of Parish of Prince George, widower, & Rebecca
Vereen, of Parish of Prince Frederick, spinster, in the house
of William Walker, 25 Apr. 1770; Elizabeth Bonhost, Jonah
Robert, wit. St. Jas PR

Bonhoste, Jacob of Parish of St. John, widower, & Judith Barnard,
spinster, at the plantation of John Coming Ball, 26 Nov. 1761;
John Gaillard, John Barnett, wit. St. Jas PR

Bonhoste, Jacob of Parish of Prince George, widower, & Hannah
Sullivan, of Parish of Prince George, in the house of Mark
Huggins, 21 Apr. 1768; Anna Huggins, Esther Sullivan, wit.
St. Jas PR

Bonhoste, Jonah & Jane Benison, 8 March 1748/9. Ch Ch PR

Bonhoste, William of Parish of Christ Church, bachelor & Mary
Bell, spinster, at the house of Mrs. Eliz. Bell, 27 March
1783; Hester Bonhoste, Eliza. Miot, wit. St. Jas PR

Bonin, John & Mary Magdalen Dess, P Licence by the Reverend
Mr. Dyson, 10 May 1727. St. Phil PR

Bonneau, Anthony & Sarah Shackelford, 4 July 1766.
OJ 1764-1771

Bonneau, Elias & Susannah Miller, 29 May 1734. T & D PR

Bonneau, Elias & Mary Darby, 30 Oct. 1746. T & D PR

Bonneau, Francis of Charleston, house carpenter, & Eleanor
Sarah Legare, widow, 7 Dec. 1797. St. Phil PR

Bonneau, Jacob & Eliz: Webb, 16 Jan. 1731/2. St. And PR

Bonneau, Jacob & Mary Miller, 11 Feb. 1746. T & D PR

Bonneau, Samuel & Frances Longuemar, 4 Dec. 1748. T & D PR

Bonnell, John & Patience Windham, 3 Dec. 1748. Pr Fred PR

Bonner, William & Marjory Wilkins, 2 Aug. 1720. St. Phil PR

Bonnetheau, Gabriel Manigault & Anna Maria Petsh, 26 Nov. 1799.
   St. Phil PR

Bonnetheau, John & Angelica Caier, P Licence, 22 Sept. 1731.
   St. Phil PR

Bonny, Thomas & Ruth Walblank, 14 Sept. 1721. T & D PR

Bonsell, Samuel & Elizabeth St. Martin, 14 March 1776.
   St. Phil PR

Bontiton, Peter & Mary Air, widow, 9 Jan. 1777. St. Phil PR

Boody, John and Sarah Evans, 22 Nov. 1741. Pr Fred PR

Boomer, Jacob & Christiana Wagner, 6 March 1762. St. Phil PR

Boomer, John & Barbara Phyfer, 21 June 1759. St. Phil PR

Boomer, John & Martha ___, 4 Feb. 1793; Samuel Stent & Benjamin
   Reynolds, trustees; Barnard Adams, David Smith, wit.
   Mar Set 2: 46-48

Boone, Capers, of Parish of Prince George, widower, & Mary
   Smith, of Parish of Prince George, widower, in the house of
   Paul Lepear, 16 June 1767; Paul Lepear, Jo Atchison, wit.
   St. Jas PR

Boone, Capers & Mary Bold, 22 Apr. 1779. St. Phil PR

Boone, James, bachelor, & Sarah Blake, spinster, in the house
   of John Blake, 10 Nov. 1785; Jas Walker, Geo McDowell, wit.
   St. Jas PR

Boone, Robert of Parish of Prince Frederick bachelor, & Elizabeth Gibbes, of Parish of Christ Church, spinster, at the
   plantation of John Boone Esqr., 9 Sept. 1784; Jno White,
   Jacob Jeanneret, wit. St. Jas PR

Boone, Samuel & Keziah Rivers, 20 Feb. 1761. St. And PR

Boone, Thomas Junr., son of Thomas and Mary Boone & Susannah
   Croft, 23 Nov. 1741. Ch Ch PR

Boone, Thomas Junr. of the Parish of Prince Frederick, bachelor,
   & Hannah Atkinson, of Parish of Prince Frederick, in the
   house of George Atkinson, 14 Sept. 1769; Geo. Atkinson,
   Jonah Woodberry, wit. St. Jas PR

Boone, William, widower, & Sarah Albergotti, 6 May 1786.
   St. Hel PR

Booth, Robert & Martha Dandridge, P Licence, 20 May 1731.
   St. Phil PR

Boquet, George Washington & Elizabeth Balantine, 10 May 1798.
  Circ Cong

Boquet, Peter & Barbara Sence, P Licence, 3 Oct. 1739.
  St. Phil PR

Boquet, Peter & Martha Smith, 3 Jan. 1766.   St. Phil PR

Borbone, ___ & Miss ___ Morrell, 30 Aug. 1798.   Trin Meth Ch

Borenair(?), John of Indianfield Swamp, & Margareth Jacobs,
  18 Nov. 1783.   St. John Luth Ch

Bosher, John & Mary Whitton, 22 July 1744.   Pr Fred PR

Bosomworth, Abraham & Susannah Seabrook, 3 Nov. 1749.
  St. And. PR

Bossard, Henry & Elizabeth Stuart, by ye Revd. Mr. Garden,
  P Licence Governr. Johnson, 26 Apr. 1720.   St. Phil PR

Bossard, Henry and Clary Wolf, 8 May 1760 by Rev. Mr. Warrin.
  Pr Fred PR

Bossard, John of Parish of Prince George, bachelor, & Elizabeth
  Screven, of parish of Prince George, at the house of Mr.
  Richard Walker, 23 June 1785; Isaac Deliesseline, William
  Murray, wit.   St. Jas PR

Bostock, Peter & Martha Trezvant, P Licence, 22 June 1749.
  St. Phil PR

Boswood, James & Martha Wood, daughter of Benja: Wood, 11 June
  1734.   St. And PR

Boswood, John & Nancy Wood, 21 Jan. 1734.   St. And PR

Bothwell, John & Susannah Hill, widow, 12 June 1774.   St Phil
  PR

Botton, Peter & Mary Decker, 10 June 1759.   St. Phil PR

Bouchoneau, Charles & Sarah Hutchison, 3 Feb. 1790; Charles
  Snowden, William Snowden, wit.   Mar Set 1: 473-474

Boucquet, George Washington & Elizabeth Ballantine, 10 May
  1798; Joseph Purcell, trustee; E. Prescot, M. Mackay, wit.
  Mar Set 3: 283-284

Boulee, Claudius & Magdalen Meinson, P Banns, 30 June 1729.
  St. Phil PR

Boulger, John Edward of Charleston, Gent., & Ann Elizabeth
  Saverance, daughter of John Saverance, of Christ Church
  Parish, 5 Dec. 1797; John Saverance, trustee; Thomas
  Whitesides, & James Bourlay, wit.   Mar Set 3: 201-202

Boulger, John Edward of Charleston, gentleman & Ann Elizabeth
  Soverince, of Christ Church, 4 Jan. 1798.   St. Phil PR

Boulton, Thomas & Elizabeth Miller, 25 July 1724.   St Phil PR

Bourdeaux, Anthony of St. James Goose Creek, & Mary Dupont of
  same, 17 Sept. 1795; Gideon Faucheraud Dupon of St. Mathews,

23

planter, trustee; J. R. May, J. Bourdeaux, wit.   Mar Set 2:
435-437

Bourdeaux, Israel of St. Thomas Parish, & Mary Rivers, spinster,
    12 Dec. 1743; license to Rev. Thomas Hasell; John Triboudet
    of Parish of St. Philip, bondsman.   MB Chas

Bourke, Alexander & Jane Miller, 24 May 1779.   St Phil PR

Bourquin, John Lewis, planter & Jane P. Donnom, of Okatie Creek,
    Granville County; 2 Aug. 1780.   James Garvey, John Mark
    Verdier, trustees; Michl Garvey, David Stoll, wit.
    Mar Set 2: 106-112

Bouston, Hugh & Ann Starling, widow, 6 Jan. 1776.   St. Phil PR

Bouti___, Jacques, & Maria Dutilly, 21 June 1772.   St. John
    Luth Ch

Boutwell, Joseph of the Parish of Prince Frederick, bachelor
    & Elizabeth Micheau, of Parish of Prince Frederick, at the
    house of Paul Micheau, 22 June 1785; Benja Guerry, Ann
    Micheau, wit.   St. Jas PR

Bowden, Thomas & Esther Powers, widow, 22 July 1757.   St Phil PR

Bowen, John & Mary Bargee, 28 Nov. 1764.   St. Phil PR

Bowen, John & Mary Robinson, 2 Sept. 1789.   St. Phil PR

Bowers, Edward & Mary Hyatt, spinr., 17 Apr. 1766.   OJ 1764-
    1771

Bowing, George & Mary For, 18 Nov. 1781.   St. Phil PR

Bowler, Charles & Elizabeth Jones, 21 Nov. 1765.   St. And PR

Bowler, James Henry of Charleston Dist., & Sarah Bradwell
    Ferguson of Beaufort, District, daughter of Wm. Ferguson;
    Barkley Ferguson, John McCullough, wit.   26 Aug. 1795.
    Mar Set 2: 448-450

Bowler, William of St. Bartholomews Parish, & Mary Nicholls,
    daughter of Saml Nicholls, 6 March 1788; Joseph & Ann Stevens,
    trustees; Susannah Donnom, John Winder, Jos. Dunnom, wit.
    Mar Set 1: 555-556

Bowles, Tobias of Charleston, attorney at law, & Susanna
    Drayton, a minor about 18 years old, daughter of Rebecca &
    John Drayton; 10 March 1795; Thomas Winstanley, trustee;
    Edwd Perry Junr, Jas Postell Junr, John L. Freazer, wit.
    Mar Set 2: 373-378

Bowls, John & Susannah Saunders, 9 Dec. 1745.   Pr Fred PR

Bowls, Tobias & Susannah Drayton, 10 March 1795.   St. Phil PR

Bowman, James & Margaret Greene, 22 Dec. 1785.   St. Hel PR

Bowman, John & Mary Davies, 6 Sept. 1762.   St. Phil PR

Bowman, John to Margaret Rosborough, daughter of Alexander
    Rosborough, 11 ___ 1794, Chester Co.   Ches Ct Min B

Bowman, Robert & Eliz: Crubin, widow, 7 June 1735.   St. And PR

Bowman, Samuell & Keziah Ladson, 18 July 1753.   St. And PR

Bowman, Thomas & Ann Black, 21 Dec. 1788.   St. Hel PR

Bowman, William & Anne Young, widow, 12 Sept. 1735.   St. And PR

Boyant, Ezechiel & Rebecca ___, 22 July 1771.   St. John Luth Ch

Boyd, James and Mehitabel Clegg, 7 Nov. 1737.   Pr Fred PR

Boyd, Robert & Ann Walker, 19 Sept. 1762.   St. Phil PR

Boyd, Robert & Anne Walker, 19 Sept. 1762.   T & D PR

Boyd, Robert & Susannah Myers, widow, 3 Apr. 1785.   St. Hel PR

Boyer, Henry & Katharine Delky, 27 May 1777.   St. Phil PR

Boyer, Henry & Mary Beil, widow, 17 Jan. 1785.   St. John Luth
   Ch

Boyneau, Michael of Santee & Elizabeth Sanders, 13 Sept. 1764.
   T & D PR

Bozman, Peter & Sarah Brown, 28 Dec. 1786.   Pugh diary

Braddock, David Cutler, mariner, & Mary Lyford, 7 Nov. 1742.
   St. Hel PR

Bradford, Charles & Mary Woodruffe, 12 July 1792.   St. Phil PR

Bradwell, Isaac & Susannah Bonneau, 1 Jan. 1778.   T & D PR

Bradwell, John & Elizabeth Loyd, 30 March 1775.   St. Phil PR

Brady, Edward & Rachael Whiteford, of Amelia, 27 Sept. 1753.
   Hist Oburg

Brailsford, Martin of Charleston, merchant, & Mary Cormack,
   daughter of Mary Donaldson, under age of 21, 8 Oct. 1788;
   Mary Donaldson, wife of James Donaldson, & Peter Bocquet,
   trustees; Alexr Chisholm, Sebastian Keeley, wit.   Mar Set 1:
   387-390

Brailsford, Samuel & Elizabeth Holmes, P Licence, 2 April 1750.
   St. Phil PR

Brailsford, William & Maria Heyward, 20 June 1786.   St. Hel PR

Braly, Thomas & Mary Bramston, widow, 20 July 1788.   St. Phil PR

Brand, John, Junior & Jame Meadows, 22 Feb. 1725/6.   St. Phil PR

Brandford, William & Mary Bryan, 18 Apr. 1746.   St. And. PR

Brandford, William & Elizabeth Savage, Spinster, P Licence,
   24 April 1751.   St. Phil PR

Brandford, Wm. & Anne Creighton, 23 March 1720/21.   St. And PR

Braun, David & Katharine Dörr(in), 3 Dec. 1764.   St. John Luth
   Ch

25

Brazier, Zachariah & Mary Anne Fairfax, P Licence, 7 April 1740.
St. Phil PR

Breed, Timothy & Sarah Hodges, 27 Jan. 1743.   St. Hel PR

Breed, Timothy & Ann Withers, widow, 21 Apr. 1765.   Ch Ch PR

Breedlove, Nathaniel & Susanna Lary, 17 Sept. 1768.   St. PhilPR

Breight, Matthew & Jane Hard, 17 Oct. 1768.   St. John Luth Ch

Breitenbach, Conrad & Mary Richards, 18 Aug. 1784.   St. John
Luth Ch

Brekenrige, Adam & Ann Carwithin, 7 July 1755.   T & D PR

Bremar, James & Vollentine Shekelford, 4 Feb. 1722-3.   T & D PR

Bremar, Peter & Elizabeth Shekelford, 9 May 1718.   T & D PR

Bremare, Francis & Martha Laurens, P Licence, 1 March 1738.
St. Phil PR

Brenan, Eugene & Mary Quire, 20 May 1774.   St. Phil PR

Bresben, William & Margaret Stewart, Oct. 1733.   St. Phil PR

Bret, Charles & Rebecca Worden, 15 Feb. 1729/30.   St. And PR

Brewer, Albert & Catharine Donolly, 26 Feb. 1772.   St. Phil PR

Brewton, John & Mary Weyman, 7 Jan. 1771.   St. Phil PR

Brewton, Miles & Mary Payne, P Licence, 24 Feb. 1742. St Phil
PR

Brewton, Robert & Mary Loughton, P Licence, 15 April 1729.
St. Phil PR

Brickell, James, Doctor of Medicine, & Susannah Mitchell,
relict of Peter Witten Esqr., then of Major Ephraim Mitchell,
8 Nov. 1792; Theodore Samuel Marion & James Gray Weare,
rustees; Peter Ray, Robert Burdell, wit. Mar Set 2: 34-37

Brickell, James of St. John's parish, Doctor of Medicine, &
Eliza Mary White, daughter of Blakeley White; 16 Dec. 1794;
Martha Hodgson, Jeremiah Dickinson, wit. Mar Set 2: 360-362

Brickin, James & Sarah Henderson, 2 Sept. 1775. St. Phil PR

Brickles, Richard & Sarah Warmingham, P Licence, January 1732.
St. Phil PR

Bridgland, David & Rebecca Skinner, 14 Jan. 1798. Trin Meth Ch

Brigs, Adam of Charles Town, carpenter, & Elizabeth Philips of
Charles Town, relict of Wm. Phillips decd., 12 March 1771;
John Nevin, Wm. Tweed, wit. Misc. Rec. OO: 530-531

Brimingham, Richard & Ann O'Neal, 14 May 1782.   St Phil PR

Brimstone, Jonathan & Martha Pickings [1740's]. Hist Oburg

Brindley, John Geo. & Sarah Jeffords, 18 June 1767. T & D PR

Brindlay, John George of St. John's Parish, & Mrs. Sarah Pope,
20 Oct. 1794; Charles Brown, trustee; W. Marshall, James
Horne, wit. Mar Set 2:330-334

Brindlay, John George & Sarah Pope, widow, 21 Oct. 1794.
St. Phil PR

Bringhurst, John & Elizabeth Shute, 8 Apr. 1754. St. Phil PR

Britten, Timothy & Mary Goddard, P Licence, 10 April 1743.
St. Phil PR

Britton, Daniel & Elizabeth Hayne, 26 Jan. 1747/8.   Pr Fred PR

Britton, Moses and Hester Jolly, 23 Apr. 1741.   Pr Fred PR

Brock, George, son of Elias decd. & Ann, m. Charity Ccok, 13
Sept. 1792. Bush R QM

Brockinton, Wm. & Jane (?) Benton, 20 Nov. 1794.   Pugh diary

Brockway, Jesse & Martha Brown, widow, 30 June 1793.   Trin
Meth Ch

Brockway, Samuel & Mary Magdaline Naser, 16 Jan. 1798.   Circ
Cong

Brockenton, William & Sarah Griffen, 5 July 1715.   T & D PR

Brooks, James & Sarah Singletary, 1 Sept. 1791.   Bush R QM

Broomhead, Robert and Rebecca Hales, widow; minister Alexander
Garden; bondsmen Robert Broomhead of Charles Town and John
Stevens (Stephens) of Charles Town, joiners. 12 Mar. 1732.
MB NY

Broughton, Andrew of Berkley Co., Gent., & Ann Singellton of
same, spinster, 19 Nov. 1750; Richard Singellton, gent.,
trustee; John Singellton, David Dean Jr., wit.   Misc.
Rec. TT: 429-433

Broughton, Edward & Sarah Weatherly, 21 Nov. 1740. St. Hel PR

Broughton, Peter & Sarah Swinton, 7 Apr. 1796.   Circ Cong

Broughton, Thomas & Sarah Heskett, P Licence by the Revd. Mr.
Alexr. Garden, 5 May 1748.   St. Phil PR

Broughton, Thomas & Elizabeth Lessene, 1 Nov. 1774. St. Phil PR

Brower, John & Mary Harvey, 17 Feb. 1791.   Circ Cong

Brown, Alexander of Prince Fredericks Parish, Craven County,
planter & Mary Belin, of Prince George Parish, spinster, 17
Feb. 1746; Jams. Belin, Geo Pawley Junr., Thomas Handlin,
wit.   Misc. Rec. HH, 230

Brown, Alexander of Parish of Prince Frederick & Mary Dutarque,
spinster, 10 Aug. 1744; license to Rev. Thomas Hasell;
Thomas Oliver, merchant, bondsman.   MB Chas

27

Brown, Alexander & Mary Dutarque, 16 Aug. 1744.   T & D PR

Brown, Casper & Mary Hullman, widow, 19 Feb. 1772.   St Phil PR

Brown, Charles & Mary O'Hara, widow, 16 Oct. 1772.   St Phil PR

Brown, Christopher & Sally Faucheraud, 8 May 1789; Peter
    Dubois, James McBride, wit.   Mar Set 1: 650-651

Brown, Francis & Eleanor Walcott, 10 Apr. 1712.   SPG

Brown, Francis & Anne Margaret Come, per Licence by the Revd.
    Mr. Alexr. Garden, 23 January 1747.   St. Phil PR

Brown, George & Mary Obart, P Licence, 1 Feb. 1748.   St Phil PR

Brown, Godfrey & Rachel Burkitt, 20 Feb. 1745/6.   Pr Fred PR

Brown, Hugh & Mary Easton, widow, 8 Oct. 1772.   St. Phil PR

Brown, Isaac & ___, 14 Apr. 1795.   Fairf Pres Ch

Brown, James, M.D., & Ann Deveaux, 8 Aug. 1786.   St. Hel PR

Brown, John & Rene Bonneau, 12 July 1757.   T & D PR

Brown, John of Allsaints Parish & Ann Bonney Monk, 22 Feb. 1785;
    William Jordan, James McCracken, wit.   Mar Set 1: 612

Brown, John Revd. & Frances Ayers, 4 Aug. 1789.   Pugh diary

Brown, John Junr. & Judith Hull, 5 May 1737.   St. And PR

Brown, Jonathan & Margaret Booth, P Banns, 15 April 1722.
    St. Phil PR

Brown, Joseph & Mary Hudson, P Licence, 22 May 1739.   St Phil PR

Brown, Joseph & Hannah Nipper, widow, 24 Sept. 1772.   St Phil PR

Brown, Joshua & Harriet Wyatt, 7 Dec. 1797.   Circ Cong

Brown, Nathaniel & Sarah Elliott, 4 Feb. 1747.   St. And PR

Brown, Ross & Elizabeth Floyd, widow, 13 Jan. 1795.   St Phil PR

Brown, Saml & Mrs. Margt. Rambert, 28 Apr. 1796.   Trin Meth Ch

Brown, Squire & Maria Eyre, 25 Dec. 1792.   St. Phil PR

Brown, Stephen widdower, & Elizabeth Tallman, widdow, 16 Sept.
    1781.   St. Phil PR

Brown, Talbott & Margeret Cuddy, P Licence, 30 January 1744/5.
    St. Phil PR

Brown, Thomas & Catharine Murray, 28 Sept. 1783.   St. John Luth
    Ch

Brown, William and Margaret Herbert, spinster; minister Timothy
    Mellichamp; bondsmen William Brown of St. Bartholomews Parish
    and John Miller (Milner) of Charles Town gunsmith; wit.
    James Michie, 17 Sept. 1733.   MB NY

SOUTH CAROLINA MARRIAGES 1688-1799

Brown, William & Esther Dupuy, P Licence, 31 January 1740. St. Phil PR

Brown, William & Sarah Barklay, 18 May 1777. St. Phil PR

Brown, William & Ann Williamson, 17 Mar. 1797. Circ Cong

Browne, Charles Fowler, of Charleston, bricklayer, and Sarah Chitty, of same, 24 Dec. 1799. St. Phil PR

Browne, Daniel & Margaret Forster, widow, 17 June 1787. St. Phil PR

Browne, James of Charleston, merchant & Elizabeth Petsch, daughter of Adam Petsch, late Chymist & Apothecary, 10 Apr. 1797; John Christopher Martin & Michael Crowley, trustees; Henry Bailey, Gabriel Bailey, wit. Mar Set 3: 56-63

Browne, William & Margaret Cole, 12 July 1795. St. Phil PR

Brownfield, Robert of George Town, Physician & Susanna Mann Heriot, 16 May 1799; John Ouldfield Heriot, Robert Heriot, trustees; Geo: Herriot, Geo H. Spierin, Jo Blyth, wit. Mar Set 3: 325-330

Bruce, Caleb & ___, 27 March 1776. Pugh diary

Bruce, Daniel of Charleston merchant, & Susannah Smith, daughter of Thomas Smith late of Winyaw, planter; 30 Oct. 1794; Thomas Cochran & Thomas Screven, planter; Charles Buckman, John Buckman, wit. Mar Set 2: 317-330

Bruce, Daniel & Susannah Smith, 2 Oct. 1794. St. Phil PR

Bruce, Donald & Margaret Lockhart, 14 Feb. 1774. St. Phil PR

Bruce, John & Jane Holbeatch, P Licence by Mr. Garden, 2 Feb. 1722/23. St. Phil PR

Bruce, John & Ann Sanders, 14 Feb. 1750-1. T & D PR

Bruce, Peter Henry & Elizabeth Fitchett, of St. Philips Parish, 5 Apr. 1757; Patrick Laird, John Patient, wit. Misc. Rec. KK: 455-456

Bruce, Peter Henry & Elizabeth Fitchett, widow, 10 Apr. 1757. St. Phil PR

Bruder, John & Eleanor Anneshele, P Licence by Mr. Garden, 28 June 1736. St. Phil PR

Brue(?), George & Betsy Benton, 20 Jan. 1799. Pugh diary

Bruneau, Paul & Elizabeth Pair, P Licence, 20 Sept. 1731. St. Phil PR

Brunet, Isaiah & Alice Thomson, P Licence by Mr. Garden, 4 March 1735. St. Phil PR

Brunett, Isaiah & Susannah Mary Leay, P Licence, 1 Jan. 1740. St. Phil PR

Brunson, John, widow, & Susanna Robinson, widow, 13 Aug. 1743. Pr Fred PR

29

Brunson, William of parish of St. James Santee, & Eliza. Cooper, spinster, 26 Apr. 1744; license to Rev. Daniel Dwight; Samuel Bowman of St. Johns parish, bondsman.   MB Chas

Bryan, Arthur & Helen Cummins, of Beaufort Dist., spinster, 8 May 1797; Daniel Carrel & Benjamin Peporn, trustees; Jane Clayton, James Troup, wit.   Mar Set 3: 154-157

Bryan, Hugh & Martha Brandford, 19 Oct. 1721.   St. And PR

Bryan, Hugh & Catherine Barnwell, 2 Jan. 1734.   St. Hel PR

Bryan, Hugh of Parish of St. Helena, Esq., & Mary Preoleau, spinster, 25 Oct. 1744; license to Rev. Alex. Garden; Samuel Prioleau, of Charles Town, bondsman.   MB Chas

Bryan, Hugh & Mary Prioleau, P Licence, 25 Oct. 1744.   St. Phil PR

Bryan, John & Elizabeth Boddett, 30 March 1756.   St. Phil PR

Bryan, John & Mary Esther Sanks, widow, 11 June 1772. St. Phil PR

Bryan, John & Rachel Simons, 24 Apr. 1777.   St. Phil PR

Bryan, John, of Charles Town & Lydia, relict of the late Edward Simons; 1 Feb. 1783; Benjamin Simons & John Ball, both of St. Thomas & St. Dennis Parish, trustees; Rebecca Jamieson, James Pring, wit.   Mar Set 2: 71-75

Bryan, John & Sarah Margareta Finlay, 11 Sept. 1748.   Pr Fred PR

Bryan, John and Sarah Atnor, 26 Oct. 1747.   Pr Fred PR

Bryan, Jonathan & Marh Williamson, P Licence, 13 October 1737. St. Phil PR

Bryan, Joseph & Mary Story, 9 Jan. 1741.   St. Hel PR

Bryan, Nicholas, of Parish of Prince George, bachelor, & Mary Williams, of Parish of Prince George, spinster, in the house of Danl. Horry Esqr., 9 June 1759, Michael Mckarty, Jane Mckarty, wit.   St. Jas PR

Bryan, Samuel & Susanna Glaze, 4 May 1790.   Circ Cong

Bryan, William & Mary Bennet, P Banns, 11 January 1735. St. Phil PR

Bryant, Gray & Nansey Webb, 19 Apr. 1787.   Pugh diary

Bryant, James of Parish of Prince Frederick, widower, & Hezekiah Sutton, of Prince Fredericks parish, spinster, at the house of Mrs. Esther Micheau, 7 Jan. 1785; Paul Michau, Ann Michau, wit.   St. Jas PR

Bryant, John & Jane Thornton, 8 Oct. 1794.   St. Phil PR

Bryant, Thos. & Martha Oglesbee, 16 June 1785.   Pugh diary

Buchanan, John of Parish of Prince George, bachelor, & Elizabeth Miott, spinster, in the house of Mrs. Eliz: Bell, 21 Aug.

1783; Mary Withers, Charlotte Withers, wit.   St. Jas PR

Buckingham, Elias & Margaret Falker, 13 June 1771.   St. Phil PR

Buckles, Thomas & Margaret Brown, 28 June 1755.   St. Phil PR

Budding, Wm. & Ann Rotherford, 29 March 1766.   OJ 1764-1771

Bulard, David & Priscilla Harwy (Harvey?), 24 Feb. 1776.
St. John Luth Ch

Bull, Arthur of St. Helena Parish, Granville Co., & Esther
Stewart, widow, 7 May 1744; license to Rev. Lewis Jones;
Jenkin Hughs of Charles Town, bondsman.   MB Chas

Bull, John & Elizabeth St. John, 2 Nov. 1797.   St. Phil PR

Bull, Stephen & Martha Godin, 27 Apr. 1731.   St. And PR

Bull, Stephen & Martha Godin, P Licence, 27 April 1731.
St. Phil PR

Bull, Stephen & Elizabeth Bryan, 10 May 1739.   St. Hel PR

Bull, Stephen, Eldest Son of the Lieutn. Governor, & Judith
Mayrant, spinster, P Licence by the Revd. Mr. A. Garden, 2
May 1747.   St. Phil PR

Bull, Stephen & Elizabeth Woodward, 18 Dec. 1755.   St. Phil PR

Bull, Stephen & Mrs. Ann Middleton, widow, 11 June 1772.
St. Hel PR

Bull, Thomas & Sarah Simpson, 11 May 1771.   St. Phil PR

Bull, William & Elizabeth Reid, spinster, daughter of James
Reid, physician, decd., 25 Aug. 1779; Stephen Bull, Mrs.
Judith Pringle, trustees; Robert Pringle, Elizabeth Pringle,
wit.   Mar Set 1: 188-189

Bull, William & Elizabeth Reid, 26 Aug. 1779.   St. Phil PR

Bull, William, junr. & Hannah Beale, spinster, per Licence by
the Revd. Mr. Robert Betham, 17 August 1746.   St. Phil PR

Bullard, Edward & Sarah Harris, widow, 16 Apr. 1757.   St. Phil
PR

Bullard, Griffith & Hibaba Young, 18 Nov. 1734.   St. Phil PR

Bullen, James & Mary Poinsett, 1 July 1726.   St. Phil PR

Bullock, Samuel & Elizabeth Bollard, 28 Dec. 1726.   St. Phil PR

Bullock, Samuel & Rhoda Hales, 12 July 1770.   T & D PR

Bullock, Samll. & Eliza Cooke, 18 May 1730.   Ch Ch PR

Bulmer, William & Elizabeth Rogers, P Licence, 23 Jan. 1734.
St. Phil PR

Bunch, Paul & Amy Winigum, 28 Apr. 1748.   Hist Oburg

Buncker, John & Catherine Wills, P Licence, 16 Nov. 1752.
   St. Phil PR

Bunness, James & Sarah Jaudon, 9 Sept. 1794.   St. Phil PR

Bur, Thos. & Rachel Bailey, 7 Feb. 1766.   OJ 1764-1771

Burch, Edward & Mary Ann Wilson, 2 May 1797.   Pugh diary

Burford, John & Ann Berches, P Licence by Mr. Garden, 27 April
   1736.   St. Phil PR

Burch, Joseph & Mary Ann Fisher, 11 May 1762.   St. Phil PR

Burch, William & Carolina Langdon, P Banns, 8 June 1747.
   St. Phil PR

Burdell, Jacob & Elizabeth Carrier, 18 Feb. 1713-4.   T & D PR

Burdell, John and Mary Lieubray, 23 Aug. 1744.   Pr Fred PR

Burdell, Jacob & Mary Joy, 30 July 1746.   Ch Ch PR

Burdell, John & Elizabeth McGrigor, 17 Apr. 1748.   T & D PR

Burdell, Thomas & Margaret Wright, 16 Jan. 1742/3.   Pr Fred PR

Burford, John & Susanah Wood, 1 Feb. 1740/1.   St. And PR

Burger, David & Catharine Cleator, 4 June 1775.   St. Phil PR

Burger, David & Mary Elms, 5 Nov. 1777.   St. Phil PR

Burgess, John of St. Bartholomews Parish & Sarah Timmons, of
   same, spinster, 31 Aug. 1763; Elijah Hartee, Thomas Crawford, trustees; William Day, John Stricland, wit.   Misc.
   Rec. MM: 76-77

Burgess, John & Mary Ann Churchill, 28 Aug. 1777.   St. Phil PR

Burgess, Samuel & Mary Givens, 26 Jan. 1733/4.   St. And PR

Burk, Tobias & Mary Vance, P Licence, 18 Aug. 1749.   St. Phil PR

Burk, Walter Capt. of Philadelphia, mariner, & Elizabeth Salter,
   12 Feb. 1799.   St. Phil PR

Burkhard, John, merchant, & Miss Catharine Wills, 5 Aug. 1784.
   St. John Luth Ch.

Burley, Richard & Frances Scott, 12 Apr. 1750.   T & D PR

Burn, John Paul & Catharine Krebs, 17 July 1785.   St. John
   Luth Ch

Burn, Samuel & Mary Ancrum, 28 Nov. 1771.   St. Phil PR

Burn, Walter and Martha Rowe, widow; minister Alexander Garden,
   bondsmen Walter Burn of Charles Town, gent., and John Salter
   of same, gent., wit. James Michie, 19 June 1733.   MB NY

Burnet, Henry & Mary Hamilton, widow, 21 May 1757.   St Phil PR

SOUTH CAROLINA MARRIAGES 1688-1799

Burnett, Henry of Charles Town, carver, & Mary Hamilton, of same,
   widow, of Robert Hamilton; Lambert Lance of Charles Town,
   trustee; Sarah Holzendorf, Albert Holzendorf, wit. 21 May
   1757. Misc. Rec. KK: 486-490

Burnham, Nicholas & Elizabeth Smith, P Licence, 31 December
   1741. St. Phil PR

Burrows, Frederick & Mary Torey, widow, 2 Feb. 1794. St Phil PR

Burrows, Jeremiah & Belinda Heap, 30 Oct. 1720. St. And PR

Burrows, John & Eliz Scott, 24 Jan. 1769. St. Phil PR

Burrows, Richard & Mary McCulloch, 18 Feb. 1770. T & D PR

Burrows, William & Mary Ward, P Licence, 20 April 1749. St.
   Phil PR

Burt, Nathaniel & Rebekah Goldsmith, P Licence by Mr. Garden,
   19 July 1736. St. Phil PR

Burt, Nathaniel, Junr. & Rebecca Mallory, per Licence, 16 May
   1746. St. Phil PR

Burt, Peter & Mary Fallows, 20 June 1769. St. Phil PR

Burt, William & Ann Jones, 20 Apr. 1775. St. Phil PR

Burton, Benjamin & Margaret Jones, 15 March 1759. St. Hel PR

Burton, Isaac & Ann Remington, 15 Jan. 1775. St. Phil PR

Burton, Thomas & Elizabeth Stewart, 11 June 1762. St. Phil PR

Bury, John & Margaret Richard, 9 July 1761. St. Phil PR

Bury, John & Susannah Roberts, 4 Nov. 1779. St. Phil PR

Bushell, Edward & Mary Bull, P Licence, 22 December 1744.
   St. Phil PR

Busk, Richard of St. James Goose Creek & Mary Ann Jones, widow,
   17 Augu. 1744; license to Rev. Daniel Dwight; James Little,
   bondsman. MB Chas

Butcher, John & Barbary Gas, spinster, per Licence by the Revd.
   Mr. Robt. Betham, 25 Sept. 1746. St. Phil PR

Butler, Charles P., silver smith, & Ann Poyas, of Charleston,
   widow, 28 Dec. 1798; Bethel Threadcraft, watchmaker, trustee;
   Isaac N. Gill, Jas Nicholson, wit. Mar Set 3: 330-334

Butler, Elisha & Eliza Miles, widow, 24 Sept. 1738. St And PR

Butler, Elisha & Mary Wright, widow, 17 Jan. 1747. St. And PR

Butler, James & Eliza. Rice, widow, 26 April 1766. OJ 1764-1771

Butler, James & Ann Bennett, daughter of Thomas Bennett, 19 Dec.
   1782. Ch Ch PR

Butler, James & Mary Hamlin, daughter of George and Mary Hamlin,
   20 May 1790. Ch Ch PR

33

Butler, James Henry & Sarah Freeman, 20 Sept. 1766. St. Phil PR

Butler, John & Mary Bowdon, 10 Feb. 1709/10.   Reg Prov 1711-15,
   p. 449(41)

Butler, Joseph & Mary LeRoach, P Licence, 23 December 1731.
   St. Phil PR

Butler, Joseph, of Charleston, mariner & Maria Tash, of same,
   26 Oct. 1799.   St. Phil PR

Butler, Peter & Elizabeth Graham, spinster, P Licence, 27 Feb.
   1749.   St. Phil PR

Butler, Samuel & Catharine Parrott, 9 Aug. 1760. St. Phil PR

Butler, Thomas & Elizabeth Elliott, 19 Dec. 1723.   St. Phil PR

Butler, Thomas & Elizabeth Gibbes, P Licence, 8 July 1734.
   St. Phil PR

Butler, Thomas & Constant Fitch, widow, 16 April 1738. St. And.
   PR

Butler, Thos. & Elizabeth Ladson, 13 June 1732. St. And PR

Butler, William & Elizabeth Elliott, 1 Dec. 1738. St. And PR

Butler, William & Ruth Ellis, 17 June 1766.   OJ 1764-1771

Butt, Peter of Parish of Prince George, bachelor, & Elizabeth
   Harvey, of Parish of Prince George, spinster, at the house
   of Mrs. Eliz. Harvey, 10 July 1782; no wit. St. Jas PR

Butter, John & Eleanor Doujon, 29 March 1759.   St. Phil PR

Butterton, Joseph & Elizabeth Margaret Touslger, 3 Nov. 1789.
   St. Phil PR

Buttler, Edward and Mary Skipper, 13 Apr. 1742. Pr Fred PR

Buttler, Thomas & Elizabeth Lunberry, 5 July 1767. T & D PR

Buttler, Thomas & Mary Miller, 7 Oct. 1773. T & D PR

Byers, Robert & Elizabeth Graham, widow, 21 Nov. 1772.
   St. Phil PR

Byers, Williamson to Martha Adams, both of York Co., 1 Aug.
   1798, William Byers, surety.   York Pro 66/3129

Bynum, Turner & Eliza Miller, 13 Aug. 1799.   St. Phil PR

Byrd, Jno(?), & Ann Watkins, 21 July 1774. Pugh diary

Byrem, William & Mary Rogers, 30 April 1725.   St. Phil PR

Byrn, Felix & Deborah Mackey, P Licence, 8 Dec. 1741. St. Phil
   PR

Byrne, Michael & Catherine Thomas, 7 Apr. 1795. Trin Meth Ch

Byrnes, James & Clementina Martha Leibert, 16 June 1793.
   Trin Meth Ch

Byrns, John & Mary Spencer, 10 June 1798.   Trin Meth Ch

Bythewood, Thomas & Sarah Mallery, 21 Dec. 1794.   Circ Cong

Caborne, George of St. Bartholomews Parish, & Sarah Esther
    Bellenger, of same, 24 July 1787; Edmond Bellenger, Esther
    Bellenger, trustees; Edmund Bellenger, Junr., Mary Myers,
    wit.   Mar Set 1:   327-328

Caborne, George of St. Peters Parish. & Catherine Cam of St.
    Andrews Parish, widow, 12 Jan. 1797; Daniel Doyley of St.
    Bartholomews Parish, & Thomas Wigfall of St. Thomas Parish,
    trustees; Thos. Miles, John H. Mitchell, Margaret Gillespie,
    wit.   Mar Set 3:   94-99

Cahusac, John of St. Stephen's Parish, Charleston Dist., to
    Elizabeth Ann Williams.   28 Jan. 1789.   James Brannon, wit.
    John Williams, surety.   York Pro 55/2452

Cahusac, Peter & Mary Manzequen, P Banns, 18 June 1749.   St.
    Phil PR

Cain, James & Sarah Colcock, 3 Dec. 1755.   St. Phil PR

Cain, John and Ann Power, 15 Apr. 1737.   Pr Fred PR

Caismire, Claimance & Susannah Lentry, 21 Aug. 1759.   St. Phil
    PR

Calder, James & Margaret Whitfield, 9 March 1782.   St. Phil PR

Caldwell, John, Serjeant, & Hanna Herrington, by Authority of
    a Certificate of permission signed by Major H. Sheridan of
    the 3d American Regiment, 9 Jan. 1782.   St. John Luth Ch

Calhoon, James of Parish of Prince Frederick, Widower, and
    Martha Monk, of Parish of Prince George, widow, in the house
    of William Hull, 5 Sept. 1771; Edmund Carr, John Simmons, wit.
    St. Jas PR

Calhoun, William of Charleston, merchant, & Lydia Cattell,
    daughter of the late Benjamin Cattell, Esqr., decd., 20
    Nov. 1792; John Ward, wit.   Mar Set 2: 83-84

Calhoun, William & Lydia Cattell, 21 Nov. 1792.   St. Phil PR

Callabeuf, Stephen & Mary Rowser, 29 Nov. 1744.   Ch Ch PR

Callibeuf, Stephen of Charles Town & Mary McDowell, spinster,
    31 July 1744; license to Rev. Levi Durand; Robert Clemens
    of Parish of Christ Church, bondsman.   MB Chas

Callibeauf, Stephen of Parish of Christ Church, chair maker, &
    Mary Roser, spinster, 7 Nov. 1744; license to Rev. Levi Dur-
    and; John Evans, of Charles Town, joiner, bondsman.   MB Chas

Callion, Jacobus, of Parish of Prince George, Widower, &
    Margaret Waller, of Parish of Prince George, widow, 9 July
    1769; Alexander ___, Benjn. Perdriau, wit.   St. Jas PR

Calvert, ___ & ___ Linthwaite, 2 Jan. 1766.   OJ 1764-1771

Calvert, John & Mary Clarke, 13 Nov. 1755.   St. Phil PR

Calvert, John of Charles Town & Jane Elizabeth Holmes, widow,
29 Jan. 1781; William Graham, trustee; Wm. Roach, Mary
Roach, wit.   Misc. Rec. TT: 7-9

Calvert, William & Mary Steinson, P Licence, 8 Sept. 1733.
St. Phil PR

Calvert, William of Goosecreek to Judith Elsin, 2 March 1794.
Trin Meth Ch

Calvin, John of Pr. William Parish, & Mary Dossette, 11 June
1758.   St. Hel PR

Calwell, Henry Senr. & Sarah Rivers, 11 March 1791.   St. Phil PR

Calwell, John & Rebecca Norman, 11 Jan. 1759.   St. Phil PR

Cam, William & Catharine Wigfall, daughter of John Wigfall of
Parish of St. Thomas & St. Dennis, & granddaughter of Catharine Wigfall, decd., 30 Jan. 1788; John Wigfall, Thomas
Wigfall, his son, trustees; Samuel Ward, Samuel Wigfall,
wit.   Mar Set 1: 328-332

Camble, Mikel & Milly Webb, 21 Dec. 1785.   Pugh diary

Camble, Robt. & Lucia Blair, 26 Feb. 1788.   Pugh diary

Cambridge, Tobias & Elizabeth Wood, 1 Jan. 1778.   St. Phil PR

Cameron, Alexander of Christ Church Parish, & Matilda Fenwicke,
daughter of Edward Fenwicke, decd., 2 July 1788 (already
married); Thomas Gadsden, Esqr., trustee; Thos. Lowndes,
Dom. A. Hall, wit.   Mar Set 1: 379-384

Cameron, Lewis of Charleston, merchant, & Amelia Murray, widow,
15 March 1799; John Prentice, trustee; Thomas Denny, Langdon
Cheves, wit.   Mar Set 3: 350-352

Cameron, Will. & Mary Young, 24 Feb. 1793.   Trin Meth Ch

Campbell, Alexander of George Town, & Martha Durand, daughter of
James Durand, decd., 8 May 1789; William Forrister, Martha
Forrister, trustees; William Magill, C. C. Forrester, wit.
Mar Set 1: 442-444

Campbell, Arch. & Phoebe Sarah Barnwell, 11 Dec. 1780.
St. Hel PR

Campbell, Archebel, & Jane Orr, 26 Jan. 1763.   St. Hel PR

Campbell, Colin of Berner Street, parish of St. Mary le bone,
County of Middlesex, & Rebecca Izard, younger daughter of
Ralph Izard, late of S. C., decd., 22 Apr. 1768; John, Duke
or Argyle, William Campbell; & Daniel Blake of S. C., trustees; Wm. Black, Wm. Fowler, wit.   Misc. Rec. TT: 241-245

Campbell, David & Ann Loughton Motte; Isaac Motte, William
Smith, James Ladson, Esqrs; 27 Sept. 1792; Wit: Ab. Motte.
Mar Set 2: 69-70

Campbell, Hugh & Cath. Delegal, 3 May 1747.   St. Hel PR

Campbell, Hugh & Eliza. Reyley, 7 April 1766.   OJ 1764-1771

Campbell, James & Judith Dwyer, 3 ___ 1749.   Pr Fred PR

Campbell, John & Catharine Lee, widow, 17 May 1762.   St Phil PR

Campbell, McCarlan, of Charleston & Sarah Fenwicke, daughter of
    Edward Fenwicke, decd.; marriage agreement made 24 Feb. 1777,
    this document dated 28 Aug. 1792; Charles Cotesworth Pinckney
    & Charles Drayton, trustees; John Burckhardt & Dalziel
    Hunter, wit.   Mar Set 2: 15-25

Campbell, Macartan & Sarah Fenwick, 24 Feb. 1777.   St. Phil PR

Campling, William & Sarah Page, 24 Apr. 1728.   St. Hel PR

Campbell, William & Mary Times, P Licence, 2 June 1749.
    St. Phil PR

Campbell, Willm. Right Honble Lord & Sarah Izard, 17 Apr. 1763.
    St. Phil PR

Cane, Barnet & Jean Wently, 5 Sept. 1774.   Pugh diary

Cannon, Arnold & Sarah Anger, 31 Oct. 1754.   St. And PR

Cannon, Daniel & Martha Winn, spinster, P Licence by the Revd.
    Mr. Garden Rector, 8 March 1749/50.   St. Phil PR

Cannon, Daniel & Mary Doughty, 30 Oct. 1755.   St. Phil PR

Cannon, George & Susanah Williamson, 21 Aug. 1794.   Pugh diary

Cannon, Henry & ___, 14 Aug. 1798.   Pugh diary

Cantey, Josiah & Elizabeth Boswood, 3 Oct. 1731.   St. And PR

Cantle, John of Charles Town, mariner & Sarah Loocock, 17 Mah
    1752; John Remington of Charles Town, trustee; John Bury,
    Wm. Remington, wit.   Misc. Rec. LL: 487-489

Cape, Brian & Mary Hetherington, 6 May 1770.   T & D PR

Capers, ___ & Susannah Morgan, 28 Apr. 1763.   St. Hel PR

Capers, Charles & Anne Thomson, 13 Nov. 1753.   St. Hel PR

Capers, Josp: Ellicot & Hannah Frampton, 21 Dec. 1740.   St. Hel
    PR

Capers, Richard & Anne Sincklar, 17 May 1730.   Ch Ch PR

Capers, Richard & Elizabeth Bonhost, 8 Jan. 1740.   Ch Ch PR

Capers, Richard of parish of Christ Church & Mary Maybanks,
    widow, 20 July 1744; license to Rev. Levi Durand; Peter
    Benoist, bondsman.   MB Chas

Capers, Richard & Mary Ann Maybank, 2 Aug. 1744.   Ch Ch PR

Capers, Richard & Rachel Spencer, 29 Nov. 1767.   St. Phil PR

Capers, Thomas & Elizabeth Guy, 8 Dec. 1767.   St. Phil PR

SOUTH CAROLINA MARRIAGES 1688-1799

Capers, William & Catharine Dutarque, 4 Dec. 1753. T & D PR

Capon, Luke & Eleanor Lasberry, 17 Aug. 1767. St. Phil PR

Cardozo, Abraham & Hannah Allen, widow, 3 Jan. 1759. St Phil PR

Carirne, Samuel & Sarah Beckett, 22 Mar. 1758. St. Phil PR

Carlton, George (Overseer), & Sarah Lassiter Sams, spinster,
    10 May 1796; Charles Chamberlain, trustee; William Lawrence,
    Thomas Elliott, wit. Mar Set 2: 526-527

Carman, Joseph & Susannah Helligess, 27 Aug. 1771. St Phil PR

Carman, Thomas & Deborah Palmetor, 21 Nov. 1722. St. Phil PR

Carn, Samuel Doctor & Catherine Bond, 18 Feb. 1759. Ch Ch PR

Carne, John, Cabinet Maker in Charles Town, & Mary Hutchinson,
    of Christ Church parish, 12 May 1765; Thomas Hutchinson,
    Mathias Hutchin [sic], trustees; Thomas Barksdale, Thomas
    Player, William Evans, wit. Misc. Rec. NN: 123-127

Carne, Samuel & Jannet Borland, P Licence, 23 February 1752.
    St. Phil PR

Carnes, Lawrence & Ann Wilkie, 15 Jan. 1782. St. Phil PR

Carpenter, Joseph & Maria Miller(in), 3 Sept. 1772. St. John
    Luth Ch

Carr, James & Mary Yeadon, 10 Jan. 1788. St. Phil PR

Carr, John & Mary Freglith, 26 Aug. 1773. St. Phil PR

Carr, William & Elizabeth Shute, P Licence, 29 Jan. 1729.
    St. Phil PR

Carruthers, William & Jean Wertzer, widow, 14 Nov. 1770.
    St. Phil PR

Carson, James of Charleston, merchant, & Elizabeth Neyle, dau-
    ghter of Elizabeth Neyle, 7 May 1796; Wm. Neyle & Sampson
    Neyle of Savannah, Ga., trustees; John Sollie, wit.
    Mar Set 2: 521-522

Carson, William of Charles Town, merchant, & Rebeckah Lloyd,
    spinster, minor, only daughter of John Lloyd, decd., 10 Jan.
    1770; Robert Rivers, John Freer, James Carson, trustees;
    James Latta, James Carson, wit. Misc Rec. oo: 560-564

Cart, John & Rachael Dallas, P Licence, 22 January 1741.
    St. Phil PR

Cart, Joseph & Anne Bird, 6 Apr. 1758. T & D PR

Cart, Joseph & Martha Walker, 14 Dec. 1760. T & D PR

Carter, Benjamin & Eliza. Carrant, 9 Feb. 1722/23. St. Phil PR

Carter, Benjamin & Rebecca Murphy, widow, 14 Jan. 1740. Hist
    Oburg

38

Carter, John and Martha Sarten, 26 March 1742.   Pr Fred PR

Carter, Stephen & Sarah Barton, 16 Apr. 1734.   St. And PR

Carter, Stepney & Mary Wilson, 30 Aug. 1781.   St. Phil PR

Cartlidge, Edmund and Elizabeth Keble, 9 Dec. 1743.   Pr Fred PR

Carwithen, William & Mary Bisset, P Licence, 14 Jan. 1729.
   St. Phil PR

Cartwright, Richd. & Kesiah Skinner, P Licence by Mr. Garden,
   23 Dec. 1735.   St. Phil PR

Casey, Benjamin of Charleston, & Maria Elizabeth Strohecker,
   18 Dec. 1799; John Geddes, John Strohecker, trustees;
   Frederick Wolf, Johann George Wurdemann, wit.   Mar Set 3:
   407-411

Caskin, John & Deborah Weston, 24 Sept. 1776.   St. Phil PR

Cassello, Henry & Margaret Mitchell, 18 July 1734.   Circ Cong

Caswell, John & Sarah Bee, 28 March 1722.   St. Phil PR

Cater, Benjamin & Mary Bedon, 11 June 1750.   St. And PR

Caton, Benjamin & Ann Vickery, 26 March 1758.   St. Phil PR

Cattel, John & Margaret Levingstone, P Licence, 3 Jan. 1737.
   St. Phil PR

Cattel, John, widower, & Sarah Hazzard, widow, 9 Dec. 1742.
   St. Hel PR

Cattel, Peter & Mary Lloyd, per Licence, 6 June 1745.   St. Phil
   PR

Cattel, William, junr. & Ann Frazer, spinster, by the Revd.
   Mr. Timothy Mellichamp, 31 July 1746.   St. Phil PR

Cattell, Andrew & Sarah Toomer, 14 July 1745.   St. And PR

Cattell, Benjamin & Rose Webb, 22 July 1778.   St. Phil PR

Cattell, Benjamin (son of William Cattell Jun.), & Mary McCall
   of Philadelphia, 25 June 1772.   St. And PR

Cattell, Charles of Parish of St. Andrews, Berkley Co., &
   Catherine Cattell, spinster, 13 March 1743/4; license to
   Rev. Thomas Thompson; John Hume, merchant, bondsman.   MB Chas

Cattell, Charles & Catherine Cattell, 25 March 1744.   St And PR

Cattell, John (son of Benjamin) & Mary Levingston, 19 Jan. 1758.
   St. And PR

Cattell, John Junr., & Margaret Livingston, 3 Jan. 1737
   [1737/8].   St. And PR

Cattell, Wm. Junr., & Anne Cattell, 17 May 1732.   St. And PR

Cattell, William (son of William Cattell Junr.), & Sabina
   Lynch, 8 March 1767.   St. And PR

39

Cattell, Willm. Junr. & Ann Frasier, 31 July 1746. St And PR

Causton, John & Mary Pestell, P Licence, 9 Nov. 1744.
St. Phil PR

Cavineau, James & Mary Douglass, widow, 9 June 1766. OJ 1764-
1771

Caw, David, Doctor & Katherine Serree, widow, per Licence by
the Reverd. Mr. Robert Betham, 27 Nov. 1746. St. Phil PR

Caw, Lewis & widow Dubois, 3 Dec. 1751. Ch Ch PR

Caylove, Frederick & Mary Ann Coffman, 26 Apr. 1778. St Phil PR

Chaddock, Thomas & Ann Modiner Christian, P Licence by the
Revd. Mr. Garden Rector, 1 August 1749. St. Phil PR

Chalmers, Gilbert & Sophia Boddington, 23 June 1774. St. Phil
PR

Chambers, Joseph & Eleanor Hamilton, 30 July 1772. St Phil PR

Chalmers, Lionel & Martha Logan, P Licence, 30 January 1738.
St. Phil PR

Chalmers, Lionel & Elizabeth Warden, 24 Aug. 1766. St. Phil PR

Chambers, William & Isabella Maceant, P Licence by Mr. Garden,
9 Feb. 1736. St. Phil PR

Chambers, William (of the 31st of Marines) & Rose Dane, 4 Sept.
1766. St. Phil PR

Champneys, John & Mary Musgrove, 31 Aug. 1731. St. And PR

Champneys, John & Sarah Saunders, 7 Jan. 1740 [1740/1].
St. And PR

Champneys, John of Charles Town, merchant & Mary Wilson, of
same, widow, 13 Aug. 1781; Alexander Harvey, of Chehaw,
trustee; Jeremiah Savage, Gilbert Wilson, wit. Mar Set 1:
1-2

Champneys, John & Mary Wilson, widow, 15 Aug. 1781. St. Phil PR

Chanler, Isaac of Charlestown, Practitioner in Physick, &
Sarah White, spinster, 15 Apr. 1771; Blake Leay White &
Joseph Veree, carpenters, trustees; James Mortimer Harris,
Charles Harris, William Morgan, wit. Mar Set 1: 86-92

Chaplin, Benjamin, & Sarah Ladson, 1 Oct. 1751. St. Hel PR

Chaplin, Benj., widower, & Eleanor Reynolds, 29 Jan. 1756.
St. Hel PR

Chaplin, John & Elizabeth Ladson, widow of B. Ladson, 24 Feb.
1756. St. Hel PR

Chaplin, William & Sarah Reynolds, widow, 30 Apr. 1741.
St. Hel PR

Chaplin, William & Ann Westcoat, widow, 19 Jan. 1769. St. Phil
PR

SOUTH CAROLINA MARRIAGES 1688-1799

Chaplin, William & Martha Fripp, 5 Feb. 1763.   St. Hel PR

Chapman, Thomas & Anne Helm, P Licence, 12 Oct. 1740.   St. Phil
PR

Chapman, William & Rebecca Storey, 28 Apr. 1735.   Circ Cong

Chapman, William of James's Island & Mary Guy, 10 May 1741.
St. And PR

Chapman, William & Elizabeth Brown, 14 Feb. 1749 [1749/50].
St. And PR

Chapman, William Snr(?), & Elenor Harris, widow, 19 Oct. 1758.
St. And PR

Chapman, Willm & Margarett Parsons, 12 July 1742.   St. And PR

Chardon, Isaac & Mary Mazyck, P Licence, 9 July 1730.   St. Phil
PR

Chardon, Isaac & Mary Woodward, 6 Nov. 1731.   St. And PR

Charles, George & Eliz Hoff, 8 May 1770.   St. Phil PR

Charls, Noulson & Sarah Lowary, 29 Jan. 1763.   St. Hel PR

Charnock, Thomas & Sibell Milner, P Licence, 2 April 1738.
St. Phil PR

Charville, John & Anne Mackay, P Banns, 15 Dec. 1734.
St. Phil PR

Chauvin, Isaac & Elizabeth Jourdan, 25 August 1751.   Ch Ch PR

Cheesborough, Aaron & Eliza. Wanlys, P Licence, 8 July 1731.
St. Phil PR

Cheney, Thomas & Elizabeth Wood, 4 Nov. 1777.   St. Phil PR

Cherright, Paul & Rebekah Magee, P Licence, 5 March 1729.
St. Phil PR

Cherry, George & Jane Cannon, 1 Jan. 1786.   Pugh diary

Chery, George & Catey Megee, 2 May 1775.   Pugh diary

Chesheiar, James & Mary Davis, 14 Oct. 1745.   St. And PR

Chesolm, Alexander & Judith Ratcliffe, P Licence, 26 Feb. 1742.
St. Phil PR

Chevillette, Johann & Mrs. Susanna Hepperditzel, 13 Jan. 1745/6;
Joseph Robinson, wit.   Hist Oburg

Chevillette, John & Sarah Yanham, P Licence, May 1734.   St. Phil
PR

Chichester, John of Charleston, Physician, & Mary Beatrix
Powell, granddaughter of William Hopton, Esqr., 10 Nov. 1794;
Nathaniel Russell, trustee; Sarah Russell, Henry A. Livings-
ton, wit.   Mar Set 2: 337-340

41

Chichester, John & Mary Beatrix Powell, 11 Nov. 1794. St. Phil
PR

Chicken, Thomas & Margret Guerry, spinster, 14 Aug. 1744;
license to Rev. John Fordyce; Paul Bruneau, William Thoms,
of Parish of St. James Santee, bondsmen. MB Chas

Chicken, William, Widower, & Elizabeth Chovin, widow, 14 May
1761; James Roberts, John DeLesseline, wit. St. Jas PR

Chisolm, Alexander Robert & Sarah Glaze Maxwell, 6 July 1789.
St. Phil PR

Chovin, Alexander & Mary Tart, 12 Nov. 1772. T & D PR

Christian, David & Frances Rochonet, P Licence, 4 Feb. 1729.
St. Phil PR

Christie, James of Beach Hill, Parish of St. Paul, & Hepzibah
Rose, daughter of Thomas Rose, decd., 22 Nov. 1768; Thomas
Savage, Maj. Samuel Elliot; (bond), Elizabeth Hyrne, Josiah
Murphy, wit. Misc. Rec. RR: 575-576

Christie, James & Hephziba Rose, 22 Nov. 1768. St. Phil PR

Christmas, Jonathan and Hester Morton, 19 June 1741. Pr Fred
PR

Christy, Hugh & Elizabeth Nichols, 12 Oct. 1752. St. Hel PR

Chitty, William (grocer) & Miss Ann Cole, both of this city,
9 Oct. 1794. Trin Meth Ch

Clan, Daniel of St. James Goose Creek & Ann Bearirn, spinster,
10 Apr. 1744; license to Rev. Timothy Mellichamp; William
Guy Junr., bondsman. MB Chas

Clancey, William & Christian Caskie, 28 May 1777. St. Phil PR

Clapp, Gilson & Sarah Ward, P Licence, 29 Jan. 1733. St. Phil
PR

Clarck, Peter, blacksmith & Anna Maria Carpenter(in), 1 Apr.
1777. St. John Luth Ch

Clarendon, Smith & Margaret Meek, widow, 9 Oct. 1773. St. Phil
PR

Clark, Archibald Campbell & Susannah Sutter, 14 Mar. 1786.
St. Hel PR

Clark, David & Martha Allen, 18 Feb. 1794. Circ Cong

Clark, Drewey & Alice Wilcox, 2 Aug. 1795. Circ Cong

Clark, Edward & Blanch Foster, 3 May 1748. Ch Ch PR

Clark, Francis & Mary Smith, P Licence, 11 Nov. 1742. St. Phil
PR

Clark, George & Sophia Edwards, 9 Apr. 1753. St. Hel PR

Clark, Henry Senr. of Claremont Co., & Charity Smith of same, 6
Dec. 1794; John Cain, trustee; John Jefferson, Benjn Oneal,

wit. Misc. Rec. A: 255-259

Clark, James & Dianna Adams, 13 May 1798. Trin Meth Ch

Clark, James & Mary Cambell, 29 Nov. 1798. Circ Cong

Clark, John & Elizbth Bowman, widow, 10 Sept. 1743. St And PR

Clark, John & Mary Collins, 2 July 1744. Ch Ch PR

Clark, John of St. James Santee, & Mary Collins, spinster;
6 June 1744; license to Rev. Levi Durand; William Buchannon
of Prince George's Parish, bondsman. MB Chas

Clark, John & Sarah Myers, 24 Nov. 1785. St. John Luth Ch

Clark, Robert & Mary Long, 13 Jan. 1770. St. Phil PR

Clarke, Edward & Lydia Viart by Mr. Garden, 29 July 1736.
St. Phil PR

Clarke, James & Rachel Hammond, 18 Sept. 1758. St. Phil PR

Clarke, Richard Revd. & Mary Roberts, 26 Dec. 1755. St. Phil PR

Clarke, William & Lucretia Hall, widow, 18 March 1778. St. Phil
PR

Clarkson, William & Ann Hutchinson, 4 May 1775. St. Phil PR

Clarkson, William & Elizabeth Anderson Harris, 30 Dec. 1794.
St. Phil PR

Clarkson, William of Charleston, & Elizabeth Anderson Harris,
daughter of Tucker Harris, 27 Dec. 1794; Tucker Harris,
William Blacklock, trustees; Alexander Bower, wit. Mar Set
2: 346-348

Clase, Samuel & Martha Remy, P Licence, 8 Sept. 1737. St. Phil
PR

Clatworthy, James & Mary, widow of ___ Rush, 15 Feb. 1756.
Hist Oburg

Clay, Joseph the younger of Georgia, & Mary Savage of Charleston, spinster, 23 Nov. 1789; Henry William Desaussure,
practitioner of law, Samuel Legare, merchant, Ralph Elliott
Esqr., trustees, Elias L. Horry, Ruth Savage, wit. Mar Set
1: 470-472

Clayton, David & Ann Roberson, 12 Feb. 1762. St. Phil PR

Cleaton, John & Sirrah Fuster, widow, [1740's]. Hist Oburg

Cleave, Nathan & Hannah Sanders, 27 Aug. 1761. T & D PR

Cleave, Nathan & Catharine Bonneau, 13 Aug. 1763. T & D PR

Cleiland, John, Doctor & Ann Simpson, P Licence, 18 Dec. 1750.
St. Phil PR

Cleiland, William & Esther Maybank of Christ Church Parish, 15
Dec. 1785; D. Ward, W. Douxsaint, wit. Mar Set 1: 198-199

43

Cleiland, William of City of Charleston, bachelor, & Esther
Maybank of Parish of Christ Church, spinster, 15 Dec 1785;
Sy. Swinton, Dan. Ward, wit.   St. Jas PR

Cleims, Martin & Mary Martin, 25 March 1786.   St. John Luth Ch

Clemens, Thomas & Anne Morgan, P Licence, 28 June 1733.
St. Phil PR

Clemenson, John, Gent., & Eunus McIver, of Charleston, widow,
14 July 1790; James Bentham & Mr. Christian Boomer, trustees;
Michael Hart, James Quin, wit.   Mar Set 1:   495-497

Clement, John & Patience Utbert, by Licence of G. Johnson, 1721.
St. Phil PR

Clement, William & Mary Callyhon, widow, 28 Jan. 1747.   Hist
Oburg

Clement, William Esqr. & Sarah Wilkenson, 20 Nov. 1799.   Circ
Cong

Clements, John & Sarah Smith, 22 Jan. 1771.   St. Phil PR

Clements, Jno & Katherine Watson, 26 Sept. 1723.   Ch Ch PR

Clemmons, Thomas, widower, & Elizabeth Baily, 15 Sept. 1769.
St. Hel PR

Clemons, Thomas and Anne Morgan, widow; minister Alexander
Garden bondsmen Thomas Clemons (Clementt) of Charles Town
pack horse man, and Edward Doyle (Doyell) of Berkley County,
plnater, wit.   James Michie, 28 June 1733.   MB NY

Clerk, John of Parish of Prince George, bachelor, & Mary Lambert
of Parish of Prince George, widow, 15 Sept. 1770; John Bell,
Lydia Perdriau, wit.   St. Jas PR

Clerk, Joseph & Anna Tyran, 25 March 1725.   T & D PR

Cleveland, Doctor William & Margaret Macnobney Widow, P Licence,
22 April 1732.   St. Phil PR

Clifford, Charles & Elizabeth Perry, 11 Sept. 1777.   St. Phil PR

Clifford, John & Martha Dandridge, P Licence by Mr. Garden, 16
Dec. 1736.   St. Phil PR

Clifford, Thomas & Martha Guerard, 8 Feb. 1721.   St. Phil PR

Clifford, William & Mary Parker, 22 June 1738.   St. And PR

Clime, Georg & Mary FitzHarris, 11 May 1783.   St. John Luth Ch

Clinch, Michael & Elizabeth Stow, widow, 6 Feb. 1718/19.
St. And PR

Cline, George & Ann Shirer, 3 Aug. 1777.   St. Phil PR

Clinton, John & Mary Birkmire, 25 June 1764.   St. Phil PR

Clitherall, James of Charleston, Practitioner of Physick, &
Elizabeth Smith, widow of Thomas Loughton, Smith; ____ 1775;
Katharin Clark, Mary Inglis, wit.   Mar Set 2: 136-140

SOUTH CAROLINA MARRIAGES 1688-1799

Clouney, Joseph & Elizabeth Trezvant, 14 Feb. 1765. St Phil PR

Clyat, Stephen & Katherine Avant, 30 July 1749. Pr Fred PR

Clyatt, Robert & Hannah Stone, 28 July 1713. T & D PR

Clyatt, Samuel of Prince Frederick parish, carpenter, & Mary
    Wilson, spinster, [no date, probably Sept. 1744]; license to
    Rev. John Gordyce; William Anderson of Parish of Prince
    George, planter, bondsman. MB Chas

Clym, Martin & Anna Christiana Goette, widow of George Goette,
    23 Dec. 1786; Barnard Beekman, trustee; Charles Desel Beek-
    man, Samuel Beekman, wit. Mar Set 1: 292-293

Coachman, James of Prince George Parish, planter & Ann Johnston,
    widow of Charlestown, 6 May 1773; Helen Rattray, widow,
    Benjamin Coachman, the elder of St. James Goose Creek &
    Benjamin Coachman, the younger of Charleston, trustees;
    Sarah Villepontoux, Rev. Robert Smith, Ann Waties, wit.
    Misc. Rec. PP. 541-547

Coachman, James & Ann Johnston, widow, 6 May 1773. St. Phil PR

Coachman, John of Georgetown Dist., & Lydia Towner of same,
    spinster, 12 July 1797; Paul Michau, & Joseph Blyth, planters,
    trustees; Jehu Postell, Peter Guerry, wit. Mar Set 3: 141-
    144

Coat, Henry, son of Marmaduke Coat, & Mary Hasket, 7 Feb. 1793.
    Bush R QM

Coats, Thomas & Catharine George, 7 March 1782. St. Phil PR

Coats, William & Mary Green, 17 Nov. 1757. St. Phil PR

Cobb, Arthur, & ___, 3 Sept. 1767. Pugh diary

Cobia, Francis & Christiana Elizabeth Spidell, 23 Oct. 1773.
    St. Phil PR

Cobia, Michael, butcher, & Juliana Elisabetha, daughter of
    Peter Diener, tanner, 23 Jan. 1774. St. John Luth Ch

Cobia, Nicholas & Ann Rumph, 8 Feb. 1780. St. Phil PR

Cobleton, Hose Francis & Jean Frasher, 25 Dec. 1799. Trin
    Meth Ch

Cobley, Jemmitt, storekeeper, & Helen Wright, (no date, before
    1750). St. Hel PR

Cobley, Jemmitt & Eleanor Wright, spinster, per Licence,
    Endorsed by the Revd. Betham to the Revd. Mr. Quincey, 31
    July 1746. St. Phil PR

Cochran, Thomas & Susanna Hawie, widow of Robert Hawie, decd.,
    21 Nov. 17777; Barnard Beekman, John McCall, Jr., trustees;
    Hext McCall, James Cox, wit. Mar Set 1: 10-12

Cochran, Thomas Jun. & Eliza Torrans, 19 Dec. 1799. Circ Cong

Cockfield, John & Anne Barton, 6 Oct. 1740. St. And PR

45

Cockfield, Willm. & Sarah Carter, widow, 24 Dec. 1740. St. And
PR

Cockran, Michael, widower, & Rebecca Sullivan, spinster, married
in the house of Thos. Spencer Senr., 11 Jan. 1759; Wm.
Roberts, Stephen Sullivan, wit. St. Jas PR

Cockran, Robert & Mary Elliott, 3 Feb. 1763. St. Phil PR

Cockran, Thomas & Susannah Hewie, widow, 18 Dec. 1777. St. Phil
PR

Codner, Charles & Anne Barnet, P Licence, 11 Aug. 1731. St.
Phil PR

Coffin, Ebenezer, of City of Charleston, merchant & Mary
Matthews, daughter of Benj. Mathews of St. Johns Parish,
Colleton; H. Leonard, Thomas Hanscome, wit. 22 May 1793.
Mar Set 2: 143-147

Coffin, Ebenezer & Mary Mathews, 22 May 1793. Circ Cong

Coffin, Henry & Mary Cane, 6 Nov. 1733. Circ Cong

Cogdell, Charles & Jane Wilkie, widow, ___ Oct. 1774; John
Cogdell, trustee; Eliza. Cogdell, Chas Jacob Lindfors, wit.
Misc. Rec. RR: 314-316

Cogdell, Charles & Jane Wilkie, widow, 1 Nov. 1774. St. Phil PR

Cogdell, George & Mary Ann Elizabeth Stevens, 11 May 1777.
St. Phil PR

Cogswell, Jeremiah & Mary Wyet, 1721. St. Phil PR

Cohen, Mordecai & Leah Lazarus, 9 Dec. 1795; Benjamin Toes,
trustee; Aaron Lazarus, Andrew Harris, Aaron Loper, wit.
Mar Set 2: 463-465

Cohen, Moses of Charlestown, merchant & Judith Delyon, spinster,
8 Feb. 1779; Isaac Delyon, & Barnet Moses, trustees; Isaac
DaCosta Junr., Jacob Jacobs, wit. Mar Set 1: 485-486

Cohen, Solomon, Gent., & Bella Moses, daughter of Meyer Moses,
13 March 1786; Abraham Cohen of Georgetown, & William Hasell
Gibbes of Charleston, trustees; Benjamin Tores, Gershen Cohen,
wit. Mar Set 1: 210-211

Coker, George & Eleaner Thomas, P Licence, 6 Nov. 1738. St.
Phil PR

Colcock, Isaac & Catherine Woodman, per Licence, 3 June 1745.
St. Phil PR

Colcock, John & Deborah Milner, P Licence, 13 July 1732.
St. Phil PR

Colcock, John, attorney of Charlestown & Millicent Jones, 29
Oct. 1768; Charles Pinckney & Jacob Motte, trustees; wit.
Elizabeth Milner, Jno Jones. Mar Set 2: 61-63

Colcock, John & Millicent Jones, 30 Oct. 1768. St. Phil PR

Cole, John & Anne Hogg, 29 Oct. 1754. St. Hel PR

Cole, Joseph & Barbara Walter, P Licence, 29 March 1745. St. Phil PR

Cole, Joseph & Rebecca Turner, 26 Feb. 1779. St. Phil PR

Cole, Richard & Sarah Oswald, widow, 5 July 1766. OJ 1764-1771

Cole, Richard & Ann Lloyd, 25 Feb. 1770. St. Phil PR

Cole, Richard & Ann Boomer, 29 May 1777. St. Phil PR

Cole, Thomas of Parish of Prince Frederick bachelor, & Sarah Hamlen, of Parish of Prince Frederick, spinster, in the house of Mr. John DeLiesseline, 9 March 1786; Anthony Ford, John Deliesseline, wit. St. Jas PR

Coleman, John & Martha Bee, P Licence, 3 Nov. 1743. St. Phil PR

Coleman, Martin & Marian Leander, P Licence, 13 Feb. 1737. St. Phil PR

Colent, Henry & ___, 23 Nov. 1775. Pugh diary

Colladon, James, widower, and Martha Fleming, in the house of John Marion, 29 Dec. 1766; Peter Guerry, Jacob Jeanneret, wit. St. Jas PR

Collea, Gabriel & Catherine Davis, P Licence, 17 April 1739. St. Phil PR

Colleton, George & Elizabeth Peterson, P Licence, 27 Jan. 1731. St. Phil PR

Colley, Robert & Mary Kelly, per Licence, 8 June 1745. St. Phil PR

Collings, John & Ann Mazick, 14 Sept. 1771. St. Phil PR

Collings, Jonathan & Anne Simons, 3 Jan. 1743-4. T & D PR

Collings, Jonathan & Mary McGrigory, 20 Oct. 1745. T & D PR

Collings, Orange & Ann Seabrook, 7 Sept. 1711. SPG

Collins, James & Mary Thomson, P Licence, 3 Jan. 1739. St. Phil PR

Collins, John & Mary McWhennie, 26 Jan. 1772. St. Phil PR

Collins, John & Mary Lovelack, Sept. 1795. Moses Waddel

Collins, Jonah & Susannah Bonhost, 31 Jan. 1751. Ch Ch PR

Collins, Jonathan of Parish of St. Thomas & Mary Ann Simmons, spinster, 3 Jan. 1743-4; license to Rev. Thomas Hasell; John Naylor, bondsman. MB Chas

Collins, Manassa, gent., & Ann Taylor, widow, 20 Feb. 1792; Bracy Singleton, trustee; James Granvill, wit. Mar Set 1: 624-625

Collins, Manasseh & Ann Taylor, widow [no date, Feb-March 1792]. St. Phil PR

Collins, Robert & Elizabeth Waters, 4 March 1727. St. Phil PR

Collins, Thomas R. of Charleston Dist., & Eliza Bowler, of same, 24 Aug. 1791; James Hamilton Jr., wit. Mar Set 1: 602-604

Collins, William and Elizabeth Smith, widows, 28 June 1744. Pr Fred PR

Collis, Robert & Elizabeth Ellis, P Licence, 24 Jan. 1733. St. Phil PR

Colman, James & Rachel Kolb, 14 Dec. 1775. Pugh diary

Colman, Wm. & Martha Howert, 20 Dec. 1798. Pugh diary

Coloney, Edward of Parish of Prince George, bachelor, & Hannah Charners, of Parish of Prince George, spinster, at the house of Daniel Willcox, 21 Apr. 1779; Jno Wilson, James Campbell, wit. St. Jas PR

Colson, Thomas & Mary OBrian, per Banns by the Revd. Mr. Robt. Betham, 3 March 1746/7. St. Phil PR

Colwell, John & Elizabeth Lewis, widow, 9 March 1758. St. Phil PR

Combe, John & Jane ___, 23 Nov. 1751. T & D PR

Combe, Paul & Charlotte Geautier, 19 July 1759. St. Phil PR

Comefoord, James & Margaret Eliz. Pendroos, 27 Feb. 1763. St. Phil PR

Comer, Robert, son of Joseph & Elizabeth, and Martha Hawkins, 9 Nov. 1797. Cane Creek MM

Comer, Stephen, son of Joseph & Elizabeth, and Mary Hawkins, 31 Oct. 1799. Cane Creek MM

Comer, Wm. & Mary Jeffrys, P Licence by Mr. Mellich, 6 Sept. 1735. St. Phil PR

Comerford, James & Mary Dering, P Licence, 5 Nov. 1744. St. Phil PR

Commander, Thomas & Sarah Griffen, 1 Apr. 1713. T & D PR

Commett, Peter & Hannah Watson, per Licence by the Revd. Mr. Robt. Betham, 8 July 174f. St. Phil PR

Compton, Joshua, son of Samuel & Elizabeth, & Rebekah Hawkins, 24 Jan. 1799. Cane Creek MM

Compton, Stephen, son of Samuel & Elizabeth & Dinah Milhous, 25 Jan. 1798. Cane Creek MM

Conaway, Robert & Juliana Easton, 26 Nov. 1771. St. Phil PR

Condy, Jeremiah & Elizath. Hall Doughty, 14 Oct. 1790. Circ Cong

Cone, Charles Godfrey, of Charleston, merchant, & Miss Margaret Metzger, under age of 21, 21 Nov. 1789; Philip & Henry Wesner & David Cruger, trustees; George Neumann, Philip

Zooler, Adam Spidel, wit.   Mar Set 1: 456-458

Coningham, Jno & Saley Maggs, 11 Feb. 1796.   Pugh diary

Connant, John & Anne Levy, 21 July 1728.   St. Hel PR

Connell, John & Ann Rannels, widow, 24 March 1761.   St. Phil PR

Conner, John and Ann Mckdaniel, 4 Aug. 1737.   Pr Fred PR

Connila, John & Mary Wood, 8 Jan. 1778.   Pugh diary

Conoley, David & Sarah Mortimore, 23 March 1757.   St. And PR

Connoly, William & Barbara Ensidler, 2 Sept. 1784.   St. John
    Luth Ch

Connore, Bryan & Anne Campbell, widow, 21 Dec. 1748.   Pr Fred
    PR

Connoway, John & Mary Lee, 7 Apr. 1760.   St. Phil PR

Conyer, John & Hanah Marriner, 4 Dec. 1726.   St. Phil PR

Conyer, John & Anne Stone, P Licence, 18 July 1739.   St. Phil
    PR

Conyers, Clement & Frances Snell, 8 Mar. 1778.   St. Phil PR

Conyers, James & Mary Mackintosh, 18 Feb. 1744.   Pr Fred PR

Conyers, John & Mary Quarterman, 15 July 1717.   T & D PR

Conyers, John, a taylor, of Ireland, & Anne Stone, widow, (no
    date).   St. Hel PR

Conyers, John & Elizabeth Hicks, widow, 10 May 1752.   St. Hel
    PR

Conyers, Thomas & Elena Scott, 10 Dec. 1744.   St. Hel PR

Cook, Amos, son of Isaac, & Elizabeth Townsend, 12 Apr. 1775.

Cook, Eli, son of Isaac and Mary, & Martha Hawkins, 12 March
    1772.   Bush R QM

Cook, Ephraim & Mehetabel Blackwell, of the Dist. of George-
    town, 13 Apr. 1798; Samuel Blackwell, trustee; Michal Black-
    well, John Dunnam, wit.   Mar Set 3: 270-271

Cook, George & Elizbth. Hull, 2 June 1739.   St. And PR

Cook, George & Eleanor Wade, widow, 17 July 1777.   St. Phil PR

Cook, Isaac, son of Isaac & Sarah, and Sarah Milhous, 7 Oct.
    1790.   Cane Creek MM

Cook, James, Provincial Surveyor, & Sarah Millhouse, spinster,
    of Town of Cambden (formerly Pine Tree), 10 Sept. 1768;
    Joseph Kershaw, Jane Milhouse, wit.   Misc. Rec. OO: 411-412

Cook, John, carpenter, & Hannah Powell, widow, 11 May 1757.
    St. Hel PR

Cook, Jno & Madam Dalton, widow, 7 Nov. 1711.   SPG

Cook, John, son of Isaac & Mary decd., and Olive Smith, 1 Aug.
   1793.   Cane Creek MM

Cook, Levi, son of Amos & Elizabeth, and Ann Fraizer, 27 Dec.
   1798.   Cane ·Creek MM

Cook, Phanuel & Elizabeth Woodward, P Licence, 7 July 1738.
   St. Phil PR

Cook, Richard & Hannah Willeby, P Banns, 29 Jan. 1738.   St.
   Phil PR

Cook, Thomas & Hannah Forbes, widow, 10 Apr. 1788.   St. Phil
   PR

Cook, Thomas, son of Isaac & Charity, & Kezia Henderson, 5
   Sept. 1792.   Bush R QM

Cook, Wright, son of Isaac & Chrity, & Rebeca Pearson, 2 Oct.
   1799.   Bush R QM

Cooke, Edward & Mary Burnham, 30 Nov. 1750.   T & D PR

Cooke, Phanuel and Ann Haddock, widow; minister Alexander
   Garden; bondsmen Panuell Cooke of Christ Church Parish and
   Henry Gibbes of Charles Town.   (N. B., but probably Apr.
   1733.).   MB NY

Cooke, Phannet & Anne Haddock, P Licence, 15 May 1733.   St. Phil
   PR

Coombs, John of Parish of Prince Frederick, bachelor & Anne
   Shields, widow, 1 Feb. 1779; Daniel Jaudon, Constant June,
   wit.   St. Jas PR

Coon, John & Eleanor Manuel, 12 July 1755.   St. Phil PR

Cooper, Benja. Allen & Jane Russell, 28 March 1776.   Pugh diary

Cooper, John & Mary Morris, P Licence by the Revd. Mr. Garden
   Rector, 21 April 1750.   St. Phil PR

Cooper, John & Sarah Smith, 9 May 1762.   St. Phil PR

Cooper, John Allen & Rachel Marshall, 16 Nov. 1799.   Circ Cong

Cooper, Joseph & Margaret N. [1740's].   Hist Oburg

Cooper, Robert Revd., & Ann Perenneau, 22 May 1760.   St. Phil
   PR

Cooper, Thomas & Eleanr. Wright, 16 November 1725.   St. Phil PR

Cooper, Thomas & Margt. Magdalen Beauchamp, 1728.   St. Phil PR

Cooper, William & Mary Hunter, 11 April 1779.   Bush R QM

Cope, John & Mary Burkett, 7 June 1749.   Pr Fred PR

Copley, Thomas and Mary Verdilly, widow; minister Daniel
   Dwight; bondsmen Thomas Copley of St. Georges Parish, and
   David Allen of Charles Town, victualer, wit. James Michie,

SOUTH CAROLINA MARRIAGES 1688-1799

20 July 1733.   MB NY

Coppock, John, son of John, & Anne Jay, 7 Jan. 1790.   Bush R
QM

Corbett, John & Mary Clifford, P Licence by the Revd. Mr. Alexr.
Garden, 19 April 1748.   St. Phil PR

Corbett, Joseph & Margaret Harrison, 22 Oct. 1761.   St. Phil PR

Corbett, Thomas, son of Thomas Corbett of Charleston, &
Elizabeth Harleston, the younger, daughter of Col. John
Harleston, late of Charleston, planter & Elizabeth Harleston,
12 May 1795; Nicholas Harleston, Edward Rutledge Jr., &
Dr. William Read, trustees; William Harleston, Edward Har-
leston, wit.   Mar Set 2: 403-411

Corbett, Thomas & Elizabeth Harleston, 21 May 1795.   St. Phil PR

Cordes, James & Eliza. Simmons, P Licence, 1 January 1729.
St. Phil PR

Cordes, John & Judith Banbury, 11 May 1775.   St. Phil PR

Cordes, Thomas & Ann Ravenell, 6 July 1749.   T & D PR

Cordes, Thomas Junr. & Rebecca Jamieson, 3 May 1797.   St. Phil
PR

Cordier, Peter of Charleston, merchant, & Julia Felicity
Stonestreet, 18 May 1799.   St. Phil PR

Coricorette, John, mariner, & Elizth. Smith, 5 Aug. 1797.
Trin Meth Ch

Corker, Richard of Parish of Prince Frederick & Elizabeth
Goodale, 20 July 1744; license to Rev. Daniel Dwight; Thomas
Doughty of Parish of St. Phillips, bondsman.   MB Chas

Corker, Thomas & Mary Hill, P Licence, 27 Nov. 1750.   St. Phil
PR

Corker, Thomas of Charleston, ship wright, & Elizabeth Glew, 31
May 1797.   St. Phil PR

Cormack, Alexander & Mary Godwin, 13 Jan. 1759.   St. Phil PR

Cornelius, John to Charity Joiner, by Revd. Thomas Stringer
or Stinger, March 1776.   Camden District (?).   Lanc DB
C & E, p. 24

Cornish, Heny. & Jean Gill, 29 June 1724.   Ch Ch PR

Corre, Johannes, & Anna Hatscheson, 27 Dec. 1777.   St. John
Luth Ch

Corsan, Robert of St. Philips Parish, & Lilles Ducant, 23 Apr.
1744; license to Rev. Alexander Garden; Robt Ducat (Duckett),
bondsman.   MB Chas

Corvasier, Barth, son of France Corvasier & Gilet Derpres,
both of Rennes in France, & Janna Grove, daughter of Samuel
Grove, late of this Town, & Jean Watson; 1 Jan. 1780; Mrs.
Mary King, Miss Mary Brown alias Powell, Francis Saunders,

51

Peter James Masson, wit.   Misc. Rec. VV: 102-105

Cosing, James & Mary Godwin, 23 Oct. 1746.   St. And PR

Cossens, Edmond & Eliza. Godfrey, P Licence, 28 March 1749.
St. Phil PR

Cosslett, Charles Mathews, & Ann Grimke, daughter of John Paul
Grimke, of Charleston, 16 Dec. 1772; John Faucheraud Grimke,
of the University of Cambridge, England, & Henry Pevrineaux,
of Charleston, trustees; Thos Knox Gordon, Edward Savage,
wit.   Mar Set 1:   8-10

Coughlan, Nathaniel & Margaret Fryley, P Licence, 30 Nov. 1752.
St. Phil PR

Coulbourn, Charles & Elizabeth Dring, 19 May 1764.   St. Phil PR

Couliatt, David & Eleanor Gunn, 7 Jan. 1762.   St. Phil PR

Couliette, Lawrence & Mary Williams, 25 Nov. 1726.   St. Phil PR

Coulson, Jacob & Betsy Sanders, 1798.   Moses Waddel

Countee, William & Ruth Leaycroft, P Licence by the Revd. A. G,
13 Oct. 1748.   St. Phil PR

Course, Isaac & Ann Prince, 14 Jan. 1789.   St. Phil PR

Courtney, Edward & Liddy Smith, 11 May 1794.   Circ Cong

Courtonne, Pierre & Mary Magdalena Peltro, by Mr. Garden, 30
Dec. 1736.   St. Phil PR

Courty, Jacques & Mary McKenzie, 6 Feb. 1795.   St. Phil PR

Cousins, John & Elizabeth Shann, 4 Jan. 1721/22.   St. And PR

Coutua, Peter & Mary Middleton, P Licence, 5 June 1738.   St.
Phil PR

Couzens, (Corsan), Robt. & Lillies Ducket, P Licence, 26 April
1744.   St. Phil PR

Couzins, George and Lucy Palmer, both of this Parish.   11 Feb.
1744/5.   Stoney Creek Pres Ch

Coveney, Thomas & Elizabeth Field, 6 Oct. 1798.   Circ Cong

Coward, Jeremiah & Elizabeth Hayes, 24 Jan. 1788.   St. Phil PR

Cowell, Henry & Ann Yeomans, 4 May 1754.   St. Phil PR

Cowen, John & Jane Cuddy, 12 June 1756.   St. Hel PR

Cox, Florentius & Sarah Lickyer, P Licence, 9 February 1741.
St. Phil PR

Cox, Jesse & ___, 27 Apr. 1793.   Pugh diary

Cox, John and Mary Wilden, 7 Nov. 1737.   Pr Fred PR

Cox, John & Mary Dick, 27 Aug. 1752.   St. Hel PR

Cox, Joseph & Hannah Liston, spinster, per Licence by the Revd. Mr. Robt. Betham, 3 July 1746.   St. Phil PR

Cox, Reynold & Margaret Bryan, P Licence by Mr. Millechamp, 3 Oct. 1735.   St. Phil PR

Cox, Thomas & Elizabeth Clark, 8 March 1755.   St. Hel PR

Coyle, Henry & Anne Young, P Licence, 14 March 1728/9.   St. Phil PR

Cragg, John and Mary Welch, widow; minister Alexander Garden; bondsmen John Cragg, Indian trader, and David Allen of Charles Town, victualar; wit. J. Hammerton, 19 June 1733. MB NY

Craggs, Jacob & Mary Welsh, P Licence, 29 June 1733.   St. Phil PR

Cramer, Tobias & Elisabetha Thomas, 16 March 1783.   St. John Luth Ch

Craston, John & Julia Miller, P Licence, 11 October 1742. St. Phil PR

Cratchley, Jonathan and Elizabeth Buckholts, 2 Aug. 1737. Pr Fred PR

Crawford, Belly & Sara. Petter, 24 Dec. 1765.   OJ 1764-1771

Crawford, Bellamy & Susannah James, 22 Feb. 1780.   St. Phil PR

Crawford, Daniel & Mary Holland, P Licence by the Revd. Mr. Alexr. Garden, 7 Feb. 1747.   St. Phil PR

Crawford, David & Isabella Maine, by Banns by Mr. Bell, Presbyterian Minister, 8 Feb. 1747.   St. Phil PR

Crawford, James & Kaziah Saunders, 15 Sept. 1739.   Pr Fred PR

Crawford, Peter & Elizabeth Coates, 25 Feb. 1782.   St. Phil PR

Crawford, Thomas & Mary Evans, 11 Dec. 1753.   Pr Fred PR

Cray, William & Mary Gignilliat, spinster, per Licence by the Revd. Mr. Robert Betham, 30 November 1746.   St. Phil PR

Creaton, James & Bella Engles, free Blacks, 9 Aug. 1798.   Trin Meth Ch

Cree, George & Judith Connely, ___ 1772.   St. And PR

Creighton, George & Clementine Robinson, 2 June 1768.   St. Phil PR

Creighton, Jams. & Lesy. Anderson, 1 Mar. 1766.   OJ 1764-1771

Creighton, William & Elizabeth Skette, widow, 17 Nov. 1767. St. Phil PR

Creighton, William & Sarah Piggot, widow, 26 Aug. 1770.   St. Phil PR

Creutzberg, Conrad & Maria Cath. Bardt(in), 18 May 1786. St.
John Luth Ch

Creutzberg, Michael & Maria Speissegger, 28 Oct. 1784.   St.
John Luth Ch

Crewett, Peter & Unity Neal, 25 March 1728.   St. Phil PR

Crisp, Townsend & Mary Cowley, P Licence, 23 Nov. 1742.   St.
Phil PR

Crofft, Edwd. & Eliza. Brewton, P Licence, 19 July 1722. St.
Phil PR

Crofft, Hill & Priscilla Mariner, 20 Oct. 1720. St. Phil PR

Croft, Abraham & Anna Maria Marston, P Licence, 25 July 1731.
St. Phil PR

Croft, Childermas & Katherine Parteridge, by Licence of the
Hcnble. Arthur Middleton, Esqr. by Mr. Garden, April 28,
1726/6.   St. Phil PR

Croft, Childermas, of Parish of Prince Frederick, bachelor, &
Mary Simmons, spinster, in the house of George Simmons, 28
May 1767; Peter Mouzon, Jon. Barnett, wit. St. Jas PR

Croft, Childermas, of the Parish of Prince George, widower &
Ellen Rawlins, spinster, in the house of Mr. Anthony Simons,
16 Aug. 1781; Anthony Simons, Wm. Cleiland, wit. St Jas PR

Croft, Edward & Lydia Wells, 22 June 1742.   Ch Ch PR

Croft, Edward, Jun. & Mary Wilson, P Licence by the Revd. Mr.
Alexr. Garden, 15 March 1747.   St. Phil PR

Croft, Hill & Rebekah Corbin, 2 June 1726.   St. Phil PR

Croft, John & Magdalen Menson, P Licence, 21 September 1743.
St. Phil PR

Croft, Peter & Mary Boone, daughter of William Boone decd.,
[no date, probably 1772].   Ch Ch PR

Croft, Robert of Parish of Prince Frederick, bachelor & Ann
Jenkins, spinster, in the house of Thomas Boone, 24 March
1763; Thos. Boone, Elizabeth Boone, wit.   St. Jas PR

Croft, William & Jane Richard, 6 May 1735.   St. Phil PR

Croftman, Thomas & Mary Cooms, P Licence, April 1734.   St. Phil
PR

Cromby, John and Mary Tompkins, 19 Apr. 1744.   Pr Fred PR

Crookshands, David & Elizabeth Florishton, 22 Dec. 1762.
St. Hel PR

Crosby, Josiah & Hannah Revell, 5 Nov. 1797.   Circ Cong

Crosby, William & Ane Swala, widow, 18 Sept. 1692; Findla Martin,
William Novell, bondsmen.   Sec Prov 1675-95, p. 493.

Croskey, John & Elizabeth Hill, 12 Aug. 1721.   St. And PR

Croskeys, John & Sarah Mathews, P Licence of G. Johnson; 2 Oct.
   1720.   St. Phil PR

Cross, Paul & Ann Nockcliffe, widow, 19 March 1774.   St. Phil PR

Cross, Thomas, widower, & Joanna Dyer, 28 March 1743.   St. Hel
   PR

Crosswell, James & Sarah Fenwick, 25 Sept. 1767.   St. Phil PR

Crosthwaite, Thomas & Mary Ward, P Licence, 27 July 1732.
   St. Phil PR

Crotty, Thomas & Jane Mackgrew, P Licence, 16 Aug. 1737.
   St. Phil PR

Cruckshanks, Wm. of Charleston, shoemaker, & Mary Minus, 28 Feb.
   1798; Charles Prince, trustee; David Abendanone, W. G. OHear,
   wit.   Mar Set 3: 243-245

Cruger, Charles Frederick & Martha Kirk, 4 Apr. 1789.   St. Phil
   PR

Cruger, Frederick David & Isabella Liston, 12 Feb. 1778.   St.
   Phil PR

Crummy, Henry & Magdalene Zorn, 9 June 1752.   Hist Oburg

Cryer, John of Parish of Prince George, bachelor & Ruth Noble,
   of Parish of Prince George, spinster, in the house of
   Alexander Anderson, 1 Nov. 1782; Martha Cryer, Alexander
   Anderson, wit.   St. Jas PR

Cryer, Thomas & Elizabeth Powell, both of Amelia Township,
   13 July 1752.   Hist Oburg

Cudworth, Benjamin Jr. & Catharine Sheppard, 5 Aug. 1775.   St.
   Phil PR

Cuhseling, Andreas, overseer & Anna Barbara Karol(in), 3 July.
   1769.   St. John Luth Ch

Culliatt, James & Ann Ladson, 20 June 1784; John Culliatt, F.
   Forget, wit.   Mar Set 2:   257

Culliatt, James of Charleston, coachmaker, & Jane Treagy, 17
   May 1798.   St. Phil PR

Cultender, Abraham & Rebecca Brit, widow, 20 March 1758.   St.
   Phil PR

Cumerford, James of Parish of St. Phillips, & Mary Dering,
   spinster, 3 Nov. 1744; license to Rev. Alexander Garden;
   Andrew Rutledge, Esq., bondsman.   MB Chas

Cuming, Benjamin & Julet Brown, 21 May 1766.   OJ 1764-1771

Cumming, Alexander & Lucy McCormick, 24 June 1789.   St. Phil PR

Cummings, John, bachelor & Ann Stuart, spinster, 13 Oct. 1760;
   Benjn. Perdriau, Michael Boineau, wit.   St. Jas PR

SOUTH CAROLINA MARRIAGES 1688-1799

Cummins, Lawrence & Ann Winton, 26 March 1762.   St. Phil PR

Cunningham, Patrick & Jane Tweedy, 16 June 1766.   OJ 1764-1771

Currant, Peter & Susanna Hope, P Licence, 15 Nov. 1732. St.
    Phil PR

Curry, George & Allen Fletcher, P Licence by Mr. Thomson, 16
    Oct. 1735.   St. Phil PR

Cusack, Adam & Frances Oran, 13 Sept. 1764.   T & D PR

Cusack, James & Anna Brown, 29 Apr. 1773.   St. Phil PR

Cussens, Richard & Esther Thompson, by Banns by A. G. Rector
    & c, 1 Aug. 1748.   St. Phil PR

Cutforth, Isaac & Martha Powel, P Licence, 27 Mar. 1732.
    St. Phil PR

Cuthbert, George & Mary Grimball, 3 Feb. 1754.   St. Hel PR

Cuthbert, James Junr. of Prince Williams Parish, Practitioner
    in Physic & Ann Bryan of same, spinster, 12 Apr. 1757; John
    Smith, William Bower Williamson, trustees; Jas Cuthbert,
    Jonan. Bryan Junr., wit.   Misc Rec. RR: 5-8

Cuthbert, James of Prince Williams Parish & Mary Wigg, widow,
    24 Feb. 1758.   St. Hel PR

Cuthbert, James Hazzard & Sarah Barnwell, 5 May 1785.   St. Hel
    PR

Cutler(?), John, mariner, & Margareth Taylor, 14 May 1783.
    St. John Luth Ch

Cutler, Benjamin Clarke & Sarah Hyrne, widow, 9 Jan. 1794.
    St. Phil PR

Cutryer, Daniel and Joyce Griffin, spinster; minister Francis
    Varnod; bondsmen Daniel Cutryer and John Pierce of Parish of
    St. Pawle, planters; wit. James Michie, 18 July 1733. MB NY

Cuttier, Joseph & Ann Mary Sahly, 27 Mar. 1741.   Hist Oburg

Cuttino, Jeremiah of George Town, Winyah, gunsmith & Ann Judith
    Boissard, spinster, 19 Oct. 1744; license to Rev. John Ford-
    yce; Francis Spencer, of St. James Santee, bondsman. MB Chas

Dabbs, Mr. & ____, 11 Nov. 1779.   Pugh diary

Dabbs, Joseph & ___, 21 July 1768.   Pugh diary

Dabbs, Wilm. & Martha Cherry, 8 March 1792.   Pugh diary

DaCosta, Abraham & Rebecca Piemento, daughter of Leah Piemento,
    15 Feb. 1765; Sarah DaCosta, Jno Remington, wit. Misc. Rec.
    MM: 222-223

DaCosta, Joseph of Charleston & Rebecca Depass, daughter of
    Ralph Depass, late of George, now of Charleston, 15 Dec. 1786;
    Jacob Jacobs, vendue master, & James Lynah, doctor of physick,
    trustees; Peter Smith, Stephen Thomas, wit. Mar set 1: 272-274

56

Dagons, Andreas & Catharina Ritfield, 6 July 1784. St. John
Luth Ch

Dalbiac, David & Catharine Coulet, P Licence, 18 Aug. 1735.
St. Phil PR

Dale, Thomas & Mary Brewton, P Licence, 28 Mar. 1733. St. Phil
PR

Dale, Thomas & Hannah Symmonds, P Licence, 30 June 1743. St.
Phil PR

Dale, Thomas, Esqr. & Anne Smith, P Licence, 26 Nov. 1738.
St. Phil PR

Dallas, Walter & Judith Padgett, 8 June 1727. T & D PR

Dalton, Darius of Parish of St. Bartholomew, & Mary Nichols,
to be married 20 June 1759, document dated 19 June 1759;
Thomas Stock, John Joulee, wit. Mar Set 1: 335-336

Dalton, James & Katherine Martin, P Licence, 6 Oct. 1729.
St. Phil PR

Dalton, William, widower, & Mary Miller, 13 March 1728.
St. Hel PR

Danford, Joseph of Charles Town, & Margaret Gray, daughter of
William Gray, of Berkley County, carpenter, 12 Dec. 1725;
John Bee, James Banbury, Judeth Banbury, wit. Sec Prv E,
p. 104

Danford, Joseph & Margaret Gray, 15 Dec. 1725. St. Phil PR

Daniel, Douglass, and Margaret Gandy, 24 Feb. 1744/5. Pr Fred
PR

Daniel, John & Sarah Raven, 22 Jan. 1735/6. St. And PR

Daniel, Jonathan & Catherine Croomy, 5 Apr. 1730. St. And PR

Daniel, Robert & Elizabeth Perryman, 7 Jan. 1721-2. T & D PR

Daniel, Robert & Elizabeth Russ, 19 Dec. 1754. T & D PR

Daniell, Joh, shipwright & Mary Arnoll, widow, by the Revd. Mr.
Natnan Basset presbyter Ministr. According to the form of
that profession, 25 Dec. 1732. St. Phil PR

Dannelly, Edward & Patience Sanders, 5 Feb. 1756. T & D PR

Danilly, Patrick & Elizabeth Gracebery, 24 Sept. 1740. Pr Fred
PR

Danzy, Richard & Sarah Crouch, 2 Oct. 1723. T & D PR

Darby, James, late of the Kingdom of Great Britain, now of
Charles Town, & Margaret Elliott, 27 Apr. 1773; Ann Elliott
& Mary Elliott, trustees; Wm Sheed, Henry Reeves, wit.
Misc. Rec. PP: 579-581

Darby, James & Margaret Elliott, 4 May 1773. St. Phil PR

Darby, John, widower, & Ann Bart(in), daughter of the late
Josua Bardt, 17 Oct. 1781. St. John Luth Ch

Darby, Michael & Mary Warnock, 21 May 1717. T & D PR

Darby, William & Margaret Evans, 17 Aug. 1797. St. Phil PR

Darrell, Edward & Sarah White, 16 Feb. 1796. St. Phil PR

Darrile, Robert & Elizabeth Cooke, 22 Jan. 1736. Ch Ch PR

Dart, Benjamin & Amelia Hext, spinster, P Licence by the Revd.
Mr. Garden Rector, 18 Jan. 1749/50. St. Phil PR

Dart, John & Mary Hext, by Licence by Revd. Mr. Betham, 24
April 1746. St. Phil PR

Dart, John & Martha Motte, 22 Jan. 1765. St. Phil PR

Dart, John Sandiford, & Mary Motte, daughter of Jacob Motte,
Esq., 22 Jan. 1765. Ch Ch PR

Darvil, Elsworth & Elizabeth Storey, P Licence, 11 Feb. 1737.
St. Phil PR

Daser, Friederich, pastor in this Charleston German St. John's
congregation, to Elisabetha, daughter of Rev. J. Severin
Hanbaum, decd., 8 March 1770. St. John Luth Ch

Dashiell, Charles & Esther Howeth, 30 Sept. 1792. St. Phil PR

Daves, Thomas Bachelor & Mary Cross, widow, 5 Feb. 1783; John
Drake, Thomas Parker, wit. St. Jas PR

David, Abraham & Elizabeth Guy, 19 Feb. 1756. St. Hel PR

David, Abraham, carpenter, & Mary Anne Williams, (no date).
St. Hel PR

David, John & ___, 9 Jan. 1777. Pugh diary

David, Peter & Ann Keating, widow, 5 May 1744; license to
Rev. Alex. Garden; John Triboudet, bondsman. MB Chas

David, Peter & Anne Keating, P Licence, 6 May 1744. St. Phil
PR

Davidson, Alexander & Elisabeth Ball, 3 Dec. 1742. Pr Fred PR

Davidson, George & Elizabeth Rogers, 25 Sept. 1773. St. Phil
PR

Davie, William & Mary Williams, widow, 14 Jan. 1777. St. Phil
PR

Davis, Alexander & Ann McClaran, 21 Apr. 1773. St. Phil PR

Davis, Benjamin of the Parish of Prince George Pee Dee, & Mary
Britton, of Prince Fredericks Parish, 11 Dec. 1782; Sarah
Giles, Hugh Giles, wit. Mar Set 2: 195-196

Davis, Benjamin & Rachel Port, 21 Feb. 1748/9. Pr Fred PR

Davis, Benjamin & Mary Ann McGregor, 4 Feb. 1762.   St. Phil PR

Davis, Charles & Elizabeth Curliss, widow, 18 Feb. 1773.   St. Phil PR

Davis, Edward & Margaret Hatcher, 9 Nov. 1752.   St. Hel PR

Davis, George & Ann Crim, 1 Nov. 1761.   St. Phil PR

Davis, Harman Capt. of Charleston, and Mrs. Dorothy Oswald, of same, widow, 31 Oct. 1799.   St. Phil PR

Davis, John & Anne Parris, 30 Dec. 1725.   St. Phil PR

Davis, John (painter) & Rebecca Collins, both of St. Thomas Parish, 23 Dec. 1794.   Trin Meth Ch

Davis, John & Theodorah Cook P Licence, 19 May 1732.   St. Phil PR

Davis, John & Martha Mann, 12 Nov. 1761.   St. Phil PR

Davis, Joseph & Mary White, 10 July 1754.   T & D PR

Davis, Samuel, & Margaret Matthew, widow, 1 Sept. 1741.   Pr Fred PR

Davis, Thomas & Catharine Oats of the Village of Hamsted, 7 Jan. 1797; Richard Wrainch, of Charleston, merchant, trustee, Matw. Hayden, Jno Watson, wit.   Mar Set 3: 37-43

Davis, Thos. & Mary Willis, 1 Oct. 1792.   Trin Meth Ch

Davis, William & Martha Watson, 16 June 1745.   St. Hel PR

Davis, William & Martha Wattson, both of this parish, 18 June. 1745.   Stoney Creek Pres Ch

Davis, William & Mary Viart, widow, 16 Sept. 1764.   St. Phil PR

Davis, William & Margaret Campbell, 11 March 1755.   St. Phil PR

Davis, William & Ann Sarverance, widow, 7 Apr. 1763.   St. Phil PR

Davis, William of Charles Town, & Mary Viart, of same, widow, 10 Sept. 1764; Christopher Rogers, Taylor, & Thomas Nethere-left of same, trustee, Wm. Ellis, Mary Bochett, wit.   Misc Rec. OO: 182-185

Davis, William Ransom of Stateburgh, Camden Dist., & Martha Cantey of same dist., spinster, 20 June 1792, Wade Hampton, Joseph Cantey & Isaac Conyers, trustees; Robert Hails, Daniel Flud, wit.   Misc. Rec. A: 205-211

Davison, John & Susannah King, widow, 15 March 1759.   St. Phil PR

Dawes, James & Elizabeth Varnor, 13 Feb. 1759.   St. Phil PR

Dawney, John of Town of Beaufort, & Sarah Story, of same, widow, 23 Sept. 1766; Thomas Middleton, Katharine Kelsall, wit. Misc. Rec. NN. 203-207

Dawson, Charles & Martha Goodbye, 17 July 1760. St. Phil PR

Dawson, John & Joanna Broughton Monk, daughter of Thomas Monck, decd., 30 Dec. 1760; Alexander Broughton, of St. James Goose Creek, guardian of sd. Joanna; Thos Broughton, Gabl Pilkington, wit. Mar Set 1: 304-307

Dawson, John Junr. & Mary Huger, 10 Feb. 1789. St. Phil PR

Daxter, William & Anne Holton, P Licence, 6 Mar. 1731. St. Phil PR

Day, George & Sarah Austin, 20 June 1759. St. Phil PR

Day, George of Charleston & Elizabeth Oats, daughter of Elizabeth Oats, decd; Jno Colhoun, Eliz. Lesesne, wit. 3 Feb. 1794. Mar Set 2: 223-227

Day, William of St. Bartholomews Parish, Colleton Co., & Elizabeth Postell, daughter of James Postell, of St. Georges, Berkley Co., 10 Dec. 1779; Philip Smith, James Stobo, planters, trustees; James Postell Jr., James Oliver, wit. Mar Set 1: 55-57

Deall, Richard & Mary Jones, 29 June 1752. Stoney Creek Pres Ch

Dealy, Robert of Parish of St. Stephen, bachelor & Hester Bailey of Parish of Prince Frederick, widow, at the house of Mr. Isaac Rembert, 22 Feb. 1780; Peter Guerry, Martha Rembert, wit. St. Jas PR

Dean, James & Dina Even [1740's]. Hist Oburg

Deane, Grafton & Mary Shrewsbury, P Licence, 13 Jan. 1740. St. Phil PR

Dearing, Colomondley Doctor & Elizabeth Bellinger, widow, 31 Oct. 1758. St. And PR

Dearington, John & Elizabeth Simons, 24 May 1772. T & D PR

Dearington, Thomas & Elizh. Bordeau, 13 May 1766. OJ 1764-1771

Dearington, Thomas & Eliz'th Bourdeaux, 25 May 1766. T & D PR

De Arques, Robert Dctr. & Elizabeth Butler, widow, 10 Apr. 1748. St. And PR

Deas, David, Merchant of Charles Town & Mary Michie, widow, P Licence, by the Revd. Mr. Alexr. Garden Rector, 12 Feb. 1750. St. Phil PR

Deas, John of Charles Town & Elizabeth Allen, spinster, 2 May 1759; George Seaman, David Deas, James Lennox, & Richard Singleton, trustees; William Lennox, Thomas McCauley, Edward Webley, wit. Mar Set 1: 548-552

Deas, John & Elizabeth Allen, 3 May 1759. St. Phil PR

Deas, John Jr. & Maria Smith, 1 Oct. 1788; William Allen Deas, Joseph Allen Smith, Barnard Elliott, trustees; Archibald Brown, James Clitherall, wit. Mar Set 1: 395-397

60

Deas, Robert & Margaret Philip Campbell, 4 Feb. 1799; Thomas A.
Somarsall, David Dees, trustees; John Ward, James M. Ward,
wit.   Mar Set 3:   314-317

Deas, William Allen & Ann Izard, 2 Nov. 1798.   St. Phil PR

Debbe, David Anton, from Hanover, & Barbara, widow of Gottlieb
Baltz, 3 May 1772.   St. John Luth Ch

DeBow, John & Ann Darby, 10 March 1791.   St. Phil PR

DeBrahm, John William Gerard & Mary Fenwicke, 22 June 1787
(already married); Thos Gadsden, trustee; John Bee Holmes,
wit.   Mar Set 1:   318-319

DeBruhl, Godard of George Town & Anna White, widow, of same, 25
March 1776; Anthony White, David Graham, trustees; Jas Stewart, Eps Nott, Mary Crook, wit.   Mar Set 1: 391-393

Deeg(?), Johann Peter & Anna Zahler(in), 23 Apr. 1765.   St.
John Luth Ch

Deevees, William & Frances Forgey, 14 July 1778.   St. Phil PR

Deha, John Andrew & Margaret Caroll of Goosecreek, 18 Dec. 1729.
St. And PR

Dehay, John Andrews & Margaret Dringat, widow, 30 Oct. 1757.
St. Phil PR

DeHon, Peter & Grace Rice, widow, 9 Nov. 1794.   St. Phil PR

Delacoe, Peter & Elisabeth Lane, 25 July 1779.   St. John Luth
Ch

Delahowe, John & Ann Boyd, widow, 23 Apr. 1767.   St. Phil PR

Delaire, James & Ann Milner, of Charleston, widow, 2 March 1796;
Thomas Jones, Esqr., trustee; Chas Carrere Fronty, wit.
Mar Set 2: 528-530

De La Motta, Isaac, son of Isaac De La Motta, & Sarah daughter
of Jacob Canter, 1st day of the Month called Swan, year of
5556; Raphael Da Costa, minister; Levi Sheftall, Abm Delyon,
Isaac Frank, wit. (original in Hebrew with translation).
Rec. 23 Sept. 1796.   Mar Set 2:   534-538

DeLancey, Peter & Elizabeth Berrisford, 1 Oct. 1770.   St. Phil
PR

Delgrass, Francis & Sarah Arno, P Licence, 23 July 1741.   St.
Phil PR

Delaney, Michael & Sarah Boatright, 6 Nov. 1798.   Circ Cong

Delany, Danl. & Amelia Mauzet, 26 Jan. 1794.   Circ Cong

Delany, Marquis & Allen Walker, 30 Dec. 1777.   St. Phil PR

DeLaval, Jacinth, of Parish of St. James Goose Creek, Bricks &
Tile Maker, & Rebecca Withers, 26 June 1786; John Withers
& Peter Tamplet, trustees; John Calvert Junr., Richard Fowler,
wit. Mar Set 1:   261-262

Delcke, Johannes, tanner, & Maria Bauer, widow, from St. Paul's
    Parish, 12 Apr. 1787. St. John Luth Ch

Delebere, John Kinard & Anne Flemming, 20 March 1736. St. Hel
    PR

Delegall, Philip Junr., Lieut., & Jane Daly, 27 May 1739.
    St. Hel PR

Delegaye, John & Catherine Gaudie, 17 Apr. 1737. St. Hel PR

Deleisseline, John of Parish of St. James Santee, merchant &
    Elizabeth Jennens, of same, spinster, 7 Apr. 1785; John
    Buchannan, physician & Isaac Deliesselin, of George Town,
    gent., trustees; Jacob Jeanneret Junr., Samuel Warren, Daniel
    McGregor, wit. Mar Set 1: 153-155

Deliesseline, Francis Gottier, of Charleston, Gent., & Ann Alls-
    ton, of Waccamaw, spinster, daughter of Josias Allston, 8 Dec.
    1785; Francis Allston, of Waccamaw, Gent., trustee; John
    Allston, Allard Belin, John Waties, wit. Mar Set 1: 202-
    204

Deliesseline, Isaac of Parish of Prince George, bachelor, &
    Anne Bossard, of Parish of Prince George, spinster, in the
    house of Mrs. Anne Cuttino, 20 Oct. 1785; John Deliesseline,
    John Bossard, wit. St. Jas PR

Deliesseline, John, bachelor & Elizabeth Jennens, spinster,
    in the house of Mr. Eward Jerman, 7 Apr. 1785; Jno Buchanan,
    Isaac Danford, wit. St. Jas PR

Deliesseline, John & Dorothy Tomson, spinster, P Licence by
    the Revd. Mr. Alexr. Garden Rector, 10 Sept. 1748. St. Phil
    PR

Delka, John & Mary Harttung, 5 Dec. 1784. St. John Luth Ch

Dellison, Robt. & Mary Russell, 19 Jan. 1709/10. Reg Prov.
    1711-15, p. 449(41)

Deloney, Aurthur & Sarah Bodington, widow, 19 Feb. 1759.
    St. And PR

Delyon, Abraham, son of Isaac DeLyon of Charleston, but now of
    Savannah & Sarah Sheftall, daughter of Levi Sheftall of
    Savannah, 23 May 1785; Benj. Sheftall & Joseph Welscher, wit.
    Mar Set 1: 224-245

Dempsey, Edward & Jane Graveell, widow, 2 Aug. 1756. St. Phil
    PR

Denholm, George of Parish of Prince George, bachelor, & Ann
    Hill, of Parish of Prince George, widow, 23 July 1778;
    William Luptan, W. Vaux, wit. St. Jas PR

Denholm, George & Alice Haines, 12 Nov. 1781. St. Phil PR

Dennison, James, mariner & Ann Elizabeth Saylor, of Charleston,
    widow, 26 Aug. 1796; James Mitchell, cooper, trustee; Mary
    Flagg, Jas. Nicholson, wit. Mar Set 3: 1-8

Dennistone, George & Mary Risby, P Licence by Mr. Garden, 13
    Jan. 1736. St. Phil PR

Denny, James & Mary Robison, 29 Oct. 1797.   Trin Meth Ch

Denny, James (Overseer) & Mary Farrow, of Doobodoo, 9 Oct. 1794.
Trin Meth Ch

Denny, Thomas of Parish of Prince George, bachelor, & Sarah Lee
of Parish of Prince George, spinster, 29 Oct. 1769; Peter
Guerry, Patrick Bower, wit.   St. Jas PR

DePalacois, Joseph & Mrs. Pinina Harris, of Charlestown, widow
of Nathan Harris, 5 Aug. 1785; Jacob Aaron, Samuel DaCosta,
trustees; John Huger, Daniel Bourdeaux, wit. Misc. Rec.
VV: 208-210

Depass, Ralph of Charleston, Gent., & wife Sarah, 24 Apr. 1799;
Isaac Dacosta & Emanuel Motta, trustees William Wyche, Malcom
McKay, wit.   Mar Set 3: 338-342

Deramus, John & Margaret Cooney, 7 Feb. 1773.   St. Phil PR

Deramus, Joseph & Ann Pfund [1740's].   Hist Oburg

Derby, John & Arabella Trimble, 27 Sept. 1795. St. Phil PR

DeRosset, Armand John Dr. & Katharine Fullerton, 1 Aug. 1799.
Circ Cong

Deruraseux, Daniel & Olivia Wood, 14 March [1740's]. Hist Oburg

DeSaussure, Henry W. & Eliza Ford, __ Apr. 1785.   St. Hel PR

DeSaussure, Louis & Sarah Toomer Chaplin, 5 March 1772. St. Hel
PR

Deschampes, Peter, bachelor & Elizabeth Simmons, in the house of
George Simmons, 2 Aug. 1759; Peter Mouzon.   St. Jas PR

DesChamps, Francis, bachelor & Susannah Joy, of Parish of
Christ Church, spinster, in the house of Mrs. Mary Simmons,
30 Dec. 1784; Geo: Sinclair Capers, Samuel Warren, wit.
St. Jas PR

Deshier, Lewis & Mary LeBruce, 4 Oct. 1778.   St. John Luth Ch

Desour, Francis, bookkeeper from Leipzig, & Margaretha Baumann
(in), 17 May 1771.   St. John Luth Ch

De Treville, John Labourlarderie, & Sarah Wilkinson, 27 Dec.
1778.   St. Hel PR

Devall, David & Katherine Lashley, 10 Feb. 1709/10.   Reg. Prov.
1711-15, p. 449(41)

Devant, John & Izabella Watson, P Licence, 11 Apr. 1740. St.
Phil PR

Devaux, Jacob & Elizabeth Barnwell, daughter of John Barnwell,
10 Feb. 1774; John Gray, Charles Shaw, wit.   Mar Set 2:
131-132.

Deveaux, Andrew & Magdalen Juneau, P Licence, 17 Feb. 1738.
St. Phil PR

Deveaux, Andrew Jun. & Catherine Barnwell, 7 Mar. 1757. St. Hel PR

Deveaux, Israel & Elizabeth Martin, P Licence, 7 Apr. 1739. St. Phil PR

Deveaux, John & Sarah Sullivant, P Licence, 25 Feb. 1737. St. Phil PR

Deverex, Andrew & Margart. Potwain, 29 Nov. 1709. Reg. Prov. 1711-1715, p. 449(41)

Dewees, William & Jane Rogers, 25 Oct. 1781. St. Phil PR

Dewes, Cornelius & Sarah Minors, widow, 29 June 1770. St. Phil PR

Dewett, Charles & Mary McCall, 23 Apr. 1771. Pugh diary

Dewick, Henry & Anne Dymes, P Licence, 8 April 1740. St. Phil PR

Dewis, William & Mary Ann Bell, 8 Apr. 1764. St. Phil PR

Dewit, Charles & Sarah Troublefield, 15 Sept. 1743. Pr Fred PR

Dewitt, Fred. & ___, 3 March 1791. Pugh diary

Dewitt, Haris & Elizth. Brockton, 8 Nov. 1781. Pugh diary

Dewitt, Joseph (Butcher) & Jane Harvey, 18 Dec. 1794. Trin Meth Ch

Dews, Bethel & Margaret Croskeys, 8 May 1740. St. And PR

Dews, William of St. Georges parish & Lois Wilkins, spinster, 2 Oct. 1744; license to Rev. William Guy; Andrew Cattell, bondsman. MB Chas

Dexter, Henry of Parish of Prince George, bachelor, & Cicely Baldy, spinster, in the house of Danl. Horry, Senr., Esqr., 19 Nov. 1761; Paul Jaudon, Danl Horry, Junior, wit. St. Jas PR

Dexter, John & Mary Buckells, 14 Feb. 1746/7. Pr Fred PR

D'Harriete, Benjan. & Anne Smith, widow, 2 March 1725/6. St. Phil PR

D'harriette, Benjamin & Martha Fowler, 16 Oct. 1755. St. Phil PR

Dial, John & Susana Morgan, 17 March 1772. Pugh diary

Dial, Thomas and Catherine McGinney, 14 March 1737. Pr Fred PR

Dick, George, practioner in Physick and Mary Allein, 12 Nov. 1743. Pr Fred PR

Dick, John & Mary Gascoigne, P Licence, 14 Apr. 1743. St. Phil PR

Dick, William & Ann Warnicke, widow, 9 Dec. 1783. St. John Luth Ch

Dickinson, Joseph Capt. & Catharine Cudworth, 13 June 1793. Circ Cong

Dicks, Ebenezer & Margaret Orr, (no date). St. Hel PR

Dicks, William & Jane Hutchins, 3 Aug. 1745. St. Phil PR

Dicksey, James & Hannah Wannel, widow, of Thomas Wannel, 15 June 1740. St. Hel PR

Dickson, Samuel & Mary Bell, 20 Nov. 1794. Circ Cong

Didier, Benja: Wilson, widower, & Hannah Cook, widow, 18 July 1778. St. Hel PR

Diener, Georg, tanner, & widower, of this city, & Christina Speidel, 15 March 1787. St. John Luth Ch

Diener, Peter & Maria Susanna, widow of Peter Ro---bach, 7 Feb. 1773. St. John Luth Ch

Diesel, Karl Ludwig, & Elisabetha, daughter of George ___, 20 March 1774. St. John Luth Ch

Dill, Joseph & Elizabeth Croskeys, 2 Jan. 1719/20. St. And. PR

Dill, Joseph & Susannah Mason, 7 Sept. 1758. St. Phil PR

Dillon, Thomas & Margareth Jeffers, 20 Feb. 1785. St. John Luth Ch

Dingle, Alexander & Elizabeth Hannahan, 13 June 1766. OJ 1764-1771

Dingle, Solomon & Elizabeth Bodington, P Licence, 9 December 1748. St. Phil PR

Dinkins, William & Sarah Tompkins, 12 Feb. 1738. Pr Fred PR

Dirr, Jacob of Amelia & Eva Catharine Keyser of Orangeburg Township, 22 Dec. 1754. Hist Oburg

Diston, Charles & Martha Canty, 16 June 1719. St. And PR

Diston, Thomas (son of Thomas Diston of Sheffeild in Yorkshire) & Elizabeth Turgis (daughter of Francis Turgis of Ringwood in Hampshire) married 21 July 1709 by John Maitland, Rector of St. Paul's Church, Colleton County. Reg Prov. 1709-12: 57

Disher, Henry & Catherine Ehney, 3 Aug. 1767. St. Phil PR

Ditcham, George & Ann McPherson, 7 Sept. 1789. St. Phil PR

Ditmere, Albert & Mary Craige, P Licence, 6 Nov. 1740. St. Phil PR

Ditmere, Oliver & Christian Laroche, 10 March 1721. St. Phil PR

Ditmore, Henry & Abigail Holmes, 24 Dec. 1795. St. Phil PR

Dixon, Christopher & Susannah Black, 8 Oct. 1760. St. Phil PR

Dixon, James & Elizabeth Wilson, 1728. St. Phil PR

Dixsey, James & Hannah Wannel, widow, 15 June 1740. St. Hel PR

D'Lahowe, John, Practitioner of Physick, & Ann Boyd, widow,
   22 Apr. 1767; Edward Martin, trustee; Sarah Lesesne, John
   Lesesne, wit. Mar Set 2: 366-371

Doane, Joseph, mariner, & Mary Finlayson, 28 March 1798. St.
   Phil PR

Doar, John, bachelor, & Esther McClellan, spinster, 30 Sept.
   1788; Sam Dupre, Archbd McClelland, Junr. wit. St. Jas PR

Dobbin, Hugh & Ann Crese, P Licence, 5 June 1747. St. Phil PR

Dobbins, John & Ann Potts [no date, Sept. 1789]. St. Phil PR

Dobbins, Joseph & Elizabeth Brown, 19 March 1777. St. Phil PR

Dobell, John & Susannah Holmes, P Licence by the Revd. Mr. Alexr.
   Garden, 1 May 1748. St. Phil PR

Dods, James of Edisto Island, & Elizabeth Miller, widow, 23 Feb.
   1743/4; license to Rev. John Quincey; Mark Guttry of Charles
   Town, bondsman. MB Chas

Dolliver, Henry Capt. of Charleston, mariner & Margaret Hazard,
   widow, 14 July 1799. St. Phil PR

Dolphin, James & Margaret Rowlin, P Licence, 2 May 1730.
   St. Phil PR

Don, Peter & Sarah Collings, 16 Oct. 1764.   T & D PR

Donaldson, James & Mary Cormack, widow of Alexander Cormack,
   1 March 1774; George Wood, trustee; Philip Henry, Peter Ross,
   wit.   Misc. Rec. RR: 618-621

Donavan, Mathew & Mary Ross, 23 May 1768.   St. Phil PR

Donnom, Ebenezer & Mary Poo, 18 May 1765.   St. Phil PR

Donnom, Jacob & Cathn. Krk, spinr., 24 Apr. 1766. OJ 1764-1771

Donhow, James & Judith Clark, P Licence, 2 Aug. 1739. St. Phil
   PR

Donovan, Isaac & Mary Cobia, 6 March 1788.   St. Phil PR

Donsal, Johanes, blacksmith & Maria Calwel, 24 Dec. 1776.
   St. John Luth Ch

Door, John & Mary Little, 22 July 1774.   St. Phil PR

Dopson, Isaac & Mary Gould, 1749. Stoney Creek Pres Ch

Dorman, Michael & Margaret Barnes, 21 Sept. 1763. St. Phil PR

Dormer, Michael of Charles Town & Margaret Garnes, of same,
   widow, 20 Sept. 1763; John Swint, Michael Katizan, wit.
   Misc. Rec. LL: 650-651

SOUTH CAROLINA MARRIAGES 1688-1799

Dornstatt, Ludwig, shoemaker, & Maria Elisabetha Neuman, widow, 13 May 1787.   St. John Luth Ch

Dorrell, Jonathan & Mary Whiteside, daughter of Thomas White-side, decd., 17 Dec. 1755.   Ch Ch PR

Dorrill, John, son of Robt Dorrill, Senr., & Elizabeth Murrell, 13 Jan. 1765. Ch Ch PR

Dorrill, Jonathan & Mary Combe, 7 Dec. 1785.   Ch Ch PR

Dorrill, Robert & Elizabeth Cook, 22 Jan. 1736.   Ch Ch PR

Dorrill, Robert, son of Robert Dorrill Senr., & Sarah Jones, 7 Apr. 1765.   Ch Ch PR

Dorrill, Robert Senr., & Martha McDowell, relict of John McDowell, 6 June 1767.   Ch Ch PR

Dorrill, William & Elizabeth Whiteside, daughter of Thomas Whiteside, decd., 24 Feb. 1778.   Ch Ch PR

Dorrill, William & Rebekah McKoy, 24 July 1785.   Ch Ch PR

Doughty, James & Ann Wilson, per Licence, by the Revd. Mr. Robt. Betham, 27 May 1746.   St. Phil PR

Doughty, William & Rachel Porcher, 22 Feb. 1770. St. Phil PR

Douse, Stephen & Sarah Stewart, P Licence, 19 Feb. 1732. St. Phil PR

Douvillier, Lewis & Theodore Vailliandet, 1 Aug. 1796.   Trin Meth Ch

Douxsaint, Paul & Mary Hendrick, 28 June 1758.   St. Phil PR

Dowdee, Richard, pumpmaker, & Judith Russ, widow, 11 Apr. 1756. St. Hel PR

Dowdin, John & Mary Franks(?), 22 Aug. 1784.   St. John Luth Ch

Downes, William & Jane Lindsay, widow, 1 Sept. 1772. St. Phil PR

Downey, William, sailor & Mary Hughs, by permission of Major Peter Trail, Commander of the Royal Artillery in Charles-Town, 11 June 1782.   St. John Luth Ch

Downing, Samuel & Catherine Singleton, 5 Dec. 1769.   St. Phil PR

Dowse, Hugh of Parish of St. Georges Dorchester, & Mary Pallett, spinster, 3 May 1744; license to Rev. Thomas Thompson; John Wheeler, bondsman. MB Chas

Dowse, Richd. & Mrs. Rebecca Partridge, 4 Jan. 1709/10. Reg Prov 1711-15, p. 449(41)

Doyley, Daniel & Anna Pinckney, 18 Jan. 1756.   St. Phil PR

Dozer, John of Dist. of Georgetown, & Ann Giles of same, widow, 24 Dec. 1791; William Davis, Abraham Dozer, trustees; Richard Godfrey, Harry Davis, wit. Mar Set 1: 617-620

67

Dragard, Pierre & Rinah Tongue, 13 Apr. 1797; Isaac Teasdale & Isaac DaCosta, trustees; Henry Bailey, Gabriel Bailey, wit. Mar Set 3: 63-70.

Drake, Edward & Ann Ruberry, __ Apr. 1753. T & D PR

Drayton, Charles Doctor & Esther Middleton, 24 Feb. 1774. St. And PR

Drayton, Henry-William, & Dorothy Golightly, 29 March 1764. St. And PR

Drayton, John & Sarah Cattell, 17 Feb. 1736 [1736/7]. St. And PR

Drayton, John & Sarah Newberry, P Licence, 22 April 1740. St. Phil PR

Drayton, John of Charleston & Hester Rose Tidyman, of same, spinster, daughter of Philip Tidyman, 5 Nov. 1794; Hugh Rose of St. Thomas & St. Dennis Parish, trustee; Sarah Bond Jon, Benjn. Huger, wit. Mar Set 2: 342-346

Drayton, John & Hester Rose Tidyman, 6 Nov. 1794. St. Phil PR

Drayton, John Junr. & Charlotta Bull, 14 Nov. 1741. St. And PR

Drayton, Stephen Esqr. & Elizabeth Waring, 24 Jan. 1769. St. Phil PR

Drayton, Thomas & Eliz: Bull, 26 Dec. 1730. St. And PR

Drayton, William & Mary Motte, 4 Oct. 1759. St. And PR

Drayton, William Henry, of Charlestown, son of John Drayton, Esqr., & Dorothy Golightly, daughter of Culcheth Golightly, 28 March 1764; Elizabeth Pinckney, John Parker, trustees; Harriott Pinckney, Sarah Butler, wit. Mar Set 2: 185-192

Drehr, John, miller & Catharine Leever, widow of Jacob Leever, Orangeburgh Dist., 31 July 1797; Barnit Hoyler, Samuel Friday, J. C. Bamberg, wit. Misc Rec. A: 308-311

Driesbeint, Daniel & Anna Flot, by authority from the commanding officer of the regiment, 22 Apr. 1777. St. John Luth Ch

Dring, Pearcival, of Parish of Prince-George, bachelor, & Elizabeth Crook of Parish of Prince-George, spinster, 18 March 1761; Georgis MackDowll, Ann MackDowll, wit. St. Jas PR

Drummond, James & Mary Seller, 19 Oct. 1772. St. Phil PR

Dry, William & Mary Jane Rhett, P Licence, 28 January 1745. St. Phil PR

DuBarthas, William & Mary Jane LeBoulinger, 20 July 1779. St. Phil

Dubois, David & Susannah Muncreef, 10 July 1777. St. Phil PR

Dubois, Isaac & Catharine Boisseau, 9 July 1749. T & D PR

SOUTH CAROLINA MARRIAGES 1688-1799

Dubois, James & Hester Guerin, 11 Dec. 1760.   T & D PR

Dubois, John & Sarah Mouzon, 16 Nov. 1758.   T & D PR

Dubois, Peter & Ann Mouzon, 11 June 1752. T & D PR

Dubose, Andrew & Elizabeth Mems(?), 4 May 1775. Pugh diary

Dubose, Daniel and Nancy Rembert, spinster; minister Thomas
    Morritt; bondsmen Daniel Dubose of Christ Church Parish and
    Gabriel Peirud (Peyrad) of Charles Town, barber; wit.
    James Michie, 12 June 1733.   MB NY

Dubose, Daniel of Parish of Christ Church, bachelor, & Frances
    Simons of Parish of Christ Church, widow, at the plantation
    of Henry Lawrence, Esq., 11 Nov. 1766; Isaac Legare, Clemons
    Brown, wit. St. Jas PR

Dubose, Isaac & Catharine Dutarque, 27 Feb. 1777. St. Phil PR

Dubose, Isaac & Catherine Dubose, both of Camden, 6 July 1797;
    Zachariah Cantey, Joseph Brevard, trustees; Sarah M. Brown,
    Saml. Mathis, wit. Misc Rec A: 311-315

Dubose, James & ___, 24 Sept. 1784.   Pugh diary

DuBose, Samuel of Parish of St. Stephens, bachelor, & Elizabeth
    Sinkler, of Parish of St. Stephens, spinster, in the house
    of Mr. James Sinkler, 24 March 1784; John Couturier, Peter
    Gaillard, wit.   St. Jas PR

Dubourdieu, Joseph of P. G. P. & Mary White of this parish,
    24 June 1746.   Pr Fred PR

Dubourdieu, Samuel & Judith Dugue, 16 Sept. 1690; Jean de Farcy,
    Susanne Marguerite de Farcy, Anthoine Bourau, P. le Salle,
    wit. (original in French, translated BHH). Sec Prov A
    1682-1690, pp. 380-381

Ducat, George Junr. & Anna Ullett, 24 Oct. 1745.   St. And PR

Duffe, James & Amerilla Macintosh, 22 May 1732.   Ch Ch PR

Duke, Robert & Maria Phillis Dudley, spinster; minister Alex-
    ander Garden; bondsmen Robert Duke and Edward Vanvelsin of
    Charles Town, shoemakers; wit. James Michie, 28 Mar. 1732.
    MB NY

Duke, Robert & Maria Phillis Dudly, P Licence, 3 July 1733.
    St. Phil PR

Duke, William & widow Halliburton, 13 Jan. 1749.   Ch Ch PR

Dulaney, James & Jane Keighly, widow, 13 Sept. 1760. St. Phil
    PR

Dunbar, Thomas of Charleston, & Mary Withers, of Prince George
    Parish, spinster, 1 Sept. 1784; John Buchannan, Physician of
    St. James Santee, William Withers of St. [sic] George Winyaw,
    planter, trustees; Rd. Withers, S. F. Warren, Albert Roux,
    wit.   Mar Set 1:   35-37

Dunbar, Thomas of Parish of St. Philips Charleston, bachelor &
    Mary Withers, of Parish of Prince George, spinster, at the

69

house of Mrs. Elizabeth Withers, 2 Sept. 1784; Jno Buchanan, Will. Withers, wit.   St. Jas PR

Dunbar, William & Elizabeth Simons of Charleston Neck, 27 Dec. 1799; Ellis Sutcliffe, John Garman, trustees; Christian Gruber, Ellis Sutcliffe, Margaret B. Gruber, wit.   Mar Set 3: 398-406

Dunbar, William of Winton County & Sarah Middleton, of Orange-burgh Dist., S.C.   7 July 1794; John Chevillette & Daniel Govan, gentlemen, trustees; Jane Thomson, Cephus Prentiss, wit. Misc. Rec. A: 259-262

Duncan, Benjamin & Elizabeth Thomson, 21 July 1782.   St. Phil PR

Dungworth, Henry & Ann Thomson, P Banns by the Revd. Mr. Alexr. Garden Rector, 4 Sept. 1748.   St. Phil PR

Dunlap, Alex'dr., & Sarah Fleming, of W. Indies, 10 Nov. 1754. St. Hel PR

Dunlop, Samuel & Ann Smith, P Licence by the Revd. Mr. Alexr. Garden, 13 Oct. 1747.   St. Phil PR

Dunnham, Ebenezer & Frances Commander, 20 Feb. 1/45/6.   Pr Fred PR

Dunning, James & Catharine Scott, widow, 24 Nov. 1776.   St. Phil PR

Dunscom, Durham & Esther Hennien, widow, 20 June 1773.   St. Phil PR

Dunwoody, William of Parish of St. Johns Colleton & Sarah Upham, spinster, 15 Aug. 1744; license to Rev. Samuel Quincey; William Ferguson bondsman.   MB Chas

Dupont, Alexander & Ann Guerry, 28 Sept. 1746.   Ch Ch PR

Dupont, Jos. & Ann Dupont, 6 March 1766. OJ 1764-1771

DuPre, Cornelius & Jean Brabant, 20 Nov. 1708.   T & D PR

DuPre, Josias & Sarah Alston, 7 March 1750-1.   T & D PR

Dupre, Samuel, bachelor & Elizabeth Mary De Liesseline, widow, 12 Apr. 1770; Jonah Robert, Benjn. Perdriau, wit.   St. Jas PR

Dupree, Daniel of Parish of Prince Frederick, bachelor, & Mary Normand, 28 June 1759; Frances Des Champs Sr., Peter Mouzon, wit.   St. Jas PR

Dupree, James & Mary Bullein, P Licence, 31 January 1732.   St. Phil PR

Dupree, James of Prince Fredericks Parish, Craven Co., & Sarah Johnson, 2 Feb. 1785; John Murray, John Hughes, trustees; John Mackay, Thomas Green, Mary Johnson, w it.   Mar Set 1: 493-495.

Durand, James & Martha Croft, daughter of the late Edward Croft and wife Lydia, 20 Feb. 1772.   Ch Ch PR

Durand, Levi Revd. & Susannah Boone, daughter of Thomas and Mary Boone, 14 May 1745. Ch Ch PR

Durtarq, John & Mary Serre, spinster; minister Thomas Hassell; bondsmen John Dutarque of Parish of St. Thoms, and Thomas Whitmarsh of Charles Town, printer; wit. James Michie, 6 June 1733. MB NY

Dutargue, John & Lydia Gaillard, 23 Aug. 1774. St. Phil PR

Dutarque, John Jr. & Mary Serre, 6 Feb. 1753. T & D PR

Dutarque see Durtarq

Dutart, John, bachelor, & Mary Boineau, spinster, at the house of Michl. Boineau, widower, 1 March 1764; James Rembert, Judith Rembert, wit. St. Jas PR

Duthy, William & Jane Boone, P Licence, 25 Sept. 1742. St. Phil PR

Duva, James & Mary Rowser, 6 July 1781. St. Phil PR

Duva, Richard & Mary Joy, widow, 27 Aug. 1741. Ch Ch PR

Duval, John & Martha Addison, 3 Nov. 1791. St. Phil PR

Duval, Stephen & Sarah Braithwaite, 27 Sept. 1755. St. Phil PR

Duval, Stephen & Catherine Tousiger, 3 Apr. 1764. St. Phil PR

Duvall, James & Eliz. Stack, widow, of ye Parish of St. Helena, 2 June 1746. Stoney Creek Pres Ch

Duvall, John & Rebecca Murray, 7 Oct. 1781. St. Phil PR

Dwight, Daniel Rev. & Hester Cordes, 21 Apr. 1747. T & D PR

Dwight, Samuel & Elizabeth Moore, 20 Nov. 1793. St. Phil PR

Dysart, George & Hannah Martin, 4 May 1732. T & D PR

Eaden, James & Elizabeth Morain, 28 Nov. 1723. Ch Ch PR

Eagan, Thomas & Ann Jeasop, 9 Jan. 1777. St. Phil PR

Earle, Wm. Capt. & Mrs. Hannah Ions, 31 May 1797. Circ Cong

Easton, Caleb & Mary Ratford, 14 Oct. 1762. St. Phil PR

Easton, Christopher & Jane Nelson, P Licence by the Revd. Mr. Clarke, 8 June 1755. St. Phil PR

Easton, Christopher & Susannah Lee, 19 Apr. 1758. St. Phil PR

Eayres, William & Rebecca Ripley, 12 March 1788. St. Phil PR

Eberhard, Johann, born in Bellheim in Electoral Palatinate (Kurpfalz) & Christina Rosina, widow of John Bernhard, 3 Sept. 1786. St. John Luth Ch

Eberhard, Thomas & Mary Moore [1740's]. Hist Oburg

71

Eberly, Hans & Ann Marckly [1740's].   Hist Oburg

Ebert, Gotlieb & Anna Amacher, 27 Dec. 1751.   Hist Oburg

Eddie, James & Mary Chris'n Bollard, 18 Dec. 1751.   T & D PR

Eddings, William & Theodora Law, widow, __ Sept. 1733. Circ Cong

Eden, James & Jane Jolly, 25 Sept. 1728.   Ch Ch PR

Eden, James Gottier & Mary Newman, 17 Sept. 1772.   St. Phil PR

Eden, Jeremiah & Sarah Rouser, 26 March 1761. T & D PR

Eden, Jeremiah & Sarah Rowser, 26 March 1761.   Ch Ch PR

Eden, John & Rebekah Player, 16 Feb. 1774.   Ch Ch PR

Eden, Thomas of Parish of St. Johns Colleton Co., & Mary Stan-yarn, widow, 24 May 1744; license to Rev. Samuel Quincey; Hugh Cartwright, bondsman.   MB Chas

Eden, William & Rachel Evans, 14 Nov. 1759.   St. Phil PR

Edes, James & Mary Goodwin, 23 Oct. 1756.   St. Phil PR

Edes, James of Charlestown, & Penelope Delesure, 28 Dec. 1743; Lewis Tanveir(?), Catherine Dalbiac, wit.   Misc Rec HH: 271-272

Edes, James & Penelope Delescure, P Licence, 29 Dec. 1743. St. Phil PR

Edes, James of Parish of St. Philip & Penelope Delescure, widow, 28 Dec. 1743; license to Alexander Garden; Lewis Janvier, bondsman. MB Chas

Edgell, Robert & Mary Hewitt, P Licence, 8 Jan. 1741. St. Phil PR

Edgley, Thomas & Penelopy Middleton, 18 Nov. 1734. St. Phil PR

Edin, William, widower, & Marsell Marg't Delegall, 13 May 1753. St. Hel PR

Edings, Abraham & Sarah Baily, P Licence by the Revd. Mr. Alexr. Garden, 18 Jan. 1747.   St. Phil PR

Edings, Joseph & Provy Docnor, 28 June 1761.   St. Phil PR

Edings, William Elliott now of State of Georgia, gent., & Mary Sanders of Parish of St. Paul, widow, 14 March 1799; Peter Smith, trustee; Sarah Hamilton, Sarah Wilkinson, wit. Mar Set 3:   360-362

Edmonson, Joseph of St. Georges Parish, Dorchester, Taylor & Ann Dunning of same, widow, 18 Aug. 1785; Elijah Bell, trustee; Martha Ward, John Ward, wit. Mar Set 1:   92-95

Edwards, Alexander Esq. & Mary M'Pherson DeSaussure, 22 May 1793.   Circ Cong.

Edwards, Alex: L. & Sarah Amelia DeSaussure, about 1795.
St. Hel PR

Edwards, Digby, mariner & Martha Fendin, 14 Feb. 1751. St. Hel
PR

Edwards, Edward & Mary Syer, 25 Sept. 1772. T & D PR

Edwards, Edward & Mary Wakefield, 8 Dec. 1796. St. Phil PR

Edwards, John & Margaret Peronneau, 11 Apr. 1758. St. Phil PR

Edwards, Job and Mary Wild, 10 Sept. 1737. Pr Fred PR

Edwards, John of Berkley Co., & Sarah Miles of same, widow, 31
Jan. 1765; Rosamund Perry, widow & Edward Perry, Esq., both
of Colleton Co., trustees; Mary Man, Robt Ladson, wit. Misc
Rec. PP: 368-361

Edwards, John & Martha Griffeth, 5 Jan. 1773. Pugh diary

Edwards, John, merchant & Rebekah Holmes, widow, 27 Dec. 1773;
Arthur Peroneau, Thomas Bee, trustees; Molcey Branford,
Susanna Donnom, wit. Mar Set 1: 120-126

Edwards, Josua [sic], & Ann Kolb, 5 May 1773. Pugh diary

Edwards, Petter & Mary Smith, 19 Nov. 1746. St. And PR

Edwards, William & Martha Watkins, P Licence, 29 Apr. 1739.
St. Phil PR

Edwards, William of Charles Town, factor, & Elizabeth Moore, of
St. George Dorchester, daughter of James Moore, late of
St. Peter's Parish, 2 March 1774; James Moore, John Moore,
William Saunders, trustees; Saml Porcher, James Edwards, wit.
Misc. Rec. RR: 212-215

Egan, Dennis & Eleanor Miller, widow, 29 March 1768. St. Phil
PR

Egan, John & Catharine Little, 18 July 1781. St. Phil PR

Ehne, Jacob & Mary Russell, 19 Oct. 1797. Circ Cong

Ehni, John. Georg & Charlotta Makin, 13 Aug. 1765. St. John
Luth Ch

Eisenbraun, Matthaus, drayman here, from Weyler Schorndorfer
Oberbach in the Duchy of Wirtemberg & Maria Kufer(in), 8
Jan. 1782. St. John Luth Ch

Ehney, Unrick & Elizabeth Hennegen, widow, 5 March 1762. St.
Phil PR

Ehrick, John Mathias & Peggy Africana Wightman, 6 Jan. 1796.
St. Phil PR

Elder, Thomas & Charlotte Hartley, (May 1773. T & D PR

Elders, William & Sarah Amory, spinster, P Licence by the Revd.
Mr. Alexr. Garden, 17 Aug. 1747. St. Phil PR

Elerson, James & Elizabeth Elerson, 7 June 1753. Hist Oburg

Elfe, Thomas & Mary Hancock, widow, P Licence by the Revd. Mr.
Alexr. Garden, 7 June 1748.   St. Phil PR

Elfe, Thomas & Rachel Prideau, 29 Dec. 1755.   St. Phil PR

Ellbert, William, widower & Hannah Sealey, widower, of St.
Helena Parish, 2 Oct. 1749.   Stoney Creek Pres Ch

Elleman, John, son of Enos & Catharine, and Susannah Coppock,
2 Aug. 1787.   Bush R QM

Ellery, Thomas & Anne Moore, 12 Oct. 1725.   St. Phil PR

Elliot, Humphrey & Catherine Booth, P Licence, 13 Nov. 1744.
St. Phil PR

Elliot, Thomas Jr., and Bulah Law, 30 April 1720.   Charleston
MM

Elliot, Thomas Sen., and Ann Clifford, 6 May 1721.   Charleston
MM

Elliott, Artimus & Mary Burnham, P Licence, 22 June 1738.
St. Phil PR

Elliott, Barnd. & Mary Eliza. Bellinger Elliott, 21 Apr. 1766.
OJ 1764-1771

Elliott, Barnard of the Island of Port Royal, & Catherine
Hazzard, daughter of the late Capt. Wm. Hazzard decd.; 12
July 1785; William Hazzard Wigg, trustee; Catharine Hazzard,
William Deceaux, James Hazzard Cuthbert, wit.   Mar Set 2:
77-80

Elliott, Major Barnard of Charlestown, & Susanna Smith, spinster,
daughter of Benjamin Smith, Esqr., decd. 30 Dec. 1775; Thomas
Smith, Jacob Motte, William Smith, trustees; Roger Smith,
Ralph Izard Junr., wit.   Mar Set 1:   163-165

Elliott, Barnard & Susannah Smith, 1 Jan. 1776.   St. Phil PR

Elliott, Barnard of Charleston & Juliet Gibbes, youngest daughter of Robert Gibbes, late of Charleston, decd., 15 March
1798; Robert Gibbes, Lewis Gibbes, trustees; Jno Gibbes,
Alex Garden, wit.   Mar Set 3:   254-257

Elliott, Benjamin & Mary Odingsells of Edisto Island, 22 Feb.
1749/50.   St. And PR

Elliott, Chas & ___ Ferguson, 3 Jan. 1766.   OJ 1764-1771

Elliott, Jehu & Mary West, 3 May 1757.   St. And PR

Elliott, John & Mary Bullock, 31 March 1757.   T & D PR

Elliott, Ralph Emms, & Susannah Parsons Savage (no date).
St. Hel PR

Elliott, Robt. & Elizabeth Scriven, 3 Feb. 1720/21.   St. And
PR

Elliott, Stephen & Elizabeth Butler, 23 Apr. 1749.   St. And PR

Elliott, Thomas & Elizabeth Prioleau, 27 Jan. 1780. St. Phil
PR

Elliott, Thomas Junr. & Mary Butler, 20 July 1738. St. And PR

Elliott, Thomas Junr. & Mary Bellinger, 19 May 1747. St. And
PR

Elliott, Thos Snr. of St. Pauls Parish & Elizabeth Bellinger,
widow, 30 Jan. 1744 [1744/5]. St. And PR

Elliott, Thomas John & Mary Pendarvis, 30 July 1724. St. Phil
PR

Elliott, Thomas Odingsell, & Mary Pinckney of Charleston, spinster, daughter of Charles Pinckney; Thomas Pinckney the elder
& Thomas Pinckney the younger, trustees. Mar Set 1: 216-
224

Elliott, William & Frances Gearing, 20 January 1725/6. St. Phil
PR

Elliott, William & Sarah Mulryne, 11 Apr. 1756. St. Hel PR

Elliott, William, widower, & Mary Barnwell, 6 Aug. 1760.
St. Hel PR

Elliott, William & Phoebe Waight, 23 May 1787. St. Hel PR

Elliott, Willm. & Elizabeth Baker, 13 Dec. 1721. St. And PR

Elliott, Wm. Junr. & Hester Butler, 24 Feb. 1721/22. St. And
PR

Elliott, William Junr. & Francis Guering, 20 Jan. 1725 [1725/6].
St. And PR

Ellis, Edmund & Elizabeth Capers, (no date). St. Hel PR

Ellis, Gideon & Eliza. Henley, P Licence, 18 Nov. 1734. St.
Phil PR

Ellis, Henry & Sarah Mills, widow, 24 Feb. 1779. St. Phil PR

Ellis, Isom & ___, 1 Sept. 1768. Pugh diary

Ellis, John & Elizabeth Reynolds, 29 Nov. 1730. St. Hel PR

Ellis, Robert & Katherine(?) Abbot, widdow, 17 Feb. 1727;
Benjamin D'Harriotte, bondsman; license directed to Rev. Mr.
Alexander Garden. Pvt Papers.

Ellis, Robert & Cathrine Abbot, 17 Feb. 1727. St. Phil PR

Ellis, Solomon & Mary Sinquefield, 1796. Moses Waddel

Ellis, Samuel & Hester Vanal, 12 Aug. 1770. T & D PR

Ellis, Saml & Ann Moss, 28 Aug. 1794. Circ Cong

Ellis, Thomas & Ann Glaze, 10 Aug. 1775. St. Phil PR

Ellis, Thomas & Elizabeth Drake, 18 Feb. 1744-5. T & D PR

Ellis, William, & Amey Edee, widow of William, 9 March 1739.
   St. Hel PR

Ellis, William & Lidia McKoy, 12 March 1761. St. Phil PR

Ellison, Robert & Elizabeth Potts, 6 Nov. 1772. St. Phil PR

Elmes, Thomas & Elizabeth Cantey, spinster, 2 Sept. 1692;
   George Cantey, planter, bondsman, J. Hobson, wit. Sec Prov
   1675-95, p. 492.

Elsinor, James & Rebekah Boggs, P Licence, 5 March 1734. St.
   Phil PR

Elsinore, Alexander & Elizabeth Blake, widow, 31 Mar. 1771.
   St. Phil PR

Elsinore, James & Margaret Worth, 7 May 1761. St. Phil PR

Embree, Isaac, son of Moses, m. Hannah Ballinger, 7 Oct. 1784.
   Bush R QM

Emer, Abraham & Ann Marronette, widow, 6 May 1764. St. Phil
   PR

Emmett, Jonathan & Sarah Evans, 26 Jan. 1744. Ch Ch PR

England, Thomas of Parish of Prince George, bachelor, &
   Elizabeth Rembert, of Parish of Prince George, widow, at the
   house of Mr. Isaac Rembert Jr., 12 Nov. 1782; Jacob Jeanneret Junr., Isaac Rembert, Junr., wit. St. Jas PR

English, John of Parish of Christ Church, widower, and Mary
   Baker, of Parish of Christ Church, spinster, 24 June 1784;
   Saml Huggins, Samuel Warren, wit. St. Jas PR

Ernst, Antony & Ann Barbara Gyer [1740's]. Hist Oburg

Ernst, Georg Adam & Ann Barbara Tapp, widow, [1740's]. Hist
   Oburg

Ernst, J. Wendel & Margarethe Kratschin, widow, 23 April 1764.
   St. John Luth Ch

Ernst, Johann, blacksmith, from Baden Burhof, & Catharina,
   daughter of Matthias Rosen, 7 May 1771. St. John Luth Ch

Ernst, Johannes, widower, & Maria Evan Pater(in), 7 Apr. 1778.
   St. John Luth Ch

Erving, Peter & Jane Leecroft, P Licence, 20 Nov. 1731. St.
   Phil PR

Evance, Thomas & Margaret Smith, 1 July 1756. St. Phil PR

Evans, Daniel & Margaret Lockhart, 3 Apr. 1794. Circ Cong

Evans, Danl. & Martha Rippon, 11 April 1766. OJ 1764-1771

Evans, David & ___, 23 Sept. 1766. Pugh diary

Evans, Elias & Mary Mordah, 27 Dec. 1772. T & D PR

SOUTH CAROLINA MARRIAGES 1688-1799

Evans, George & Ann Smith, widow of Thomas Rigdon Smith, 23
    July 1766; Philip Smith & William Clay Snipes, of St. Bartho-
    lomews Parish, trustees; Sarah Conrad, Mary Smith, wit.
    Mar Set 1: 425-431

Evans, James & Elizabeth Bennett, daughter of John Bennett,
    ___ 1775.   Ch Ch PR

Evans, John & Sarah Spencer, 7 Jan. 1744/5.   Ch Ch PR

Evans, John & Hannah Christian Young, widow, 9 Aug. 1758.
    St. Phil PR

Evans, John & Elizabeth Chaplin, 30 Apr. 1741.   St. Hel PR

Evans, John & Sarah Fripp, 27 Nov. 1766.   St. Hel PR

Evans, Joseph & Rachel McCool, 3 Jan. 1799.   Bush R QM

Evans, Josiah & Margaret Larkins, of Prince Fredericks Parish,
    17 Feb. 1755.   Hist Oburg

Evans, Middleton, & Hannah, widow of Josp. Ellicott Capers (no
    date).   St. Hel PR

Evans, Philip & Mary Clay [no date, Jan-Feb. 1719/20].   St. And
    PR

Evans, Samll. & Ann Ford, 7 Dec. 1711.   SPG

Evans, Stephen & Rebecca Chapman, 15 June 1765.   St. Phil PR

Evans, William & Sarah Cox, P Licence, 3 June 1738.   St. Phil
    PR

Evans, William & Priscilla Cook, 27 Apr. 1749.   Ch Ch PR

Eveleigh, George & Elizabeth Whiting, 19 Aug. 1742.   Ch Ch PR

Eveleigh, Nicholas & Mary Shubrick, 5 May 1774.   St. Phil PR

Eveleigh, Samuel & Elizabeth Eveleigh, 31 May 1733.   Circ Cong

Eveleigh, Thomas & Ann Simmons, 23 March 1773.   St. Phil PR

Evelins, Frederick, of St. Paul's Parish, & Anna Christina
    Swindershine, of same, widow, 26 Aug. 1776; Christian Sig-
    well, trustee; Jacob Shaffer, George Hanieser, wit.   Misc.
    Rec. SS: 407-410

Evins, John & Ann Dashwood, widow, 17 Aug. 1727.   Ch Ch PR

Evins, Stephen & Rebeccah Chapman, 24 June 1765.   St. And PR

Ewins, George & Priscilla Cox, P Licence, by the Revd. Mr.
    A. Garden, 6 March 1753.   St. Phil PR

Eycott, John & Mary Jeys, P Licence, 29 July 1742.   St. Phil
    PR

Fair, William & Catharine Devaux, 11 Oct. 1760.   St. Phil PR

Fairchild, Morris & Kate Noble, [no date, Feb. - March 1792].
St. Phil PR

Fairchild, Robert, widower, & Sarah Wigg, 14 Feb. 1754. St. Hel
PR

Fairchild, Robert, widower, & Christiana McLoud, 19 March 1772.
St. Hel PR

Fairchild, William & Martha Elliott, 14 March 1726. St. Phil
PR

Fairread, Samuel & Mary Aires, directd. to Mr. Garden, 3 March
1722/23. St. Phil PR

Fairy, John & Ann Yssenhut, 5 Feb. 1743. Hist Oburg

Fall, John & Margaret Welsh, 20 Apr. 1796. St. Phil PR

Fanen, William & Elizabeth Obryan, 17 July 1756. St. And PR

Farkenson, Joseph & Elisabeth Clark, widow, 10 Apr. 1768.
St. John Luth Ch

Farley, Thomas & Mary Morrice, P License by Mr. Garden, 2 June
1725. St. Phil PR

Farley, Saml. & Elizabeth North, ___ Dec. 1709. Reg Prov 1711-
15, p. 449 (41)

Farmer, James of Parish of Prince Frederick, bachelor, &
Rebekah Ellis, of Parish of Prince Frederick, spinster, 27
Jan. 1774; Thos Jones, Benja. Perdriau, wit. St. Jas PR

Farquhar, George & Eliz. Sharwood, 5 Feb. 1770. St. Phil PR

Farquharson, Francis of Parish of Prince George, Winyah, &
Deborah Franks, spinster, 8 June 1744; license to Rev. John
Fordyce; John Craft, of Parish of St. Philips, bondsman.
MB Chas

Farr, Nathaniel & Elizabeth Smith, widow, 24 Sept. 1779. St.
Phil PR

Farr, Thomas & Elizabeth Holmes, 23 Nov. 1760. St. Phil PR

Farr, Thomas Jr. & Elizabeth Waring, 18 Nov. 1773. St. Phil
PR

Farrar, Field, planter & Elizabeth Hext, widow, 10 May 1787;
Peter Youngblood, Wm. Steele, trustee; Eliza Childs, Thos
Mills, wit. Mar Set 1: 324-326

Farrow, Stephen & Elisabeth Woodford, 1 Feb. 1779. St. John
Luth Ch

Farrow, William & Rachel Callebeuff, P Licence, 16 Dec. 1739.
St. Phil PR

Farrow, William & Elizabeth Burnham, 22 Dec. 1763. St. Phil
PR

Faures, Laurent, son of Jean Faure, of Bordeaux, & Sophie
Jeanne marie Elizabeth Pigeot de Louisburg, daughter of

Jean Baptiste Pigeot de Louisbourg, of St. Domingo, 3 Feb. 1786. (Original in Franch, translated by BHH). Mar Set 4: 146-150.

Fawkner, John & Anne Bint, per Licence, 18 March 1745. St. Phil PR

Fearis, Denham & Mary Hendley, 6 Feb. 1764. St. Phil PR

Fearow, John & Sarah Ross, 22 Apr. 1773. St. Phil PR

Felder, Henry & Mary Elizabeth Shaumlöffel, 15 Dec. 1747. Hist Oburg

Feltham, Joseph & Honra Dike, 30 Oct. 1765. St. Phil PR

Fendin, Abraham & Mary Ann Norton, 26 Jan. 1765. St. Phil PR

Fendin, John of Johns Island & Elizabeth Thomas, spinster, 31 July 1744; license to Rev. Samuel Quincey; John Spencer, bondsman. MB Chas

Fendin, John & Elizabeth Thomas, 7 Aug. 1744. St. Hel PR

Fendin, John & Sarah Toomer, 3 Nov. 1785. St. Hel PR

Fenn, Joseph & Elizabeth Hamean, per Licence, 7 Feb. 1744. St. Phil PR

Fenney, James & Ann Goin, 17 Oct. 1771. Pugh diary

Ferguson, Charles & Chloe Williamson, 15 Apr. 1784. St. John Luth Ch

Ferguson, Hugh & Sarah Burley, 1 June 1738. St. And PR

Ferguson, John & Mary Bowman, P Licence, 18 Oct. 1733. St. Phil PR

Ferguson, Thomas & Mary Leay, P Licence, 14 Feb. 1740. St. Phil PR

Ferguson, Thomas & Hannah Sterland, P Licence, 26 Sept. 1742. St. Phil PR

Ferguson, Thomas & Kathrine Elliott, widow, 30 Oct. 1757. St. And PR

Ferguson, Thomas & Elizabeth Rutledge, 4 Aug. 1774. St. Phil PR

Ferguson, William of Colleton County, & Mary Broadbelt, widow, 7 March 1769; David Ferguson, trustee; Martha McPherson, Samuel Dunlap, wit. Misc. Rec. PP. 558-559

Ferguson, William of St. Bartholomews Parish, & Catharine Eaton of St. Paul's Parish, widow, 25 Oct. 1766; Albert Duynmire, of St. Paul's Parish, planter, trustee; Andrew McCullough, Andrew McCarley, John Thomson, wit. Mar Set 1: 205-207

Ferris, James & Margaret Wainwright, 9 Apr. 1772. St. Hel PR

Ferris, William, widower, & Janet Orr, 3 July 1744. St. Hel PR

Fesh, John & Sarah Varnon, 18 Nov. 1768.   St. Phil PR

Fesner, Joseph & Eave Weaver, both of Orangeburgh Dist., 13
    June 1787; John Wallace, William Fitzpatrick, wit. Mar Set
    1: 399-400

Fibs, Johannes, & Lidia Freyson, 9 Apr. 1787.   St. John Luth Ch

Fickland, George & Elizabeth Elphinston, widow, 21 July 1774.
    St. Phil PR

Fickline, George & Jane Cammell, P Licence, 13 May 1742.
    St. Phil PR

Fickling, Francis & Elizabeth Bridget, 30 Nov. 1781.   St. Phil
    PR

Fickling, George & Mary Coomer, 21 Apr. 1756.   St. Phil PR

Fickling, Joseph of Edisto Island & Mary Evans, widow, 8 March
    1788; William Joseph Mikell, trustee; Ephraim Mikell, Abigail
    Mikell, John Mikell, wit.   Mar Set 1: 349-352

Fickling, William & Sarah Johnson [no date].   St. Hel PR

Fidling, Jacob & Rebecca Edenburgh, P Licence, 23 April 1741.
    St. Phil PR

Fielding, Charles & Anne Waight, (no date).   St. Hel PR

Field, John & Elizabeth Betterson (no date).   St. Hel PR

Field, William & Sarah Chaplin, 1 Oct. 1751.   St. Hel PR

Fields, Charles & Anne Waight, [before 1752].   St. Hel PR

Fields, John Junr. & Rebecca Trunker, 29 Dec. 1784.   St. John
    Luth Ch

Fields, William Brown & Ann Mowhinny Black, 18 Feb. 1796.
    Circ Cong

Fillery, Stephen & Elizabeth Harriot, 15 Apr. 1782.   St. Phil
    PR

Finch, William & Isabel Lea, P Licence, Feb. 1733.   St. PHil PR

Fincher, Francis, son of Armil & Elizabeth Byshop, 10 Sept. 1788.
    Bush R QM

Findley, Henry & Martha Jerry, 22 May 1790.   St. Phil PR

Findley, James E. B. Dr., of Charleston & Mary Young, of same,
    29 Dec. 1797; Jacob Ford, trustee; Wm. Peronneau, Henry
    Peronneau, wit. Mar Set 3: 195-200

Finlay, John & Mary Sparks, 17 June 1720.   St. Phil PR

Findley, Sparks, & Sarah Boone, widow, 22 Oct. 1791; James
    Jaudon, John Mell, trustees; Daniel Anderson, David J. Jones,
    John Anderson, wit. Mar Set 1:   623-624

Finley, James E. B. of Wiltown, St. Paul's Parish, Physician,
    & wife Mary, formerly Mary Peronneau, daughter of Mary &

Arthur Peronneau, decd., 15 Nov. 1799; Jacob Ford, trustee; Benjamin Porter, wit.   Mar Set 3:   388-396

Finley, John & Eleanor Smith, per Licence, 2 Oct. 1745.   St. Phil PR

Finley, William & Hester Taylor, 18 June 1757.   St. And PR

Finnekin, Edward & Margaret Marshall, widow, P Licence, by the Revd. Mr. Alexr. Garden, 14 Nov. 1747.   St. Phil PR

Finny, William & Mary Poor, 15 Sept. 1740.   St. Hel PR

Fisher, Edward & Prudence Nash, widow of William Nash, 12 Jan. 1736/7; James Williams, Joshua Morgan, wit.   Misc. Rec. II: 113-114

Fisher, Edward & Prudence Nash, P Licence, 10 Jan. 1736.   St. Phil PR

Fisher, Ferdinand & Rosannah Minnick, widow, 8 Oct. 1772. St. Phil PR

Fisher, Peter & Margaret Mcpherson, widow, P Licence by the Revd. Mr. Alexr. Garden, 1 Oct. 1747.   St. Phil PR

Fisher, Thomas & Henrietta Holland, P Licence, 31 Dec. 1733. St. Phil PR

Fitch, James & Ann Rose, 16 Sept. 1756.   St. Phil PR

Fitch, James & Helena Campbell, 28 July 1764.   St. Phil PR

Fitch, John & Ann Holmes, 16 Jan. 1748/9.   Hist Oburg

Fitch, Jonathn. Junr. & Ann Elliott, ___ Dec. 1709. Reg. Prov. 1711-15, p. 449(41)

Fitch, Jonathan & Frances Nelson, 22 July 1734.   St. And PR

Fitch, Joseph & Constant Williamson, 5 March 1718/19. St. And PR

Fitchett, Giles & Elizabeth Danford, P Licence by the Revd. Mr. Alexr. Garden, 14 Sept. 1747.   St. Phil PR

Fitchett, James & Jane Armstrong, 18 Jan. 1738 [1738/9]   St. And PR

Fittich, Nicholaus & Susanna Muckenfuss(in), no date, 1774. St. John Luth Ch

Fitts, John & Elizabeth Burns, 16 June 1761.   St. Phil PR

Fitzgerald, James & Elizabeth Stanton, 26 May 1742. St. Hel PR

Fitzgerald, John & Grace Butlar, widow, P Licence by the Revd. Mr. Robt. Betham, 15 Feb. 1746.   St. Phil PR

Fitzgerald, John, mariner & Sarah Ayres of Charleston, widow, 6 March 1792; Joseph Pope, wit. Mar Set 1: 625-626

Flagg, George & Mary Magdelene Anderson, 14 July 1770. St. Phil PR

Flagg, Samuel Hawk & Elizabeth McCleish, 3 Jan. 1793. St. Phil
PR

Flanigan, Patrick of Charleston & Rebecca Gaborial, 1 Dec. 1784;
Henry Welsh, wit.   Mar Set 1: 6-7

Fleming, Maurice of Parish of Christ Church & Elizabeth James,
spinster; 4 Aug. 1744; license to Rev. Alexander Garden;
John Nelme, of Charles Town, bondsman.   MB Chas

Fleming, Maurice & Elizabeth James, 12 Aug. 1744.   Ch Ch PR

Fletcher, William & Elizabeth McIntoish, 22 Nov. 1761. St.
Phil PR

Fletcher, Willm. & Sarah Best, 21 July 1791. Pugh diary

Fleurison, Daniel & Cybil Neufuille, 1 March 1726. St. Phil PR

Fley, Samuel & Elizabeth Poinset, P Licence, 2 April 1730.
St. Phil PR

Flick, Johann Michael, widower & Anna Maria Alber(?), widow,
10 May 1768.   St. John Luth Ch

Fling, John & Judith Butler, 22 Jan. 1725/6.   St. Phil PR

Flinn, John & Mary Winter, 19 June 1739.   St. Hel PR

Flinn, William, of George Town, carpenter & Ann, daughter of
Thomas Pagett Senr; Thomas Pagett Junr., trustee; Thomas
Hasell, William Crook, wit.   Misc. Rec. II: 156-158

Flint, Joseph, Mercht., & Jane Mylne, 1 March 1792.   Trin Meth
Ch

Flint, Thomas & Sarah Forshaw, 3 Jan. 1797.   Circ Cong

Flood, William & Mary McElvey, 4 Feb. 1729/30. St. And PR

Florentine, Simeon & Ann Bishop, 19 Sept. 1770.   St. Phil PR

Flower, Joseph Edwd. & Elizabeth Woodward, 22 Dec. 1737.
St. And PR

Flowers, Jacob & Anne Hutson, 18 Dec. 1794.   Pugh diary

Flowers, Jno & ___, 25 Jan. 1787.   Pugh diary

Floyd, John, widower, & Anne Parmenter, 9 Dec. 1733. St. Hel
PR

Floyd, Richard & Anne Howard, 4 May 1735.   St. Phil PR

Flud, Daniel & Elizabeth Stanyarne Mathews, of Charleston,
daughter of John Raven Mathews, of John's Island, 1 Jan.
1795; Isaac Holmes, William Washington, trustees, James
Stanyarne, John S. Brisbane, Algernoon Wilson, wit. Mar Set
2: 378-384

Flutt, George & N. Pickings [1740's]. Hist Oburg

Fly, Samuel & Frances Guignard, widow, 5 July 1758.   St. Phil
PR

SOUTH CAROLINA MARRIAGES 1688-1799

Fogartie, David & Mary Nailor, 20 July 1749.   T & D PR

Fogartie, David & Rebecca Green, 2 May 1759.   T & D PR

Fogartie, David, widower & Mary Perdriau, widow, at the planta-
    tion of John Dutarque, Junr., 12 June 1763; Joseph Fogartie,
    Stephen Fogartie, wit.   St. Jas PR

Fogartie, James & Marg't Ame'a Garden, 25 Aug. 1776.   T & D PR

Fogartie, Joseph & Martha Barnet, 25 Feb. 1750-1.   T & D PR

Fogartie, Stephen & Esther Dutarque, 9 May 1721.   T & D PR

Fogarty, John & Mary Harris, P Licence, 3 Feb. 1723.   St. Phil
    PR

Fogatye, James & Margreatt Phorde(?), 7 Nov. 1693; Findaly
    Marton, Daniel Fraisor, bondsmen.   Sec Prov 1675-95, p. 483.

Foissin, Elias & Mary L. Roche, P Licence, June 1732.   St. Phil
    PR

Foissin, Elias & Esther Mathews, of Prince George Parish, widow,
    27 Jan. 1774; Lewis Bochet & Thomas Ballew, trustees; Jacob
    Bonhoste, Joseph Sulliven, wit.   Mar Set 1:   75-78

Fole, Thomas Capt. & Catherine Melachamp, 1 Nov. 1764.
    St. And PR

Follingsby, John & Ann Cadman, 25 Feb. 1772.   St. Phil PR

Follingsby, John & Rhoda Johnson, 24 Nov. 1781.   St. Phil PR

Fomea, Andrew & Elizabeth Taylor, widow, 5 March 1777.   St.
    Phil PR

Footman, John Waggaman, & Mary Turpin, 10 Jan. 1798.   St. Phil
    PR

Ford, Anthony of Parish of Prince Frederick, bachelor & Lydia
    Boone, of Parish of Prince Frederick, spinster in house of
    Mrs. Susanna White, 22 Sept. 1785; Thos Cole, Wm. Anthy
    Atkinson, wit.   St. Jas PR

Ford, George & Sarah Oliver, 13 April 1722.   St. Phil PR

Ford, George of Parish of Prince George, widower & Mary Boone,
    spinster, at the house of Mr. Capers Boone, 13 Oct. 1778;
    William Boone, John Shackelford Jun., wit.   St. Jas PR

Ford, George, of Parish of Prince Frederick, widower, &
    Katherine Wayne, of Parish of Prince George, spinster, in
    the house of Mr. Wm. Wayne, 6 May 1784; Jno Shackelford,
    Willm. Murray, wit.   St. Jas PR

Ford, Jacob Esqr., of Charleston, & Ann Motte Ford, his wife,
    daughter of Arthur Peronneau, of Charleston, 28 Dec. 1797;
    William Edward Hayne, Gent., trustee; Wm. Peronneau, wit.
    Mar Set 3: 225-241

Ford, Joseph & Mary Turkitt, 5 March 1716-7.   T & D PR

Ford, Nathaniel & Mrs. Mary King, 6 May 1714.   T & D PR

Ford, Preserved & Mary ___, 14 Dec. 1709.   Ch Ch PR

Ford, Stephen of Parish of St. Bartholomew, bachelor, & Sarah
     Barton of Parish of Prince Frederick, spinster, 25 Jan. 1761;
     Isaac Ford, ___, it.   St. Jas PR

Ford, Stephen òf Parish of Prince Frederick, widower, & Mar-
     garet White, of Parish of Prince George, spinster, at the
     house of Mr. Anthony Martin White, 8 July 1779; Geo Ford,
     William Barton, wit.   St Jas PR

Ford, William of Parish of St. Andrews, bricklayer, & Kezia
     Cartwright, widow, 7 Sept. 1744; Mumford Milner of Charles
     Town, bondsman; license to Rev. William Guy.   MB Chas

Ford, William & Keziah Cartret, widow, 11 Sept. 1744.   St. And
     PR

Fordham, Richard & Mary Sharp, widow, 9 July 1778.   St. Phil PR

Fordyce, The Revrd. John to Mary Karwon, widow, 20 Oct. 1748, by
     Rev. Mr. Alexr Keith, Minister of Pr. George Parish.   Pr Fred
     PR

Forest, George of Charleston, merchant & Charity Lushington, of
     same, widow, 7 May 1794; William Mason, Thomas Karwon of
     St. Thomas Parish, trustees; Sarah Latham, Ann Moss, wit.
     Mar Set 3: 165-173

Forest, Michael & Joanna Clancy, widow, 26 June 1790.   St. Phil
     PR

Forrest, George & Charity Lushington, 8 May 1794.   Circ Cong

Forrester, William & Martha Durand alias Gillespie, of Prince
     Fredericks Parish, widow of James Durand, 26 Feb. 1788; Ann
     Brown, Childermas Croft, trustees; Ann Minott, Wm. Taylor,
     wit.   Mar Set 1: 375-376

Forst, Henry & Elizabeth Wiat, widow, 23 Dec. 1769.   St. Phil
     PR

Foskey, Bryan & Mary Underwood, widow, 5 Sept. 1762.   St. Phil
     PR

Fosky, Brian & Ann Powell, widow, 13 Oct. 1776.   St. Phil PR

Foster, John Robert & Ann Doryherty, 23 Feb. 1797.   Circ Cong

Fountain, Alexr. & ___, 24 Nov. 1791.   Pugh diary

Fountain, Demsey, & ___, 28 Apr. 1796.   Pugh diary

Fountain, John & Jane Lewis Chapnis, P Banns, 9 January 1727.
     St. Phil PR

Fountain, John & Susanna Matthews, P Licence, September 1733.
     St. Phil PR

Fowler, Edward & Elizabeth Yates, P Licence, 5 Nov. 1738.
     St. Phil PR

Fowler, James & Martha Widdicomb, P Licence, 5 March 1723.
     St. Phil PR

Fowler, John & Dorothy Gary, P Licence, 19 July 1724.   St. Phil
   PR

Fowler, Jonathan & Ann Watkins, widow, 20 May 1764. St. Phil PR

Fowler, Richard & Catherine Grant, P Licence, 9 April 1730.
   St. Phil PR

Fowler, Richd. & Ann Jerves, 28 Jan. 1766. OJ 1764-1771

Fowler, Richard & Ann Jervis, 23 Jan. 1766.   St. Phil PR

Fowles, John & Frances Gifford, 31 July 1720.   St. Phil PR

Fowzer, John George & Sarah Lawry, 24 May 1759. St. Phil PR

Fox, David & Mary Dill, P Licence by Mr. Garden, 17 Sept. 1737.
   St. Phil PR

Fox, Davis & Catherine Potter, of this parish. 27 March 1748.
   Stoney Creek Pres Ch

Fox, Henry and Martha Keen, widow, 20 Aug. 1738.   Pr Fred PR

Fracia, Francis & Ann Bisset, 8 July 1724.   St. Phil PR

Fraik, Thomas & Maria Werner(in), widow, 26 May 1767. St. John
   Luth Ch

Frampton, John & Hannah Adams, P Licence, 30 June 1732. St.
   Phil PR

Francis, John & Anne Basset, P Banns, 10 June 1742.   St. Phil
   PR

Frank, Jacob & Sarah Flood, widow, 14 May 1750.   Hist Oburg

Frank, Simon & Rebecca Lybfritz, widow, 15 Nov. 1763. St. Phil
   PR

Frankland, Captn. Thomas & Sarah Rhett, P Licence, 27 May 1743.
   St. Phil PR

Franklin, Richard & Susanna Gilbert, widow, 5 Dec. 1731. St.
   Hel PR

Franks, John & Catherine Hoats, widow, 11 Jan. 1762. St. And
   PR

Franks, Simon, of "Solomon parish," planter, & Rebecca Syfrith(?)
   of Charles Town, widow, 15 Nov. 1763; Mark Anthony Besseleu,
   Christian Gruber, wit.   Misc. Rec. MM: 8

Franks, Ulrick & Sophia Sabina, widow, 23 Dec. 1772.   St. Phil
   PR

Fraser, Rev. Hugh & Elizabeth Clegg Porter, only daughter of
   Benjamin Porter, late of Georgetown Dist., planter, decd.,
   31 March 1796; John Porter of Georgetown Dist., & wife Anzy,
   trustees; Manasseh Michau, Wm. Dunlop, wit. Mar Set 2:
   509-513

Fraser, James & Ann Vinson, 4 Feb. 1766.   OJ 1764-1771

Fraser, John & Sarah Ladson, 10 Apr. 1770.   St. And PR

Fraser, William & Eleanor Corker, widow, 13 Dec. 1779.   St. Phil
   PR

Frasier, John & Mary Duke, 8 Aug. 1771.   T & D PR

Fray, George & Christian Pyfrin, 9 Feb. 1758.   St. Phil PR

Frazer, Alexander & Ann Harvey, P Licence, 10 Nov. 1749.   St.
   Phil PR

Frazer, Frederic & Mary DeSaussure, 27 Jan. 1791.   Circ Cong

Frazer, Isaac, son of James decd., & Mary Pearson, 7 July 1774.
   Bush R QM

Frazer, John Milligan, of Charleston, house carpenter, &
   Rebecca Eairr, widow, 6 Apr. 1797.   St. Phil PR

Frazier, Alexander & Margaret Forbes, 25 May 1760.   St. Phil
   PR

Frazier, James, widower, & Mary Ash, 27 Feb. 1772.   St. Hel
   PR

Frederick, Andris of Orangeburgh Dist., & Charlotte Foggle,
   widow, 13 Jan. 1778; Melicha Warley of Charleston, trustee;
   Lewis Golsan, Emanuel Abrahams, wit.   Mar Set 1: 249-250

Frederick, Samuel, planter & Sarah Bradwell, of St. George
   Parish, Dorchester, 4 April 1767; Jacob Bradwell, Isaac
   Bradwell, John Bradwell, planters, trustees; Elizabeth
   Bradwell, Sarah Bradwell, Harriet Bradwell, wit.   Misc. Rec.
   TT: 435-437

Freeman, Richard & Anne Loroach, P Licence, 4 June 1740.   St.
   Phil PR

Freeman, William & Jane Lewis, widow, 22 Dec. 1742.   St. And
   PR

Freer, Solomon of St. Johns Parish, Colleton Co., & Ann Mathews
   of Charles Town, widow, 1 Feb. 1777; Benjamin Mathews, John
   Raven Matthews, George Matthews, trustees; James Air, William
   Print, wit.   Misc. Rec. RR: 406-408

Freer, Solomon & Ann Mathews, widow, 2 Feb. 1777.   St. Phil PR

Freer, William & Charity Gibbson, 2 Dec. 1784.   St. John Luth
   Ch

Freers, Joseph & Eleanor Gibson, P Licence by Mr. Garden, 18
   March 1725/6.   St. Phil PR

French, John & Sarah Johnson, 1 July 1741.   St. And PR

Frew, John, cabinet maker, & Mary Ann Bullock, spinster, 1 Aug.
   1798; John Singleton, silver smith, trustee; Cs. Stewart,
   Jean Singleton, wit.   Mar Set 3: 277-278.

Frewin, Charles, Esqr., & Anne Simons, of Parish of St. Thomas
   & St. Dennis (extract from Parish Register), by Alexr.
   Garden, Rector, 10 Feb. 1767. Misc. Rec. NN: 339-340

Frewin, Charles & Ann Simons, 10 Feb. 1767.   T & D PR

Frick, ___ & ___ Hinckle, 13 Oct. 1774.   St. And PR

Frick, Jacob, son of Mr. Thomas Frick, & Christian Hinckel(in), daughter of Mr. Jacob Hinckel, 10 Oct. 1774, by Henrick Muhlenberg.   St. John Luth Ch

Friend, George & Catharine Muckenfuss, widow, 29 June 1779. St. Phil PR

Frier, John & Susanna Boone, 14 Apr. 1757.   St. Phil PR

Friley, John & Mary Dent, widow, 23 June 1744.   St. And PR

Frink, Thomas & Rebecca Eliza Kirk, 20 Sept. 1795.   St. Phil PR

Fripp, John & Elizabeth Hand, 19 Apr. 1747.   St. Hel PR

Fripp, John & Elizabeth Hunn, spinster, P Licence by the Revd. Mr. Alexr. Garden, 19 April 1747.   St. Phil PR

Fripp, John of St. Helena Island, planter, & Elizth. Grive of Ladys Island, Parish of St. Helena, widow, 23 Sept. 1776; Thomas Bell of Ladys Island, trustee; G. Christie, Eliz. Tobias, wit.   Misc. Rec. RR: 368-371

Fripp, Paul & Amey Reynolds, 27 June 1768.   St. Hel PR

Fripp, Paul & Elizabeth Jenkins, (no date).   St. Hel PR

Fripp, William & Tabitha Edings, 1 Oct. 1761.   St. Hel PR

Fripp, William & Madolen Magott, 10 May 1770.   St. Hel PR

Frish, Charles & Elizabeth Yesekus, 10 June 1783.   St. John Luth Ch

Frith, Samuel & Anne Croskeys, 6 June 1720.   St. And PR

Frogatt, Addin & Ann Wood, 11 Apr. 1790.   St. Phil PR

Frost, Thomas Rev. & Elizabeth Downes, 15 Nov. 1787.   St. Phil PR

Frost, William & Mary Townshend, P Licence by Mr. Garden, 31 Oct. 1736.   St. Phil PR

Fry, Paltor & Martha Charity, P Licence, 15 Aug. 1749.   St. Phil PR

Fryer, John & Rachel Gray, P Licence, 28 Oct. 1731.   St. Phil PR

Fryerstone, John and Sarah Dial, 22 Nov. 1741.   Pr Fred PR

Fullalove, Thos. & Alice Graham, 16 Jan. 1766.   OJ 1764-1771

Fuller, Nathaniel of St. Andrews Parish, Berkley Co., & Sarah Lloyd, spinster, 17 March 1743/4; license to Rev. Alexander Garden; Alexander Levie, of Charlestown, bondsman.   MB Chas

Fuller, Nathanel & Sarah Loyd, per Licence, 17 March 1743.
    St. Phil PR

Fuller, Nathaniel & Anne Fuller, 10 Apr. 1768.   St. And PR

Fuller, Richd. & Mary Drayton, 21 Dec. 1721.   St. And PR

Fuller, Thomas of St. Andrew's Parish, & Elizabeth Middleton,
    19 June 1786.   St. Hel PR

Fuller, Thomas Collo. & Elizabeth Miles, widow, 7 Sept. 1766.
    St. And PR

Fuller, Thomas Col. & Catherine Foley, ___ 1773. St. And PR

Fuller, Whitmarsh, & Judith Simpson, 2 July 1761.   St. And PR

Fullwood, William & Alice Wells, 8 Oct. 1727.   St. Phil PR

Furcher, Peter & Catherine Daniel, widow, 22 Feb. 1731/2.
    St. And PR

Furgusson, John & Hannah Cordoza, widow, 10 Apr. 1765. St.
    Phil PR

Furman, Josiah & Sarah Hartmann, 10 Nov. 1765.   St. Phil PR

Furnas, John, son of John decd., and Esther Wilson, 25 Nov.
    1780.   Cane Creek MM

Furnas, John & Ruth Cook, 3 Jan. 1798.   Bush R QM

Furnas, Joseph, son of John decd., & Sarah Pearson, 30 Sept.
    1790.   Bush R QM

Furnas, Robert, son of John & Mary decd., and Hannah Wilson,
    11 Feb. 1796.   Cane Creek MM

Fuster, John & Sirrah Hatcher, [1740's].   Hist Oburg

Futhy, James and Margaret Glenn, 4 March 1738.   Pr Fred PR

Fyfe, John & Sarah Dott, widow, 2 July 1775.   St. Phil PR

Fyffe, Charles of Craven Co., Practitioner in Physick, & Anne
    Rowe of Charles Town, spinster, 26 Nov. 1751; Col. George
    Pawley of Craven Co., planter, trustee; Jos Brown, Jno
    Neufville, wit.   Misc. Rec. II: 215-217

Gabeau, Anthony & Elizabeth Henley, 23 Sept. 1778.   St. Phil
    PR

Gadelius, Sven & Abbey Everott Banister, 4 Oct. 1790. St. Phil
    PR

Gadsden, Christopher & Jane Godfrey, spinster, per Licence by
    the Revd. Mr. Robt. Betham, 28 July 1746.   St. Phil PR

Gadsden, Christopher & Mary Hazel, 29 Dec. 1755.   St. Phil PR

Gadsden, Christopher & Ann Wragg, daughter of Joseph Wragg,
    9 Apr. 1776; Gabriel Manigault, trustee; Wm. Burrows, Wm.
    Print, wit.   Mar Set 1: 63-69

Gadsden, Christopher & Ann Wragg, 14 Apr. 1776.   St. Phil PR

Gadsden, James William & Rebecca Coachman of Charleston, 29 Nov.
1797; Rebecca Smith, widow, trustee; John Singelton, Junior,
John Singleton, wit.   Mar Set 3: 205-207

Gadsden, Thomas & Collins Hall, 11 April 1728.   St. Phil PR

Gadsden, Thomas & Alice Mighells, P Licence, 25 July 1732.
St. Phil PR

Gadsden, Thomas & Martha Fenwicke, 16 Oct. 1778.   St. Phil PR

Gafkin, Henrich Christoph, widower, & Christina Mttutzin, daughter of the late Friedrich Mattutz, 12 July 1778. St. John
Luth Ch

Gaignard, Gabriel & Frances De Lesslienne, spinster, P Licence
by the Revd. Mr. Levi Durante, 10 Nov. 1746. St. Phil PR

Gaillard, Alcimus & Eliza Gendroon, spinster, 30 July 1744;
license to Rev. Thomas Hasell; Munford Milner, bondsman.
MB Chas

Gaillard, Bartholomew, bachelor, & Elizabeth Webb, spinster,
in the house of Elizabeth Webb, 19 Feb. 1769; Peter Mouzon,
Frances Bochet, wit.   St. Jas PR

Gaillard, Charles, bachelor, & Ann Dupre, spinster, in the
house of Samuel Dupre, 13 Sept. 1770; Jonah Robert, Benj.
Perdriau, wit.   St. Jas PR

Gaillard, David of Parish of St. Stephens, bachelor, & Joanna
Dubose, of Parish of St. Stephens, spinster, at the planta-
tion of Theodore Gaillard Sr., 23 Sept. 1773; James Rivers,
Isaac Dubose, wit.   St. Jas PR

Gaillard, James, bachelor, & Mary Jones, widow, at the house
of Saml. Fenner Warren, 19 July 1763; Allen Mackee, Wm.
Jones, wit.   St. Jas PR

Gaillard, John, bachelor, & Susanna Boone, spinster, in the
house of Thomas Boone, 10 Nov. 1768; Thos Boone Junr., Chas
Gaillard, wit.   St. Jas PR

Gaillard, John & Harriott Lord, 24 Nov. 1791.   St. Phil PR

Gaillard, John & Mary Loyd, 22 Nov. 1792.   St. Phil PR

Gaillard, John Junr., bachelor, & Susanna Boone, by Licence,
10 Nov. 1768, by S. F. Warren, rector; Thomas Boone, Chas
Gaillard, wit. (from Register of St. James Santee Parish).
Misc. Rec. VV: 125

Gaillard, Theodore of Charleston, barrister, & Cornelia Marshall
6 Nov. 1799; John Gaillard of St. Stephens Parish, William
Robertson, of Charleston trustees; A. E. Miller, Peyre
Gaillard, wit. Mar Set 3: 386-387

Gaillard, Theodore the younger, of Charlestown, merchant, &
Eleanor Cordes, of St. John's Parish, spinster, daughter of
John Cordes, decd; Samuel Cordes & Peter Porcher, of St.
Stephens Parish, planters, trustees; James Cordes, James
Cordes, Junr., wit. 6 June 1764.   Mar Set 2: 239-241

Gaillard, Theodore Junr. & Martha Doughty, 1 Nov. 1792. St. Phil PR

Gairdner, Edwin, of Charleston, merchant, & Jane Drummond Gordon, daughter of John Gordon; James Gairdner, John Alexander Ogilvie, trustees, 23 Dec. 1795; Chas Dundas Deas, J. J. Debesse, wit. Mar Set 2: 454-456

Gairdner, James & Mary Gorden, eldest daughter of John Gorden, 1 Nov. 1790; Alexander Rose, Edward Pennan, Elihu Hall Bay, John Alexander Ogelvie, trustees; Wm. Robertson, Ro Mitchell, wit. Mar Set 1: 520-523

Galaspie, David & Mary Rogers, widow, 12 May 1770. St. Phil PR

Galloway, Alfred, pilot & Elizabeth Gleason, widow, 27 June 1798. St. Phil PR

Galloway, David & Mary Stocks, 12 Sept. 1719. St. And PR

Galloway, Thomas & Anne Wingwood, spinster; minister Alexander Garden; bondsmen Thomas Galloway (Gallwey), mariner, and Jeremiah Milner of Charles Town, victualler; Wit. James Michie, 11 June 1733. MB NY

Galloway, Thomas & Anne Winigood, P Licence, 17 June 1733. St. Phil PR

Galphin, George & Bridget Shaw, P Licence, 1 July 1742. St. Phil PR

Gandy, Samuel & Rosina Zellwegerin, 14 March [1740's]. Hist Oburg

Garden, Alexander & Elizabeth Peronneau, 25 Dec. 1755. St. Phil PR

Garden, Alexander & Sarah Lesesne, 3 Nov. 1791. St. Phil PR

Garden, Alexander & Harriett Hockley Cochran, 9 March 1796. St. Phil PR

Garden, the Reverend Alexander & Martha Guerard, P Licence by the Reverent Mr. Thomas Morritt, 8 June 1725. St. Phil PR

Garden, Alex., Rev. & Amey Hartley, 14 Dec. 1749. T & D PR

Garden, Benjamin & Eliza Harry Bremar, 16 Sept. 1759. St. Phil PR

Garden, Benjamin of Prince William Parish, Granville Co., & Amelia .Godin, daughter of Benjamin Godin, decd., and granddaughter of Isaac Mazyck, 16 Jan. 1765; Stephen Bull of Sheldon, & Wm. Lennox of Charlestown, trustees; Sampson Neyle, Copeland Styles, wit. Mar Set 2: 486-490

Garden, Johannes, & Margar. Findin (Einden?], widow, 27 Nov. 1765. St. John Luth Ch

Gardiner, Daniel of Parish of St. Mark, Craven Co., planter, & Ann Hart, widow of Benjamin Hart, 3 March 1772; Henry Hunter, trustee; Charles Woodmason, Rector of the Parish of St. Mark, wit. Misc. Rec. RR: 391-394

Gardner, Daniel & Frances Hackett, P Licence by A. Garden, 23
May 1747.   St. Phil PR

Gardner, John & Rachael Heatley, P Licence, 19 Nov. 1741.
St. Phil PR

Gardner, John & Margt. Whitney, 30 March 1794.   Trin Meth Ch

Garner, Melcher, of St. Paul's Parish, planter, & Ann Smith,
(under age of 21), daughter of Ann Evans of St. Georges
Parish; 14 July 1768; Ann Evans & Wm. Clay Snipes, trustees;
Elizabeth Palmer, Joanna Garner, wit. Mar Set 2: 9-12

Garner, William of St. Pauls Parish, Gent., & Sarah Murray,
spinster, 18 Dec. 1771; Edward Griffith of Prince Williams
Parish, trustee; Melcher Garner, Roger Parker Saunders, Bryan
Cape, wit.   Misc. Rec. PP: 222-223

Garner, William & Sarah Murray, 19 Dec. 1771.   St. Phil PR

Garnes, William & Rachel McDaniel, P Licence, 22 Sept. 1742.
St. Phil PR

Garnes, William & Hannah Spencer, 11 Jan. 1756.   St. Phil PR

Garnier, John of Prince George's parish, widower, & Anne
Keen, of Prince George's Parish, spinster, in the house of
Mrs. Eliz: Withers, 27 June 1786, James Withers, William C.
Shackelford, wit.   St. Jas PR

Garns, William & Margaret D'Hay, widow, 9 June 1760.   St. Phil
PR

Garrett, Richard & Mary Davis, widow, 26 Apr. 1789.   St. Phil
PR

Garvey, John & Elizabeth Gilbert, 16 March 1736.   St. Hel PR

Garvey, John, widower, & Martha Rich, widow, 24 Oct. 1751.
St. Hel PR

Garvin, Ebenezer & Margaret Day, widow, 11 Jan. 1778. St. Phil
PR

Gascoyne, Charles Richard of New Windsor & Sarah Tipper,
spinster, 25 July 1744; license to Rev. Alex. Garden; Richard
Linter of Charles Town, bondsman.   MB Chas

Gascoyn, Charles Richmond & Sarah Tipper, P Licence, 23 July
1744.   St. Phil PR

Gaskins, Daniel of Charleston Dist., & Elizabeth McCullough,
15 Feb. 1798; Jas Green, William Ferebe, wit. Mar Set 3:
241-243

Gates, John & Catharine Mintz, 19 March 1786.   St. John Luth
Ch

Gates, Thomas, Doctor of Divinity & Elizabeth Postell, spinster,
7 Nov. 1792; Susannah Postell, widow and William Postell,
Esq.; Elias Lynch Horry, Ann Waring, wit.   Mar Set 2:
80-83

Gates, Thomas Revd. & Elizabeth Postell, __ Nov. 1792.
   St. Phil PR

Gatz, George & Barbara N., widow [1740's]. Hist Oburg

Gaultier, Joseph & Mary Esther Portal, 31 March 1746. St. Phil
   PR

Gaultier, Joseph & Mary Nichols, 7 May 1772.   St. Phil PR

Gaunt, Nebo & Elizabeth Brooks, 4 March 1790.   Bush R QM

Gaunt, Samuel, son of Zebulon, m. Abigail Kelly, 30 Apr. 1785.
   Bush R QM

Gaunt, Zebulon, late of Camden Dist., & Mary Kelly, 2 Nov. 1780.
   Bush R QM

Gaunt, Zimri, son of Zebulon, m. Sarah Cook, 3 Nov. 1785.
   Bush R QM

Gauthier, Joseph, taylor, & Elisabeth Bursote(?), widow, 20 Nov.
   1768.   St. John Luth Ch

Gee, Charles of Parish of Prince George, bachelor, & Catherine
   Bond of Parish of Prince George, widow, in the public school-
   house of Prince George, 24 Apr. 1770; Thomas Webb, Peter
   Maume(?), wit.   St. Jas PR

Geliou, Saml. & Mrs. Jane Russell, 11 March 1797.   Trin Meth
   Ch

Gelzer, Daniel & Margaret Brick, widow [1740's]. Hist Oburg

Gemmel, John & Sarah Simpson, 12 Feb. 1782.   St. Phil PR

Genscel, John & Margaret Jeyser, 20 Apr. 1775.   St. Phil PR

Georg, Johann Heinrich, shoemaker, & Magdalena, widow of Jacob
   Bohler, 28 Jan. 1783.   St. John Luth Ch

George & Eliz., free Negroes, 3 Sept. 1738.   St. And PR

George, Edward & Rebecca Smidmore, 9 June 1762.   St. Phil PR

George, James & Elizabeth Hamilton, widow of David Hamilton, of
   Charleston, shipwright, 16 Sept. 1795; Wm. Pritchard Jun.,
   Samuel Harvey, trustees; George Nicholls, wit.   Mar Set 2:
   438-442

George, James & Elizabeth Hamilton, widow, 17 Sept. 1795. St.
   Phil PR

George, John & Mary Skipper, 17 Aug. 1738.   Pr Fred PR

Geyer, Wm. (Mariner) & Elizth. Glover, widow, of this city,
   6 Oct. 1794.   Trin Meth Ch

Gibberns, John & Elizabeth Bennett, 9 Nov. 1736.   Ch Ch PR

Gibbes, Benjamin & Elizabeth Bail, 20 Oct. 1790.   St. Phil PR

Gibbes, Henry & Mary Dunbar, widow, 30 Aug. 1791. St. Phil PR

Gibbes, John & Mary Ann Stephens, 2 May 1754. St. Hel PR

Gibbes, John & Ann, widow of Thomas Wigg [no date]. St. Hel PR

Gibbens, John & Elizabeth Bennett, P Licence by Mr. Garden, 9
    Nov. 1736. St. Phil PR

Gibbes, John & Elizabeth White, 6 July 1760.   Ch Ch PR

Gibbes, John & Mary Metheringham, 2 Dec. 1760.   Ch Ch PR

Gibbes, John & Mary Smith, daughter of Benjamin Smith, Esqr.,
    decd., 27 Nov. 1787; William Smith, James Ladson, trustees;
    Alexr. Barden, Nathl. Heyward, wit. Mar Set 1: 397-399

Gibbes, Col. John of Parish of St. Johns, Colleton Co., &
    Elizabeth Jenys, widow of Paul Jenys, late of Berkley County,
    23 Aug. 1743; Henry Bedon & Bramfield Evans, trustees;
    Stephen Bedon Junr., John R. Bedon, wit. Misc. Rec. II:
    239-243

Gibbes, John Walters & Amarinthia Baddely, 20 Oct. 1776. St.
    Phil PR

Gibbes, Robert & Elizabeth Haddrell, 2 Apr. 1741.   Ch Ch PR

Gibbes, Robert Reeves, of Charleston, planter, & Anne Smith, of
    sare, 28 Nov. 1799.   St. Phil PR

Gibbes, William & Mary Bennison, spinster, 7 Feb. 1743/4;
    license to Rev. Liev Durant; Robert Gibbes, bondsman. MB
    Chas

Gibbes, William & Mary Benison, 8 March 1744. Ch Ch PR

Gibbes, William & Elizabeth Hasell, daughter of Rev. Thomas
    Hasell, of St. Thomas' Parish, 18 Feb. 1747/8.   Ch Ch PR

Gibbes, William of Christ Church Parish, & Elizabeth Hasell,
    spinster, 17 Feb. 1747; Thomas Hasell, of Prince George
    parish, trustee; Robt Gibbs, Jno Hasell, wit. Misc. Rec. HH:
    399-400

Gibbes, William & Elizabeth Hasell, 18 Feb. 1747. T & D PR

Gibbes, William Hasell of Parish of Prince George, bachelor &
    Elizabeth Allston, Parish of All Saints, spinster, at the
    house of Mrs. Alston, 29 Aug. 1782; Benjn. Allston, Ann All-
    ston, wit. St. Jas PR

Gibbs, Daniel & Mary Cozzins, 24 May 1798.   Circ Cong

Gibbs, John & Mary Woodward, 25 July 1719.   St. And PR

Gibson, Ambrose of Parish of St. Bartholomew, & wife Elizabeth,
    formerly widow of Thomas Elliott; Thomas Patterson of
    Saltcatcher Bridge, trustee; William Patterson, Mary T.
    Patterson, wit.   Mar Set 3: 202-203

Gibson, Edward & Susanna Schwartz, 22 Dec. 1741; Christian &
    Joseph Schwartz & John Souderecker, wit.   Hist Oburg

Gibson, John & Margaret Fludd, both below Orangeburgh Township
    19 Dec. 1754.   Hist Oburg

Gibson, Robert & Anne Maria Black, 19 May 1771.   St. And PR

Gibson, Thomas & Anne Stocks, 30 Jan. 1720/21.   St. And PR

Gibson, William & Margaret Arnold, P Licence, 24 Feb. 1733.
   St. Phil PR

Gibson, William & Mary Burnett, 8 Jan. 1762.   St. Phil PR

Giddens, Samuel & Elizabeth Ellis, spinster, per Licence by the
   Revd. Mr. Robert Betham, 19 Aug. 1746.   St. Phil PR

Giegelman, Hans & Ann Elizabeth Shuler [1740's].   Hist Oburg

Giessendanner, George Jun. & Agner Diedrich, widow, [1740's].
   Hist Oburg

Giessendanner, Henry & Elizabeth Rumph, 25 Feb. 1767.   Hist
   Oburg

Giessendanner, John Ulrick & his housekeeper, 15 Nov. 1737.
   Hist. Oburg

Gignilliat, James & Charlotte Pepper, 8 May 1766.   St. Hel PR

Gilbriath, Robt. & Ann Harrisson, 23 Sept. 1797.   Trin Meth Ch

Gissendanner, Henry & Mary Larry, 21 Jan. 1796.   Hist Oburg

Gignilliat, Gabrel & Eliza. Cahusac, 12 May 1766.   OJ 1764-1771

Gignilliatt, James & Charlotte Pepper, 17 Apr. 1766.   OJ 1764-
   1771

Gilbert, Francis & Sophia McIntosh, 18 Aug. 1782.   St. Phil PR

Gilchrist, Bryan & Eliz Hanson, 27 March 1770.   St. Phil PR

Giles, Abraham & Elizabeth Fletcher, widow, 8 Feb. 1747/8.
   Pr Fred PR

Giles, John & Jane Rennie, P Licence by the Revd. Mr. A. Garden,
   23 March 1753.   St. Phil PR

Giles, Othniel & Jane Colleton, widow, 5 Jan. 1778.   St. Phil PR

Giles, Robert & Matilda Cameron, widow, 31 Dec. 1795.   St. Phil
   PR

Gill, John & Rebecca Pearce, widow, 11 March 1795.   St. Phil PR

Gillcrist, Robert & Rebekah Underwood, P Licence, 28 Aug. 1729.
   St. Phil PR

Gillespie, Robert of Parish Prince George, bachelor & Martha
   Durand, of parish of Prince George, widow, at the house of
   Mrs. Martha Durand, 26 July 1785; Saml Cooper, Childermas
   Croft, wit.   St. Jas PR

Gillibeau, James of Charleston, taylor, & Elizabeth More, 22 Apr.
   1797.   St. Phil PR

Gillon, Alexr. & Mary Cripps, widow, 5 July 1766.   OJ 1764-1771

Gillon, Alexander & Ann Purcell [no date, Feb. 1789]. St. Phil PR

Gills, Hugh & Sarah Ball, 4 Feb. 1772. Pugh diary

Gilmore, John & Elizabeth Hartman, 28 May 1778. St. Phil PR

Gilmore, John & Eliz'th Hartman, 28 May 1775. T & D PR

Gilmore, John & Mary Ripley, 23 July 1782. St. Phil PR

Giraldeau, James & Mary Postell, 22 March 1740. St. Hel PR

Girardeau, Peter Bohun, & Elizabeth Hyrne, 17 Nov. 1795; Daniel Doyley, trustee; Anna Doyley, Charles Webb, wit. Mar Set 2: 442-448

Girerdeau, Peter & Elizabeth Bohun, 19 Dec. 1730. St. And PR

Girerdeau, Petter & Elizabeth Heap, 19 March 1746 [1746/7]. St. And PR

Gissendanner, John of Charleston & Susannah Besselleu, of same, widow, 20 Dec. 1795; Daniel Miscally, trustee; Joseph Darby, Isaac Dumons, wit. Mar Set 3: 51-52

Gissendanner, John & Susannah Bessileau, 31 Dec. 1795. St. Phil PR

Gittins, Nathaniel & Mary Lawrens, P Licence, Sept. 1733. St. Phil PR

Given, David & Arabella Steuart, 15 Nov. 1798. Circ Cong

Givens, Charles & Mary Barlow, 10 Nov. 1785. St. Hel PR

Givens, John & Mary Stone, 18 Sept. 1751. St. Hel PR

Givens, Philip, widower, & Martha Bowman, 3 Oct. 1734. St. Hel PR

Givin, John, widower & Catherine Ricketts, 17 March 1739. St. Hel PR

Glandal, Richard & Hannah Gibson, widow, 29 Apr. 1730. St. And PR

Glaspell, Neal & Elizabeth O'Hearne, 16 June 1788. St. Phil PR

Glasier, Samuel & Sarah Louisa Roy, P Licence, 6 March 1731. St. Phil PR

Glaze, William & Ann Nevin, widow, 23 Aug. 1778. St. Phil PR

Glazier, Frederick & Mary Wildiers, 4 Dec. 1763. St. Phil PR

Glen, John and Anna Thompson, 16 Apr. 1745. Pr Fred PR

Glen, William of Charlestown, merchant & Martha, daughter of Stephen Miller, 7 Apr. 1770; Brian Cape, trustee; A. Downs, John Glen, wit. Mar Set 1: 159-160

Glen, William & wife Margaret, 19 July 1773; Alexander Michie, trustee; Robt Crab, Thos Phepoe, wit. Mar Set 1: 253-254

Glen, William & Martha Miller, 12 Apr. 1770.   T & D PR

Glenn, John & Mary Bocquet, 21 Apr. 1796.   St. Phil PR

Glenn, John & Sarah Wittimar, 16 Nov. 1797.   Circ Cong

Glenn, Thomas & Mary Guadee, 28 March 1743.   St. Hel PR

Glenwright, John & Elizabeth Maddutz, by Authority of a Certifi-
    cate from Major Trails of the Royal Artillery, 26 Dec. 1781.
    St. John Luth Ch

Glidden, Richard & Mary Barrows, P Licence by the Revd. Mr.
    Alexr. Garden, 9 Oct. 1747.   St. Phil PR

Glover, Joseph of Parish of Prince George, widower & Elizabeth
    Jeanneret, of Parish of Prince Frederick, spinster, in the
    house of Francis Marshall, M.D., 15 April 1784; Francis
    Marshall, John ___, wit.   St. Jas PR

Glover, Joseph of Parish of Prince George, widower, & Jean
    Sinkler, of Parish of St. Stephen, spinster, in the house
    of Mr. James Sinkler, 30 Sept. 1786; Edwd Drake, Peter Sink-
    ler, wit.   St. Jas PR

Glover, Moses, planter, & Mary Sophia Hepburn of Nassau, widow,
    14 Oct. 1799; Alexander Taylor of same, & Wilson Glover, of
    South Carolina, trustees; Tho Foster, Mary Foster, Thos Hunt,
    wit.   Mar Set 3: 368-372

Glover, Moses, of Georgetown & Sarah Henrietta Bonneau of
    Georgetown, 28 Nov. 1792; Hugh Horry Esqr., trustee; Sarah
    Horry, Patrick Golding, wit.   Mar Set 2: 45-46

Glover, William & Margaret Young, 24 June 1777.   St. Phil PR

Glover, William & Jane Packrow, P Licence, 22 June 1749.   St.
    Phil PR

Gobe, Louis Claude Giles, son of Giles Gobe & Marie Plante, &
    Louise Agnis le Noir, daughter of Leonard Le Noir & Jeanne
    Orval, no date. Extract from Register of the Chancellor of
    Consulate of the French Republic. Rec. 24 July 1795.
    (original in French, translated BHH). Mar Set 2: 411-414

Godard, Rene, son of Rene Godard & Jeanne Sondy, native of
    Nantes, department of Loire, & Marie Juhan, daughter of
    Jacques Juhan & Marie Paysau, native of Halifax, Nova Scotia,
    no date. Extract from Register of the Chancellor of Consu-
    late of the French Republic. Rec. 29 July 1795. Mar Set
    2: 414-417

Godber, Wm. & Loveridge VillePontoux, 30 Dec. 1790.   Circ Cong

Goddard, Francis & Mary Manwaring, 14 Jan. 1713-4.   T & D PR

Goddard, Francis & Mary Pight, P Licence, 20 Dec. 1732.
    St. Phil PR

Goddman, Thomas & Barbara Parry, P Licence by Mr. Jon, 22 Aug.
    1735.   St. Phil PR

Godfrey, Benjamin & Margaret Fossin, P Licence, by the Reverend
    Mr. Alex. Garden, 22 Feb. 1725/6.   St. Phil PR

Godfrey, Benjamin, planter, & Mary Robinson Estes, widow of Richard Estes, 10 June 1790; Joseph Compton, Turner Meyrick, trustees; Frans Myrick, James Forrett, wit. Mar Set 1: 487-490

Godfrey, Benjamin & Abigail Darling, 3 Feb. 1773. St. Phil PR

Godfrey, Benjamin Harrington, of Georgetown Dist., and Elizabeth Campbell, 28 Apr. 1792; Jacob William Harvey, trustee; Serajah Hasford, Robert Carr, wit. Mar Set 2: 1-2

Godfrey, John of Parish of St. Andrews, & Mary Chapman, spinster, 12 May 1744; license to Rev. William Guy; Richard Godfrey, bondsman. MB Chas

Godfrey, John & Mary Chapman, 14 May 1744. St. And PR

Godfrey, John of Prince Fredericks Parish, & Mary ____ (already married), 24 Aug. 1761; William Wilson, William Green, trustees; Edmund Mathewes, Jannet Harrinton, wit. Misc. Rec. LL: 513-515

Godfrey, John & Mary Harrinton, 29 July 1761 by Revrd. James Dormer. Pr Fred PR

Godfrey, John & Patience DelaChappelle, widow, 25 Sept. 1762. St. Phil PR

Codfrey, John & Elizabeth Chappell, widow, ___ Oct. 1762. St. And PR

Godfrey, Richard & Rebeccah Guy, spinster, 27 Jan. 1743/4; license to Rev. William Guy; William Bonneau, bondsman. MB Chas

Godfrey, Richard & Rebecca Guy, 31 Jan. 1743 [1743/4]. St. And PR

Godfrey, Thomas alias Garnear & Elizabeth Chapman, 9 July 1752. St. And PR

Godfrey, Thomas & Sarah Donnom, 14 Jan. 1787. St. Phil PR

Godfrey, William & Ann Saxbey, 22 Oct. 1741. St. And PR

Godin, Isaac & Mara. Matthewes, 4 Oct. 1759. St. Phil PR

Goelett, James & Mary Handcock, P Licence, 28 Feb. 1743. St. Phil PR

Goetzinger, Adam & Franzine Russel, 26 Dec. 1782. St. John Luth Ch

Goff, John & Margaret Cords, 6 Jan. 1766. OJ 1764-1771

Goldin, John & Mary Robertson, P Licence, 3 Oct. 1748. St. Phil PR

Goldrick, Bryan & Mary Shortey, 6 Feb. 1728. St. Hel PR

Golightly, Colsheth & Mary Elliott, widow, 30 Mar. 1746. St. And PR

Goldsmith, John & Rebekah Mallory, P Banns, August 1731. St. Phil PR

Golsen, Lewis & Elizabeth Stehely, 19 Dec. 1752. Hist Oburg

Golsman, John & Margaret Bomgardner, 13 Jan. 1767. St. Phil PR

Goodale, Thomas and Frances Richardson; spinster; minister Alexander Garden; bondsmen Thomas Goodale, Indian Trader, and Nicholas Haynes of Charles Town, victualer, 25 June 1733. MB NY

Goodbie, Alexander & Anna Daniel, 9 Dec. 1725. T & D PR

Goodbie, John & Hannah Wallbank, 29 Dec. 1713. T & D PR

Goodin, John & Elizabeth Street, widow, 29 Aug. 1743. St. And PR

Goodson, Arter & ___, 14 July 1791. Pugh diary

Goodson, Thos. & Sarah Jenkins, 24 Oct. 1782. Pugh diary

Goodwin, John & Lydia Wilds, 4 Apr. 1743. Pr Fred PR

Goodall, William & Elizabeth Greenwood, 24 Dec. 1739. Pr Fred PR

Gordon, John & Bridget Batsford, 10 Aug. 1745. St. And PR

Gordon, John & Elizabeth Wright, 2 Apr. 1751. St. Hel PR

Gordon, John & Elizabeth Scott, 26 June 1769. St. Phil PR

Gordon, John of Charlestown, Taylor, & Penelope Gordon, spinster, legatee of John Gordon, of Charlestown, tavernkeeper, decd., 17 Jan. 1776; William Moultrie, Barnard Elliott, trustee, John Troup, Joseph Gaultier, wit. Misc. Rec. SS 7-10

Gordon, John & Penelope Gordon, 18 Jan. 1776. St. Phil PR

Gordon, John & Elizabeth Reilly, widower, 14 March 1787. St. Phil PR

Gordon, John Jnr., factor, & Nancy Williams, 27 May 1792. Trin Meth Ch

Gordon, Peter & Sarah Reed, 14 Jan. 1778. St. Phil PR

Gordon, Thomas & Ann Nelme Widow, P Licence by the Revd. A. G., 9 July 1752. St. Phil PR

Gordon, Thomas & Mary Hawkes, 14 Jan. 1765. St. Phil PR

Gordon, William & Margaret Hawthorn, 4 Apr. 1771. St. Phil PR

Goreing, Thos. & Jane Heydon, widow, 9 Sept. 1731. St. And PR

Gording, Thomas & Martha Wright als D'Oily, 14 Dec. 1725. St. Phil PR

Goring, Thomas & Mary Cheshire, widow, 1 March 1746 [1746/7]. St. And PR

Gosling, William J. & Mary Ann Roof, 24 June 1782. St. Phil PR

Gotier, Francis & Isabel Gordon, per Licence, 4 Feb. 1743.
St. Phil PR

Gottier, Francis of Charles Town & Isabell Gordon, widow, 4 Feb.
1743/4; license to Rev. Alex. Garden; Gabriel Guignard,
bondsman. MB Chas

Götzinger, Georg & Esther Howardt, 25 Dec. 1781. St. John
Luth Ch

Gough, John & Rebecca Hext, 2 Dec. 1776. St. Phil PR

Gough, Thomas & Lesly Creighton of St. Bartholomew's Parish,
21 Aug. 1783; Margaret Cunningham, James Postell Junr.,
Richard Singellton, trustees; Sarah Postell, Benjamin Postell,
wit. Mar Set 1: 160-162

Gough, Thomas & Lisley Creighton of St. Bartholomews Parish,
21 Aug. 1783; Margaret Cunningham, James Postell, Richard
Singelton, Andrew Cunningham, trustees; Sarah Postell,
Benj. Postell, wit. Mar Set 1: 235-237

Gough, William & Mary Bearsley, 19 Jan. 1727, (in London).
St. Hel PR

Gough, William & Susannah LeFond, widow, 24 Oct. 1735. St. Hel
PR

Gough, William & Magdalen Hamilton, widow, 7 May 1749.
St. Hel PR

Gough, William, widower, & Magdalena Hamilton, widow, 6 May
1749, of St. Helena Parish. Stoney Creek Pres Ch

Gould, John & Elizabeth Evans, both of this parish, 16 Oct. 1755.
Stoney Creek Pres Ch

Goulling, John & Ann Lawson, 28 July 1766. St. Phil PR

Gourdin, Samuel & Mary Doughty, 7 Nov. 1793. St. Phil PR

Gouron, Philip & Charlotte Jortin, by Mr. Garden, 25 June 1722.
St. Phil PR

Gowdey, William & Lucina Barlow, 15 Oct. 1758. St. Phil PR

Gowdy, John & Ann Beedle, 20 Dec. 1761. St. Phil PR

Graaff, Peter Caspar, merchant, & Lucy Buskin, ___ 1791;
Francis Ryckboth, trustee; John Frederick Kern, wit. Mar
Set 1: 546-548

Graber, Samuel Ernst & Anna Barbara Scheurers, widow, 29 Jan.
1769. St. John Luth Ch

Gracia, Anthony & Elizabeth Riggs, widow, 30 Apr. 1744; Matthew
Beaird, bondsman; License to Rev. Timothy Mellichampe.
MB Chas

Graeme, David Esqr. & Ann Mathews, 21 Jan. 1759. St. Phil PR

Graeser, Conrad Jacob & Ann Maria Clements, 7 Jan. 1792. St. Phil PR

Graham, David of Parish of Prince George, bachelor, & Elizabeth Hunter of Parish of All Saints, widow, at the house of Percival Pawley, 9 Jan. 1770; John Postell Junr., Edw. Drake, wit. St. Jas PR

Graham, Francis & Catherine Bull, widow, 13 Apr. 1758. St. Hel PR

Graham, James, Gent., Lieutenant in His Majesty's 64th Regt. of Foot, & Hester Howorth, spinster, daughter of Col. Probart Howorth, of Charleston, 7 Nov. 1782; Thomas Ferguson & Roger Parker Saunders, trustees; Elizth. Pinckney, Thos Winstanley, wit. Mar Set 1: 135-137

Graham, Mungo & Sarah Amory, P Licence by the Revd. Mr. Alexr. Garden, 18 Oct. 1749. St. Phil PR

Graham, William & Elizabeth Diana Raven, 1 Jan. 1771. St. Phil PR

Grainger, James & Eleanor Ekall, 20 Aug. 1791. St. Phil PR

Grainger, James & Ann Eyre, 13 Jan. 1793. St. Phil PR

Grange, Hugh and Ann Saunders; minister Timothy Mellichamp; bondsmen Hugh Grange and Wm. Elliot, Esqr., of St. Andrews Parish; wit. J. Hammerton, 10 March 1732. MB NY

Grant, John & Elizabeth Filbing, widow, 26 Feb. 1775. St. Phil PR

Granville, James & Elizabeth Forbes, 14 March 1790. St. Phil PR

Gratia, Francis & Mary Scriven, P Licence, 28 August 1733. St. Phil PR

Graven, Friedrich & Ursula Aberlin, widow, 6 May 1773. St. John Luth Ch

Graves, Joseph & Mary Bennet, 29 Apr. 1743. Pr Fred PR

Graville, Samuel & Mary Pendarvis, 23 Aug. 1773. St. John Luth Ch

Gray, Henry & Ann Villepontoux, 24 Apr. 1745. Ch Ch PR

Gray, Henry of Charlestown, Gentlemen, & Mary Ann Withers of Goose Creek, spinster, a minor; William Johnston, John Calvert, trustees; H. Peroneau, Robt. Williams Junr., wit. 10 Feb. 1780. Mar Set 1: 126-128

Gray, James & Mary Simmons, 15 Jan. 1723. St. Phil PR

Gray, James & Elizabeth Watson, 15 March 1764. St. Hel PR

Gray, Levy & Ann Newbery, 21 Sept. 1797. Pugh diary

Gray, William & Ann Shaw [1740's]. Hist Oburg

Grayall, James & Charity Fickling, P Licence, 5 July 1737. St. Phil PR

Grayson, John, from West Indies, & Sarah Wigg, 14 Apr. 1754.
    St. Hel PR

Grayson, John & Susannah Greene, 9 Oct. 1787.   St. Hel PR

Grayson, Thomas Wigg & Mary Hill, 27 Feb. 1794.   St. Hel PR

Gready, James & Judith Postell, 11 July 1781.   St. Phil PR

Green, Benjamin & Jennet Cooper, P Banns, 1 Jan. 1740.
    St. Phil PR

Green, Benj. & Elizabeth Fripp, 17 Aug. 1752.   St. Hel PR

Green, George, & Mary Britt, 15 Dec. 1742.   Pr Fred PR

Green, Henry & Elizabeth Butler, 15 Apr. 1782.   St. Phil PR

Green, John & Mary Elms, 28 Nov. 1719.   St. And PR

Green, John of Port Royal, clerk & Sarah Wigg, spinster, grand-
    daughter of William Hazard, 27 Oct. 1762; James Cuthbert,
    William Wigg, trustees; John Story, John Hoy, wit.
    Misc. Rec. MM: 216-220

Green, John Rev. & Sarah Wigg, 28 Oct. 1762.   St. Hel PR

Green, Josiah & Catherine Beal, 18 March 1754.   St. Hel PR

Green, Nathaniel & Susannah Huthinson, P Licence, 4 April 1745.
    St. Phil PR

Green, Peter & Cathn. Rolang, 11 Feb. 1766.   OJ 1764-1771

Green, Samuel & Sarah Norton, 27 Feb. 1752.   St. Hel PR

Green, Samuel of the Island of Hilton Head, planter, & Susannah
    Chanler, daughter of Rev. Mr. Isaac Chanler, late of Charles
    Town decd. (already married), 25 Jan. 1770; Charles Grimball,
    Isaac Chanler, trustees; William Morgan, James Taylor, wit.
    Misc. Rec. OO: 325-327

Green, Thomas & Anne Jenkins, P Licence, 6 Nov. 1744.   St. Phil
    PR

Green, William of Prince George Parish & Lydia Avant of Prince
    Frederick, 31 March 1741.   Pr Fred PR

Green, William & Jane Thompson, 17 July 1752.   T & D PR

Green, William & Jane Thomson, 19 Aug. 1752.   Pr Fred PR

Green, Wm. & Elizabeth Finkley, 8 Sept. 1774.   Pugh diary

Greene, Charles of Prince Williams Parish, Beaufort Dist., &
    Anna Ladson of St. Bartholomew's Parish, Dist. of Charleston;
    4 Nov. 1793; James Bowman of Port Royal, trustee Sarah H.
    Bay, Wm. Bowman, wit.   Mar Set 2: 179-181

Greene, Daniel John & Elizabeth Ellis, widow of David Adams,
    Apr. 1784.   St. Hel PR

Greene, Daniel John & Sarah Capers, 29 Jan. 1786.   St. Hel PR

101

Greene, Edward & Ann Bell, widow, 28 Aug. 1786; William Bell, Barnard Lindsey, Josh Edmanson, wit. Mar Set 1: 246-247

Greene, James F., & Margt. Givens, 15 May 1764. St. Hel PR

Greene, Ray & Mary Magdeline Flagg, 25 July 1794. St. Phil PR

Greene, Russell & Ann Hansor, widow, 24 Dec. 1795. St. Phil PR

Greene, Thomas of Charles Town & Ann Jenkins, spinster, 6 Nov. 1744; license to Rev. Alexander Garden; Thomas Willoughby, bondsman. MB Chas

Greene, William & Martha Sams, P Licence, 21 Dec. 1732. St. Phil PR

Greenland, George of Parish of St. Michael, Charlestown, bachelor, & Patience Simmons, spinster, at the plantation of George Simmons, 6 Dec. 1770; John Drake, Peter Simmons, wit. St. Jas PR

Greenland, John & Elizabeth Forrest, 26 Apr. 1728. St. Phil PR

Greenland, Walter Mondet & Ann David Hamilton, 2 June 1793. St. Phil PR

Greensword, Samuel & Ann Fellows, 9 Nov. 1769. St. Phil PR

Greenwood, John & Elizabeth Wilson, 26 Feb. 1765. St. Phil PR

Greenwood, William, the elder of Charleston, & Mrs. Ann Lord, widow, _____ 1796; Nathaniel Russell, Thomas Corbett, trustees, Mary Gaillard, John Gaillard, wit. Mar Set 2: 493-496

Greenwood, William & Ann Lord, widow, 28 Apr. 1796. St. Phil PR

Greer, James Carey of Charleston, merchant, & Margaret Manson Farquhar, 17 March 1797. St. Phil PR

Gregory, John & Elizabeth Williams, 12 Jan. 1726. St. Phil PR

Gregory, John, planter, of St. Pauls Parish, & Mary Dunmere, 24 Jan. 1743/4; license to Rev. John Quincey; William Inns, bondsman. MB Chas

Greiter, Joseph & Susanna Shuler, 1740. Hist Oburg

Gregg, John of Charleston, & Bridget Godfrey, of Parish of St. Helena, spinster, 27 Apr. 1789; William Sams, Thomas Winstanley, trustees; William Sams Junr., John Sams, wit. Mar Set 1: 467-468

Greggs, George, Mariner & Margareth Welsh, 6 Jan. 1784. St. John Luth Ch

Gregorie, James & Mary Christiana Hopton, 22 Feb. 1789; Nathaniel Russell, Samuel Legare, trustees; Eleanor Sarah Legare, J. Ward, wit. Mar Set 1: 408-414

Gregory, Jeremiah & Margaret Dennis, P Licence, 24 Oct. 1731. St. Phil PR

Gregory, William & Ameliah Lecraft, 24 Oct. 1765.   St. Hel PR

Grenier, Peter Francis & Margaret Younker, 24 Nov. 1778.   St. Phil PR

Grey, Charles & Elizabeth Greenland, widow, 8 Dec. 1742.   St. Hel PR

Grey, Henry & Mrs. Jolly, 11 Apr. 1794.   Trin Meth Ch

Grey, William & Ruth Mann, 5 Oct. 1797.   Circ Cong

Grey, Wm. & Hannah Andrew, 11 June 1721.   St. And PR

Grice, James & Mary Burce, widow, 24 Apr. 1770.   St. Phil PR

Grieffous, Peter & Anna Hottow, 25 May 1742.   Hist Oburg

Grieffous, Peter & Anna Otto, 25 [May?], 1742; Peter Hurger, Jacob Kuhner, wit.   Hist Oburg

Grierson, James & Elizabeth Wasson, 8 Nov. 1794.   St. Phil PR

Griffeth, Joseph & Mary Lemmon, 27 Sept. 1737.   Circ Cong

Griffin, Willm. & Eliza Stevens, 10 June 1735.   St. Phil PR

Griffith, David & Hannah Middleton, both of Berkly Co., 11 June 1750.   Hist Oburg

Griffith, Morgan & Mary Walford, P Licence, 25 May 1743.   St. Phil PR

Griffith, Thomas & Rebecca Ridgill, widow, P Licence, 9 March 1740.   St. Phil PR

Griffith, Thomas Jones of Charleston, gentleman, & Elizabeth Brewer Wyatt, 10 Dec. 1797.   St. Phil PR

Griffiths, Thomas & Allen Walker, widow, 30 Dec. 1777.   St. Phil PR

Griggs, Clemard of the Parish of Prince George, widower, & Lydia Jenkins of Parish of Prince George, spinster, in the house of Peter Lesesne, 8 June 1771; Petr. Lesesne, Ann Alston, wit.   St. Jas PR

Griggs, John, of St. Bartholomew's Parish, merchant, and Sarah Webb, spinster, 22 Jan. 1784, William Webb, physician, trustee; Daniel Doyley, Wm. Godfrey, Rebecca Bellinger, wit.   Mar. Set 1: 102-104

Grimbal, Paul & Ann Jenkins, 8 July 1756.   St. Phil PR

Grimbal, Thomas & Sarah Pert, 8 Aug. 1721.   St. Phil PR

Grimball, John of the Dist. of Beaufort, planter, & Miss Elizabeth Berkley, daughter of Mr. John Berkley, of Wilton, planter, 21 April 1797; Paul Hamilton of St. Bartholomews Parish, & Morton Waring of Charleston, trustees; Jean Slann, Susanna Wilkinson, wit.   Mar Set 3: 129-131

Grimball, John & Elizabeth Berkley, 21 Apr. 1797.   Circ Cong

Grimboll, Joshua & Hannah Rippon, widow, 29 Oct. 1765. St. Phil PR

Grimke, John Paul of Charles Town & Ann Grimball, spinster, 19 June 1744; license to Rev. Alexander Garden; Ribton Hutchinson, bondsman. MB Chas

Grimke, John Paul & Anne Grimboll, P Licence, 20 June 1744. St. Phil PR

Grimmer, Peter & Dorothea Huber, daughter of Johannes Huber, 31 Jan. 1738. Hist Oburg

Grindlay, James & Christian Govan, 11 Oct. 1755. St. Phil PR

Grinnin, Charles & Dorothy Whitaker, P Licence, 31 Dec. 1733. St. Phil PR

Grive, Joseph of Ladys Island, St. Helena Parish, & Elizabeth Bell of same, widow, 22 March 1770; John Grives, trustee; Allen Meckee, David McKee, wit. Misc. Rec. PP: 364-367

Gross, Carl & Catharina Dubbertin, 28 Feb. 1786. St. John Luth Ch

Grossman, John & Margaret Stephen, both of Berkeley County, 11 Oct. 1753. Hist Oburg

Grove, Samuel of Charles Town, Mariner & Jean Keen, widow of Jean Kean [sic], mariner & shopkeeper, 24 Aug. 1757; Edward Cain of Liverpoole, England, trustee; Mary Rybould, Elizabeth Mills, wit. Misc. Rec. LL. 67-69

Grove, Samuel & Jean Kean, widow, 26 Aug. 1758. St. Phil PR

Gruber, Christian, of Charleston, butcher, & Margaret Barbara Cobia, widow of Daniel Cobia, 27 March 1799; John Burkmyer, butcher, trustee; E. L. Sutcliffe, Henry W. Mann, wit. Mar Set 3: 334-335

Gruber, Karl Adam & Katharina Steidel(in), 14 May 1765. St. John Luth Ch

Gruber, Samuel & Maria Dorothea Pring(in), widow, in Amelia township, 18 Feb. 1783. St. John Luth Ch

Gruber, Samuel, house carpenter, & Elizabeth Finley, 23 June 1799. St. Phil PR

Gruber, Samuel Ernst & Kath. Sabina Rolle, 4 June 1765. St. John Luth Ch

Gruber, Samuel Ernst, cooper, & Maria Dorothea, Werner(in), 19 Feb. 1777. St. John Luth Ch

Guerard, Jacob of St. Helena Parish, Beaufort Dist., & Miss Lucia Bull, sister of John Bull, 17 Mar. 1782; John Bull, trustee; Ben: Geurard, wit. Mar Set 1: 431-432

Guerard, John & Elizabeth Hill, P Licence, 13 Feb. 1734. St. Phil PR

Guerey, Peter & Mary Ann LeGrand, 15 Dec. 1757. St. Phil PR

Guerin, Andrew & Elizabeth McMurdy, widow, 26 Dec. 1758. St. Phil PR

Guerin, Elisha & Lucretia Kelly, 29 Oct. 1749. T & D PR

Guerin, Francis & Agnes Bush of St. Andrews Parish, 31 Dec. 1782; John Lewis, Mathurin Guerin, wit. Mar Set 1: 357-358

Guerin, Henry & Magdalene Bonneau, 5 Dec. 1760. T & D PR

Guerin, Isaac & Martha Mouzon, 15 Apr. 1730. T & D PR

Guerin, James of Parish of Prince Frederick, bachelor, & Martha Guerin, of Parish of Prince Frederick, spinster, 2 March 1784; Saml Jaudon, Wm. Anthony Atkinson, wit. St. Jas PR

Guerin, James of Parish of Prince Frederick, widower, & Anne Perdreau, of Parish of Prince Frederick, widow, 23 Feb. 1786; Lemuel Wilks, Peter Guerin, wit. St. Jas PR

Guerin, John & Eliz'th Johnston, 20 May 1746. T & D PR

Guerin, Mathurin, of Charles Town, Gardiner & Susanah Desserx, of same, widow, 18 May 1708; John Boisseau, trustee; Nicholas Trott, Pierre Manigault, wit. Sec Prov 1709-25, 3-9

Guerin, Mathurin, Senr., & ___ Peacock, ___ 1774. St. And PR

Guerin, Peter & Mary Marion; minister Timothy Melechamp; bondsmen Peter Guerin and Peter Marion of St. James's Parish Goosecreek, planters; wit. J. Hammerton, 4 July 1733. MB NY

Guerin, Peter & Mary Ann Norman, 4 Jan. 1749-50. T & D PR

Guerin, Robert & Sarah Sanders, 12 July 1759. T & D PR

Guerin, Samuel & Frances Bochett, 3 March 1774. T & D PR

Guerin, Vincent, & Judith Guerin, 12 July 1703. T & D PR

Guerin, Vincent of St. Thomas Parish, Berkley Co., & Esther Dubois, widow of James Dubose, and daughter of Isaac Guerin; Robert Guerin trustee, 10 Aug. 1773; Wit. Duncan McDougall, Peter Joudon. Mar Set 2: 63-67

Guerin, Vincent & Hester Dubois, 19 Aug. 1773. T & D PR

Guerin, William of Charles Town, merchant, & Mary Elliott, spinster, sister of Barnard Elliott, 7 Sept. 1763; Samuel Elliott, Richard Bolin Baker & Barnard Elliott, trustees; Benjamin Williamson, Wm. Logan, wit. Misc. Rec. MM: 132-133

Guerin, William & Mary Elliott, 24 Nov. 1763. St. Phil PR

Guerry, Benjamin of Parish of St. Stephens, bachelor & Lydia Micheau, of Parish of Prince Frederick, spinster, in the house of Mr. Paul Micheau, 1 April 1784; Elizabeth Michau, A. Caleb Guerry, wit. St. Jas PR

Guerry, LeGrand, of Parish of Prince George, bachelor & Dorothy Guerry, of Parish of St. Stephens, spinster, 4 Dec. 1783; Elizabeth Michau, Esther Perdriau, wit. St. Jas PR

Guerry, Peter of Parish of St. Stephens, widower, & Judith
  Croft, of Parish of Prince Frederick, widow, in the house of
  Isaac Rembert Senr., 30 July 1778; Manasseh Michau, C. Wm.
  Lenud, wit.   St. Jas PR

Guerry, Peter Jr., of Prince George Parish, bachelor &
  Catherine Rembert, of Parish of Prince Frederick, spinster,
  at the house of Isaac Rembert, 12 Nov. 1782; Legrand Guerry,
  Jacob Jeanneret junr., wit.   St. Jas PR

Guerry, Stephen, bachelor, & Mary Sanders, spinster, in the
  house of Isaac Legrand, 9 Sept. 1769; Peter Robert Junr.,
  Stephen Dumay, wit.   St. Jas PR

Guerry, Stephen of Parish of St. Stephens, bachelor & Frances
  Micheau of Parish of Allsaints, spinster, at the house of
  Mr. John Guerry, 3 Dec. 1779; H. Lenud, Benj. Guerry, wit.
  St. Jas PR

Guinard, Gabriel & Fanny Lesesseline, 10 Nov. 1746.   Ch Ch PR

Guino, John of Charles Town & Sarah Crabb, widow, of William
  Cragg, of Edisto Island, 2 Feb. 1687/8; Paul Grimball, Lewis
  Price, & William White, wit.   Sec Prov 1675-1695, p. 294

Gumbles, William & Elizabeth Partridg, 23 Jan. 1734.   St. Phil
  PR

Gunter, Edward Docr. & Martha Melachamp, 12 Apr. 1772.   St. And
  PR

Gurrean, Thos. & Mary Ford, 8 Feb. 1709/10.   Reg Prov. 1711-15,
  p. 449(41)

Guy, Christopher of St. Andrews Parish, & Mary Godfrey,
  spinster, 20 June 1744; license to Rev. William Guy, William
  Guy of Charles Town, bondsman.   MB Chas

Guy, Christopher & Mary Godfrey, 21 June 1744.   St. And PR

Guy, Christopher & Jane Chapman, 6 June 1751.   St. And PR

Guy, Christopher & Mary Mars, 1 March 1794.   Trin Meth Ch

Guy, James & Sarah Hargrave, 10 Dec. 1771.   St. Phil PR

Guy, James, taylor, & Mary Yates, 4 Apr. 1785.   St. John Luth
  Ch

Guy, William Revd. & Elizabeth Cooper, of St. James Goose Creek,
  __ Aug. 1747.   St. And PR

Guy, The Revd. Mr. William, Rector of St. Andrews & Elizabeth
  Cooper, spinster, by Licence by the Revd. Mr. Alexr. Garden,
  6 Aug. 1747.   St. Phil PR

Guy, Zebulon & Anne Allein, 13 Jan. 1730/31.   St. And PR

Gwin, John, widower, & Catherin Rickets, 17 March 1737.   St.
  Hel PR

Gygee, Rene & Elizabeth Ker, P Banns, 25 Dec. 1742.   St. Phil
  PR

Gyger, Hans Jacob & Margaret Shuler, widow [1740's]. Hist Oburg

H___, George & Maria Hallmann(in), 20 Apr. 1786. St. John
    Luth Ch

H___, Martin, mason, & Elisabetha Simonsinn, 2 June 1771.
    St. John Luth Ch

Hacket, Thos. & Jane Spence, 18 Sept. 1794. Trin Meth Ch

Hackett, Michael & Elizabeth White, widow, 14 Feb. 1765. St.
    Phil PR

Hadderett, George & Mary Pheasant(?), 21 Dec. 1711. SPG

Hagen, Dennis & Catharine McCartney, widow, 21 June 1760.
    St. Phil PR

Hager, Saml. & Mrs. Elizabeth Gendron, 19 Jan. 1709/10.
    Reg. Prov. 1711-15, p. 449(41)

Hagood, Gideon of Charleston & Harriet Peckham Yonge, daughter
    of Francis Yonge, the eldest, late of St. Pauls Parish, decd.
    & Susanna Yonge, 16 March 1796; George Reid, trustee; Wm.
    Rowe, James Moore, wit. Mar Set 2: 477-481

Hagood, Gideon & Harriet Yonge, 17 March 1796. Circ Cong

Hagood, Johnson & Martha Riley, 1 Dec. 1797; Geo F. Hahnbaum,
    Isaac Griggs, wit. Mar Set 3: 192-193

Hahnbaum, D. Christian & Mary Haire, 25 Dec. 1785. St. John
    Luth Ch

Hahnbaum, Georg Ernst, medic. practicus, & Catharina Barbara,
    daughter of Friederich Schraden, 5 Sept. 1769. St. John
    Luth Ch

Haines, Mark & Eliza. Porter, P Licence, 8 March 1744/5.
    St. Phil PR

Haines, William & Deborah Carman, 5 May 1727. St. Hel PR

Hale, Janes, & Ann Westbarry, 6 Feb. 1763. St. Hel PR

Haler, Siphorus & Sarah Coulin, 16 June 1763. St. Phil PR

Hales, Daniel & Sarah Johnson, 6 Sept. 1791. St. Phil PR

Hales, John & Margaret Rupp, 23 Dec. 1777. T & D PR

Hales, William & Rebekah Ireland, P Licence, 29 Dec. 1731.
    St. Phil PR

Haliburton, William & Joan Watkins, 10 Apr. 1743. Ch Ch PR

Hall, Alexander & Henrietta Ward, by Comissry Bull, 26 Apr.
    1722. St. Phil PR

Hall, Daniel & Susanna Mathews, 23 Feb. 1775. St. Phil PR

Hall, George Abbott & Lois Mathewes, daughter of John Mathewes,
    late of St. Michaels Parish, decd., & Sarah Mathewes,

14 Feb. 1764; James Carson, Sarah Reeve, wit. Mar Set 1: 580-584

Hall, John of Charles Town, & Mary Ann Dodd, widow, 9 Apr. 1774; Peter Fayssoux, physician, trustee; Wm. Rudhall, wit. Mar Set 1: 181-183

Hall, Richd. & Mary Rise, 7 March 1795. Trin Meth Ch

Hall, Thomas & Mary, widow of John Fripp Junr. & 3 Mar. 1740. St. Hel PR

Hall, Thomas & Mary Fendin, 4 Feb. 1741. St. Hel PR

Hall, Thomas & Deborah Hancock, P Licence, 27 Aug. 1741. St. Phil PR

Hall, Thomas & Elizabeth Hale, P Licence, 8 Dec. 1744. St. Phil PR

Hall, Thomas of St. James Santee, & Priscilla Bruce, of St. Thomas Parish, Berkley Co., 25 Oct. 1753; Benj. Simons, Rev. Alexander Garden, trustees; Mary Ann King, John Guerin, Stephen Hartley, wit. Misc. Rec. II: 605-608

Hall, Thomas & Priscilla Bona, 25 Oct. 1753. T & D PR

Hall, Thomas & Susanna Glare, 6 Sept. 1770. St. Phil PR

Hall, Thomas of Charleston & Mary Newton of St. Bartholomews Parish, spinster, 12 Oct. 1785; John Gibbons, trustee. Mar Set 1: 238-241

Hall, William & Sarah Taveroone, P Licence, 5 June 1731. St. Phil PR

Hall, William & Susanna Treasvant, P Licence by the Revd. Mr. Alexr. Garden, 21 May 1748. St. Phil PR

Hallam, Henry, bachelor & Mary Bonhoste, spinster, in the house of Mr. Jonah Collins, 24 July 1783; Jno Jonah Murrell, Daniel M'Gregor, wit. St. Jas PR

Halliday, Hugh of Charleston, grocer, & Eleanor Halliday, widow, 12 Dec. 1798. St. Phil PR

Halsey, James, Widower, & Frances Grant, widow, 12 July 1764; John Barnett, Stephen Sullivan, wit. St. Jas PR

Ham, Thomas & Sarah McConnell, 6 Nov. 1762. St. Phil PR

Ham, Thomas & Margaret Addison Ralph, ___ June 1791. St. Phil PR

Hambleton, John & Patience French, P Licence by Mr. Garden, 3 May 1737. St. Phil PR

Hamelton, John & Catharine Myers, widow, 1 July 1741. Hist Oburg

Hamelton, John Esqr. of Craven County, & Rosanna Manning, widow, 20 Nov. 1769; Jacob Agnes (Eagner), trustee; Geo. Spagner, Mary Agner, wit. Misc. Rec. OO: 208-209

Hamerser, Cramer & Sarah Coats, 27 Sept. 1720.   St. Phil PR

Hamett, Thomas & Charlotte Kirk, widow, 1 Dec. 1776.   St. Phil
PR

Hamilton, Archibald & Bridget Roche, 10 Jan. 1726-7.   T & D PR

Hamilton, Archibald, widower, & Anne Palmer, widow, 6 Apr. 1735.
St. Hel PR

Hamilton, David & Elizabeth Reynolds, 20 Nov. 1774.   St. Phil
PR

Hamilton, James of Camden Dist., Craven Co., & Mary Ferguson of
Charleston Dist., Colleton County, 14 March 1782; Park Pepper
of Charlestown Dist., Colleton trustee; Sarah Holman, Jo:
Donnom, wit.   Misc. Rec. UU: 131-133

Hamilton, James of Prince Williams Parish, & Sarah Swinton,
10 June 1790; Joseph Slann, trustee; S. Sanders, Joseph
Wilkinson, Jean Slann, wit.   Mar Set 1: 530-534

Hamilton, Robert & Mary Derber, 8 Sept. 1745.   St. Phil PR

Hamilton, Robert & Margaret Fleming of George Town Dist., widow,
3 July 1798; Paul Durant of George Town Dist., trustee;
James Malcomson, Benjn Durant, wit.   Mar Set 3: 278-281

Hamilton, Stephen & Eliz: Verdal, 16 June 1734.   St. And PR

Hamilton, William & Mary Macrea, widow, 6 May 1766.   St. Phil
PR

Hamilton, Wm. & Mary M'Crea, widow, 6 May 1766.   OJ 1764-1771

Hamilton, William of Pon Pon & Rachel Buer, widow of Thomas
Buer of St. Bartholomew's Parish, 16 June 1772; John Liddle,
Audeon St. John, William Beatty, wit.   Mar Set 1: 104-107

Hamlin, George & Mary, daughter of John and Mary Metheringham,
31 Dec. 1765.   Ch Ch PR

Hamlin, Thomas & Mary McDowell, 3 Jan. 1750.   Ch Ch PR

Hamlin, Thomas of Parish of Christ Church, widower, & Margaret
Jaudon, of Parish of Prince Frederick, widow, 23 Aug. 1780;
Alex. Chovin, Geo. McDowell, wit.   St. Jas PR

Hammet, William Revd., & Miss C. Darrell, 14 Jan. 1794.   Trin
Meth Ch

Hammilton, John & Catherina Myers, widow, 1 July 1741.   Hist
Oburg

Hampton, Henry to Susanna Andrews, 30 May 1780 by Robert Chapman, Minister of the Gospel.   Wit. William Fowler, George
Louis Hochhimer, Camden Dist.   Camden Dist WB, p. 145

Hampton, John & Gracia King, 7 Aug. 1777.   St. Phil PR

Hancock, Richard & Prudence Mortimer, 29 March 1726.   St. Hel
PR

Hancock, Robert & Elizabeth Elsinore, widow, 14 Oct. 1779.
St. Phil PR

Hand, Obadiah, carpenter, of Georgetown Dist., & Sarah Butler,
widow; 10 Jan. 1792; John G. Britten, trustee; W. Whitefield,
Rachel Blalock, wit.   Mar Set 2: 4-6

Handlen, Thomas & Elisabeth King, 5 ___ 1749.   Pr Fred PR

Handy, Thomas of Charleston, rigger, & Dorothy Gilchrist, widow,
6 Aug. 1799.   St. Phil PR

Hangwald, Johann, from Königsberg, taylor, & Catharina, widow
of William ___, 8 Jan. 1769.   St. John Luth Ch

Hanly, John & Margaret Duggan, widow, 2 Aug. 1789.   St. Phil PR

Hanover, John & Deborah Sharpe, P Licence, 3 Sept. 1730.   St.
Phil PR

Hans (apparently no surname) & Magdalene Piercey, maiden name
Bush, 10 Dec. 1740.   Hist Oburg

Hanscombe, William & Margaret Gray, widow, 31 March 1778.   St.
Phil PR

Hanser, Elias & Elizabeth Younker, 25 July 1772, St. Phil PR

Harcout, John & Mary Boyer, widow, 8 March 1762.   St. Phil PR

Harden, Thomas & Anne Nelson, P Licence by Mr. Garden, 15 Sept.
1736.   St. Phil PR

Harden, William of Prince Williams Parish, & Mary Miles, 6 July
1791; James Miles, Robert Miles, trustees; Jos Brailsford,
Jro McPherson, wit.   Mar Set 1: 606-608

Hardin, Thomas & Angel Scott, P Licence, 28 Sept. 1740.   St.
Phil PR

Hardman, Valentine & Mary Picking, by Rev. Francis Varnod,
11 Dec. 1730 (extract from register of St. George's Parish),
James Sharp, wit. Misc Rec. KK: 479

Hardwick, Thomas & Sarah Watson, widow, of Samuel Watson, 27
June 1727.   St. Hel PR

Hardy, Robert & Hannah Jenkins, 17 May 1761.   St. Phil PR

Hargrave, Thomas & Mary Cox, P Licence, 20 Dec. 1729.   St. Phil
PR

Harleston, Edward & Anna Bella Moultrie, 31 May 1787.   St. Phil
PR

Harleston, John & Elizabeth Faucherard, 17 April 1766.   OJ 1764-
1771

Harleston, John & Elizabeth Fauchereaud, 17 Apr. 1766.   St.
Phil PR

Harleston, John of Charlestown & Elizabeth Lynch, daughter of
Thomas Lynch, decd., 1 May 1777; Thomas Lynch, William
Cattle, trustees; John Sandford Dart, Jacob Motte, wit.
Misc. Rec. RR: 438-439

Harleston, John & Elizabeth Lynch, 1 May 1777.   St. Phil PR

Harleston, Nicholas & Anne Ashby, 9 Sept. 1756.   T & D PR

Harleston, William of Charleston, gent., & Elizabeth Pinckney,
    daughter of Roger Pinckney decd., Esqr., 9 Dec. 1789;
    Robert Quash, Hopson Pinckney, & Roger Pinckney, trustees;
    Roger Parker Saunders, Sarah Quash, wit.   Mar Set 1: 463-467

Harleston, William & Elizabeth Pinckney, 9 Dec. 1789.   St. Phil
    PR

Harleston, William of St. John's Parish, & Sarah Quash, daughter
    of Robert Quash, 31 March 1794; Evan Edwards, wit.   Mar Set
    2: 261264

Harleston, William & Sarah Quash, 13 March 1794.   St. Phil PR

Harley, Joseph & Elizabeth, daughter of Henry Jackson, 9 Jan.
    1768; James Skirving & William Skirving, trustees; Edward
    Dempsey, John Houston, wit.   Misc. Rec. NN: 145-149

Harley, Joseph & Jane Jackson, 7 Dec. 1749; (document in poor
    condition). Misc. Rec. KK: 272-275

Harley, Joseph & Elizabeth Jackson, 9 Jan. 1768.   St. Phil PR

Harper, Donald & Mary Spencer, 3 March 1770.   St. Phil PR

Harper, Thomas & Elizabeth Edwards, 19 Jan. 1776.   St. Phil PR

Harramond, Henry & Mary Fisher, 8 April 1735.   St. Phil PR

Harremond, Henry & Elizabeth Montcrief, P Licence, 3 January
    1741.   St. Phil PR

Harresperger, John & Elizabeth Frichman, 30 Apr. 1751.   Hist
    Oburg

Harrington, Whitmill & Jennet Shaw, 2 Feb. 1741/2

Harriot, William of Georgetown, merchant, & Mary, minor dau-
    ghter of Edward Thomas, 10 May 1792; Robert Smith, Henry
    Gibbes, wit.   Mar Set 2: 371-373

Harris, Charles & Elizabeth Christie, 31 Dec. 1772.   St. Phil
    PR

Harris, Christr. & Margart. Rachael Dugle, 30 Dec. 1709.   Reg.
    Prov. 1711-15, p. 449(41)

Harris, George & Rachel Lance, p Licence, 13 Apr. 1740.   St.
    Phil PR

Harris, Henry of Berkley County & Elizabeth Hayes, 23 Apr. 1692;
    Thomas Smith Esqr., John Lovell (Lowell?), joyner, bondsmen.
    Sec Prov 1675-95, p. 485

Harris, John & Eleanor Watson, P Licence, 15 Dec. 1748.   St.
    Phil PR

Harris, John & Margaret Donner, widow, 29 May 1788.   St. Phil
    PR

Harris, Samuel & Mary Stillman, 2 Sept. 1761.   St. Phil PR

Harris, Thomas & Susannah Wirth, widow, 4 Dec. 1770.   St. Phil PR

Harris, Thomas of All Saints Parish, George Town Dist., planter & Phereby Pool alias Giles of Prince George Parish, 17 Aug. 1779; James Thompson, Elijah Cox, wit.   Mar Set 1: 437-438

Harris, Thomas & Martha Carpenter, 30 Dec. 1779.   St. Phil PR

Harris, William & Mary Ladson, 3 July 1729.   St. And PR

Harris, William & Mary Wilkinson, P Licence, 11 Sept. 1737. St. Phil PR

Harris, William & Sarah Tucker, P Licence, 19 Aug. 1739. St. Phil PR

Harris, William & Anne Graves, 19 March 1752.   St. Hel PR

Harrison, Edward & Elander Gorden, 9 June 1762.   St. Phil PR

Harrison, Isaac & Hannah Gladdin, widow, 17 June 1790.   St. Phil PR

Harrison, John & Sarah Evans, 11 Aug. 1771.   St. Phil PR

Harrison, Thomas, widower, & Judith Brown, widow, 24 Jan. 1743. St. Hel PR

Harrison, Thomas, widower, and Hannah Sealey, both of this Parish, 12 Nov. 1745.   Stoney Creek Pres Ch

Harry, David & Dinah Boston(?), 19 Dec. 1765.   Pugh Diary

Harry, James & ___, 11 July 1771.   Pugh Diary

Hart, Arthur & Mary Williams, 7 March 1765.   St. Phil PR

Hart, Arthur & Elizabeth Williams, 21 Apr. 1771.   Pugh diary

Hart, William & Mary Coursey, spinster, P Licence by the Revd. Mr. Robert Betham, 20 Feb. 1746.   St. Phil PR

Hartburg, Johann Philipp Hartburg & Maria Agnes Gossmann, 13 Aug. 1772.   St. John Luth Ch

Harth, John of Charlestown, merchant & Elizabeth Holson, widow of Christopher Holson, 29 July 1779; Robert Howard, trustee; James Guy, Alexr. Forrester, wit.   Mar Set 1: 148-153

Harth, John & Elizabeth Holson, widow, 1 Aug. 1779.   St. Phil PR

Harth, William, from St. Mathias' Parish, & Maria Lancaster, from Dorchester, in Mr. Johannes Harth's house, 11 March 1787.   St. John Luth Ch

Hartley, James & Mary Needland, belonging to the Parish of Christ Church, P Licence by Mr. Garden, 23 Sept. 1726. St. Phil PR

Hartley, Stephen & Elizabeth Newton, 13 Jan. 1731.   Ch Ch PR

Hartley, Stephen & Eliz; Newton, 13 Jan. 1731/2.   St. And PR

Hartman, John & Sarah Joy, 13 Apr. 1732.   Ch Ch PR

Hartman, William & Ruth ___, 5 Nov. 1740.   Ch Ch PR

Hartman, William & Ruth Scanlen, P Licence, 5 Nov. 1740.
   St. Phil PR

Hartning, Sigmund, & Catharine Andersen, 12 Feb. 1785.   St.
   John Luth Ch

Harttung, Philip & Mary Gotsman, widow, 13 Aug. 1772.   St. Phil
   PR

Harvey, Andrew & Sarah Delany, widow, 8 Apr. 1779.   St. Phil PR

Harvey, Benja. & Mary Mortimore, P Licence, 3 Dec. 1748.   St.
   Phil PR

Harvey, George & Sarah Drain, widow, 8 Jan. 1759.   St. Phil PR

Harvey, John & Catherine Croft, P Licence, 17 Jan. 1744/5.
   St. Phil PR

Harvey, John & Catherine Rawlins, spinster, 28 June 1766.
   OJ 1764-1771

Harvey, John Boyd of Georgegown, mariner & Charlotte Villepontoux of Dist. of Georgetown, spinster, 20 Sept. 1797; Benjamin Allston the younger, planter, trustee; Paul Michau Junr.,
   Saml Allston, wit.   Mar Set 3: 190-192

Harvey, Robert & Mary Stevenson, P Licence, 16 January 1739.
   St. Phil PR

Harvey, Samuel & Ann Greenland, widow, 21 May 1795. St. Phil
   PR

Harvey, William of St. Helena Parish & Elizabeth Mikell, widow,
   6 Feb. 1743/4: Jemmet Cobley, merchant, bondsman; license
   to Rev. Lewis Jones.   MB Chas

Harvey, William & Elizabeth Mikell, widow, 16 Feb. 1743.   St.
   Hel PR

Harvey, Wm. Junr. & Mary Seabrook, 23 Aug. 1739.   St. And PR

Harwood, Thomas & Jane Johnston, P Licence, 28 May 1732.
   St. Phil PR

Hasel, Thomas Junr. in St. Thomas's Parish & Alice Morritt,
   eldest daughter to the Rev. Mr. Thomas Morritt, Apr. 26,
   1744.   Pr Fred PR

Hasell, Andrew & Sarah Wigfall, 28 March 1751.   T & D PR

Hasell, Andrew & Sarah Wigfall, 28 March 1751.   Ch Ch PR

Hasell, John & Hannah Simons, 27 Apr. 1749.   T & D PR

Hasell, Thomas & Alice Morrit, 26 Apr. 1744.   T & D PR

113

Hasell, Thomas Junr. of Parish of St. Thomas, Berkley Co., &
    Alice Morritt, spinster, 5 Apr. 1744; license to Rev. John
    Fordyce; Capt. Thomas Sommersett, of CharlesTown, bondsman.
    MB Chas

Hasell, Thomas Rev. & Elizabeth Ashby, 21 Jan. 1714-5. T & D
    PR

Hasell, Thomas of Parish of Prince George, bachelor, & Margaret
    Summers of Parish of Prince George, at the house of Miss
    Judith Trapier, 2 Feb. 1772; Jos. Dubourdieu, P. Trapier, Jr.
    St. Jas PR

Haselton, Richard & Susanna Gilbert, P Licence, 31 May 1740.
    St. Phil PR

Haselwood, Edward & Elizabeth Mills, P Licence, 27 April 1732.
    St. Phil PR

Hasford, Samuel of Parish of All Saints, widower, & Mary Pawley,
    of the Parish of Allsaints, spinster, 19 July 1778; Frances
    Michau, Elizabeth Pawley, wit. St. Jas PR

Hasfort, Joseph & Naomi Carlisle, 13 June 1738.   St. And PR

Hasfort, Joseph & ___, 14 Apr. 1741.   Hist. Oburg.

Hasfort, Richard & Barbara Diedrick, 3 Jan. 1740.   Hist Oburg

Haslett, John & Mary Audley Gunter, 27 Apr. 1799.   Circ Cong

Haslett, John, painter, & Mary Wilson, 2 Aug. 1799.   St. Phil
    PR

Hastie, Nassau & Mary Still, P Licence, 13 Juen 1739.   St.
    Phil PR

Hatcher, ___ & Sela Megee, 3 July 1776.   Pugh diary

Hatcher, James & Jane Jervey, 30 Sept. 1758.   St. Hel PR

Hatcher, Joseph & Mary Sarah (?) Taylor, widow, 30 Apr. 1741.
    Ch Ch PR

Hatten, John & Elizabeth Richardson, widow, 15 Dec. 1771.   St.
    Phil PR

Hatter, John of Charles Town, mariner, & Elizabeth Richardson,
    widow, 10 Dec. 1771; John Syme, of Parish of St. Thomas,
    Practitioner in Physic, trustee; John Remington, Andrew
    Dillient, wit. Misc. Rec. PP: 285-291

Hattfield, John & Mary Sheppard, 24 Sept. 1763.   St. Phil PR

Hatton, Joseph Capt. & Mary Wood, 17 Jan. 1748.   Ch Ch PR

Hausmann, Heinrich, & Giehne (Jane) Thomson, 23 Dec. 1777.
    St. John Luth Ch

Hautreux, Peter & Sarah Horry of Georgetown, widow, 30 Apr.
    1796; John Shackelford & Richard Shackelford, trustees;
    Cleland Kinloch, Thos. Mitchell, wit. Mar Set 2: 506-509

Harvey, Dennis & Mary Henry, widow, 13 June 1794.   St. Phil PR

Haward, Daniel & Mary Miles, 8 March 1743 (1743/4].   St. And PR

Hawes, Saml & Elizabeth White, 1 Feb. 1796.   Trin Meth Ch

Hawie, Robert of Charlestown & Susannah Lesesne, daughter of
    James Lessesne, late of St. Thomas Parish, 6 Dec. 1769;
    Geo. Duncan, Mm. Brown, wit.   Misc. Rec. SS: 183-187

Hawie, Robert & Susanna Lessesne, 14 Dec. 1769.   St. Phil PR

Hawkes, William & Martha Coleman, P Licence by the Revd. Mr.
    Garden Rector, 30 July 1749.   St. Phil PR

Hawkins, Benjamin, son of James and Marther, & Martha Hollings-
    worth, 10 Oct. 1771.   Bush R QM

Hawkins, Amos, son of James & Martha, and Anne Comer, 9 June
    1791.   Cane Creek MM

Hawkins, Amos, son of John & Mary, and Ann Milhous, 8 June 1797.
    Cane Creek MM

Hawkins, Amos, son of Isaac & Margaret, and Phebe Wilson, 6
    Dec. 1791.   Cane Creek MM

Hawkins, Benjamin, son of James & Martha, & Olive Cook, 26
    Sept. 1799.   Cane Creek MM

Hawkins, James & Rebekah Tipper, per Licence, 21 Feb. 1744.
    St. Phil PR

Hawkins, James, son of James & Martha, and Sarah Wilson, 7 June
    1792.   Cane Creek MM

Hawkins, John, son of John & Mary, and Lydia Comer, 30 Nov. 1799.
    Cane Creek MM

Hawkins, John, son of Nathan & Ann and Sarah Kenworthy, 38 July
    1796.   Cane Creek MM

Hawkins, Nathan, son of James & Marther, and Ann Cook, 8 July
    1773. Bush R QM

Hayden, Mathew & Jane Watson, of the village of Hamsted, spin-
    ster, 6 Feb. 1797; Richard Wrainch, trustee; Thos. Davis,
    Jno Watson, wit.   Mar Set 3: 43-47

Hayes, Charles & Eliz'th Goodbie, 12 May 1730.   T & D PR

Hayes, Wm. & Mary De Filleau, P Banns, 5 Nov. 1724.   St. Phil
    PR

Hayne, Isaac of St. Bartholomew's Parish, Doctor in Physick, &
    Mary Hopkins, under age 21, of Prince George Parish, Dorches-
    ter, spinster; Isaac Walter, of St. George Parish, & Wm.
    Peronneau, of Charleston, merchant, trustees; Thos. Simons,
    Wm. Edward Hayne, wit.   Mar Set 2: 208-210

Hayner, John George & Eva Catharine Barrin, both of Orangeburgh
    Township, 24 Aug. 1755.   Hist Oburg

Haynes, Nicholas & Martha Fryar, 20 Aug. 1721. St. Phil PR

Haynsworth, John & Elisabeth Davison, 5 July 1747. Pr Fred PR

Hays(?), Wm. & Elizabeth Wear, 3 June 1776. Pugh diary

Hays, John of Parish of Prince George, bachelor, & Penelope
    Bernard, of Parish of Prince George, spinster, 8 March 1779;
    Thomas Hoddey, Lydia Perdriau, wit. St. Jas PR

Hays, Thomas & Mary Thompson, widow, 25 Sept. 1763. St. Phil PR

Hayward, Thomas & Anne Miles, 14 Feb. 1747 [1747/8]. St. And
    PR

Haywood, Thomas & Hester Taylor, 4 June 1719. St. And PR

Hayward, Thomas & Ann Sinclair, 26 Apr. 1770. St. Phil PR

Hazard, Rd. & Isabella Watson, 14 Nov. 1711. SPG

Hazell, William & Susannah Brandford, 8 Feb. 1764. St. Phil PR

Hazzard, Harvey & Catherine Smyth, 29 Nov. 1764. St. Hel PR

Hazzard, William & Sarah Cowen, 27 Jan. 1728. St. Hel PR

Hazzard, William & Catherine Wigg, 22 Apr. 1750. St. Hel PR

Hazzard, William of St. Luke's Parish, & Mary Fuller of St.
    Andrew's Parish, daughter of Thomas Fuller, decd; 18 Oct.
    1792; William Miles of St. Andrew's Parish, trustee;
    Charles Elliott, John Potter, wit. Mar Set 2: 29-34

Hazzard, William Coll: & ___ Rose, [before 1757]. St. Hel PR

Hazzard, William, Coll: & Elizabeth Russell [second wife, before
    1757]. St. Hel PR

Heape, Benjamin & Mary Wood, spinster, per Licence by the Revd.
    Mr. Alexander Garden, 7 April 1747. St. Phil PR

Heape, William & Sarah Drayton, 11 March 1738. St. And PR

Heard, John & Esther La Pierre, 10 July 1722. St. Phil PR

Hearin, Zacheriah & Margaret Manduvel, 29 Aug. 1775. T & D PR

Hearn, John and Elizabeth Beddise, spinster; minister Francis
    Varnod, bondsmen John Hearn of Colleton County, and John
    Fairchild of Charles Town, 22 Feb. 1732. MB NY

Hearne, Peter & Elizabeth Rivers, 18 Dec. 1781. St. Phil PR

Heart, William of the Congrees & Sirrah Young, of Edistoe Fork,
    3 Oct. 1750. Hist Oburg

Healthly, Thomas & Susannah Monroe, P Licence, 23 April 1741.
    St. Phil PR

Healthly, William & Mary Vinin, P Licence, 12 Oct. 1731. St.
    Phil PR

Heatley, Richard & ___, 5 Nov. 1714. T & D PR

SOUTH CAROLINA MARRIAGES 1688-1799

Hedderly, Phillips & Mary, widow of Charles Williams, 7 Nov. 1768. St. Hel PR

Heep, Benjamin & Mary Wood, 7 Apr. 1747. St. And PR

Hegerman, Jasper & Froney Craven, widow, per Licence by the Revd. Mr. Robert Betham, 22 Dec. 1746. St. Phil PR

Heidelberg, Christian & Isabel Oliver, P Licence, 24 Feb. 1733. St. Phil PR

Heinelmann, Valentin & Elizabeth Dow, 8 Sept. 1785. St. John Luth Ch

Heinrich, Philips, cooper & Elisabetha Kaufmann (in), 15 June 1777. St. John Luth Ch

Heinrichson, Botgia(?), born in Bremen, carpenter & Anna Maria Schweitardt(in), 26 Aug. 1787. St. John Luth Ch

Heisaker, Peter Heinrich & Anna Banders(in), soldier of the 5th regiment with the permission of the captain, 15 July 1777. St. John Luth Ch

Hellerd, Andrew & Hanah Jerome, P Licence, 26 December 1723. St. Phil PR

Helldrup, Thomas Goseelin & Susannah Eliza Larry, 6 Apr. 1799. St. Phil PR

Heller, John & Esther Ott, ___ 1752. Hist Oburg

Helm, George & Anne McCullock, P Licence, 18 July 1738. St. Phil PR

Henderson, James & Hannah Sands, widow, 10 May 1774. St. Phil PR

Henderson, Richard, son of Nathaniel & Rebecca, & Rachel Hollings-worth, 26 Apr. 1794. Bush R QM

Henderson, Robert & Ann Remington, of Charleston, 7 March 1792; Patrick Byrne, James Nicholson, trustees; Mary Wells, Richd. Wells, wit. Mar Set 1: 640-646

Henderson, Samuel & Jane Mattrass, widow, P Licence by the Revd. Mr. Alexr. Garden, 30 June 1748. St. Phil PR

Henderson, William & Sarah Cook, P Licence, 25 Nov. 1750. St. Phil PR

Hendlen, Thomas & Amy Arnold, widow, 13 July 1777. St. Phil PR

Hendlin, Thomas & Isabel Graey, 15 Jan. 1778. St. Phil PR

Henion, Peter & Esther Willis, widow, 18 Feb. 1773. St. Phil PR

Henkinson, Joseph & Elizabeth Stevens, 8 Jan.1768; Philip Helverson, Wm. Farmer, wit. NN: 405-407.

Henley, John & Margaret Thompson, spinster; minister Thomas Morritt; bondsmen John Hanley (Handlen) and Edward Henley

117

(Handlen) of Prince Georges Parish, planters; wit. James
Michie, 22 Feb. 1732. MB NY

Henrichs, Gorlieb Franz, from Hamburg, & Mrs. Ro___, formerly
Kaufmann(in), 30 Oct. 1771. St. John Luth Ch

Henry, Alexander, of Charleston, merchant, & Elizabeth Flemming,
5 Jan. 1797. St. Phil PR

Henzie, Bigoe & Elizabeth Murray, 8 May 1787. St. Hel PR

Heriot, William & Mary Thomas, 21 March 1792. St. Phil PR

Herbert, William & Elizabeth Oram, 31 December 1744. St. Phil
PR

Herman, Michael & Barbary Gutstrings, widow, 12 Dec. 1778.
St. Phil PR

Hern, ____, & Margaret Burn, 26 Dec. 1756. St. Phil PR

Herrel, Georg, taylor & Anna Barbarra Muil(in)(?), 24 Feb.
1778. St. John Luth Ch

Herries, Peter of Parish of Prince George, Widr. & Mary Cains,
of Parish of Prince George, widow, 4 June 1761; John Cains,
Eliz: Warren, wit. St. Jas PR

Herry, Robert & Margaret Pope, per Licence, 6 June 1745. St.
Phil PR

Hertzog, Barnard & Anne Mary, widow of Warner Ulmer, of Orangeburgh Township, 18 Feb. 1755. Hist Oburg

Haskett, John & Martha Russ, 2 March 1762. T & D PR

Hesman, Johannes, soldier in General Pulaski's Legion, &
Catharina Bart(in), widow, 15 June 1779. St. John Luth Ch

Hess, Hans George Henry & Miss Catharine Magdalena Shuler, 12
Oct. 1742; Peter Hurger, Michael Larry, Valentine Justus,
Elias Schnell, wit. Hist Oburg

Hessy, Hans George & Catharina Margaret Shuler, 12 Oct. 1742.
Hist Oburg

Hethcock, Volentine & _____, 13 Sept. 1792. Pugh diary

Hetherington, John & Mary Miller, 16 Aug. 1763. T & D PR

Hewet, Hill, of Parish of Prince George, bachelor & Martha
England, of Parish of Prince George, spinster, 30 Oct. 1782;
Joseph DeLessline, Susanna England, wit. St. Jas PR

Hewgill, John & Eleanor Lindsay, 23 March 1778. St. Phil PR

Hewitt, James & Elizabeth Rosetter, 27 June 1793. Trin Meth CH

Hews, Patrick & Rebeccah Anger, 5 July 1756. St. And PR

Hewson, Wm. & Elizabeth Bevel, 29 June 1775. Pugh diary

Hewster(?), William & Ann Sutton, 12 Aug. 1765. Pugh diary

Hext, Alexander of Colleton County, & Jane Weaver, spinster, 13 Dec. 1743; license to Rev. Alex. Gordon; Walter Dunbar of Charles Town, bondsman. MB Chas

Hext, Alexander & Jane Weaver, per Licence, 15 Dec. 1743. St. Phil PR

Hext, Hugh & Susannah Brersford, widow, 29 Apr. 1742. Ch Ch PR

Hext, John of Parish of St. Bartholomew, bachelor & Elizabeth Cheesborough of Parish of Prince George, spinster, at the house of Mrs. Mann, 20 Apr. 1779; John Gough, John Cheesborough, wit. St. Jas PR

Heyward, Daniel of Granville Co., & Mary Miles, spinster, 7 March 1743/4; license to Rev. William Guy; John Beswicke, merchant, of Charles Town, bondsman. MB Chas

Heyward, Daniel & Mary Miles, 8 March 1743. St. Hel PR

Heyward, Daniel & Elizabeth Simons, 8 Sept. 1771. St. Phil PR

Heyward, John & Elizabeth, widow of John Cattell, 12 Oct. 1758. St. Hel PR

Heyward, Nathaniel & Harriet Manigault, legatee of Hon. Peter Manigault, late of Charlestown, decd., 27 Feb. 1788; Gabriel Manigault & Joseph Manigault, trustees; Thos Heyward Junr., wit. Mar Set 2: 395-397

Heyward, Nathaniel & Henrietta Manigault, 27 Feb. 1788. St. Phil PR

Heyward, Thomas & Ann Stobo, widow, 30 March 1746. St. And PR

Heyward, Thos. & Ann Gignilliat, 23 Jan. 1766. OJ 1764-1771

Heyward, Thomas Jr., & wife Elizabeth, daughter of Mary Elliott Savage & Thomas Savage, granddaughter of Elizabeth Butler, late of Georgia, decd., 9 May 1790; James Heyward of Combahee & Ralph Elliott of Port Royal, trustees; Nathl. Heyward, John Casper Springer, wit. Mar Set 1: 497-499

Heyward, William & Hannah Shubrick, 1 Jan. 1778. St. Phil PR

Heyward, William, of Prince Winyaw parish, & Charlotte Manby Villepontoux, of Charleston, 1 June 1797. St. Phil PR

Hibben, Andrew & Elizabeth Wingood, widow of John Wingood, 12 Jan. 1766. Ch Ch PR

Hibben, Andrew & Elizabeth Wingood, widow, 13 Jan. 1766. St. Phil PR

Hickbo, Isaac Barre, of Charleston, mariner, & Catharine McClieth, 13 Oct. 1797. St. Phil PR

Hickey, James & Charlotte Lestargette, 25 Feb. 1797. St. Phil PR

Hickey, William & Rebecca Gant [1740's]. Hist Oburg

Hickling, Ephraim & Hannah Thorpe, 20 Aug. 1774. St. Phil PR

Hickman, Geo & Mary White, 2 March 1772. Pugh diary

Hicks, Hew & Sarah Boone, 21 Nov. 1723. Ch Ch PR

Hicks, John & Hannah Murdock, P Licence, 28 Nov. 1731. St. Phil PR

Hicks, Matthew & Anne Barrow, widow, daughter of Phi. Givens, 7 June 1754. St. Hel PR

Hidelson, the Rev. John & Rachel Howard, widow of Georgetown District, 3 Feb. 1795; Samuel Smith of Georgetown, merchant & Patrick Dollard, planter, trustees; Levi Durand, B. Forrester, wit. Mar Set 2: 384-387

Higgins, George & Anne Collis, P Licence, 21 July 1734. St. Phil PR

Higgins, Seth & Isabella Lockens, 30 Apr. 1788. St. Phil PR

Higgins, Thomas & Rachel Quash, 8 Nov. 1772. St. Phil PR

Higginson, Samuel & Margery Hamilton, P Licence, 27 June 1739. St. Phil PR

Hildyard, William & Hannah Wills, P Licence, 4 July 1749. St. Phil PR

Hill, Charles of Berkley County, & Mrs. Elizabeth Godfrey, daughter of Capt. John Godfrey, decd., and Elizabeth late wife of sd. John Godfrey, now wife of Col. Robert Gibbs, 14 Jan. 1714; Richard Godfrey, John Godfrey, trustees; Saml Eveleigh, Jno Fenwicke, wit. Misc Rec. II: 68-72

Hill, Charles & Elizabeth Godfrey, 13 Jan. 1714/15. St. And PR

Hill, Charles & Sarah Smith, per Licence by A. G., 6 March 1745. St. Phil PR

Hill, Charles & Charlotte Finlayson, 19 May 1793. St. Phil PR

Hill, Duncan, now of Charleston, mariner & Elizabeth Butler, of Charleston, widow, late Elizabeth Lyon, 3 Dec. 1785; James Hamilton, & Angus McLeod, trustees; Rafel Hernandes, Richard Davis, wit. Mar Set 1: 171-175

Hill, Edward & Jane Clare, 3 Nov. 1732. St. And PR

Hill, H. & Laney Reeves, 8 July 1789. Pugh diary

Hill, Henry & Hannah Berry, 8 Feb. 1742. St. Hel PR

Hill, Jacob & _____, 29 Sept. 1791. Pugh diary

Hill, James & Susannah Gregory, P Licence by the Revd. Mr. Alexr. Garden Rector, 1 Nov. 1750. St. Phil PR

Hill, John & Susannah Burrey, 8 Apr. 1761. St. Phil PR

Hill, Paulus, from Franckfurth, on the Mayn, & Elisabetha Echardt(in), 8 Apr. 1783. St. John Luth Ch

Hill, Thomas & Susannah Green, widow, 5 Dec. 1776. St. Phil PR

Hill, Thomas Revd. & Jane Wells, 5 July 1785. St. John Luth Ch

Hill, Wm. & Sarah Evans, 22 Nov. 1711. SPG

Hiltonbrand, Adam & Margaretta Henrykinn, 30 June 1777. St. Phil PR

Himeli, Bartholomew Henry Revd., & Rachel Russ, 8 Jan. 1764. St. Phil PR

Hind, John & Jane Wilson, Licence, of G. Johnson, 7 July 1720. St. Phil PR

Hinds, Patrick, shoemaker, & Margt: McHerry, 23 Aug. 1742. St. Hel PR

Hinds, Patrick, widower, & Jane Douglass, 4 July 1750. St. Hel PR

Hinds, Patrick & Sarah Brush, P Licence by the Revd. A. Garden, 8 Oct. 1752. St. Phil PR

Hinds, Patrick & Anne Rivers, 1 Jan. 1761. St. Phil PR

Hines, Orson & Catharine Knight, 7 June 1798. Pugh diary

Hines, Steven & Mary Cooper, 28 Sept. 1786. Pugh diary

Hines, William & Ann Farey, 20 Dec. 1761. St. Phil PR

Hinsen, Joseph & Martha Stiles, of James Island, 1 Apr. 1797. Circ Cong

Hinson, Alexander & Mary Graves, widow, 14 July 1737. St. Hel PR

Hird, Mark & Marg't Daniel, 11 Feb. 1742. St. Hel PR

Hiscock, Edward & Martha Wickers, P Licence, 11 Sept. 1749. St. Phil PR

Hislop, Robert & Mary Warnock, 24 Sept. 1796. Trin Meth Ch

Hitchins, James & Margaret Longhair, P Licence, 7 May 1729. St. Phil PR

Ho____, Johann & Eleonora Haily, 2 Nov. 1771. St. John Luth Ch

Hodge, Ro't & _____, 21 Oct. 1779. Pugh diary

Hodgens, William & Ann Bent, widow, 9 March 1775. St. Phil PR

Hodges, G. & _____, 29 Dec. 1796. Pugh diary

Hodgson, John & Esther Randles, P Licence, 6 Oct. 1721. St. Phil PR

Hoffman, Jacob & Mary Ramely, 12 Oct. 1784. St. John Luth Ch

Hogan, Patrick & Sarah Wood, 3 May 1773. St. Phil PR

Hogarth, Wm. & Mary Turner, 12 Oct. 1797.   Trin Meth Ch

Hogg, John & Hannah Painter, 28 Dec. 1721.   St. And PR

Hogg, John & Anne Crosskeys, 1 Jan. 1731.   St. Hel PR

Hogg, John & Margt: Burton, widow, 6 July 1764.   St. Hel PR

Hoggatt, William & Mary Loddemore (Larimore) widow, 14 Apr. 1743.   Ch Ch PR

Hoi, George Frederic & Juliet Steirer, 18 May 1797.   Trin Meth Ch

Holaway, James & Elizabeth Watkins, 1 Jan. 1795.   Pugh diary

Holland, Edmudn & Henrietta Hall, 24 Sept. 1727.   St. Phil PR

Holland, Hugh & Miss Sarah Fields, 12 May 1785.   St. John Luth Ch

Holliday, Hugh of Charleston, & Eleanor Holliday of same, widow, 1 Dec. 1798; Francis Mulligan, trustee; Jno Mitchell, John L. Mulligan, wit.   Mar Set 3: 323-325

Hollingsworth, Abraham, son of Joseph and Eunice Steddom, 12 Sept. 1799.   Bush R QM

Hollingsworth, Isaac, son of George, and Ann Cox, 11 Aug. 1774. Bush R QM

Hollingsworth, James, son of George decd., and Jane, and Sarah Wright, 16 Nov. 1786.   Bush R QM

Hollingsworth, John, son of George decd. and Jane, and Rachel Wright, 12 March 1789.   Bush R QM

Hollingsworth, Joseph, son of George and Hannah, and Margaret Hammer, 4 June 1768.   Bush R QM

Hollins, Thomas & Hannah Moore, by Mr. Garden, 22 July 1736. St. Phil PR

Holman, Conrad & Eve Mary Hoof, widow, 14 Nov. 1774.   St. Phil PR

Holman, Thomas & Mary Wells, 15 May 1740.   St. And PR

Holman, Thomas of St. Bartholomews Parish, planter, & Mary Holman, daughter of Thomas Holman decd., 11 Mar. 1762; Thomas Hutchinson, trustee; Joseph Ladson, Thomas Stock, wit.   Mar Set 1: 444-446

Holman, Willm. & Rachel Clare, 2 June 1734.   St. And PR

Holmes, Frances & Elizabeth Brandford, 20 March 1739.   St. And PR

Holmes, Francis & Elizabeth Symmons, 8 March 1721.   St. Phil PR

Holmes, Isaac & Elizabeth Peronneau, 19 Jan. 1723.   St. Phil PR

Holmes, Isaac & Susanna Poinset, 28 Jan. 1726.   St. Phil PR

Holmes, Isaac & Rebeccah Bee, 8 May 1759.   St. Phil PR

Holmes, Isaac & Elizabth. Baker, 6 Nov. 1797.   Circ Cong

Holmes, Jack & Mary Esther Simons, 6 June 1798.   St. Phil PR

Holmes, James & Ann Griffin, 16 Apr. 1764.   St. Phil PR

Holmes, John & Katherine Fowler, relict of Richard Fowler, 20
    July 1720. Ch Ch PR

Holmes, John & Ann Coachman, of Prince George Parish, 3 March
    1796; Jehu Postell, John Coachman, & John Keith, trustees;
    Peter Lewis, John S. Budd, wit.   Mar Set 4: 366-369

Holmes, Ralph & Elizth Caroline Holmes, 11 Dec. 1794.   Circ
    Cong

Holmes, Sack of Charleston, Gent., & Mary Esther Simmons, of
    same, spinster, 6 June 1798; Revd. Thomas Frost, Henry
    Vailey, trustees; Wm Johnston, Gabriel Bailey, wit. Mar Set
    3: 252-254

Holmes, Samuel & Elizabeth Morgan, P Licence, 2 August 1733.
    St. Phil PR

Holmes, William & Miss Margaret Edwards, 31 March 1791;
    Alexander Edwards, trustee; Henry Bailey, wit. Mar Set 1:
    560-561

Holmes, Wm. & Marga. Edwards, 31 March 1791.   Circ Cong

Holroyd, Turpin & Elizabeth Nicols, 6 May 1781. St. John Luth
    Ch

Holsen, Christopher & Eliz. Hamilton, 23 Sept. 1762. St. Phil
    PR

Holt, John & Jane Howe, 9 May 1795.   Trin Meth Ch

Holton, Thomas & Anne Mindemen, 6 Dec. 1721. St. Phil PR

Holzendorf, Frederick & Mary Ann Miller, 26 July 1758.
    St. Phil PR

Hones, Wm. & Ann Nunamaker, 14 July 1759. St. Phil PR

Honeywood, Arthur & Elizabeth Howser, 7 May 1782. St. Phil PR

Honour, Thomas & Mary Stock's, widow, 14 July 1762. St. Phil
    PR

Honyhorn, Thomas & Sarah Woodbury, P Licence, 24 Feb. 1741.
    St. Phil PR

Hood, William & Catherine Bunker, 30 Nov. 1755.   St. Phil PR

Hope, William & Catherine Smyth, 25 Oct. 1765. St. Hel PR

Hopkins, Christopher & Ann Cadell, P Licence by Mr. Garden,
    13 Nov. 1736.   St. Phil PR

Hopkins, Jo. Steward & Jane Lloyd, 23 Jan. 1786. St. John Luth
    Ch

Hopton, William & Sarah Clapp, widow, 28 March 1744; license to
    Rev. Alex. Garden; Thomas Smith of Charlestown bondsman.
    MB Chas

Hopton, William & Sarah Clap, P Licence, 3 April 1744. St.
    Phil PR

Horger, Jacob & Lovisian Shaumloffel [1740's]. Hist Oburg

Horger, Jacob & Margaret Inabnit, 17 Oct. 1771. St. Phil PR

Horn, Donald & Mary Conroy, widow, 26 Aug. 1771. St. Phil PR

Horn, Peter & Elizabeth Pulla, widow, 19 Aug. 1765. St. Phil
    PR

Hornsby, Laben & Pheby Roach, 4 Apr. 1793.   Trin Meth Ch

Horry, Daniel gent. & Elizabeth Garnier, spinster, 23 Aug.
    1692; Isaac Massique (Mazyck), Peter LaSalle, bondsmen.
    Sec Prov 1675-95, p. 490

Horry, Daniel of Parish of St. James Santee, & Sarah Ford,
    spinster, 20 Dec. 1743; license to Rev. Thomas Hasell;
    John Atchison, Esqr., bondsman.   MB Chas

Horrey, Daniel & Sarah Ford, 12 Jan. 1743-4.   T & D PR

Horry, Daniel & Harriot Pinckney, 15 Feb. 1768.   St. Phil PR

Horry, Daniel Jr., bachelor & Judith Serre, spinster, in the
    house of Daniel Horry, Esqr., 9 Dec. 1759; John Dutarque
    Junr., Elias Horry, wit.   St. Jas PR

Horry, Hugh, of Parish of Georgetown, bachelor, & Sarah Bonneau
    of Parish of Georgetown, widow, 23 Apr. 1786; Peter Horry,
    H. Lenud, wit. St. Jas PR

Horry, Jonah & Sarah Burnett, 5 Nov. 1788.   St. Phil PR

Horry, John of Parish of Prince George, widower, & Ann Royer,
    widow, married in the house of John Mayrant Esqr., 5 July
    1759; Elias Horry, Elizabeth Perdreau, wit.   St. Jas PR

Horry, Peter & Martha Romsey, P Licence, 23 June 1737. St.
    Phil PR

Horry, Peter, of Waccamaw, & Margaret Guignard, 9 Feb. 1793;
    William Mayrant & George Ioor of High Hills; Samuel Fley,
    Wm. Richardson, wit.   Mar Set 2: 75-76

Horry, Thomas & Anne Branford, 13 June 1772.   St. And PR

Horsey, Thos. & Elizth Newball, 21 July 1791.   Circ Cong

Horsfort, Richard & Miss Barbara Diedrick, daughter of John
    Diedrick, 3 Jan. 1740.   Hist Oburg

Hort, William & Alice Gibbes, spinster, 7 Jan. 1772; William
    Gibbs, & Sarah Rutledge, widow, trustees; J. Rutledge,
    Hugh Rutledge, Roger Smith, wit.   Misc. Rec. PP: 349-353

Hort, William & Alice Gibbes, 7 Jan. 1772.   St. Phil PR

SOUTH CAROLINA MARRIAGES 1688-1799

Hort, William of Charleston, & Miss Catharine Simons, daughter
of Benjamin Simons, decd., 22 March 1790; his late wife Alice,
daughter of Robert Gibbes decd. and wife Elizabeth, granddaughter of George Haddrell and wife Alice; niece of Culcheth
Gibbes; Rev. Robert Smith, Hugh Rutledge, Edward Rutledge,
trustees; Abm Alexander, Thomas Hasell Junr., wit. Mar Set
1: 473

Hort, William & Catharine Simons, daughter of Benjamin Simons,
late of Christ Church Parish, decd., 22 March 1790. Mar
Set 2: 278-282.

Hort, William & Catharine Simons, 23 March 1790. St. Phil PR

Hosford, Joseph & Hanah Pendarvis, P Licence, 26 Sept. 1725.
St. Phil PR

Hoskins, James & Elizabeth Streater, 22 March 1747 (1747/8].
St. And PR

Hoskins, John & Sarah Taylor, 9 Apr. 1748. Pr Fred PR

Hoster, William & Angelica Marit, 19 Nov. 1758. St. And PR

Hottow, Charles & Ann Tshudy [1740's]. Hist Oburg

Hottow, Peter & Margaret Barbara Shuler [1740's]. Hist Oburg

Houghton, John & Mary Sheppard, P Licence, 31 Aug. 1738. St.
Phil PR

How, Daniel & Elizbth. Guines, widow, 18 Dec. 1747. St. And
PR

How, Robert & Elizabeth Guerin, 3 July 1729. T & D PR

Howard, Edward & Letties Jones, 23 Sept. 1716. T & D PR

Howard, Edward & Ann St. Martin, 28 March 1727-8. T & D PR

Howard, Edward and Rebecca McKleveney, 25 Apr. 1738. Pr Fred
PR

Howard, Experience & Rachel Bee, widow, 7 May 1727. St. Phil
PR

Howard, James & Jemima Harker, 18 March 1771. St. Phil PR

Howard, John, wigmaker, & Elisabetha Chapmann, widow, 7 Sept.
1786. St. John Luth Ch

Howard, Richard & Sarah Hawkins, P Licence, 21 May 1739. St.
Phil PR

Howard, Robert & Mary Norris, 13 Apr. 1764. St. Phil PR

Howard, Robert & Ann Cartman, 26 Apr. 1770. St. Phil PR

Howarth, Henry & Martha Mayne, widow, 6 Apr. 1761. St. Phil PR

Howarth, Probert & Ann Croft, 27 May 1756. St. Phil PR

Howe, James & Mary Yarder, P Licence of G. Johnson; 13 Aug. 1720.
St. Phil PR

Howel, William & Almey Vickers, 29 March 1738.   Circ Cong

Howell, John & Elizabeth Philips, P Licence by Mr. A. Garden
Rector, 29 July 1751.   St. Phil PR

Hows, Robt. & Mrs. Mary Moore, 2 Jan. 1709/10.   Reg Prov
1711-15, p. 449(41)

Howser, Elias & Elizabeth Lindt, 22 June 1783.   St. John Luth
Ch

Hoyland, Thomas & Anna Maria Linthwaite, P Licence, 26 Dec. 1745.
St. Phil PR

Huber, John Frederick & Barbara Kreyter, 7 Aug. 1750.   Hist
Oburg

Huber, Joseph & Elizabeth Horrmutt, 4 Sept. 1753.   Hist Oburg

Hudson, Samuel & Margaret Maxwell, widow, __ July 1746.   Hist
Oburg

Hudson, Thomas & Elizabeth Mell, ___ Oct. 1741.   St. And PR

Huey, Samuel & Gennet Brown, 7 July 1760.   St. And PR

Huger, Benjamin & Mary Kinloch, 1 Dec. 1772.   St. Phil PR

Huger, Benjamin of All Saints Parish, Esqr., & Mary Allston,
widow, 17 Feb. 1796; Benjamin Allston & Joseph Blythe,
trustees; Alexr. Collins, William Cuttino, wit.   Mar Set
2: 499-503

Huger, Sir Daniel, son of Sire Daniel Huger & Marguerite Huger,
and Elizabeth Gendron, daughter of Sire. Phillipee Gendron,
Esq., and Madelaine Gendron, agreement dated 22 May 1710.
Sec Prov 1714-1717; 170

Huger, Daniel & Anne LeJeau, 18 Oct. 1749.   T & D PR

Huger, Isaac & Elizabeth Chalmers, 23 March 1762.   St. Phil PR

Hugg, George & Mary Hogg, widow of Andrew Hogg, 6 Oct. 1737.
St. Hel PR

Huggins, John & Precila Rooper, __ Dec. 1709.   Reg. Prov.
1711-15, p. 449(41)

Huggins, Joseph & Elizabeth Murrell, 2 July 1773.   Ch Ch PR

Hughes, Henry & Susannah Bothwell, widow, 28 March 1779.
St. Phil PR

Hughes, Jenkin & Margaret Danford, P Licence by Mr. Garden,
19 Jan. 1736.   St. Phil PR

Hughes, Meredith of Prince Frederick, bachelor, & Anne Ford, of
the Parish of Prince-George, spinster, at the plantation of
George Ford, 9 Jan. 1772; Peter Bonneau, Thos Poten, wit.
St. Jas PR

Hughes, Solomon & Elizabeth Thornwell, 17 May 1792.   Pugh diary

Hughes, Thomas & Anne Hawkins, 29 June 1747.   Pr Fred PR

Hughes, Thomas and Catherine Neany, 1 Aug. 1739.   Pr Fred PR

Hughes, William and Sarah Potts, 2 June 1747.   Pr Fred PR

Hull, William & Ann Bonny, 1 May 1745.   T & D PR

Hull, Willm. & Elizabeth Johnson (no date).   St. Hel PR

Hull, William Junr., of Colleton County, St. Bartholomews
    Parish & Elizabeth Johnson of same, 17 Nov. 1770; John
    Bowler, Thomas Kinge, wit. Misc. Rec. OO: 473-474

Hume, Robert & Sophia Wiggington, 1721. St. Phil PR

Hume, Robt. & Susanh Quash, 20 March 1766.   OJ 1764-1771

Hume, Robert & Susannah Quash, 24 Apr. 1766.   T & D PR

Hume, Robert & Frances Susanna Quash, 24 Apr. 1766.   St. Phil
    PR

Humphreys, Benjn., planter & Rebecca Gabrail, 26 July 1792.
    Trin Meth Ch

Humpress, Thomas & Anne Armestrong, P Licence to Mr. G.,
    4 Dec. 1740.   St. Phil PR

Hunsinger, Michael, baker & Catharine Leitner, from Goose
    Creek, 28 Jan. 1787.   St. John Luth Ch

Hunt, Daniel & Christian Thompson, P Licence, 23 Dec. 1737.
    St. Phil PR

Hunt, Jesse & Elizabeth Rippley, widow; Anthony Labbe, trustee,
    30 Aug. 1794; Caleb Smith, Jas Nicholson, wit. Mar Set 2:
    299-304

Hunt, John & Ann Ball, 25 Dec. 1766. St. Phil PR

Hunt, Joseph & Mary Field, 2 Sept. 1741. St. Hel PR

Hunt, Joseph & Miss Martha Gray, 10 Apr. 1772.   St. John Luth
    Ch

Hunt, Ralph and Mary Cook, 3 Jan. 1793.   Cane Creek MM

Hunt, Samuel, son of Ralph, and Margaret Townsend, 11 Feb. 1789.
    Bush R QM

Hunt, Thomas & Hannah Nott, 31 Jan. 1787.   St. Phil PR

Hunter, James & Frances Fayssoux, widow, per Licence by the
    Revd. Mr. Robert Betham, 6 Dec. 1746.   St. Phil PR

Hunter, Samuel of Craven County, planter, & Mary Martin, of
    Colleton County, widow of Moses Martin, 11 March 1752;
    James Skirving & Joseph Scott, trustees; James Hunter,
    John Troup, wit. Misc. Rec. II: 194-199

Hunter, Thomas & Mary Lingard Wiatt, 26 Jan. 1793.   St. Phil PR

Hunter, William & Mary Kennedy, 27 June 1793.   St. Phil PR

Hurst, Joseph & Margaret Cartwright by the Revd. Mr. Garden, 27 April 1727.   St. Phil PR

Hurst, Robert & Jean Igen, 19 Aug. 1772.   St. Phil PR

Hurst, Samuel & Mary Henderson, P Licence, 8 Oct. 1741.   St. Phil PR

Hussey, Edward & Mary Barton, widow, 8 Apr. 1739.   St. And PR

Hust, Thomas & Elizabeth Bretten, widow; minister Mr. Fulton; bondsmen Thomas Hust, pettyauger man; and Nicholas Haynes of Charles Town, victualer; wit. James Michie, 5 Mar. 1732.   MB NY

Hutchens, Joseph & Catherine Cuttice, P Licence, 15 January 1740.   St. Phil PR

Hutchins, Hillman & Elizabeth, White, relict of Blake Leay White, of Charleston; ____ 1799; Theodore Trezevant & James Brickell, trustees; Mrs. Ann Heyward, Rev. Edmund Mathews, wit. Mar Set 4: 28-30

Hutchins, John & Elizabeth Watts, 1 March 1765.   St. Phil PR

Hutchinson, Axtell & Anne Williams, 27 June 1756.   St. Hel PR

Hutchinson, Jno Doctr. & Mrs. Ann Holland, 9 Apr. 1712.   SPG

Hutchinson, Dr. John, widower & Charlotte Foisin, spinster, P Licence of His Excellency Governr. Nicholson by the Reverend Mr. Garden, 21 December 1724.   St. Phil PR

Hutchinson, Mathias of St. George Parish, Dorchester, Esqr., & Louisa Tucker of same, widow of Benjamin Tucker, 25 July 1786; Archibald Salters of St. George Parish, Dorchester, trustee; Benjn L. Perry, Edward Smith, wit. Mar Set 1: 438-442

Hutchinson, Mathias of St. Georges Dorchester parish, & Elizabeth Ioor, widow of John Ioor, 5 June 1798; Joseph Waring, trustee; Eliza Provaux, Eliza Nelmes, wit. Mar Set 3: 264-267

Hutchinson, Matthias Major & Mrs. Elizabeth Ioor, 5 June 1798.   Circ Cong

Hutchinson, Ribton & Providence Dennis, P Licence, 25 Nov. 1734.   St. Phil PR

Hutchinson, Thomas of St. Bartholomew's Parish & Ann Stock, widow of Thomas Stock, 31 March 1781; William Skirving, trustee; Elizth. Mackintosh, Eleanor Oneal, wit. Mar Set 1: 118-120

Hutchinson, Thomas the younger of St. Bartholomews Parish, & Elizabeth Love Leger, daughter of Peter Leger decd., 17 Apr. 1783; George Haig, John James Haig, trustees; Jno Blake, Thoms Bourke, wit.   Mar Set 1: 499-500

Hutson, William of Charles Town & Mary Bryan, of Prince Williams Parish, Granville County, widow of Hugh Bryan, 10 Oct. 1758; Francis Pelot of St. Helena Parish, trustee; John Joachim Zubly, Josiah Rogerson, wit. Misc. Rec. LL: 264-272

Hutt, Thomas & Esther Leper, P Banns, 5 April 1727. St. Phil PR

Huxham, William, late of Great Britain, now of Charleston &
Elizabeth Baker, widow of Richard Behun Baker, 27 Oct. 1784;
Miss Emily Ladson, Thomas Ladson, William Fraser, trustees;
Jacob Dilgore, Mary Dilgore, wit. Mar Set 1: 48-53

Hyde, Samuel & Sarah Moncrieff, P Licence, 5 Nov. 1738. St.
Phil PR

Hyrne, Henry & Susannah Bellinger, 8 May 1733. St. And PR

Hyrne, Henry Collo. & Mary Golightley, widow, 26 June 1759.
St. And PR

Hyrne, William Alexander of Parish of Prince George, bachelor,
& Sarah Mitchell, of Parish of Prince George, 3 June 1779;
Benjn. Young, Anth F. Mitchell wit. St. Jas PR

Iklar, John & Ann Palmer, 16 Aug. 1774. St. Hel PR

Imrie, John of St. Philips Parish & Margaret Esmond, widow, of
George Esmond, decd., 13 Sept. 1774; Christopher Holson,
trustee; John Walker, John Groning, wit. Misc. Rec. RR:
166-170

Inabnet, John & Miss Marguretta Negly, 30 Nov. 1742; Hans
Danner, Simon Sanger, ___ Wardz, Henry Strowmann, Isaac Otto,
wit. Hist Oburg

Inabnit, Andrew & Mary Nägely [1740's]. Hist Oburg

Inabnit, Hans, & Margaret Nägely, 30 Nov. 1742. Hist Oburg

Inglis, George & Elizabeth Parker, P Licence, 3 Sept. 1743.
St. Phil PR

Inglis, William of Charleston & Jane Maxwell, daughter of Sarah
Chisolm, late Sarah Maxwell (wife of Alexander Chisholm Sr.)
2 June 1791; James Rivers Maxwell, trustee; Thos Hanscome,
James Clitherall, wit. Mar Set 1: 561-563

Ingram, William & Elizabeth Hooke, 6 Nov. 1781. St. John Luth
Ch

Inman, Abel & Mary Mullet, P Licence by A. Garden, 29 May 1747.
St. Phil PR

Imrie, John & Elizabeth Russell, 9 Sept. 1771. St. Phil PR

Imrie, John & Margaret Esdmond, widow, 2 Oct. 1774. St. Phil PR

Innis, Thomas & Unity Ridley, P Licence, 22 Dec. 1740. St. Phil
PR

Insco, Able, son of John decd. & Mary (now Pearson), and Ann
Pearson, 11 Dec. 1783. Bush R QM

Ireland, Edward & Sarah Peterson(?), 4 March 1786. St. John
Luth Ch

Ireland, Thomas & Gartright O Bryan of St. Helena Parish,
(no date, 1748 or 49). Stoney Creek Pres Ch

Irons, Stephen & Barbara Rupp, 6 Aug. 1777.   T & D PR

Irving, Jacob Aemilius, of the Island of Jamaica, but now of
    Charleston & Hannah Margaret Corbett, daughter of Thomas
    Corbett of Charleston; 18 Apr. 1796; Thomas Corbett Senr.,
    Thomas Corbett Junr., & Adam Tunno, trustees; James Male,
    Humpy. Minchin, wit. Mar Set 2: 492-493

Irving, Jacob Emelius & Hannah Margaret Corbett, 19 Apr. 1796.
    St. Phil PR

Irving, James & Elizabeth Motte, spinster, P Licence by the
    Revd. Mr. Levi Durant, 22 Feb. 1746.   St. Phil PR

Irwin, John & Mary Ann Vernoid, 19 Sept. 1739.   St. Hel PR

Isching, Willhelm & Judith Farmer, widow of Johannes Farmer,
    1 Aug. 1775.   St. John Luth Ch

Iten[?], David & Winrifred Knights, widow, 23 June 1785.
    St. Hel PR

Iten, Thomas & Mary Stanyarne, 27 May 1744.   St. Hel PR

Izard, Henry & Emma Philadelphia Middleton, 1 June 1795. St.
    Phil PR

Izard, Joseph & Eliz: Gibbes, 28 Sept. 1738.   St. And PR

Izard, Ralph & Madam Magdalen Eliza Pasquereau, 7 Apr. 1712.
    SPG

Izard, Walter & Mary Fenwick, 7 Nov. 1779.   St. Phil PR

Jackson, Hen: Pr. Wm. Par, & Elizabeth Davis, 16 Aug. 1753.
    St. Hel PR

Jackson, Johannes, butcher, & Anna Wirsching, in Georg Wirsching's
    house, 14 Jan. 1787.   St. John Luth Ch

Jackson, John & Martha Crofts Minorr, 21 Jan. 1792. St. Phil PR

Jackson, Thos & _____, 1 Mar. 1785.   Pugh diary

Jacob, Frederick & Mary Younker, 20 Oct. 1778.   St. Phil PR

Jacob, Hans & Mrs. Elizabeth Collins, 31 May 1797.   Circ Cong

Jacobs, Abraham, son of Raphael Jacobs, & Shankey, daughter of
    Joshua Hart, 19 Oct. 1785; Jacob Cohen, wit. Mar Set 1:
    348-349

Jacobs, Philip & Amelia Racus, 25 June 1771.   St. Phil PR

Jaffray, James & Mary Adams, 18 Apr. 1795; James Lee, Leighton
    Wilson, trustees; Danl Jas Ravenel, wit. Mar Set 2: 422-424

Jahn, Andreas, baker & Magdalena Heinik(in), 29 Jan. 1765.
    St. John Luth Ch

James, George & Sarah Wingat, 23 Dec. 1794.   Pugh diary

James, John & Mary Dargan, 3 Dec. 1766.   St. Phil PR

James, John & Elizabeth Turnbull, 23 Aug. 1767.   St. Phil PR

James, John & Katharine Burkhart, 8 Sept. 1798.   Circ Cong

Jamison, James & Rebecca Simons, 25 May 1773. St. Phil PR

Jancotsiy, Franz Antony, locksmith (or mechanic) & Anna
    Catharina Niffert(in), 30 Aug. 1777.   St. John Luth Ch

Jarman, John & Jane Wilkinson, widow, 7 Aug. 1794.   St. Phil PR

Jarvis, Edmund and Rebecca Stanyarne, spinster; minister
    Andrew Lesly; bondsmen Edmund Jarvis and Arthur Bull of St.
    Pauls Parish, planters; wit. James Michie, 7 March 1732.
    MB NY

Jaudon, Daniel, bachelor & Anne Dubosque, spinster, married in
    the house of Isaac Rembert Senr., 31 May 1759; Isaac Rembert,
    Paul Jaudon, wit. St. Jas PR

Jaudon, James & Mary Pedriau, 9 Feb. 1769.   T & D PR

Jaudon, James of Parish of St. John, widower, & Alley Semple,
    widow, 6 Oct. 1785; Roger Sanders, Ches Chovin, wit. St.
    Jas PR

Jaudon, John of Parish of Prince Frederick, bachelor & Mary
    Gaillard of Parish of Prince Frederick, widow, 19 Apr. 1770;
    Paul Jaudon Junr., Peter Michau, wit. St. Jas PR

Jaudon, John of Parish of Prince Frederick, widower, & Anne
    Steel, of the parish of Prince Frederick, spinster, at the
    plantation of Thomas Lynch, 4 July 1773; Benjn. Perdriau,
    Wm. Steel, wit. St. Jas PR

Jaudon, Paul of Parish of Prince Frederick & Mary Leibrey,
    spinster, 21 Dec. 1743; license to Rev. John Fordyce; Thomas
    Boone, bondsman. MB Chas

Jaudon, Paul and Margaret Lieubrey, 28 Dec. 1743. Pr Fred PR

Jaudon, Paul & Martha Guerin, 5 Jan. 1772.   T & D PR

Jaudon, Samuel of Christ Church Parish, planter, & Mary Bon-
    hoste; 11 May 1793; Gabriel Capers & Clement Brown, trustees;
    Thos Murrell, Eli Higgins, wit. Mar Set 2: 121-122

Jay, John, son of William decd., & Mary, and Betty Pugh,
    4 March 1773.   Bush R QM

Jay, James and Jemima Mills, 7 April 1791.   Bush R QM

Jay, Jessy, son of John, & Sarah Brooks, 5 Apr. 1798. Bush
    R QM

Jay, Layton, son of William & Elizabeth Mills, 30 May 1793.
    Bush R QM

Jayes, Peter & Martha Nash, P Licence, 4 May 1732. St. Phil PR

Jean, Wm. & Elizabeth Bradsher, 17 Sept. 1724. Ch Ch PR

Jeannerett, Jacob of St. James Santee, & Mary DePlesis, widow, 6 Oct. 1744; license to Rev. James Tisseaux; John Triboudet, Joseph Mary, shopkeeper, bondsmen. MB Chas

Jeanneret, Jacob Senr. of St. James Santee, & Mary Simmons, of same, widow, 10 July 1787; John Buchanan, trustee; Margaret Rembert, Martha Greenland, Isaac Rembert, wit. Mar Set 1: 320-322

Jeanneret, Jacob, widower, & Mary Simmons, widow, 2 Aug. 1787; Jno Buchanan, S. Warren, wit. St. Jas PR

Jefferds, John & Magdalen Miller, 1 June 1749. T & D PR

Jeffers, John & Margaret Howard, 12 Aug. 1714. T & D PR

Jeffords, Daniel & Judith Bona, 28 June 1764. T & D PR

Jeffords, John & Mary Jaudon, of Christ Church Parish, widow of Samuel Jaudon, decd., 23 Oct. 1798; Eli Huggins, Robert Murrell, planters, trustees; William Griffin, John Murrell, wit. Mar Set 3: 306-311

Jeffrys, James & Mary Morrell, 12 Dec. 1771. St. Phil PR

Jehne, August & Elizabeth Phillips, widow, 24 Feb. 1763. St. Phil PR

Jelford, John & Mary Vanderhorst, 16 July 1751. Ch Ch PR

Jenes, John & Ann Spencer, 7 Oct. 1762. St. Hel PR

Jenkens, Edward & Elizabeth Savy, P Licence, 15 Nov. 1741. St. Phil PR

Jenkins, Amos, son of David and Elizabeth Russell, 14 Nov. 1799. Bush R QM

Jenkins, Benjamin & Hannah Fripp (no date). St. Hel PR

Jenkins, David, son of David & Elizabeth, and Martha Evans, 8 Oct. 1789. Bush R QM

Jenkins, Isaac, son of David & Elizabeth, and Rebecah Herbart, 10 Nov. 1785. Bush R QM

Jenkins, Jacob of Anson County, N. C., & Jean Westfield of Pedee River, Craven County, widow, 1 Jan. 1760; Robert Westfield of Craven Co., trustee; John Aken, Claudius Pegues, wit. Misc. Rec. LL: 297-298

Jenkins, Jesse, son of David, and Hannah Russell, 8 June 1797. Bush R QM

Jenkins, John & Elizabeth Adams, 12 April 1727. St. Phil PR

Jenkins, John Junior & Mary Adams by Revd. Mr. Morritt, 23 May 1727. St. Phil PR

Jenkins, Joseph & Phebe Chaplin, 31 May 1735. St. Hel PR

Jenkins, Joseph & Sarah Toomer, 31 May 1770. St. Hel PR

Jenkins, Jos. of Edisto & Elizabeth Evans, 4 July 1782. St. Hel PR

SOUTH CAROLINA MARRIAGES 1688-1799

Jenkins, Joseph John, of Ladies Island in the dist. of Beaufort.
planter & Martha Oswald of St. Helena, same dist; 3 Sept.
1793; John Jenkins, trustee; William Chaplin, Wm Oswald, wit.
Mar Set 2: 153-155

Jenkins, Thomas & Mary Johnson, 30 March 1719.   T & D PR

Jenkins, Thomas, son of David & Elizabeth, and Maria Gaunt,
2 Dec. 1784.   Bush R QM

Jennby, James & ___ Summers, widow, ___ 1733.   Circ Cong

Jennens, John, bachelor & Martha Murrell, of Parish of Christ
Church, spinster, in the house of Mary Jennens, widower, 15
Jan. 1767; Aaron Littell, Charles Maynard, wit. St. Jas PR

Jenner, or Jeno, James and Frances Brown 1 Aug. 1744. Pr Fred
PR

Jennings, John & Mary Dutarque, 20 Jan. 1765.   T & D PR

Jennings, Phillip & Elizabeth, a half breed Indian woman near
Orangeburgh, 19 Nov. 1746; Joseph Hasfort, wit. Misc. Rec.
KK: 270

Jennings, Philip & Elizabeth Late Hasfort, 7 Feb. 1746/7,
Joseph Hasforts, Frogat, Brand Pendarvis & Lucas Wolf, wit.
Hist Oburg

Jennings, Thomas & Elizabeth Murrill, 23 Jan. 1744/5. Ch Ch PR

Jeno or Jenner, James and Frances Brown, 1 Aug. 1744. Pr Fred
PR

Jenys, Paul of St. Pauls Parish, Colleton Co., & Elizabeth Raven,
widow of John Raven, 19 Jan. 1735; Stephen Bedon & Henry
Bedon, shopkeepers, trustees; John Daniel, Wm. Trevin, wit.
Misc. Rec. HH: 183-189

Jenys, Paul & Elizabeth Raven, widow, by the Revd. Mr. Wm.
Guy, 25 January 1735.   St. Phil PR

Jenys, Paul & Elizabeth Raven, widow, 25 Jan. 1735/6. St. And
PR

Jermain, Edward & Susannah Satur, 18 Apr. 174__.   Ch Ch PR

Jerman, Ralph & Margaret Graham, 19 Jan. 1721.   St. Phil PR

Jervey, John & Elizabeth Gilbert, 16 Mar. 1736. St. Hel PR

Jervey, Thomas & Grace Hall, 22 July 1770.   T & D PR

Jervis, John & Priscilla Ash, 20 Feb. 1777.   St. Phil PR

Jeyes, Peter and Mary Brand, spinster, minister Alexander Garden,
bondsmen Peter Jeyes of Charles Town, carpenter, and Lawrence
Coliet (Coulliette) of Charles Town, gent., wit: James
Michie. 9 June 1733.   MB NY

Jeyes, Peter & Mary Brand, P Licence, 10 June 1733.   St. Phil
PR

Joel, Thomas & Hester Dutarque, 22 May 1763.   T & D PR

133

Johannes, Peter & Sarah Margaretha ___, widow, 6 Sept. 1768.
St. John Luth Ch

John, Philip (negro) & Rebecca Royal, widow (negro), 23 Apr.
1753. St. Hel PR

Johnson, George & Rowdy Pitt, widow, 9 July 1778. St. Phil PR

Johnson, Jacob of Colleton Co., & St. Bartholomews Parish,
planter & Martha Bowler, 17 Nov. 1770; Wm. Hull Junr., &
Thos. Kinge, wit. Misc. Rec. OO: 477-479

Johnson, Jacob Withers, of Charleston, Watch-maker, & Catherine
Quackenbush, 10 Nov. 1796; Eleanor Cooke, trustee; Oliver
Cromwell, Charles Wittick, wit. Mar Set 2: 551-553

Johnson, Jabez Withers & Catharine Quackenbush, 25 Dec. 1796.
Circ Cong

Johnson, Jacob & Martha Boller, 22 Nov. 1770. St. Hel PR

Johnson, John & Catherine Stevens, P Licence, 12 Feb. 1739.
St. Phil PR

Johnson, Mathias & Sarah Mackenzie, spinster, per Banns by the
Revd. Mr. Betham, 28 Dec. 1746. St. Phil PR

Johnson, Peter & Sarah Connors, 21 March 1798. Trin Meth Ch

Johnson, Richard & Catharine Forester, widow, 24 Jan. 1771.
St. Phil PR

Johnson, Richard & Elizabeth Schacho, widow, 26 Sept. 1773.
St. Phil PR

Johnson, William & Mary Webb, 9 Nov. 1791. St. Phil PR

Johnsone, William & Anne Symmons (2 negro's), P Ban, 27 Dec.
1742. St. Phil PR

Johnston, Arthur & Martha Taylor, 2 Jan. 1733. St. Phil PR

Johnston, James of Charles Town, baker & Margaretta Farwell,
spinster, 3 Oct. 1764; Robert Stedman & John Booner, barbers,
trustees; Ann Johnston, Jno Patton, wit. Mar Set 1: 352-356

Johnston, John & Sarah Glazier, P Licence, 26 April 1740.
St. Phil PR

Johnston, John & Mary Hunter, widow, 22 Apr. 1767. St. Phil
PR

Johnston, Richard & Rebecca Thomson, 23 March 1761. T & D PR

Johnston, Robert & Elizabeth Aiken, 1 Feb. 1759. T & D PR

Johnston, Robert & Sarah Collins, P Licence, 14 March 1731.
St. Phil PR

Johnston, Robert & Susannah Blanchard, 1 Sept. 1761. St. Phil
PR

Johnston, Samuel & Mary Thompson, widow, 13 Jan. 1767. St. Phil
PR

Johnston, Samuel & Frances Garner, 18 Oct. 1781. St. Phil PR

Johnston, William & Arn Smith, 20 March 1773. St. And PR

Johnston, William, gent., & Anna Maria Pinckney, daughter of
   Hopson Pinckney, late of St. Thos Parish, 5 Dec. 1797;
   Daniel Cannon & Thomas Doughty of Charleston, trustees;
   W. Logan, Jr., James Matthews, wit. Mar Set 3: 183-190

Johnston, William & Anna Maria Pinckney, 5 Dec. 1797. St. Phil
   PR

Jones, Alexander & Mary Farquhar, 28 Jan. 1790. St. Phil PR

Jones, Benjamin, widower, & Sarah Peters, widow, 29 Oct. 1740.
   St. Hel PR

Jones, Benja. & Pattey Marsingall, 2 May 1775. Pugh diary

Jones, Charles & Rachel Edghill, 16 Dec. 1729. St. And PR

Jones, Charles & Sarah Page, 11 March 1766. OJ 1764-1771

Jones, Christopher & Catherine Brown, per Licence, 3 Feb. 1744.
   St. Phil PR

Jones, Edward & Margaret Goodson, 20 Feb. 1779. St. Phil PR

Jones, Edward, of Charleston, Practitioner of Physick, & Ann
   Jamieson of same, spinster, 28 Dec. 1796; Keating Simons
   & Rev. Thomas Frost, trustees; Elizth. Frost, Roger Smith
   Junr., wit. Mar Set 3: 31-35

Jones, Edward of Charleston, physician & Ann Janieson, 28 Dec.
   1796. St. Phil PR

Jones, Francis, widower, & Mary Lewis, widow, 14 June 1785,
   Rd Withers, Charles Lewis, wit. St. Jas PR

Jones, Francis & Mary Lewis, 8 Oct. 1765. Ch Ch PR

Jones, George, of Charlestown, mariner, & Rebecca Campbell,
   tavernkeeper, 26 May 1777; Catherine Preston, trustee;
   Paul Preston, Charles Duncan, wit. Misc. Rec. SS: 107-110

Jones, John & _____, 28 June 1768. Pugh diary

Jones, John & Dorothy Christian, spinster, per Licence by the
   Revd. Mr. Robt. Betham, 22 July 1746. St. Phil PR

Jones, John & Ann Brandford, 6 Apr. 1756. St. Phil PR

Jones, John & Sarah Miller, widow, 10 Jan. 1786. St. John
   Luth Ch

Jones, Joseph & Mary Brewton, 6 Jan. 1741/2. Ch Ch PR

Jones, Joseph to Miss Nancy Boyd, daughter of William Boyd
   (surveyor), 12 July 1794, Chester Co. Ches Ct Min B

Jones, Joseph, son of Francis & Sarah, and Mary Taylor, 29 Sept.
   1792. Bush R QM

Jones, Joseph & Mary Norris, P Licence, 4 Oct. 1749. St. Phil PR

Jones, Joseph to Patsy Stevens, 27 Dec. 1789, Rev. David Lilly, Marlboro Co.

Jones, Joshuah & Mary Hary, 11 July 1771.   Pugh diary

Jones, Lewis Rev. & Margaret Evans, widow, 11 Sept. 1733. St. Hel PR

Jones, Richard & Mary Nutcher, 23 May 1765.   St. And PR

Jones, Robert & Elizabeth Fly, P Licence, 2 July 1749.   St. Phil PR

Jones, Roger & Phebe Parrey, P Licence, 20 Sept. 1741.   St. Phil PR

Jones, Samuel & Mary Vincent, 27 June 1735.   St. And PR

Jones, Samuel & Susannah Scott, spinster, P Licence by the Revd. Mr. Alexr. Garden, 28 Sept. 1747.   St. Phil PR

Jones, Samuel & Rebecca Holmes, P Licence, 29 June 1740. St. Phil PR

Jones, Samuel & Elizabeth McKee, 27 Jan. 1771.   St. Hel PR

Jones, Simon & Elizabeth Wilkinson, widow, 12 Oct. 1733.   St. Hel PR

Jones, Thomas & Hanah Fidling, widow, 30 Jan. 1745 [1745/6]. St. And PR

Jones, Thomas & Sarah Collins, __ Dec. 1745.   Ch Ch PR

Jones, Thos. & Elizabeth Davis, 19 Feb. 1746/7; Samuel Wright, Capt. Thompson, wit.   Hist Oburg

Jones, Thos. & Abigail Townsend, 5 June 1766.   OJ 1764-1771

Jones, William & Ann Bates, widow, 17 May 1742.   Ch Ch PR

Jones, William & Sarah Woolf, P Licence, 24 May 1752.   St. Phil PR

Jones, William & Elizabeth Hamleton, widow, 3 Oct. 1764. St. Hel PR

Jones, William & Mary Jones, widow, 14 June 1766.   St. Phil PR

Jones, William & Mary Jones, 17 June 1766.   OJ 1764-1771

Jones, William & Jane Thompson, 13 Nov. 1785.   St. John Luth Ch

Jones, William Cox, & Mary Lampert, 29 Nov. 1781.   St. Phil PR

Jonson, Briten & Mary Lewis, 30 Jan. 1769.   Pugh diary

Jordan, Christopher & Catharine Hier, widow, 27 Nov. 1776. St. Phil PR

Jordan, Robert of Parish of Prince George, bachelor, & Martha Murrill of Parish of Prince George, spinster, at the plantation of John Marant, Esqr., 18 Sept. 1763; Wm. Bell, Mary Smith, wit.   St. Jas PR

Joulce, Daniel, bachelor, & Constant June, spinster, at the house of John Jaudon, 13 March 1783; John Jaudon, Edward June, wit. St. Jas PR

Jouneau, James & Magdalen Beauchamp, 2 Jan. 1721. St. Phil PR

Joy, Benjamin & Elizabeth Gibson, 1 Nov. 1726. Ch Ch PR

Joy, Daniel & Lydia Rembart; 6 Feb. 1794; John Eberly, trustee; Henry Legg, Elizabeth Strohacker, wit. Mar Set 2: 250-253

Joy, Daniel, of Ch. Church Parish, & Miss Lydia Rambert, of Charleston, 8 Feb. 1794. Trin Meth Ch

Joy, Moses & Mary Rowser, 18 June 1724. Ch Ch PR

Joyner, Daniel to Miss Margeret Haberman, 2 June 1799 by Rev. J. P. Franklow, Orangeburg Dist. St. Mat Ch Rec

Joyner, Ezekiel to Miss Anne White, 13 June 1799, by Rev. J. P. Franklow, Orangeburg Dist. St. Mat Ch Rec

Joyner, James & Elizabeth Fairchild, 8 Jan. 1778. St. Hel PR

Joyner, John & Benedicta Russlett, widow, 25 Sept. 1777. St. Phil PR

Joyner, John Junr. & Naomy Bunch, both of Amelia Township, 23 Dec. 1754. Hist Oburg

Joyner, Joseph & Miles Jackson, 1 Jan. 1742; John Hammelton, John Fiarchild, Richard Hasfort, William Martins, Thomas Jackson, wit. Hist Oburg

Joyner, Nathan & Winifred N. [1740's]. Hist Oburg

Joyner, Thomas & Faithy Carse, in Amelia Township, 1740. Hist Oburg

Joyner, William & Elizabeth Joyner, widow, 23 Jan. 1783. St. Hel PR

Joyner, Willm: & Susannah Greene, widow of John Grayson, 11 Sept. 1798. St. Hel PR

Jozie, Patrick & Rebecca Egan, 8 Jan. 1782. St. Phil PR

Jubb, John & Eve Catherine Shuler [1740's]. Hist Oburg

Jucks, Thomas & Violets Crawford, 10 March 1747 [1747/8]. St. And PR

Julian, Alexander & Eliza Bourdeaux, 29 Feb. 1792. Circ Cong

June, Edward, bachelor & Rebecca Egan, widow, 30 Oct. 1788; Danl Joulee, John Steel, wit. St. Jas PR

June, George of Parish of St. James Santee, & Mary Brian, widow, 30 March 1744; license to Rev. Thomas Hasell; Alexander Dupont of Prince Fredericks parish, bondsman. MB Chas

June, John & Anna Howard, 5 March 1718-9. T & D PR

June, John & Lucy Kennel, 28 Dec. 1743. Pr Fred PR

June, Solomon & Anna Stanley, 30 May 1727.   T & D PR

June, Stephen & Lydia Steele, widow, 12 May 1757.   St. Phil PR

K____, B___, & Sarah Edwards, 21 March 1779.   Pugh diary

Kaiser, John Jacob & Catherine Philips, 1 Dec. 1797; John
    Eberly of Charleston, baker, trustee; Samuel Browne, Wm.
    Yeadon, wit.   Mar Set 3: 173-180

Kalckhoffen, John Jacob & Rebecca Rodamon, 14 July 1783.
    St. John Luth Ch

Kalckoffen, Jacob & Jane Elbert, 10 July 1779.   St. John Luth
    Ch

Kannady, John & Mary Godfrey, 29 Sept. 1747.   Hist Oburg

Karle, John Castor(?), & Barbara, widow of the late Johannes
    Kirchner, 24 Dec. 1782.   St. John Luth Ch

Karlington, Henry & Margaret Winter, P Banns, 21 Dec. 1737.
    St. Phil PR

Karren, Simon Michaels & Mrs. Robler(in), 16 Dec. 1769.
    St. John Luth Ch

Karwon, Thomas & Mary Marion, 3 Jan. 1773.   T & D PR

Karwon, Thomas of Parish of St. Thos. & St. Dennis, &
    Catharine Bonneau, of Parish of St. Johns, spinster, 16
    Dec. 1774; Benjamin Bonneau & Thomas Ashby, trustees; Samuel
    Bonneau & Thomas Ashby, trustees; Samuel Bonneau, Anthony
    Ashby, wit.   Mar Set 1: 142-144

Kattman, Anthonius & Catharine, widow of Mr. Sass, 9 Feb.
    1773.   St. John Luth Ch

Kay, Joseph & Jane Moore, widow, 10 June 1794.   St. Phil PR

Kayler, Henrick & Ann Beaty, 1 March 1778.   T & D PR

Kaylor, Richard & Mary Johnston, 19 Feb. 1777.   St. Phil PR

Keane, Martin and Martha Morgan; minister Alex. Garden, bonds-
    men Martin Keane of Carolina, Indian trader and Nicholas
    Haynes of Charles Town, victualer; wit. J. Hammerton, 2 July
    1733.   MB NY

Keating, Maurice & Mary Jones, per Licence, 19 Nov. 1745.
    St. Phil PR

Keatly, John & Jane Troublefield, 16 Dec. 1747.   Pr Fred PR

Kecheley, George of Parish of St. Thomas, bachelor & Catherine
    Barnett, spinster, in the house of Elisha Barnett, 8 July
    1788; Elisha Barnett, Chs Chovin, wit.   St. Jas PR

Keckel, Johann & ___ MOs(in), widow, 5 Apr. 1770.   St. John
    Luth Ch

Keckley, George & Margaret McKinfuss, 21 Apr. 1777.   St. Phil
    PR

138

Keeble, Kary & Mary Kelly, 23 Dec. 1748. Pr Fred PR

Keen, John & Elizabeth Pelleo, 2 July 1738. Pr Fred PR

Keen, Joseph of Parish of Prince George, bachelor, & Anne Crook
of Parish of Prince George, spinster, in the house of Mrs.
Eliz Crook, 29 July 1779; Godard Delworth(?), John Robinson,
wit. St. Jas PR

Keen, Thomas & Mary McKenzie, 21 July 1782. St. Phil PR

Kefkin, Henrich Christof, cabinetmaker, son of Mr. Johann
Fridrich Kefkin, inhabitant of Osterholtz in Electoral
Hanover, & Maria Margaretha, daughter of Mr. Johann Georg
Munch [Minnick], inhabitant of Crims Creeq in Oranienburg
Caunty [crims Creek in Orangeburgh County, actually
District], 28 March 1775. St. John Luth Ch

Keill, John, tanner, & Rebecca Woods, widow, 1 May 1785. St.
John Luth Ch

Keith, Alexander & Susanna Bullin, 2 Dec. 1779. St. Phil PR

Keith, Cornelious & Ednah Jurder(?), 3 Dec. 1789. Pugh diary

Keith, I. S. Rev. & Katharine Legare, 3 Apr. 1798. Circ Cong

Keith, James & widow Dwight, 1 Dec. 1751. Ch Ch PR

Keith, John Esqr., of George Town & Miss Magdalene Elizabeth
Trapier, 5 Jan. 1793; Paul Trapier the younger, the Hon.
Thomas Waties, Esqr., of George Town, trustees; Eliz Martin,
Mary Dudley, wit. Mar Set 2: 113-116

Keith, Jno & _____, 8 July 1784. Pugh diary

Keller, Jacob to Miss Christina Houser, 30 July 1799, by Rev.
J. P. Franklow, Orangeburg Dist. St. Mat Ch Rec

Keller, Mathias & Maria Handshy, 1740. Hist Oburg

Keller, Paul & Gottliebe Kirchner(in), 8 March 1764.
St. John Luth Ch

Kelley, William & Frances McCrott, widow, 6 Jan. 1765. St. Phil
PR

Kelly(?), Carl King, from Philadelphia, & Maria Barbara Weiss
(in), 12 Apr 1768. St. John Luth Ch

Kelly, Daniel Jr. of Charleston Dist., & Ann Marion, 26 Jan.
1797; aunt Mary E. Marion, trustee; Wm. Paulling, Francis
Marion, Mary Seeds, wit. Mar Set 3: 22-23

Kelly, John & Regina Stoosin, 1 June 1762. St. Phil PR

Kelly, Robert, son of John dec., and Sarah Paty, 1 Sept. 1791.
Bush R QM

Kelly, Samuel, son of Samuel, & Elizabeth Milhouse, 16 Dec. 1785.
Bush R QM

Kelly, Samuel, Jr., and Hannah Pearson, 1 Jan. 1789. Bush R QM

Kelsal, John & Mary Bellinger, of St. Pauls Parish, 24 May 1738. St. And PR

Kelsall, John & Agnes Barry of Prince Williams Parish, 30 June 1763; Stephen Bull Senr., Stephen Bull Junr., trustee; Sarah Story, Margaret Scanlan, wit. Misc. Rec OO: 444-447

Kelsall, William & Elizabeth Desaussure, 23 Apr. 1772. St. Hel PR

Kelsey, William & Eleanor Murrah, 25 March 1788. St. Phil PR

Kemmelmeyer, Johann Friderich Christian, Med. Pract. from the Duchy of Wirttemberg, & Maria, widow of the late Christian Gruber, 28 Feb. 1783. St. John Luth Ch

Kemmerling, Daniel & Maria Wussert(in), 20 June 1773. St. John Luth Ch

Kemp, Peter & Catharine Pipung, 19 March 1779. St. John Luth Ch

Kempton, George & Henrietta Warner, 17 Oct. 1799; Philip Moore, Penelope Warner, trustees; Charles Snetter & Philip Hackell, wit. Mar Set 3: 384-385

Kenedy, William & Mary Zopham, 12 March 1793. Trin Meth Ch

Kenely, John & Arrabella Bonner, widow, 18 Sept. 1794. Trin Meth Ch

Kenna, John Brett & Mrs. Ann Usher, 29 March 1796. Trin Meth Ch

Kennan, Henry & Susannah Godin, P Licence by the Revd. Mr. Alexander Garden Rector, 3 June 1751. St. Phil PR

Kennan, Henry & Elizabeth Sarah Bonnefons, 12 Nov. 1789; Jacob Guerard of Parish of St. Helena, trustee; Martha Stewart, wit. Mar Set 1: 536-537

Kenneday, Jno & Lula Brasher, 25 Aug. 1791. Pugh diary

Kennedy, James of Round O, St. Bartholomews Parish, & Ann Bemley Chalmers (already married), 1 July 1791; Johnson Hagood, William Nibbs, wit. Mar Set 1: 585-587

Kennedy, Thomas of Edisto Island, phusician, & Ann Jeffords, widow, 8 Aug. 1785; Ephraim Mikell, trustee; Abigail Mikell, John Mikell, wit. Mar Set 1: 199-202

Kennedy, Wm., widower, & Sarah Fureau, widow, both of this parish, 4 July 1754. Stoney Creek Pres Ch

Kenworthy, David, son of Joshua & Mary, and Dinah Cook, 12 March 1795. Cane Creek MM

Kenworthy, Jesse, son of David & Tamar, and Rachel Cook, 1 Nov. 1792. Cane Creek MM

Keowin, John & Sarah Eshmore, 25 July 1781. St. Phil PR

Keown, Robert & Elizabeth Harvey, P Licence by the Revd. Mr. Alexr. Garden, 14 June 1748. St. Phil PR

Keppen(?), Alan & Maria Wrade, 28 July 1769. St. John Luth Ch

Ker, James & Hester Gibbons, 26 Jan. 1731/2. St. And PR

Kerr, Isaac and Abigail Hawkins, 31 Dec. 1741. Pr Fred PR

Kerr, James & Mary Bertram, P Licence, 8 Sept. 1732. St. Phil
   PR

Kerk, William & Mary Bennoit, P Licence by the Revd. Mr. Alexr.
   Garden, 1 Dec. 1747. St. Phil PR

Kershaw, Charles & Mary Eyre Breton, 24 March 1792. St. Phil PR

Kershaw, Charles & Frances Ramage, 24 Dec. 1797. St. Phil PR

Kerwon, Crafton & Mary Hall, 16 May 1737. Pr Fred PR

Keys, Joseph of Charles Town & Margaret Hayward, widow of
   Thomas Hayward, 18 Nov. 1700; Lewis Pasquereau, Simon
   Valentyn, Henry Wigington, wit. Reg Prov 1696-1703; 176-177

Kilpatrick, James & Elizabeth Hepworth, 4 May 1727. St. Phil
   PR

Kimberly, Thomas & Isabell Goll, 24 June 1716. Charleston MM

Kimmel, John & Rachel Long, 24 May 1781. St. John Luth Ch

King, Benjamin & Benina Bell, 23 May 1798. Circ Cong

King, Charles & Mary Johnson, 13 Feb. 1732. T & D PR

King, Edward & Jerusha Rock, 29 Sept. 1721. St. And PR

King, Elding & Eleanor Norman, 4 Jan. 1732/3. St. And PR

King, George & Elizabeth Mahan, 22 Oct. 1752. T & D PR

King, James & Elisabeth Thompson, 19 Oct. 1745. Pr Fred PR

King, John & ___, 1 Nov. 1787. Pugh diary

King, Richard & Mary Beresford, 26 Apr. 1709. T & D PR

King, Richard & Margaret Ferguson, 28 May 1766. OJ 1764-1771

King, Robert & Hannah Marbeust, 29 Dec. 1714. T & D PR

King, Samuel & Elizabeth Preston, 17 May 1706. T & D PR

King, Thomas & Martha Graves, 18 Oct. 1762. St. Hel PR

King, Thomas & Mary Ellis, 4 June 1796. Circ Cong

Kingland, John & Elizabeth Flood, P Licence, 8 Jan. 1731.
   St. Phil PR

Kingman, Eliab & Ann King, 17 March 1793. Trin Meth Ch

Kingston, John of Charles Town & Ann Camren, spinster, 13 Jan.
   1743/4; license to Rev. Alexander Garden; Joseph Tobias,
   bondsman. MB Chas

141

Kingston, John & Anne Camren, P Licence, 15 Jan. 1743. St.
    Phil PR

Kinloch, Cleland of Charleston, & Harriet Simmons, daughter of
    Ebenezer Simmons, decd., 13 Apr. 1786; Francis Kinloch,
    Thomas Simmons, trustees; Thomas Eveleigh, John Parker Junr.,
    wit.   Mar Set 1: 262-263

Kinninburgh, John, Serjt of the Royal Artillery, & Margareth
    Dixon, 30 Oct. 1781. St. John Luth Ch

Kipp, Jacobus & Elizabeth Millen, P Licence by Mr. Garden, 16
    March 1735.   St. Phil PR

Kirchner, Johannes, widower, & Maria Elisabetha Rischang(in),
    5 Dec. 1765. St. John Luth Ch

Kirk, Edward & Charlotte Bennet, 19 Nov. 1770.   St. Phil PR

Kirk, John, merchant & Waldburga Schultze, widow, 31 Oct.
    1789; John Randolph Switzer, sadler, trustee; George Taylor
    Junr., C. Richiez, wit. Mar Set 1: 461-463

Kirk, Thomas & Mariam Lubbock, 6 Feb. 1748; William Glen,
    Stephen Cater, wit. Misc. Rec. GG: 402

Kirk, Thomas & Marian Lubbeck, P Licence, 6 Feb. 1748. St.
    Phil PR

Kirk, William of Parish of St. Paul & Mary Deleback, spinster,
    17 Aug. 1744; John George Delebach, of parish of St. Philips,
    bondsman; license to Rev. Alexander Garden. MB Chas

Kirk, William & Mary Doloback, P Licence, 18 Aug. 1744.
    St. Phil PR

Kirkedge, Edward & Mary Eveleigh, widow, 28 Oct. 1792. St.
    Phil PR

Kirkland, Joseph & Marianne Guerard, widow of Benjamin Guerard,
    10 March 1795; Henry Kennan, trustee; James Mathews, Martha
    Stewart, wit. Mar Set 2: 432-435

Kirkland, Joseph & Maryanne Guerard, widow, 12 March 1795.
    St. Phil PR

Kissick, Francis & Miss Margret Campbell, 7 March 1797.   Trin
    Meth Ch

Kitchen, Charles & Eugenia Megrew [1740's].   Hist Oburg

Kitchin, John & Barbara Pfund, widow [1740's].   Hist Oburg

Kleim, Martin, widower, taylor, & Anna Christiana Goette, widow,
    from Combohee, 24 Dec. 1786. St. John Luth Ch

Kline, Martin & Elizabeth Herron, 6 Sept. 1798.   Circ Cong

Knapp, Timothy, of Beaufort & Margaret Burke, widow of Raymond
    Burke, physician, decd., 23 Dec. 1789; Daniel Stevens,
    trustee; Belcher Noyes, Richd Wall, wit.   Mar Set 1: 458-459

Knauff (Knauss?), Conrad, from Homburg in Hesse-Darmstadt, &

Anna Maria, daughter of Johannes Barth, 7 Jan. 1783. St. John Luth Ch

Knapp, Timothy & Margaret Burke, widow, 25 Dec. 1789. St. Hel PR

Kneeshaw, Jno. & Elizth. Sutcliffe, 18 Feb. 1783. St. Phil PR

Knight, John & Sarah Gascoign, 31 Oct. 1771. St. Phil PR

Knignt, John & Rachel Anderson, 6 Jan. 1774. Pugh diary

Knight, Samuel & Ann Ginnis, widow, 8 Feb. 1778. St. Phil PR

Knight, William & Elizabeth Grandon, 15 Oct. 1768. St. Phil PR

Knobel, George Frederick & Elizabeth Fichter, both lately come into this Township from Germany, 25 March 1753. Hist Oburg

Knox, Archibald & Elizabh. Croft, per Licence, 15 June 1745. St. Phil PR

Knox, Thomas, mariner & Mary Tech(?), widow, 2 Nov. 1783. St. John Luth Ch

Knox, Thomas & Sarah Tucker, 16 March 1786. St. John Luth Ch

Koelle, Johannes, baker & Maria, daughter of Jacob Woerner, planter, 23 Jan. 1774. St. John Luth Ch

Kolb, Benja. & Elizabeth Murfee, 12 June 1771. Pugh diary

Kolb, Jehu & ___, 22 March 1787. Pugh diary

Kölle, Johann, baker, from Wirttemberg Cloister Blaubeuren & Maria Elisabetha Kitbim(?), from K___ in Electoral Palatinate, 11 Feb. 1770. St. John Luth Ch

Koller, Benedict, & Magdalina Springin, daughter of Johannes Springin, 1 Jan. 1740; Jacob Pier, Hans Fridig, & Jacob Kuhn, wit. Hist Oburg

Kolp, Tinman and Beersheba Watkins, widow, 19 Dec. 1738. Pr Fred PR

Koonen, Francis & Ann Maria Hagin, 1 Sept. 1748. Hist Oburg

Koonen, Jacob & Catharina Negely, 1 Sept. 1748. Hist Oburg

Kooner, Jacob Senr. & Anna, widow of Martin Tshudy, both of Orangeburg Township, 21 July 1752. Hist Oburg

Koonen, Martin & Mary Joyner, 24 Feb. 1746/7. Hist Oburg

Kooner, Martin & Mary Joyner, 24 Feb. 1746/7; Nathan Joiner, Ja's Cars, Francis Kooner, wit. Hist Oburg

Kornelius, Reinhard & Veronica Silberling(in), widow, 22 Apr. 1765. St. John Luth Ch

Kramer, Josuah, from New England a tobacco merchant(?), & Susannah Reinhardt(in), 2 Apr. 1782. St. John Luth Ch

Kranick, John Valentin & Anna Mary Heckler, all of Orangeburg
Township, ___ 1753. Hist Oburg

Krauss, Conrad & ___, 27 March 1771. St. John Luth Ch

Kreatner, Friderich, canditor, & Catharina Wirtz(in), 19 Apr.
1768. St. John Luth Ch

Kreiger, Charles Frederick, Doctor of Physick, of Charleston &
Martha Kirk, daughter of John Kirk, 31 March 1789; John Kirk,
Nicholas Hane, trustees; Lewis Popenhim, John Troup, John
Ballentine, wit. Mar Set 1: 420-421

Kreitner, Frederick of Charlestown & Barbra Eohner, of same,
3 Sept. 1774; Dr. John Swint, of same, trustee; John Kesson,
wit. Misc. Rec. SS: 17-19

Kreitner, Frederick, widower, & Mrs. Anna Barbara Boner, widow,
inhabitiants of Charles Town by Henry Muhlenburg, of St.
Michaels and Zion in Philadelphia, 6 Oct. 1774. St. John
Luth Ch

Kreuter, Joseph & Susannah Shuler [1740]. Hist Oburg

Kuhn, Casper & Anna Barbara Ernest, late wife of George Adam
Ernst, 28 June 1750. Hist Oburg

Kurner, George Jacob & Ann Catharine Larrywecht, widow, both
lately arrived from Germany in Orangeburg Township, 12 Apr.
1753. Hist Oburg

Kysell, Conrod & Hester Fulker, 24 Oct. 1769. St. Phil PR

LaCroix, William, of George Town, shopkeeper, & Sarah Burrows,
widow; 31 Jan. 1793; Archibald Taylor, trustee; James Madan,
F. Matthews, wit. Mar Set 2: 84-85

Labruce, Joseph of Parish of Prince George, Craven Co., &
Elizabeth Bremar, widow, 2 July 1744; license to Rev. Thomas
Hasel; James Bremar of St. Thomas, bondsman. MB Chas

Lacey, Samuel of Charles Town & Hannah Hogg, spinster, 14 Jan.
1743/4; license to Rev. Lewis Jones; David Brown, bondsman.
MB Chas

La Chapelle, James & Patience Hutchins, per Licence by Revd. Mr.
Garden, 26 April 1746. St. Phil PR

Lackalair, James (free Coulored man) & Catne Sheily (white woman),
3 Nov. 1793. Trin Meth Ch

Lacy, John & Anne Miller, P Licence, 2 April 1738. St. Phil PR

Lacy, John & Anne Lowe, P Licence, 7 Aug. 1739. St. Phil PR

Lacy, Samuel, widower, & Hannah Sealey, widow, 14 Mar. 1741.
St. Hel PR

Lacy, Samuel & Hannah Hogg, 2 Feb. 1743. St. Hel PR

Ladson, Abraham & Elizabeth Rose, 2 May 1771. St. And PR

Ladson, Benjamin & Elizabeth Perry, 19 March 1749. St. Hel PR

Ladson, Francis of the Parish of St. Andrews, planter & Margaret
   Musgrove of same, 25 June 1743; Richard Fuller, planter, of
   same & Robert McKewn of Colleton Co., trustees, Wille;
   Power, Tho Fuller, wit. Misc Rec. EE: 355-365

Ladson, Frances Junr., & Elizabeth Manning, 22 Dec. 1744.
   St. And PR

Ladson, Frances Snr. & Margaret Musgrove, widow, 28 June 1743.
   St. And PR

Ladson, Isaac & Rachel-Ladson Perry, 20 May 1742.   St. And PR

Ladson, Jacob & Elizabeth Perry, 18 Feb. 1719/20. St. And PR

Ladson, James & Judith Smith, 1 Oct. 1778. St. Phil PR

Ladson, Capt. James of Charlestown & Judith Smith, spinster,
   daughter of the late Benjamin Smith, 30 Sept. 1778; Thomas
   Smith, Isaac Motte, William Smith, trustees; John F. Grimke,
   Wm. Heyward, wit.   Mar Set 1: 144-146

Ladson, John & Charlotte Bew, P Licence, 24 Feb. 1724/5.
   St. Phil PR

Ladson, John Cannaway & Mary Ussher Hughes, 24 Nov. 1789. St.
   Hel PR

Ladson, Joseph, widower, & Elizabeth Rivers, of St. Bartholomews
   Parish, 21 Oct. 1750.   Stoney Creek Pres Ch

Ladson, Joseph of St. Pauls Parish, Colleton County, planter &
   Mary Brozett of St. Bartholomews Parish, widow, 29 Sept. 1745;
   Rachel Stock, Rebecker Holman, wit.   Misc. Rec. FF: 426-427

Ladson, Robert & Martha Ladson, 10 Feb. 1742.   St. And PR

Ladson, Robt & Sabina Rose, 3 Aug. 1732.   St. And PR

Ladson, Robert the elder of Colleton Co., planter, & Elizabeth
   Miles of Horse Savannah, widow of Wm. Miles, 3 Sept. 1768;
   Andrew Leitch, trustee; Josiah Miles, Patrick Griffin, wit.
   Misc. Rec. OO: 149-152

Ladson, Samuel & Sarah Norton, 7 July 1746.   St. And PR

Ladson, Samuel & Sarah Fendling, 18 Nov. 1756. St. Phil PR

Ladson, Thomas of Parish of St. Pauls Colleton Co., & Elizabeth
   Miles, spinster, 14 Aug. 1744; license to Rev. William Orr;
   Robert Ladson, of Parish of St. Andrews, Berkley Co., bonds-
   man. MB Chas

Ladson, Thomas & Elizabeth Capers, 24 Feb. 1785. St. Hel PR

Ladson, Zaccheus & Sarah Battoon, 12 Jan. 1736 [1736/7]. St.
   And PR

Laffelle, Nicholas & Mary Oats, 17 Sept. 1775. St. Phil PR

Lafield, George & Hannah Garnes, 17 Sept. 1770. St. Phil PR

La Fountain, Lewis & Mary Galloway, widow, 26 Aug. 1733. St. And PR

Lagord, John of Charlestown, Surgeon & Elizabeth Blanchard, widow, of Stephen Blanchard, 19 March 1768; Andrew Delient, James Gullardeau, wit. Misc. Rec. NN: 245

Laier, Samuel & Dorothy Caen, P Licence, 4 March 1744/5. St. Phil PR

Laine, Daniel of Prince George Parish, Craven Co. & Judith Grier, widow, 23 June, 1774; Richard Singleton, James Grier, trustees; Jona. Laurence, Jonth. Stuges, wit. Misc Rec. RR: 384-390

Lake, Richard & Mary Houghton, widow, per Licence by the Revd. Mr. Robert Betham, 19 Aug. 1746. St. Phil PR

Lake, Thos. & ___, __ Dec. 1709. Reg Prov. 1711-15, p. 449(41)

Lamb, Gibs & Margareth Mansby, 18 Sept. 1781. St. John Luth Ch

Lamb, Edward Alexander & Mary Moncrieffe, 3 Oct. 1797. Circ Cong

Lamboll, Thomas & Margaret Edgar, 14 Apr. 1737. St. And PR

Lamboll, Thomas & Mary Detmar, P Licence, 31 Sept. 1742. St. Phil PR

Lamboll, Thomas & Elizabeth Pitts, P Licence, 29 Nov. 1744. St. Phil PR

Lambson, Thomas & Martha Stone, P Licence by Mr. Garden, 22 May 1737. St. Phil PR

Lambton, Richard & Ann Walters Widow, P Licence by the Revd. Mr. Alexander Garden, Rector, 27 Nov. 1750. St. Phil PR

Lambwright, Beltshazzar & Mary Anne Smith, 14 Oct. 1736. St. And PR

Lammon, Robert & Barbara, widow of Jacob Brunzon, decd., both living upon Edistoe River, 28 May 1751. Hist Oburg

Lamons, Francis & _____ [1740's]. Hist Oburg

Lancaster, Joshua, carpenter, & Sibella Gray, of St. Bartholomew's Parish, Colleton County, 16 Aug. 1744; George Jackson of Jacksonburgh, Colleton County, trustee; Willm Guy Junr., Mumford Milner, wit. Misc. Rec. FF: 115-119

Lancaster, William & Elizabeth Currant, 17 Feb. 1726. St. Phil PR

Lance, Lambert & Mary St. John, widow, 2 June 1757. St. Phil PR

Lance, Lambert & Ann Magdelene Carne, 21 Feb. 1765. St. Phil PR

Landels, James, bachelor & Darmaris Murrall, spinster, in the house of Capt. Richard Withers, 23 Feb. 1780; Benjamin Webb, Sarah Piercey, wit. St. Jas PR

Lander, Francis & Elizabeth Simpson, 16 Oct. 1757.   St. Phil PR

Lane, James of Parish of Prince Frederick, & Ursula ___ (already married), 19 Jan. 1758, married after 29 Dec. 1756. Misc. Rec. KK: 550-551

Lane, James and Ursula Henning, 3 Feb. 1757.   Pr Fred PR

Lane, Peter and Sarah Johnston, 24 Feb. 1736.   Pr Fred PR

Lane, Samuel & Charity Cotten, 6 Sept. 1798.   Circ Cong

Lane, Willm. & Miss Elizth Stephenson, 5 March 1796.   Trin Meth Ch

Lang, William & Susannah Crawford, widow, 21 June 1787. St. Phil PR

Langley, Thomas & Mary Mitchell, P Licence by Mr. Garden, 13 May 1725.   St. Phil PR

Langly, George & Margaret Stirling, 4 Dec. 1754. Stoney Creek Pres Ch

Lankester, Joshua of Parish of St. Bartholomews & Sibella Gray, spinster, 16 Aug. 1744; license to Rev. William Guy; George Jackson, bondsman. MB Chas

Lankestir, Josheua & Sibella Grey, widow, 16 Aug. 1744. St. And PR

Larey, Peter & Elizabeth James, per Licence by Mr. Garden, 14 April 1746. St. Phil PR

Larkin, Francis & Martha Card, 11 Dec. 1727. St. Phil PR

Larkin, Samuel & Sarah Gray, 4 Jan.1762. St. Phil PR

La Roch, James & Christian Woodrow, 2 Apr. 1712.   SPG

Laroche, John & Mary Horrey, 28 Aug. 1714. T & D PR

Larod, John & Mary Warrant, 17 Nov. 1761.   St. Phil PR

Larry, Michael & Regula Koch [1740's]. Hist Oburg

Latham, Joseph & Martha Rolaine, 8 Feb. 1794.   Circ Cong

Laurens, Henry & Eleanor Ball, P Licence, 25 June 1750. St. Phil PR

Laurens, Henry Junr. & Eliza Rutledge, 26 May 1792. St. Phil PR

Laurens, James, batchelor & Hanah Rivers, widow, P Licence, of His Excelcy, the Governor by the Reverend Mr. Alexr. Garden, 30 Jan. 1724/5.   St. Phil PR

Laurens, James & Mary Broughton, P Licence by the Revd. Mr. Levi Durand of St. Johns Berkley County, 10 March 1752. St. Phil PR

Laurens, John & Elizabeth Wicking, P Licence, 3 July 1742. St. Phil PR

Laurens, Peter & Lydia Laurens, P Licence, 1 March 1741.
St. Phil PR

Laverick, John & ___ Duff, 15 Nov. 1746.   Ch Ch PR

Lavis, William & Lavinia Dawson, 31 March 1728.   St. Hel PR

Law, Benjamin & Elizabeth Watson, 12 Aug. 1725.   Ch Ch PR

Law, Jno & Mrs. Eliza Russill, 25 Oct. 1711.   SPG

Law, Joseph & Sarah Henley, 17 Jan. 1754.   T & D PR

Law, Joseph & Mary Jones, 16 Feb. 1758.   St. Phil PR

Law, Richard & Mary Gill, 9 Jan. 1766.   St. Phil PR

Lawrimore, Andrew & Mary Mackdowel, P Licence, 9 April 1730.
St. Phil PR

Lawton, Winborn, planter, & Mary Mathewes, of Colleton Co.,
widow, of Anthony Mathewes, late of John's Island, St.
John's Parish, Colleton Co., 28 Feb. 1771; Robert Randal,
Daniel Holmes, trustees; Thomas Farr, Stephen Evans, wit.
Misc. Rec. OO: 523-525

Lawyer, Thomas & Martha Kirk, 29 Apr. 1778.   St. Phil PR

Layson, George Thos. & Mary Callibuff, 30 March 1730.   Ch Ch PR

Lea, Joseph & Isobel Sherriffe, 2 Apr. 1726.   St. Phil PR

Leacraft, John Esq. Sheriff, & Elizabeth Black, 24 Oct. 1784.
St. Hel PR

Leacroft, Vincent of St. Phillips Chas. Town, & Elizabeth
Righton, spinster, 13 Sept. 1744; license to Rev. Alexander
Garden; Joseph Redman, bondsman.   MB Chas

Leander, William & Marian Stewart, P Licence, 21 Feb. 1731.
St. Phil PR

Leay, John & Mary Blake, 14 Feb. 1711-2.   T & D PR

Leaycroft, Jeremiah & Anne Sterling, P Licence, 12 October 1740.
St. Phil PR

Leaycroft, Vincent & Elizabeth Righton, P Licence, 23 Sept. 1744.
St. Phil PR

Lebby, Nathaniel & Eliz. Howard, 4 March 1764.   St. Phil PR

LeBrasseur, Francis & Anne Splatt, P Licence, 31 Jan. 1730.
St. Phil PR

LeBruce, Joseph & Elizabeth Bremar, 3 July 1744.   T & D PR

Lee, George & Elizabeth Godfrey, 10 June 1741.   St. And PR

Lee, Nicholas of George Town district, Craven County, & Mary
Willcox, widow, of same, 21 Mar. 1777; John Tamplet, Richd.
Singleton, wit. Misc. Rec. SS: 103-104

Lee, Thomas & Jane Bee, widow, 20 July 1758.   St. Phil PR

Lee, William & Ann Theus, 26 Feb. 1769.   St. Phil PR

Lee, William & Mary Bennet, 18 Jan. 1798.   Circ Cong

Leeck, Samuel, carpenter, & Anna Egerter(in), 2 Apr. 1777.
St. John Luth Ch

Leecraft, John & Amelia Flower, 17 May 1752.   St. Hel PR

Leepard, Stephen & Martha Parsons, P Licence, 22 Dec. 1729.
St. Phil PR

Lees, Robert of Charleston, & Catharine Ecklin Grattan, spinster,
11 Apr. 1791; Daniel Grattan, trustee; Violetta Wyatt, James
Troup, wit.   Mar Set 1: 557-559

Lees, Robert & Kitty Ecklin Granttin, 14 Apr. 1791.   St. Phil
PR

Legare, Daniel & Elizabeth Redford, 1 Jan. 1753.   T & D PR

Legare, Isaac Junr. of Parish of Christ Church, bachelor, &
Martha White, spinster, at the house of Mr. John White, 3
Oct. 1782; Geo McDowell, Jno Buchanan, wit.   St. Jas PR

Legare, John of Christ Church Parish & Ann Blake, daughter of
Richard Blake Junr., late of St. James Santee & grand-
daughter of Richard Blake; Alexander Chovin, Alexander
Collins & Samuel Warren, trustees; 31 Dec. 1792.   Wit:
Joseph Legare Junr.   Mar Set 2: 56-61

Legare, Samuel & Eleanor Sarah Hoyland, 21 May 1776.   St. Phil
PR

Legare, Thomas & Eleanor Ioor, 22 Feb. 1737.   Circ Cong

Legare, Thomas & Mary Seabrook, widow, 26 Feb. 1756.   St. Phil
PR

Legare, Thos Jun. & Ann Eliza Berewic [Berwick], 16 Sept. 1793.
Circ Cong

Legay, Lewis Augustin, of Charleston, Esqr., & Rebecca Sawyer
Whippy, 8 Apr. 1796; Benjamin Seabrook & Thomas Banyard,
trustees; Margaret Jenkins, Mary Jenkins, wit.   Mar Set 2:
485-486

Legay, Louis Augustin & Rebecca Sawyer Wippey, 9 Apr. 1796.
Circ Cong

Legear, Petter & Elizabeth Hague, 16 Nov. 1760.   St. And PR

Leger, James of Parish of Prince Frederick, bachelor & Kesia
Stewart of Parish of Prince Frederick, spinster, 25 March
1779; Wm. Leger, Daniel Dupre, wit.   St. Jas PR

Leger, Peter & Mary Evans, P Licence, 31 Dec. 1730.   St. Phil
PR

Leger, Samuel & Mary Tucker, P Licence, 22 Apr. 1739.   St. Phil
PR

Legford, Adam & Margaretha Wandissen, from New York, 16 Dec.
1771.   St. John Luth Ch

Legg, Edward, of Parish of St. Andrews, & Mary Porter, daughter
of Thomas Porter, decd; 29 Apr. 1775; Elizabeth Porter of
St. George Parish, spinster, trustee; Maurice Lee, Mary Haly,
wit.   Mar Set 1: 71-75

Legg, Samuel & Mary Dewees, 29 June 1771.   St. Phil PR

Legge, Edward & Elizabeth Smith, 6 Jan. 1757.   St. Phil PR

Lehre, John & Mary Brown, widow, 14 Sept. 1758.   St. Phil PR

Lehre, William of Charleston, Physician & Ann Miller of same,
widow, 24 Dec. 1795; Thomas Lehre & Jacob Martin, trustees;
Andrew Norris, Laurence Ryan, wit. Mar Set 2: 502-506

Lehre, William of Charleston, physician & wife Ann, 7 May 1799;
Thomas Lehre Sr., Jacob Martin, trustees; William Parker,
Stephen Dueston, wit.   Mar Set 3: 372-383

Leigh, Benjamin & Mary McGruder, June 1799.   Moses Waddel

Leigh, Egerton, & Martha Bremar, 15 Jan. 1756.   St. Phil PR

Leigh, William, of Parish of Prince Frederick, bachelor, &
Esther Bernard, of Parish of Prince Frederick, widow, 27
Aug. 1778; George McDowell, Peter Lenud, wit. St. Jas PR

Lejeau, Francis & Mary Ashby, 14 Apr. 1726.   T & D PR

LaBruce, Joseph of the Parish of Allsaints, bachelor & Hannah
Allston, of Parish of Allsaints, spinster, at the house of
Mr. William Allston, 3 Feb. 1780; Frans. Allston, Wm. Allston,
Junr., wit.   St. Jas PR

Lemon, George & Esther Watts, 3 Apr. 1779.   St. Phil PR

Lemprier, Clement Capt. & Elizabeth Vanor, 5 Feb. 1744/5.
Ch Ch PR

Lemprier, Clement Capt. & Ann Wilks, 20 Dec. 1746. Ch Ch PR

Lennox, William of Charleston, merchant, & Judith Godin,
spinster, daughter of Benjamin Godin, decd., 12 Sept. 1761;
John Guerard, James Lennox, trustees, David Deas, James
Grindlay, wit.   Mar Set 1: 572-576

LeNud, Henry of the Parish of Prince George, bachelor, &
Elizabeth Croft, of Parish of Prince George, widow, at the
plantation of Elizabeth Croft, 13 June 1782; Peter Guerry,
Anthony Bonneau, wit.   St. Jas PR

LeNud, Peter of Parish of Prince Frederick, bachelor & Lydia
Jaudon, of Parish of Prince Frederick, spinster, at the house
of Mr. Wm. Leigh, 9, Jan. 1783; Geo M'dowell, Thomas Leigh,
wit.   St. Jas PR

Leonard, George & Susannah Benet, 30 Nov. 1761.   St. Phil PR

Leperre, Wm. & Eliza Henderson, P Licence, 8 Aug. 1735.
St. Phil PR

Lepper, John & Elizabeth Painter, P Licence, April 1734.
St. Phil PR

Lequeux, Sims, of St. Stephens Parish & Harriott Walter of same, daughter of Richard & Harriot Walter; 21 Nov. 1793; John Glaze of Charleston, trustee; Peter Gaillard, Richd Chs Walter, wit. Mar Set 2: 197-200

Lequieu, Peter & Amelia Capers, widow, 3 July 1763. Ch Ch PR

Leroux, John & Elizabeth Vanall, 26 June 1757. T & D PR

Lesesne, Daniel & Mary Simons, 22 Jan. 1756. T & D PR

Lesesne, Isaac & Frances Netherton, 30 Aug. 1722. T & D PR

Lesine, Casper, linen weaver, & Ester Stewert, widow, from St. Bartholomew's Parish, living in Round O, 5 March 1787. St. John Luth Ch

Leslie, Charles & Nancie Elmes, widow, 14 Jan. 1733/4. St. And PR

Lessesne, James & Sarah Walker, P Licence, 21 Dec. 1742. St. Phil PR

Lessesne, John & Mary Frederick, 2 July 1778. St. Phil PR

Lestarjette, Lewis & Elizabeth Burnham Elliott, 9 Sept. 1773. St. Phil PR

Leutz, Bernhard, taylor, & the spinster Maria Götzinger(in), 16 March 1783. St. John Luth Ch

Levi, Isaac & Elizabeth Robertson, 16 July 1783. St. John Luth Ch

Levi, Joseph & Mary Groom, 8 July 1784. St. John Luth Ch

Levins, John & Elizabeth Thornton, P Bans by Mr. Garden, 2 July 1725. St. Phil PR

Levy, Lyon & Leah Tobias, 26 July 1790; Joseph Tobias Senior, & Isaac son of sd. Joseph, trustees; Isaac Delyon, Isaac DaCosta, wit. Mar Set 1: 518-520

Lewes, Stephen C. Rev. & Mary Green, 27 Feb. 1785. St. Hel PR

Lewis, Abel & Sarah Baker, 6 June 1773. Pugh diary

Lewis, Charles & Eliz'th Mary Horrey, 8 Aug. 1713. T & D PR

Lewis, Charles, bachelor & Mary Jones, spinster, 5 Aug. 1785; Francis Jones, Samuel Warren, wit. St. Jas PR

Lewis, Daniel, of Parish of St. Johns, bachelor & Hannah Lewis, spinster, 29 June 1783; Daniel M'Gregor, Samuel Warren, wit. St. Jas PR

Lewis, Elias, bachelor & Mary Logan, widow, 29 July 1761; J. Lewis, Martha Dumay, wit. St. Jas PR

Lewis, Gershon of Parish of Prince George Winyah, & Mary Avant, widow, 3 July 1744; license to Rev. John Fordyce; Peter Sanders of Charles Town, bondsman. MB Chas

Lewis, Henry of Charleston & wife Elizabeth, 20 July 1798; William Lewis, Robert Byers, trustees; Daniel McGivering, Charles H. Deveaux, wit. Mar Set 3: 285

Lewis, James & Jane Atkins, P Licence, 24 Sept. 1732. St. Phil PR

Lewis, James & Hannah Brownluff, 29 July 1746. T & D PR

Lewis, James & Esther, widow of John Jones, late of Amelia Township, 5 Sept. 1751. Hist Oburg

Lewis, James & Jeney Chambless, 18 May 1797. Pugh diary

Lewis, John & Judith Lee Roche, P Licence, 17 Apr. 1729. St. Phil PR

Lewis, John & Sarah Linter, P Licence, 13 May 1749. St. Phil PR

Lewis, John & Mary Gannaway, widow, 2 Sept. 1758. St. Phil PR

Lewis, John & Elizabeth Crooke, 23 Sept. 1784. St. John Luth Ch

Lewis, Joseph & Sarah You, 15 Dec. 1795. Circ Cong

Lewis, Maurice & Jane Hill, P Licence by Mr. Garden, 3 May 1736. St. Phil PR

Lewis, Robert & Susannah Dubusk, 8 Dec. 1746. Pr Fred PR

Lewis, Thomas, & Rachel Cook, 28 Feb. 1793. Bush R QM

Lewis, William, bachelor & Ann Murrell, spinster, in the house of Thomas Pacy, 14 May 1767; Jas Halsey, S. Lewis, wit. St. Jas PR

Leysath, John William & Ursula Giessendanner, 3 Oct. 1752. Hist Oburg

Liblong, Henry & Miss Sarah Miller, 19 Oct. 1799. Trin Meth Ch

Lide, Hugh & Elizabeth Pugh, 12 May 1796. Pugh diary

Lide, James & Jane Holloway, 22 Aug. 1793. Pugh diary

Lide, Robert & Mary Holloway, 24 June 1790. Pugh diary

Liens, Isaac & Martha Taylor, spinster, per Licence by the Revd. Mr. Robt. Betham, 13 Oct. 1746. St. Phil PR

Lightburn, Francis of Charleston & Sarah Long, daughter of William Long decd. (already married,) 17 Jan. 1799; Simeon Theus, trustee; Wm. Lee Jr., Stephen Lee Jr., wit. Mar Set 3: 335-338

Lightwood, Edward & Ann Fishburn, P Licence by the Revd. Mr. Alexr. Garden, 1 May 1748. St. Phil PR

Lightwood, Edward of Charlestown & Elizabeth Peronneau, of same, spinster, 28 Dec. 1769; William Wells, trustee; Thos Young, Jacob Axson, William Axson Junr. Misc. Rec. SS: 448-451

Lillibridge, Hampton of the Province of North Carolina, but now of Charles Town & Theodora Ash, of Charles Town, spinster, 12 Nov. 1774; John Ash, Henry Burden, trustees; Joseph Dill, John Jones, Edward Fitzgerald, wit.   Misc. Rec. RR: 220-223

Lindauer, Georg Heinrich, baker & Maria Mayer(in), 10 July 1766. St. John Luth Ch

Linder, Daniel & Sarah Hill of Berkeley County, 14 March 1754. Hist Oburg

Lindfors, Charles Jacob & Ann Martin, widow, 3 Oct. 1773. St. Phil PR

Lindsay, Barnard & Mary Pendervais, 27 Jan. 1787.   St. Phil PR

Lindsay, Thomas & Elizabeth Tipper, 7 May 1734.   Circ Cong

Lines, Morgan, of the State of Georgia, Gent., & Esther Randolph of St. John's Parish, Berkley, widow; 8 May 1794; Paul Marion, planter, trustee; Susa. Brown, Ann Pottifear, Eliz. Linerox, wit. Mar Set 2: 105-106

Lining, John Dr. & Sarah Hill, 28 June 1739.   St. And PR

Lining, Thomas, cabinet-maker, of Chas Town & Ann Ware, P Licence, 1 March 1753.   St. Phil PR

Linkly, Christopher & Mary Holman, 31 July 1735. St. And PR

Linn, Thomas & Agnew Bower, 7 May 1757.   St. Phil PR

Linning, John & Mary Rivers, 23 May 1771.   St. And PR

Linter, Richard & Sarah Williams, P Banns by the Revd. Mr. Alexr. Garden, 29 Dec. 1747.   St. Phil PR

Linthwaite, Thomas & Ann Withers, 31 Mar. 1754.   St. Phil PR

Liston, Robert & Mary Toomer, 1 May 1756.   St. Phil PR

Littell, Aaron of Parish of St. Thomas, bachelor, & Elizabeth Jennens, of Parish of St. Thomas, spinster, in the house of Mary Jennens, widow, 27 Nov. 1766; John Barnett, John Jennes, wit.   St. Jas PR

Little, James & Ann Gough, 29 Oct. 1763.   St. Phil PR

Little, Robert & Widow Hoggatt, 27 March 1746. Ch Ch PR

Litz, Barnard, & Mary Edon, 31 March 1754.   T & D PR

Livie, Alexander & Catherine Philip, spinster, by Licence by the Revd. Mr. Robt. Betham, 24 May 1746.   St. Phil PR

Livingston, Henry & Anne Harris, 2 Sept. 1726. St. Phil PR

Livingston, Henry & Anne Bell, widow, 11 Dec. 1733. Circ Cong

Livingston, William & Mary Fitch, 1 Feb. 1747.   T & D PR

Lloyd, John, widower, & Anne Parmenter, 8 Dec. 1733.   St. Hel PR

Lloyd, John & Henny Burt, 4 Apr. 1782.   St. Phil PR

Lloyd, John & Mary Trusler, 1 Jan. 1789.   St. Phil PR

Lloyd, John, Capt. & Rebecca Boone, P Licence, 23 Nov. 1752.
   St. Phil PR

Lloyd, Martin & Elizabeth Conolly, 24 Mar. 1771.   St. Phil PR

Lloyd, Thomas & Mary Mathews, P Licence by the Revd. Mr. Robt.
   Betham, 23 July 1746.   St. Phil PR

Llcyd, Thomas of Charles Town, Gent., & Mary, daughter of James
   Mathews, 23 March 1749; Anthony Mathews, trustee; Wm. Boone
   Junr., Charles Pryce, wit.   Misc. Rec. II: 83-86

Locher, Jakob & Katharine Krehner(in), 20 May 1766.   St. John
   Luth Ch

Lochon, Veireus, & Mary Poyas, widow, 14 Oct. 1756.   St. Phil PR

Locker, John & Mary Grege, 11 Oct. 1747.   Ch Ch PR

Lockton, Austin Robert & Margaret Strahan, P Licence, 24 Nov.
   1743.   St. Phil PR

Lockwood, Joshua & Mary Lee, 23 June 1757.   St. Phil PR

Lockwood, Joshua Junr. & Amarinthea Lowndes Lockwood, 9 Feb.
   1792.   Circ Cong

Lodge, John & Hannah Doorne, 10 Feb. 1778.   T & D PR

Logan, George Col. of Berkly Co., & Martha Daniell Senr., widow,
   of Robert Daniel, late Deputy Govr. of S.C., 28 May 1719;
   William Blakeway, trustee; Thos Hepworth, Hannah Wrath, wit.
   Sec Prov 1714-1719; 373-388

Logan, George & Martha Daniel Junr., 30 July 1719.   Ch Ch PR

Logan, George, of Christ Church Parish & Elizabeth Baker of
   this parish, 3 Feb. 17__ (1742/3?),   Pr Fred PR

Logan, George, carpenter, & Lydia Creighton, 22 Mar. 1798.
   St. Phil PR

Logan, John Esqr. & Catharine Postell; 12 Oct. 1795; William
   Fishburne, trustee; Cephas Prentiss, wit.   Mar Set 2: 484-485

Logan, Joseph, widower & Anne Dutart, spinster, in the house
   of John Dutart, 15 Jan. 1786; Daniel Sullivan, Daniel
   McGregor, wit.   St. Jas PR

Logan, Peter & Ann Langdon, P Licence, 30 Mar. 1749.   St. Phil
   PR

Logan, William & Margaret Crockatt, 21 June 1757.   St. Phil PR

Logan, William Esqr., & Mary Doughty Webb, daughter of John
   Webb, 26 Apr. 1798; Miss Martha Cannon, William Webb, Daniel
   Cannon Webb, trustees; Wm. Logan Junr., John Webb, William
   B. Baker, wit.   Mar Set 3: 271-276

Logan, William Junr. & Mary Doughty Webb, 26 Apr. 1798.
   St. Phil PR

Lomitt, Thomas & Martha Watkins, P Licence, 29 Jan. 1738. St.
   Phil PR

London, Robt. & Frances Moungin, P Licence, 29 Dec. 1744. St.
   Phil PR

Long, Edward & Fanny Werkham, 5 Feb. 1773. St. John Luth Ch

Long, Samuel & Elizabeth Dart, 30 June 1768.   St. Phil PR

Long, William & Elizabeth Kirkwood, 22 June 1777. St. Phil PR

Loocock, William & Henriette Harramond, 3 May 1764. St. Phil
   PR

Lord, Benjamin & Ann Mace, 24 June 1759. St. Phil PR

Lord, Richard & Maria Lord, 27 Dec. 1798.   St. Phil PR

Lormier, Lewis & Jane Marignac, daughter of Abraham Merignac,
   decd., ___ 1733(?). Misc. Rec. GG: 229-231

Lothrop, Seth & Sarah Weyman, 31 March 1785.   St. John Luth
   Ch

Loup, John & Martha Clayter, P Licence, 7 May 1745.   St. Phil
   PR

Love, John & Elizabeth Lloyd, 20 Dec. 1787.   St. Phil PR

Loveday, John & Sarah Butler, of Charleston, widow of Henry
   Butler, 1 Jan. 1788; George Hahnbaum, Practitioner of
   Physick, trustee; John Horlbeck, Elizabeth Horlbeck, wit.
   Mar Set 1: 358-365

Loveday, John & Sarah Butler, widow, 6 Jan. 1788.   St. Phil PR

Lovelace, Thomas & Susanna Wood, P Licence by the Revd. Mr.
   Dyson, 10 Feb. 1726. St. Phil PR

Lovell, William & Elizabeth Mackay, widow, 22 Sept. 1757. St.
   Phil PR

Lovely, William (Grocer), & Margaret Cullen, 17 Oct. 1795.
   Trin Meth Ch

Lowcock, Joseph & Sarah Irish, widow, 27 Jan. 1758. St. Phil
   PR

Lowe, Thomas & Sarah Collins, P Licence, 9 Jan. 1744. St. Phil
   PR

Lowndes, Thomas of Charleston, & Sarah Bon Jon, of Christ Church
   Parish, daughter of Hon. Jacob Bond Jon, decd., 8 March 1798;
   John Bond Randell of St. James Santee, trustee; James Lowndes,
   William Lowndes, wit. Mar Set 3: 220-225

Lowndes, Thomas & Sarah Bond I'on, 8.March 1798.   St. Phil PR

Lownds, Rawlins & Amarintha Elliott, spinster, P Licence, by

the Revd. Mr. Alexr. Garden Rector, 15 Aug. 1748. St. Phil
PR

Lownds, Rawlins, Esqr., & Mary Cartwright, P Licence, 23 Dec.
1751. St. Phil PR

Lowrey, Robert & Ann Barr, 12 Apr. 1770. St. Phil PR

Lowrey, Uzzel & Wenifred Edmons, 17 Feb. 1772. Pugh diary

Lowther, Charles & ___, 10 Aug. 1769. Pugh diary

Loyd, Abraham & Mary Diana, 11 July 1790. (free mulattoes).
St. Hel PR

Loyd, Caleb & Esther Boon, 22 Apr. 1762. St. Phil PR

Loyer, Adrian of Charles Town & Catherine Dalbrae, widow, 6
Apr. 1744; license to Rev. Alex. Garden; Lewis Lorimer,
bondsman. MB Chas

Loyer, Adrian & Catherine Dalbiac, widow, per licence endorsed
by the Revd. Mr. Alexr. Garden to Henry Chiffelle French
Minister, 24 April 1744. St. Phil PR

Loyer, Adrian, Gent., & Katherine Dalbiac, widow, 24 Apr. 1744;
Jacob Martin, Chirugeon, trustee; Edward Fowler, Thomas
Lamboll, wit. Misc. Rec. GG: 40-45

Lucas, Jno & Mary Wilds, 25 May 1775. Pugh diary

Ludlam, the Revd. Richard & Anne Carter, 5 Apr. 1728. St. Phil
PR

Lluellin, Samuel & Sarah Crosskeys, 10 Oct. 1725. St. Phil PR

Lullams, David & Patience Palmer, P Licence, 22 Jan. 1730.
St. Phil PR

Lupton, William & Alice North, per Licence, 2 March 1744.
St. Phil PR

Luscombe, Geo. Cap. & Elizth. Waggoner, 12 May 1798. Trin Meth
Ch

Lusk, James & Hannah Williamson, P Licence by Mr. Garden, 13
Feb. 1735. St. Phil PR

Luter, William & Elizabeth Holworth, P Licence, 2 Apr. 1738.
St. Phil PR

Luyten, William & Maryan Collins, 29 May 1764. T & D PR

Lyford, William and Anne Watt, spinster; minister Lewis Jones;
bondsmen William Lyford, mariner and Jeremiah Milner of
Charles Town vintner; wit. James Michie, 23 May 1733. MB NY

Lyford, William, Capt., widower, & Ann Watt, 6 Jan. 1733. St.
Hel PR

Lyford, William Junr. & Martha Cattell, both of this parish,
29 May 1745. Stoney Creek Pres Ch

Lynch, Thomas Junior & Elizabeth Shubrick, 14 May 1772. St. Phil
PR

Lyon, John & Elizabeth Embleton, 2 Jan. 1772. St. Phil PR

Lyon, Mordecai of Camden Dist., Storekeeper, & Judith Cohen,
    widow, 26 Feb. 1790; Moses Levy, storekeeper, of Charleston
    trustee; E. Abrams, Samuel Myers, wit. Mar Set 1: 525-527

Lyons, Joseph & Barbara Gartman, widow, 31 Dec. 1741, in Amelia
    Township; Benjamin Carter, wit. Hist Oburg

Lyons, Joseph & Susannah Grim, widow, 1 Jan. 1740. Hist Oburg

Lyttlejohn, Duncan, of Charleston, merchant, & Ann Kennedy of
    Edisto Island, widow, ___ March 1787; Ephraim Mikell, Bailey
    Clark, wit. Mar Set 1: 297-300

McAlister, John & Ann Keith, 23 Aug. 1789. St. Phil PR

McBeth, James of Charleston, merchant, & Katharine Johnston,
    eldest daughter of Charles Johnston, 23 Apr. 1798; Robert
    McKenzie Johnston, trustee; Wm. Robertson, wit. Mar Set 3:
    250-252

McCall, Charles & ___, 27 Dec. 1798. Pugh diary

McCall, George & Elizath. Sanders, 10 Nov. 1796. Pugh diary

McCall, Hext of Charleston, attorney at law & Miss Elizabeth
    Pickering, daughter of Joseph Pickering Esqr., decd., 15
    Oct. 1783; William Washington, John Splatt Cripps, Trustees;
    John Massey, Charles Brown, wit. Mar Set 1:168-170

McCall, James & Ann Amelia Dart, 5 May 1777. St. Phil PR

McCall, John Jr. & Ann Lesesne, 3 Apr. 1777. St. Phil PR

McCall, Jno & Mary Dewett, 2 May 1773. Pugh diary

McCants, James & Agnes Donnald, widow, 18 Jan. 1770. St. Phil
    PR

McCants, William, planter, & Martha Sulivant, both of St.
    Bartholomews Parish, 24 June 1799; James Price, trustee;
    Elenor Scott, Henry Johnson, sit. Mar Set 3: 367-368

McCarthy, Garman & Jane Collins, widow, 24 Nov. 1791. St. Phil
    PR

McCarthy, Thomas & Mary Webb, widow, 26 Jan. 1758. St. Phil PR

McCarty, Thomas & Jane Budge, 9 Aug. 1779. St. Phil PR

McCay, Joseph Ringland & Frances Bacot, 9 May 1798. St. Phil PR

McCee, ___ & Mrs. Zealy, 20 March 1795. Trin Meth Ch

M'Clelland, Archibald, bachelor & Esther Des Champes, spinster,
    in the house of Francis Des Champes Senr., 3 July 1759;
    Francs. Des Champes Sr., Paul Jaudon, wit. St. Jas PR

McClenachen, James & Eleanor Beckworth, widow, 1 July 1759.
    St. Phil PR

McClencher, Alexander of the Parish of Prince George, bachelor, & Mary Falks, of Parish of Prince George, widow, at Clement Brown's ferry, 10 Jan. 1782; no wit. St. Jas PR

McCluer, John & Mary Davies, 21 Apr. 1767. St. Phil PR

McComb, James Junr. & Mary Stoll, 10 June 1788. St. Phil PR

McConnell, Thomas & Mary Blakeley, 6 Apr. 1774. St. Phil PR

McCord, John of Saxa-Gotha & Sophinisba Russell, of Amelia Township, at the house of Mrs. Mary Russell, 5 Feb. 1751. Hist Oburg

M'Cormick, Nathaniel of Parish of Prince Frederick, widower, & Mary Spencer, spinster, married in the house of James Anderson, 28 Dec. 1758; Michael Cockran, Rebecca Sullivan, wit. St. Jas PR

McCormick, Samuel, practitioner of Physick, & Mary McCullough, widow of John McCullough, of St. Johns Parish, 19 Aug. 1786; Peter Fayssoux, Zachariah Villepontoux, trustees; Keatg. Simons, George Tunno, wit. Mar Set 1: 255-258

McCormick, Samuel & Dorothy Walter, widow of Thomas Walter of Parish of St. Johns, 27 May 1790; Thomas Cooper, of St. Stephens, trustee; George Mathewes, ONeal Gough Stevens, wit. Mar Set 1: 508-509

Macracken, Arthur & Ann McGee, widow, 28 July 1799. St. Phil PR

McCrady, Robert of Jacksonborough, merchant, & Ann Riley of same, 8 Dec. 1796; Martha Riley, Johnson Hagood, trustees; Thos Gordon, John Chrisr. Smith, wit. Mar Set 3: 16-19

McCray, Alexander & Susannah Fitig, 27 March 1777. St. Phil PR

McCrea, Thomas & Mary Wells, widow, 3 Sept. 1777. St. Phil PR

McCready, John of Charleston, attorney at Law, & Jane Johnson, 2 March 1797. St. Phil PR

McCullough, Andrew & Elizth. Collier, 15 Aug. 1759. St. Phil PR

McCullough, Hugh & Jane McKnight, 1 Jan. 1773. St. Phil PR

McCullough, John & Mary McKenzie, 18 Oct. 1764. St. Phil PR

McCullough, John of St. Johns Parish, & Mary Stocker, spinster, 11 Sept. 1783; Zachariah Villepontoux, of St. Johns Berkley, trustee; M. Simons, Keating Simons, wit. Mar Set 1: 98-101

McCune, James & Mary Goold, P Licence of Govr Johnson, 14 May 1720. St. Phil PR

McDaniel, Daniel & Mary Lewis, 4 June 1723. T & D PR

McDaniel, Daniel & Sarah Evans, 13 Aug. 1742. Pr Fred PR

McDaniel, John & Magdalen Lenud, 25 Apr. 1749. Pr Fred PR

Mcdonald, Adam & Anne Wood, P Licence, 23 Nov. 1743. St. Phil PR

McDonald, Adam & Izabellah Fitch, 15 Oct. 1762. St. And PR

McDonald, Charles & Mary Burn, 15 Oct. 1778. St. John Luth Ch

McDonald, William, son of Thomas decd., and Jemima Parkins, 9 Nov. 1780. Bush R QM

McDonnald, Joseph, son of Mary & Elizabeth Parkins, 11 March 1779. Bush R QM

McDonold, Alexander & Elizabeth McNaught, 23 Oct. 1763. St. Phil PR

McDougall, Duncan & Mary Morgan, 14 July 1793. St. Phil PR

McDowell, Archibald & Sarah Hamlin, 23 Dec. 1750. Ch Ch PR

McDowell, John & Martha Hamlin, 25 March 1750. Ch Ch PR

McEnzie, Daniel & Mary Strouber, 7 July 1755. Stoney Creek Pres Ch

McEwen, John & Jannett McGregere, 2 March 1752. Stoney Creek Pres Ch

McFarlane, Robert of Little River, gent., & Sarah Starrat, widow, of Thomas Starrat, 13 March 1790; Francis G. Deliesseline, trustee; Lewis DuPre, Saml. J. Thurston, George Starrat, wit. Mar Set 1: 480-481

McGaver, Donald & D. Smith, 9 May 1782. St. Phil PR

MaGaw, James & Ann Brown, 15 May 1740. Ch Ch PR

McGaw, James & Cartwright Ireland, 11 Feb. 1754. St. Phil PR

Macgie, William & Rebekah Fell, P Licence, 20 Feb. 1731. St. Phil PR

McGill, Samuel & Elizabeth Gambell, 2 Oct. 1767. St. Phil PR

McGill, William of Georgetown, & Ann Britton, spinster, 12 May 1790; George Skinner of Peedee, planter, trustee; Alexander Campbell, John McGinney, wit. Mar Set 1: 481-485

McGilveray, Alexander & Elizabeth Patchabel, P Licence, 4 June 1750. St. Phil PR

McGilvery, Alexr. & Mary Laroche, P Licence, 12 Oct. 1749. St. Phil PR

McGilveray, Alexander & Elizabeth Chandler, 11 Mar. 1756. St. Phil PR

Macgilvery, John & Elizabeth Hassard, P Licence, 13 Dec. 1733. St. Phil PR

Mcgilvery, John & Elizabeth Hazzard, [no date]. St. Hel PR

McGinney, John of Dist. of Georgetown, merchant, & Sarah Bosher, spinster, 20 Oct. 1791; Alexander Colclough, trustee;

James McCauley, John Moore, James Richbourgh Senr., wit.
Mar Set 1: 604-606

McGrath, James of Charleston, mariner & Jane Kennedy, widow,
8 Feb. 1798.   St. Phil PR

McGregor, Alexander of St. James Parish, & Dorothy Guerry of
St. Stephens Parish, widow, 17 Aug. 1786; John Guerry,
trustee; Theod Guerry, Daniel McGregor, wit.   Mar Set 1:
247-249

McGregor, Alexander, of Parish of St. James Santee, widower, &
Dorothy Guerry, of Parish of St. Stephen widow, 14 Sept. 1786;
A. C. Guerry, Samuel Warren, wit.   St. Jas PR

McGregor, Alexander & Margaret McElvin, 13 Feb. 1738.   [1738/9].
St. And PR

McGregor, Alexr. & Hannah Bestat, 29 July 1745.   St. Phil PR

M'Gregor, Daniel, bachelor, & Phebe Smith, spinster, in the
house of Jonah Collins, 25 March 1761 [sic, for 1762?];
Jonah Atchiscn, Stephen Sullivan, wit.   St. Jas PR

McGregor, Daniel, bachelor & Magdalen Jeanneret, spinster,
in the house of Jacob Jeanneret, Sr., 31 Jan. 1786; John
Deliesseline, Saml DuPre, wit.   St. Jas PR

McGregor, Daniel, widower, and Susannah Laurense, spinster, in
the house of Richard Withers, 25 Feb. 1768; James Bell,
Alexandr. McGregory, wit.   St. Jas PR

McGruder, Basil & Betsy Graves, 2 Dec. 1799.   Moses Waddel

McGuire, John of Ashepoo, & Mary McThie, 5 July 1787.   St. Phil
PR

McInry(?), Jno & ___, 4 June 1797.   Pugh diary

McIntire, Thomas & Cornelia Cohen, 19 Dec. 1799.   Circ Cong

Mackintosh, Alexr. & Elizabeth Smith, ___ Nov. 1765.   St. And
PR

McIntosh, Alexr. Capt. & Rachel Young, 21 May 1765.   Pugh diary

McIntosh, Lachlan & ___, 13 Sept. 1781.   pugh diary

McIntosh, Lachlin of St. Bartholomew's Parish, & Martha
Proctor, 29 Dec. 1789.   St. Hel PR

McKally, William & Jane Priesley, 14 Nov. 1745.   Ch Ch PR

McKants, James and Agnes Moneally, 1 July 1740.   Pr Fred PR

Mackartey, William & Anne Dennis, P Licence, 19 Dec. 1740.
St. Phil PR

Mackay, John & Elizabeth Hamilton, spinster, P Licence, by the
Revd. Mr. Robert Betham, 18 Dec. 1746.   St. Phil PR

Mackay, Lawrence & Deborah Honour, 19 Feb. 1722/23.   St. Phil PR

McKay, William & Elizth. Parsons, 11 March 1759. St. Phil PR

McKee, Archibald of Craven County, planter, & Mary Willson, widow of David Willson, 25 Apr. 1757; Robert Willson, Robert Witherspoon, trustees; Joseph Mickis, Mary Dick, wit. Misc. Rec. KK: 475-476

McKee, David & Hannah Furnival, 12 Apr. 1772. St. Hel PR

McKee, John & Margaret Johnson, 9 March 1784. St. Hel PR

McKee, John & Harriott Rivers, 1 Jan. 1793. St. Phil PR

McKee, Paull & Elizabeth G. Seyres, 9 Aug. 1792. St. Hel PR

McKee, Saml & Jane Stafford, 19 May 1792. Circ Cong

McKellar, James & Elizabeth Potts, of Georgetown, widow, 10 Apr. 1797; Charles Lesesne, of Georgetown, trustee; James Lesesne, Mary Esther Grant, wit. Mar Set 3: 73-78

McKelvey, John to Elisabeth Tomm, daughter of Alexander Tomm, deceased, 3 Oct. 1794. Chester Co. Ches Ct Min B

McKelvey, Robert of St. Johns Parish & Susanna Cahusac, of St. Stephens Parish, 15 March 1792; William Ransom Davis, of High Hills of Santee, trustee; Thos Couturier, wit. Mar Set 1: 634-635

McKenny, Michael & Margt. Grant, 22 Apr. 1759. St. Phil PR

McKenny, William & Agnes Blake, 1 Sept. 1759. St. Phil PR

McKenzie, Geo. & Mary Coker, 8 March 1766. OJ 1764-1771

Mackenzie, John, junr., & Elizabeth Green, spinster, P Licence by the Revd. Mr. Robert Betham, 2 May 1747. St. Phil PR

McKenzie, Kennedy & Ann Mylley, 5 Feb. 1782. St. Phil PR

M'Kenzie, Patri & Elizath. Connelly, 4 Oct. 1790. Circ Cong

McKewn, Archibald of the Cypress, & Jane Hurst of St. James Goose Creek, 10 Jan. 1794; Susanna E. McDonald of Charleston, trustee; Elizabeth Ross, Joseph McDonald, wit. Mar Set 2: 206-207

McKewn, Robert of Colleton Co., & Mary Bellinger, of same, widow, 14 May 1741; Thomas Elliot & David Crawford, planters, trustees; Mary Crawford, wit. Misc. Rec. EE: 8-14

McKintoch, Lachlin & Elizabeth Smith, 17 Oct. 1765. St. Phil PR

McKinzie, Alexander & Jean Chapman, 6 Dec. 1777. St. Phil PR

Mackinzie, John & Sarah Smith, 3 Apr. 1769. St. Phil PR

McKnilidge, Alexander & Margareth Field, 23 Sept. 1784. St. John Luth Ch

Mackoy, John & Elizabeth Lee, P Licence, 22 March 1739. St. Phil PR

McKrott, John Lewis & Frances Underwood, 7 June 1761. St. Phil
PR

McLane, John & Elizabeth Page, 28 Sept. 1748. St. Hel PR

Maclane, John & Mary Nichols, both of this parish. 18 July 1745.
Stoney Creek Pres Ch

McLane, John & Elizabeth Page, 28 Sept. 1748. St. Hel PR

McLaron, Thomas & Agnes McNab, 17 March 1764. St. Phil PR

McLaughlan, Hugh & Johanna Kelly, 7 Feb. 1756. St. Phil PR

McLaughlin, William of St. Bartholomews Parish, planter, &
Elizabeth Miles of same, spinster, 17 July 1777; Robert Miles
& Isaac McPherson, trustees; Elizth. Miles, Elizth. Bowman,
wit. Misc. Rec. SS: 474-477

Macleod, Donald, of Edisto Island, Gent., & Elizabeth Bailey
Seabrook, widow, 5 Sept. 1795; Jas Murray, Wm. Seabrook,
trustees; Wm. Blackstock, George Buist, wit. Mar Set 2:
428-432

McLoud, John & Margaret Johnson, 28 June 1727. St. Hel PR

McMahan, Arthur & Eleanor Grimes, 19 Jan. 1775. St. Phil PR

McMuldrow, Hugh & Jane McDowel, 12 Jan. 1775. Pugh diary

McMurdy, Robert of Parish of St. Pauls & Elizabeth Shepperd,
widow, 1 May 1744; license to Rev. Thomas Thompson; William
Glen of Charles Town, bondsman. MB Chas

McNally, Edward to Elizabeth Huestess, 17 Jan. 1794, Rev.
Joshua Lewis, Marlboro Co.

Macnamara, Michael & Christian Arthur, 29 Nov. 1726. T & D PR

McNeill, John, late of Larne, County Antrim, Ireland, now
of South Carolina, & Martha Griffith of Prince Williams
Parish, widow of Edward Griffith, 4 July 1783; William Smith
of said parish, trustee; Jas Bradford, Sophia Miles, wit.
Misc. Rec. VV: 23-26

McNilage, Alexander of Christ Church Parish, & Margaret Fields,
20 Sept. 1784; John Barnet Esqr., John Fields, trustees;
Robt. Bruce, William Fraser, wit. Mar Set 1: 529-530

McNish, Henry of St. Peters Parish, Beaufort Dist., & Jane
Dupree Dupont of St. Luke's Parish, same Dist., 8 Feb. 1798;
Thomas Coachman, trustee; Jane Mary Coachman, Mary Eliza
Patridge, Peter Colleton, wit. Mar Set 6: 67-69

McNish, John & Ann Black, 18 May 1765. St. Phil PR

McPherson, Alexander & Sarah Bray, P Licence, 4 Jan. 1731.
St. Phil PR

McPherson, Alexander & Jane Nichols, widow, 24 Sept. 1738.
St. Hel PR

McPherson, James and Elizabeth Brown, 11 Feb. 1740/1. Pr Fred
PR

McPherson, James of Parish of Prince Frederick, bachelor, & Lydia Jean Glen of Parish of Prince Frederick, spinster, at the plantation of Dr. James Crokatt, 10 Jan. 1772; Elias McPherson, John Futhey, wit. St. Jas PR

McQueen, Alexander & Elizabeth Fuller, 14 Jan. 1774. St. And PR

McQueen, Robert & Eleanor Crawley, 18 March 1789. St. Phil PR

Macquoid, Samuel & Abigail Goble, P Licence, 9 Sept. 1740. St. Phil PR

McTueros, John & Mary Anne Sherman, widow, 26 July 1786. St. Hel PR

McTyre, Holland & Sarah Sinqfield, 1796. Moses Waddel

McWhanach, John & Mary Barns, widow, 10 Jan. 1786. St. John Luth Ch

McWhann, William of Charleston, & Jane Thomson, widow, 2 Oct. 1786; John Smith, merchant, trustee; James Madan, William Monies, wit. Mar Set 1: 274-277

Ma___, Alexander & Maria Margaretha ___, widow, 28 Feb. 1771. St. John Luth Ch

Macho, Bernard & Arabella Allen, 12 May 1785. St. Hel PR

Mack, John & Sarah Brickles, P Licence, 4 June 1740. St. Phil PR

Mackall, John & Martha Hext, P Licence, 22 April 1739. St. Phil PR

Mackelish, Thomas & Mary Colfin, 27 Jan. 1763. St. Phil PR

Mackenzie, William & Sarah Founds, 16 Jan. 1723. St. Phil PR

Mackgirt, James & Priscilla Davison, P Licence, 12 Oct. 1732. St. Phil PR

Mackrodd, Henry Christian & Susannah Maria Durousseau, P Licence, 24 Nov. 1737. St. Phil PR

Maduz, Fridrich, butcher, & Elisabetha Dickson, 1 Aug. 1777. St. John Luth Ch

Mahler, Rev. & the late Captain Eulert's widow, 21 June 1786. St. John Luth Ch

Mallery, Joseph & Mary Russel, 20 Feb. 1771. St. Phil PR

Mallery, Seamour & Mary Scrogins, 7 Aug. 1737. St. Phil PR

Man, John of this Parish Chirurgeon &c & Susannah Laroche of Prince George Parish, 7 Apr. 1743. Pr Fred PR

Man, John & Anne Vincent, 16 Nov. 1732. St. And PR

Man, John & Martha Fairchild, widow, 9 Feb. 1748. St. And PR

Man, John-Vincent & Anne Westbury, 31 May 1770. St. And PR

Mandervill, John & Mary Winter, 19 June 1733. St. Hel PR

Mandevill, Cornelius & ____, 13 Sept. 1792. Pugh diary

Manigault, Gabriel & Ann Ashby, 29 Apr. 1730. T & D PR

Manigault, Gabriel & Margaret Izard, daughter of Ralph Izard, of St. James Goose Creek, 30 Apr. 1785; Cleland Kinloch, Thos Middleton, wit. Mar Set 1: 263-272

Manigault, Peter & Elizabeth Wragg, 8 June 1755. St. Phil PR

Mann, Henry & Margaret Carpenter, widow, 22 Jan. 1770. St. Phil PR

Manning, William & Jane Blunt, P Licence, March 1733. St. Phil PR

Manson, George, of Charleston, ship carpenter, & Sarah Milligan, widow, 28 Jan. 1797. St. Phil PR

Marbeust, Joseph & Elizabeth Alston, 6 Apr. 1721. T & D PR

Marckhard, Johannes, & Christian Barbara Betz(in), 22 May 1781. St. John Luth Ch

Marckow, Christian & Sara Bollen, 29 Oct. 1786. St. John Luth Ch

Marcon, Peter & Mary Voloux, P Licence, 1 Nov. 1744. St. Phil PR

Marcus, Samuel & Priscilla Burnly, 18 June 1732. St. And PR

Marden, Thomas & Jane Langley, 1 Dec. 1765. St. Phil PR

Maria, ___ & ___, 9 Aug. 1798, Trin Meth Ch

Mariner, Nathaniel & Anne Leverage, 8 March 1721. St. Phil PR

Marion, Benjmain & Hester Bonneau, 22 Nov. 1752. T & D PR

Marion, James of St. James Goose Creek & Rebecca Shingleton, spinster, 3 March 1743/4; license to Rev. Timothy Melli-champe; Gabriel Guignard of Charles Town, bondsman. MB Chas

Marion, James & Mary Bremar, 13 Apr. 1749. T & D PR

Marion, Job of Parish of St. John, widower, & Elizabeth Gaillard, spinster, in the house of Theodore Gaillard, Senr., 14 Dec. 1762; Catherine Gaillard, Franc. Marion, wit. St. Jas PR

Marion, John & Mary Sanders, 14 Feb. 1760. T & D PR

Marion, Joseph & Elizabeth Collis, 22 Sept. 1772. St. Phil PR

Marion, Paul & Elizabeth Peronneau, 19 Apr. 1734. Circ Cong

Marion, Peter of St. James Goose Creek, & Mary Vouloux, spins-ter, 1 Nov. 1744; license to Rev. Alexander Garden; Gabriel Guignard, cooper, bondsman. MB Chas

SOUTH CAROLINA MARRIAGES 1688-1799

Marion, Robert Esqr., of St. Stephen's Parish, & Hester, relict of Stephen Deveaux; Thomas Cordes Junior, Esqr., trustee; 9 May 1792; Benjn Gignilliat, Stephen Ravenel, wit. Mar Set 2: 3-4

Marison, Lorenz & Susana ___, widow, 16 Apr. 1766. St. John Luth Ch

Markey, Jacob & Jane McKelvey, 3 Dec. 1746. St. And PR

Markis, Joseph & Ann Pickings, 19 July 1750. Hist Oburg

Markland, John & Eliza Childs, 18 March 1790. Circ Cong

Markley, Abraham & Mary Gasser, 5 Oct. 1777. St. Phil PR

Marky, Philip & Katharine Francis, 28 Aug. 1799. Circ Cong

Marlow, James & ___, 4 July 1784. Pugh diary

Marlow, James & Hannah Newbery, 12 July 1792. Pugh diary

Marlow, John & Mary Green, 16 Dec. 1779. St. Phil PR

Marr, Timothy & Mary Dawson, P Licence, 13 Jan. 1740. St. Phil PR

Marriner, Edward & Mary Harris, 12 Apr. 1725. St. Phil PR

Marrino, Charles & Mary Henriette Gaultier, P Licence, 18 Jan. 1752. St. Phil PR

Marsh, James of Charles Town & Susannah Bisset, widow, 10 Jan. 1743/4; license to Rev. Mr. Alexander Garden; John Thompson, bondsman. MB Chas

Marsh, James & Susannah Bisset, P Licence, 14 Jan. 1743. St. Phil PR

Marshall, Adam & Mary Gregg, 19 May 1791. Pugh diary

Marshall, James & Isabella Graham, widow, 16 Feb. 1758. St. Phil PR

Marshall, John & Dorothy Boomer, 21 March 1771. St. Phil PR

Marshall, Thomas & Mary Susanna Chanler, 19 Feb. 1794. St. Phil PR

Martell, Michael Philip & Elizabeth Battoon, 3 Jan. 1787. St. Hel PR

Martin, Charles & Sarah Fowler Robertson, 13 Jan. 1797. Circ Cong

Martin, Christian, tanner, & Ester Johns, both of the city, 6 May 1777. St. John Luth Ch

Martin, Christian & Elizabeth Miller, 16 Dec. 1781. St. John Luth Ch

Martin, Edward & Elizabeth Walker, 20 Jan. 1763. T & D PR

165

Martin, Edward of Parish of Prince George, widower, & Elizabeth Trapier of Parish of Prince George, spinster, at the house of Paul Trapier, 17 Sept. 1778; John Waties Jun., Jos. Wragg, wit. St. Jas PR

Martin, Henry & Eve Kaller, widow, 26 Nov. 1776. St. Phil PR

Martin, Henry & Mary Swinger (Swieger?), 19 Aug. 1779. St. John Luth Ch

Martin, Jacob, merchant & Rebecca Solzer of Charleston, widow, 11 May 1789; George Hahnbaum, Practitioner of Physick, trustee; Mary Lindauer, Daniel Strobel, wit. Mar Set 1: 452-455

Martin, James & Rebecca Freis, widow, 16 June 1781. St. John Luth Ch

Martin, John & Margaret Reid, P Licence, 15 Dec. 1739. St. Phil PR

Martin, John & Esther Dubberline, P Licence, 26 March 1749. St. Phil PR

Martin, Laughlin & Margaret Scott, widow, 1 Apr. 1779. St. Phil PR

Martin, Richard & Mary Clarke, P Licence, 5 March 1734. St. Phil PR

Martin, William & Leah Williams, 25 Nov. 1777.   T & D PR

Martin, Captn. William & Anne D'la Con, P Licence, by Mr. Garden, 27 Oct. 1723.   St. Phil PR

Martinangle, Philip & Mary Foster, 8 May 1743. St. Hel PR

Martine, Moses & Martha Jones, 27 Nov. 1746.   Pr Fred PR

Martineau, Jean Baptiste, native of Monte Andre, Diocese of St. demeurrant, Capt. Francis, Santa Domingo, now resident of Charleston, son of Pierre Martineau, & Marie Boucheau, native of Bordeaux, Parish of St. Colombe, daughter of Joseph Bouchet, 16 Sept. 1793. (original in French, translated by BHH).   Mar Set 2: 181-185

Martyn, Charles Revd. & Sarah Fuller, 13 Apr. 1755.   St. And PR

Mary, Joseph & Jane Albert, P Licence, 1 May 1742. St. Phil PR

Mason, Richard, bachelor & Susanna Sumner, spinster, P Licence, by the Reverend Mr. Alexander Garden, 18 May 1727. St. Phil PR

Mason, William (schoolmaster), & Mary Jenkins, widow, 25 Aug. 1757.   St. Phil PR

Mason, William & Susanna Fairchild, 12 July 1766. St. Phil PR

Mason, William of Charleston & Sarah Timothy of same; 23 March 1793; Revd. Robert Smith, Charles Lining, Esq. trustees. Mar Set 2: 276-278

Mason, Wm. & Susanna Fairchild, spinster, 11 July 1766.
OJ 1764-1771

Massey, William & Catherine Holmes, 27 Feb. 1756. St. Phil PR

Mason, William & Sarah Timothy, 24 March 1793. St. Phil PR

Massey, Philip & Jane Hopkins, P Licence, 20 Jan. 1733. St.
Phil PR

Masson, Richard & Margaret Morgan, P Licence, 10 Sept. 1737.
St. Phil PR

Matheringham, John & Mary Mackmortree, 19 Aug. 1725. Ch Ch PR

Mathew, William & Catharine Coats, 27 Sept. 1760. St. Phil PR

Mathews, Anthony Jr. & Anne Brandford, 13 March 1721. St. Phil
PR

Mathews, Benjamin & Ann Holmes, spinster, by the Revd. Mr.
Josiah Smith, presbyter Minister according to the form of
their profession, 5 Feb. 1744/5. St. Phil PR

Mathewes, Benjamin of John's Island & Edith Mathewes, of Charles
Town, widow, 18 Nov. 1778; Daniel Hall, wit. Mar Set 1: 147-
148

Mathews, Benjamin of Johns Island, & Mary Mathews, daughter of
Edith Mathews, widow, 5 Aug. 1790; John Ward, Joshua Ward,
wit. Mar Set 1: 506-507

Mathews, Charles & Mrs. Lucy Cooper, 21 Nov. 1711. SPG

Mathews, Edmund of Edisto, Clergyman, & Miss Mary Winborn Wells,
of Charleston, 17 Nov. 1798. St. Phil PR

Mathews, George & Mary Saltus, 2 May 1776. St. Phil PR

Mathews, James & Elizabeth Royal, 31 Oct. 1772. St. Phil PR

Mathews, James & Charlotte Godin, P Licence by the Revd. Mr.
Garden Rector, 29 March 1750. St. Phil PR

Mathews, John & Mary Brodie, P Licence, 10 May 1753. St. Phil
PR

Mathews, John & Elizabeth Holmes, 8 June 1775. St. Phil PR

Mathews, John of Charleston & Sarah Rutledge, now of Christ
Church Parish, 1 May 1799; Hugh Rutledge, Robert Hazlehurst,
trustee; Charlotte Huger, wit. Mar Set 3: 364-367

Mathews, Joseph Raven, of Parish of Prince George, bachelor, &
Faith Smith, of Parish of Prince George, spinster, 15 March
1783; Isaac Delisseline, Lydia Perdrieau, wit. St. Jas PR

Mathews, William & Mary Loughton, P Licence by Mr. Garden,
10 Nov. 1736. St. Phil PR

Mathews, William & Sarah Knelson, P Licence, 2 Nov. 1751.
St. Phil PR

Mathews, William of St. Jouns Parish, Colleton Co., & Elizabeth

Coachman, widow, of St. Johns Parish, Berkley County, 14 Jan. 1777; James Sanders of St. George Parish, trustee; Mary Evans, Saml. Hart, A. Vanderhorst, wit. Misc. Rec. RR: 457-459

Mathews, William & Martha Ann Osborne, 30 Nov. 1792; John Mathews & wife Mary, William Skirving, George Savage, trustees; Chas Lesesne, Saml. Jacob Axson, wit. Mar Set 2: 85-98

Mathis, Samuel & Margaret Cathcart Miller, 21 Jan. 1793; John Macnair of Stateborough, Claremont County, planter & Zachariah Cantey of Camden, trustees; Mary C. Bush, wit. Misc. Rec. A: 227-229

Mathyson, Nicholas & Bridget Duncook, P Licence, 2 April 1742. St. Phil PR

Matthewes, Rev. Philip & Frances Lesesne, of All Saints Parish, spinster, Benjamin Allston the younger, trustee; Frans. Allston, John Magill Junr., wit. 19 June 1794. Mar Set 2: 286-292

Matthews, John & Elizabeth Guthrie, 24 July 1749. T & D PR

Matthews, John & Ann Ragnous, widow, 24 Feb. 1759. St. Phil PR

Matthews, John of Charles Town, son of James Mathews, & Sarah Scott of same, spinster, 4 Jan. 1770; John Matthews, son of John, Humphrey Sommers, trustees; Jno Tong, Jno Sommers, wit. Misc. Rec OO: 199-201

Matthews, John & Sarah Rutledge, 5 May 1799. St. Phil PR

Matthews, William of Parish of Prince George, widower, & Esther Sullivan, of Parish of Prince George, spinster, at the plantation of Coll. Shingleton, 25 Apr. 1769; Wm. Bell, Joseph Sullivan, wit. St. Jas PR

Matthias, Georg & Elisab. Marg. Gregorius, widow, 14 Apr. 1766. St. John Luth Ch

Mattrass, James & Jane Chechez, per Licence, 9 May 1745. St. Phil PR

Maul, David, of Charleston & Mary Bessilew, of same, 2 Nov. 1799. St. Phil PR

Maverith, Samuel Stone & Catherine Cayer, P Licence, 12 July 1741. St. Phil PR

Maw, John & Judith Weatherford, 19 May 1798. Trin Meth Ch

Maxcey, Joseph & Amelia Ellisson, 30 July 1768. St. Phil PR

Maxwell, James & Mary Simons, 7 Sept. 1722-3. T & D PR

May, John, of St. Barthomoew's, & Elizabeth Baynard, widow, of Edisto Island, 16 Dec. 1770. St. Phil PR

May, William & Elizabeth Harding, P Licence, 2 Mar. 1730. St. Phil PR

Maybank, David of Christ Church Parish & Mary Simons, daughter of Benjamin Simons, late of same, planter, 9 Feb. 1797; Elias Ball, John Ball, Edward Thomas & Mrs. Catherine Simons,

SOUTH CAROLINA MARRIAGES 1688-1799

widow of Benjamin Simons decd., trustees; Arnoldus Bonneau,
Peter B. Maybank, wit. Mar Set 3: 78-81

Maybank, Joseph & Mary Ann Dupuy, P Licence, July 1731. St.
Phil PR

Maybank, Joseph & Hester Bonneau, 16 Dec. 1795. T & D PR

Mayer, John George & Charlotte Theus, 27 Aug. 1788. St. Phil
PR

Mayer, Michel & Catharina Beter(in), 10 June 1776. St. John
Luth Ch

Mayers, John of Parish of Prince George, bachelor & Ann Highback,
of Parish of Prince George, spinster, 21 Feb. 1761; Alex.
Miot, Lydia Perdriau, wit. St. Jas PR

Mayers, Thomas & Elizabeth Jonson, 15 Aug. 1790. St. Phil PR

Mayne, Charles & Martha Michie, 2 Oct. 1755. St. Phil PR

Mayrant, John & Ann Stone, 27 Sept. 1753. St. Phil PR

Mayrant, John & Ann Woodroope, 25 Oct. 1758. St. Phil PR

Mazer, David of Charlestown, Merchant & Sarah DaCosta, (under
21 years), daughter of Abraham DaCosta, and granddaughter
of Moses Paminto, 19 Aug. 1778; Isaac DaCosta the younger,
trustee; Jas Bentham, & Phil Prioleau, wit. Mar Set 2: 48-52

Mazicq (Mazyck), Isaac and Marriane Le Surrerier; James Le Surrerier enters a caveat against ye marriage of his daughter
Marriane & Isaac Mazicq, 10 Oct. 1693. October 15, 1693
caveat renounced and "Lysence may be granted." Sec Prov
1675-95, p. 444

Mazyck, Isaac & Jane Mary St. Julien, 1728. St. Phil PR

Mead, Edward & Catherine Salter, P Licence, 28 Oct. 1742. St.
Phil PR

Meara, James of Racefield in the Liberties of the City of
Limerick, & Elizabeth Carroll, eldest daughter of Daniel &
Mary Carroll, of the County of Tipperary, 3 May 1788; Car-
bery O'Brien, James Carroll, eldest son of Daniel & Mary
Carroll, trustees; John Shortt, Brian Kennedy, wit. Mar Set
1: 414-420

Mears, John & Mary Eckhard, 28 May 1786. St. John Luth Ch

Mecket, William & Ann Roth, 6 Dec. 1750. Hist Oburg

Medforth, George & Sarah Boast, widow, 20 Feb. 1788. St. Phil
PR

Meeks, Joseph & Mary Fittermus, 31 March 1788. St. Phil PR

Meeks, Joseph & Jane McNabb, 20 Jan. 1792. St. Phil PR

Mege, Claude Francois & Rebecca Morris, of Charleston, widow,
1 Dec. 1796; Peter Freneau, printer, trustee; Thos H.
McCalla, Hy. Kennan, wit. Mar Set 3: 12-16

Megee, James & ____, 21 Jan. 1781.   Pugh diary

Meguire, Joseph & Sarah Glason of this Parish. 15 Sept. 1752.
   Stoney Creek Pres Ch

Meleken, George & Jane Hatcher, 2 Jan. 1752. St. Hel PR

Melekin, George & Janet Melekin, P Banns, 27 July 1720. St.
   Phil PR

Mell, Henry & Mary Catharine, widow of Isaac Huttow, late of
   Orangeburgh Township, decd., 24 Apr. 1753. Hist Oburg

Mell, John of St. Pauls Parish, & Elizabeth Bearman, spinster,
   11 May 1790; Alexander Chovin, & Alexander Collins, trustees;
   Paul Bernard, Sparks Findley, wit. Mar Set 1: 490-492

Mell, Tho: & Mary Boswood, 23 Dec. 1718.   St. And PR

Mell, William & Elizabeth Richmond, 3 Feb. 1755. St. And PR

Mellens, Benjan. & Sarah Price, 22 Sept. 1726. St. Phil PR

Mellichamp, Saintlc & Rebecca Styles, 7 Feb. 1782. St. Phil PR

Melligan, George, bachelor & Mary Hambleton, spinster, P
   Licence of the Governor, by the Reverend Mr. Garden, 9 Feb.
   1724/5.   St. Phil PR

Mellory, David & Rebeka Smith, 23 Feb. 1727.   St. Phil PR

Melvin, David & Jane Mctier, 2 Sept. 1742.   St. Hel PR

Menott, John & Sarah Butler, 28 May 1761.   St. Phil PR

Menson, John & Anne Trusler, P Licence, 11 March 1743. St. Phil
   PR

Menson, John & Margaret Snelling, P Banns, 4 July 1738. St.
   Phil PR

Merckley, Henry & Margareth Wagner, 21 March 1785. St. John
   Luth Ch

Merritt, John & Sarah Bates, widow, 1 Dec. 1765. St. Phil PR

Metcalf, William and Sarah Bosher, 3 Aug. 1738. Pr Fred PR

Metchel, George & Hannah Hill, 17 March 1799.   Circ Cong

Metheringham, John & Elizabeth Beauchamp, 7 Sept. 1748;
   John Champneys & William George Freeman, trustees; Thos
   Corbett, trustees; Thos Corbett, Peter Manigault, wit. Misc.
   Rec HH: 136-143

Metheringham, John & Elizabeth BeauChamp, widow, P Licence by
   the Revd. Mr. Alexr. Garden Rector, 8 Sept. 1748. St. Phil PR

Metheringham, John Junior & Nancy Bennett, daughter of Thomas
   and Ann Bennett, 9 July 1749.   Ch Ch PR

Meurset, Peter & Eberhardina Haunbaum, 16 May 1773. St. Phil PR

SOUTH CAROLINA MARRIAGES 1688-1799

Mews, Henry & Anne Thornton, 10 March 1721.   St. Phil PR

Meyer, Daniel & Susannah Westbury, 26 Jan. 1786.   St. John
    Luth Ch

Meyer,Friederich & ___ Schmidt(in)(?), 12 Mar. 1786.   St. John
    Luth Ch

Meyer, John Jacob, son of Henry Meyer, & Miss Anna Bustrin
    (Buser), 1 Jan. 1740.   Hist Oburg

Meyer, Joseph, shoemaker, & Sara Burns, 16 Dec. 1770.   St. John
    Luth Ch

Meyers, Charles & Mary Ann Muckinfuss, 29 Aug. 1767.   St. Phil
    PR

Meyers, Christian, son of Johannes Meyers, & Rebecca Young,
    daughter of William Young, 12 Apr. 1738.   Hist Oburg

Meylly, John of Charleston, constable & Ann Black, widow,
    20 Apr. 1797.   St. Phil PR

Meynier, Peter & Dorothy Playstowe, by Licence by the Revd. Mr.
    Alexr. Garden Rector, 5 September 1751.   St. Phil PR

Michau, Paul of Parish of Allsaints, bachelor & Lydia Towner, of
    Parish of Allsaints, widow, at the house of Jacob Michau,
    24 Aug. 1784; Jacob Michau, Esther Collins, wit. St. Jas PR

Miche, John & Sarah Hill, 9(?) Sept. 1798.   Pugh diary

Michael, Lambert & Priscilla Stronach, 3 Feb. 1761.   St. Phil
    PR

Micheau, Daniel & Mary Jennings, 6 Apr. 1756.   T & D PR

Micheau, Jacob of the Parish of Prince Frederick, bachelor,
    & Esther Cromwell, spinster, of Parish of Prince Frederick,
    in the house of Oliver Cromwell, 11 June 1778; Manasseh Mich-
    eau, Jacob Jeannerette, wit.   St. Jas PR

Micheau, Manasseh, of Parish of Prince George, bachelor & Anne
    Guerry, of Parish of Prince George, spinster, at the house
    of Peter Guerry Senr., 19 July 1782; Geo McDowell, Edward
    Croft, wit.   St. Jas PR

Michew, Peter & Constant Sutton, widow, 26 Jan. 1758.   St.
    Phil PR

Michi, Kenneth & Mary Clapp, per Licence, 4 Feb. 1745.   St.
    Phil PR

Michie, James & Martha Hall, P Licence 3 Nov. 1737.   St. Phil
    PR

Michill, Flowers & Elizabeth Warren, 1 Feb. 1747/8. Hist Oburg

Middleton, Henry & Mary Ainslie, widow, 16 Jan. 1776.   St. Phil
    PR

Middleton, Horatio Samuel & Anne Sutton, P Licence, 28 Feb. 1737.
    St. Phil PR

Middleton, John & Sirrah Goodby [1740's]. Hist Oburg

Middleton, Lewis & Priscilla Mary Mongin, 8 May 1758. St. Phil PR

Middleton, Solomon & Mary White, 12 Feb. 1795. Circ Cong

Middleton, Thomas & Ann Manigault, daughter of Peter Manigault, decd., (already married, 9 Apr. 1783; Charles Cotesworth Pinckney, wit. Mar Set 1: 2-3

Middleton, Thomas & Ann Manigault, 15 June 1791; Hon. Gabriel Manigault, & Joseph Manigault, trustees; Henry Deas, Frederick Rutledge, wit. Mar Set 1: 567-570

Middleton, Wm. & Mary Izard, of Goosecreek, 21 Apr. 1730. St. And PR

Miers, ___ & _____, 12 Dec. 1768. Pugh diary

Miers, George & ___, 17 Aug. 1784. Pugh diary

Mikell, Ephraim, widower, & Elizabeth McGilvery, widow of John McGilvery, 22 June 1736. St. Hel PR

Miles, David, son of William & Catharine, and Elizabeth Chandler, 4 Dec. 1783. Bush R QM

Miles, Edward & Elizabeth Melachamp, 17 Apr. 1760. St. And PR

Miles, James, a free negro & Hannah Norman, a free mulatto, 25 Dec. 1783; Margaret Singellton, Richard Singellton, trustees; Frederick Grunzweig, Thos Broughton, wit. Mar Set 1: 365-367

Miles, John of St. Andrew's Parish, & Ann Fitch, of Colleton Co., spinster, child of Jonathan Fitch, the younger & granddaughter of Ann Wait, 7 Sept. 1753; Thos Lamboll, wit. Misc. Rec. MM: 351-352

Miles, John & Anne Fitch, 9 Sept. 1753. St. And PR

Miles, John, planter & Kezia Perry, widow of Joseph Perry, decd., 27 Jan. 1774; Sarah McPherson, Isaac McPherson, wit. Misc. Rec. RR: 9-12

Miles, John & Anne Butler, 21 May 1745. St. And PR

Miles, John & Eliz: Ladson, 10 Feb. 1734 [1734/5]. St. And PR

Miles, John & Sophia Sarah Guy, 7 March 1750/51. St. And PR

Miles, Lewis, bachelor, & Ann Simmons, spinster, at the house of George Simmons, 4 Apr. 1765; Wm. Roberts, Moses Miles, wit. St. Jas PR

Miles, Samuel, son of William & Catharine, and Mary Taylor, 1 Jan. 1771. Bush R QM

Miles, Thomas & Mary Fairchild, 3 May 1749. St. And PR

Miles, Thomas, son of Thomas Miles & Mary McTeer, 19 Nov. 1750. St. And PR

Miles, Thomas Junr. & Ann Ladson, 4 Aug. 1735, St. Pauls Parish.
St. And PR

Miles, William of Parish of St. Pauls in Colleton Co., & Mary
Mackewn, 15 March 1743/4; license to Rev. William Orr;
John Champneys, bondsman. MB Chas

Miles, William & Mary Ann Blake Rose, 3 Nov. 1799. St. Phil
PR

Miles, William Senr. & Martha Godfrey, widow, 19 May 1748.
St. And PR

Miles, William & Mary Elliott, 26 Oct. 1769. St. And PR

Miles, William of the Parish of St. Andrews, Berkley Co.,
planter & Martha Godfrey, of same, 17 May 1748; Nathaniel
Brown, trustee; Christopher Guy, wit. Misc. Rec. GG: 415-
418

Miles, William, son of William & Catharine, and Jane Taylor,
3 Dec. 1778. Bush R QM

Miles, William Junr. of Parish of St. Bartholomew, & Elizabeth
North, spinster, 20 Dec. 1743; license to Rev. William Orr;
William Miles Senr. of Parish of St. Andrew bondsman. MB
Chas

Miles, William and Rachel Elmore, 24 June 1797. Bush R QM

Milford, William & Susannah Croskey, P Licence by A. Garden,
10 May 1747. St. Phil PR

Milhouse, Robert, son of Henry & Rebecca, and Sally Nelson
Compton, 11 Jan. 1792. Bush R QM

Milikan, Moses & Mary Murrell, 9 Sept. 1721. T & D PR

Millar, Nicholas & Elenor Henox, P Licence, 21 Feb. 1743.
St. PHil PR

Millekin, George & Mary Watson, P Licence, 19 Nov. 1749.
St. Phil PR

Miller, Adam & Susannah Sarah Bachmann(in), 13 Apr. 1766.
St. John Luth Ch

Miller, Christopher to Angelia Zeigler, widow, 4 Nov. 1753.
Hist Oburg

Miller, Daniel & Martha Wood, 25 Feb. 1790. Circ Cong

Miller, Emanuel & Mary, widow of Andrew Inabnet, 31 Mar. 1752.
Hist Oburg

Miller, Jacob & Odelia Houscausen, 12 Apr. 1748. T & D PR

Miller, James & Mary Trenholm, 2 Oct. 1787. St. Phil PR

Miller, Johann Georg, & Philipina Sofia Willhelmina Vandams,
31 March 1777. St. John Luth Ch

Miller, John & Margaret Briegle, widow, 6 June 1772. St. Phil
PR

Miller, John & Jane Lord, 25 Nov. 1777.   St. Phil PR

Miller, John David & Ann Bounetheau, 10 Aug. 1782.   St. Phil PR

Miller, John, storekeeper, & Jane Gray, 26 Nov. 1791.   Trin Meth Ch

Miller, Moses, & Ann Jeffords, 20 Aug. 1747.   T & D PR

Miller, Nicholas of Johns Island, Colleton Co., & Elenor Herox, spinster, 27 Feb. 1743/4; license to Rev. Alexander Garden; Daniel Gayssoux of Charles Town, bondsman. MB Chas

Miller, Peter & Anna Maria Lutzen, P Licence by the Revd. Mr. Robt. Betham, 11 March 1746/7. St. Phil PR

Miller, Richard & Judity Lambol, 29 Dec. 1725.   St. Phil PR

Miller, Robert & Elizabeth Hains, 15 Sept. 1720.   St. Phil PR

Miller, Samuel & Hester Morgan, 14 May 1777.   St. Phil PR

Miller, Samuel & Ann Findlay, 10 May 1792; Peter Gaillard, trustee; Edwd Ellington, Jno Peyre, wit. Mar Set 2: 6-7

Miller, Solomon & Ann Ash, 9 Jan. 1777.   St. Phil PR

Miller, Stephen & Elizabeth Mary Vanderhorst, widow, 6 June 1744; license to Rev. Levi Durand; Walter Dunbar, bondsman. MB Chas

Miller, Stephen & widow Vanderhorst, 14 June 1744.   Ch Ch PR

Miller, Major Stephen of St. Thomas Parish, & Mary Roache daughter of Francis Roache, late of St. Thomas Parish, decd., 15 Sept. 1776; James Simon & Charles Motte, trustees; Francis Roche, Thomas Roche, wit. Misc. Rec. SS: 12-14

Miller, Stephen & Mary Roche, 27 Sept. 1770.   T & D PR

Miller, Stephen & Martha Dutarque, 19 June 1746.   T & D PR

Miller, William & Rene Brown, 13 Sept. 1763.   T & D PR

Miller, William & Susannah Stead, 18 June 1774.   St. Phil PR

Milles, John & Rebecca Swansey, widow of John Shawney, 11 May 1767; Andrew McCullough of Warmalla [sic] Road, trustee; William Dillon, John Greensword, wit. Misc. Rec. NN: 48-49

Milligan, Jacob & Sarah Shaw, widow, 11 June 1795. Trin Meth Ch

Milligan, John & Sarah McMillan, 7 May 1782. St. Phil PR

Mills, Andrew of Parish of Prince George, widower, & Susanna England, of Parish of Prince George, widow, 13 May 1783; Samuel Warren, Lydia Perdrieau, wit. St. Jas PR

Mills, John & Elizabeth Williams, 4 July 1779.   St. Phil PR

Mills, William, son of John, and Lydia Perkins, 17 Aug. 1786. Bush R QM

Mills, William Henry of Parish of Allsaints, widower, &
Elizabeth McGomery, of Parish of Allsaints, widow, married
in the house of Joseph Allston, 22 July 1769; Joseph Alston,
Andw Johnston, wit. St. Jas PR

Miller, George & Anna Tucker of this parish. 24 Nov. 1747.
Stoney Creek Pres Ch

Miller, Samuel and Helen Hughes, 26 Dec. 1743. Pr Fred PR

Mills, Alexander, son of John and Eunice Pearson, 6 Nov. 1788.
Bush R QM

Mills, John and Mary Taylor, 28 Feb. 1793. Bush R QM

Mills, Marmaduke, son of John and Patience O'Neal, 31 Dec.
1789. Bush R QM

Mills, Thos. & Sarah Breed, 29 March 1766. OJ 1764-1771

Mills, William & Grace Parker, P Licence, Sept. 1732. St. Phil
PR

Mills, William & Ann Taylor, 24 Sept. 1772. St. Phil PR

Mills, William, taylor, & Rebecca Shrewberry of Charleston, 31
March 1795; Stephen Shrewberry, trustee; Wm. Price Junr.,
Rd. Wicksteed, wit. Mar Set 2: 391-395

Millure, Michael & Mary West, P Licence, 10 Oct. 1734. St. Phil
PR

Milne, James & Jane Vanderhorst, widow, 16 Jan. 1768. St. Phil
PR

Milne, William & Carolina Brown, widow, 6 Dec. 1767. St. Phil
PR

Milner, Mumford & Elizabeth Brewton, 27 Sept. 1741. Ch Ch PR

Milner, Solomon & Mary Petty, widow, P Licence by the Revd. Mr.
Alex Garden Rector, 16 Dec. 1749. St. Phil PR

Milton, Henry & Sarah Benion, 9 Jan. 1799. Trin Meth Ch

Mimmack, John, School master, of Berkley County, Parish of
St. James Goose Creek, & Anna Goodbe, spinster, of same,
23 Feb. 1738; Anna Goodbe, Ellenor Elders, wit. Misc. Rec.
FF: 217-218

Mineor, Emanuel & Rachel Hatcher, both of Edistoe Fork, 27 Oct.
1754. Hist Oburg

Minick, Christian & wife Rebecca, were married "twenty nine or
thirty years ago" by John Ulrich Gisentanner, oath of
Elizabeth Oneal, 8 July 1766. Misc. Rec. PP: 489

Minors, Robert, widow and Elizabeth Leopard, widow, 23 Dec. 1742.
Pr Fred PR

Minors, Robert of Prince Georges Parish, bachelor, & Elizabeth
Nicholose, spinster, 13 Nov. 1760; Benjn Perdriau, Lydia
Perdriau, wit. St. Jas PR

Minson, John of Charles Town, carpenter, & Ann Trusler, spinster,
10 March 1743/4; license to Rev. Alexander Garden; Thomas
Doughty, victualer, bondsman. MB Chas

Miot, Alexander, bachelor & Rachel Fitch, spinster, at the plantation of Jean-Elizabeth Dumay, widow, 22 Dec. 1763; Peter
Dumay, James Bell, wit. St. Jas PR

Mitcham, Colin & Dorcas Herrington, 14 Oct. 1779. St. Phil PR

Mitchel, John of Colleton County, Schoolmaster & Sarah Lowle,
widow of Samuel Lowle, 10 March 1761; James Donnom, John
Martin, & Samuel Spry, trustees; Sarah Way, John Donnom,
wit. Misc. Rec. LL: 450-453

Mitchel, John & Elizabeth Johnson, 28 Oct. 1781. St. John Luth
Ch

Mitchel, Thomas of P. G. P. & Elisabeth Atkinson of this Parish,
11 July 1745. Pr Fred PR

Mitchell, Charles of Parish of St. Bartholomew & Martha Tamelson,
spinster, 29 June 1744; license to Rev. Alexander Garden;
James Porter, of Charles Town, bondsman. MB Chas

Mitchell, Charles & Martha Tamilson, P Licence, 29 June 1744.
St. Phil PR

Mitchell, Edward of Parish of All Saints, bachelor & Mary
Moore, of Parish of St. Thomas, spinster at the house of
Mrs. Allston, 29 July 1782; Tho. Waties, Peter M. Neufville,
wit. St. Jas PR

Mitchell, Ephraim & Rhoda Dodd, spinster, 13 July 1782; John
Hall, trustee; James Perry, wit. Mar Set 1: 192-193

Mitchell, Ephraim of Little River, Esqr., & Susanna Tharin,
widow, 20 May 1789; William Boone Mitchell, of Charleston,
trustee; Judith Villepontox, Sarah Burdell, wit. Mar Set 1:
432-435

Mitchell, James & Ann How, 2 Sept. 1799. St. Phil PR

Mitchell, John & Elizabeth Roper, 20 Dec. 1758. St. Phil PR

Mitchell, John & Mary Somervill, 3 Feb. 1771. St. Phil PR

Mitchell, John of Colleton Co., planter, & Ann Fabian, widow of
Joseph Fabian, planter, 30 March 1782; Joseph Fabian, trustee;
Thomas Henderson, John Mitchel, Junr., wit. Misc. Rec. UU:
34-36

Mitchell, Moses & Sarah Hincley, __ Nov. 1760. St. Phil PR

Mitchell, Robert & Mary Ann O'Bryan, 30 March 1752. St. Hel PR

Mitchell, Thomas of Parish of Prince George, bachelor & Anne
Rothmahler, of Parish of Prince George, spinster, at the
house of Job Rothmahler, 13 Aug. 1778; Edward Mitchell,
Jos. Wragg, wit. St. Jas PR

Mixan, Michael & Sarah Britton, 3 Nov. 1748. Pr Fred PR

Mixon, Michel & Marg. Russell, 25 Aug. 1778. Pugh diary

Mixon, Saml. & Kesiah Smith, 26 Jan. 1775.   Pugh diary

Moles, James & Elizabeth Caveneau, 2 Nov. 1788.   St. Phil PR

Molholand, Patrick & Anne More, widow, 14 Sept. 1743. St. And
   PR

Moncreef, John & Elinor Elders, P Licence, 4 Aug. 1744. St.
   Phil PR

Mondey, William & Eleanor Duncan, widow, 13 Sept. 1778. St.
   Phil PR

Mongin, Daniel William of St. Luke's Parish, planter &
   Shepaliah Rivers, of Charleston, 15 Apr. 1798. St. Phil PR

Mongin, David of Charlestown, watchmaker, & Elizabeth Edwards,
   spinster, 18 Nov. 1749; Richd Waters, James Robertson, wit.
   Misc. Rec. LL: 173-174

Mongin, John Andrew & Martha Bull, 23 Nov. 1786. St. Hel PR

Monheim, Christopher & Catharine Fry, both lately arrived from
   Germany in Orangeburg Township, 26 Dec. 1752.   Hist Oburg

Monk, James & Margaret Elizabeth Weston, 13 Sept. 1789. St.
   Phil PR

Monk, John of Parish of St. Stephens, bachelor, & Magdalen
   Boineau, spinster, in the house of Michl. Boineau, 20 Oct.
   1767; Thos Boone, Junr., Isaac Rembert, wit. St. Jas PR

Monroe, Daniel & Sarah Neilson, widow, 29 March 1761. St. Phil
   PR

Monroe, Alexander & Mary Anne Cameron, P Banns, 26 Oct. 1742.
   St. Phil PR

Monroe, John and Susannah Stewart, spinster; minister Alexander
   Garden; bondsmen John Monroe of Charles Town, tailor, and
   William Leander of Charles Town, barber; wit. James Michie,
   9 Apr. 1733. MB NY

Montgomery, John & Mary Commander, 20 Aug. 1770. St. Phil PR

Montier, Lewis & M. Biddys [1740's]. Hist Oburg

Moody, Jno & ____, 4 June 1795.   Pugh diary

Moody, Joseph & Katherine Dunn, widow, (having been three
   times published) by the Revd. Mr. Josiah Smith, presbyter
   Minister According to the form of their profession, 8 Sept.
   1746.   St. Phil PR

Mookinfost, Joseph & Cathrine Smith, 11 July 1758.   St. Phil PR

Moon, Patrick of Christ Church Parish, & Frances Scott, of same,
   widow, 13 Jan. 1792; Thomas Hunter Forrest, cooper, of
   Charleston, trustee; Thos Nicholls, Thos M. Woodbridge, wit.
   Mar Set 1: 613-617

Moon, Patric & Frances Scott of Christ Church [Parish], 14 Jan.
   1792.   Circ Cong

Moonys, Thomas and Rebecca Brown, 13 Aug. 1742. Pr Fred PR

Moor, Alexander, and Sarah Martin, widow; minister Andrew
    Lashley; bondsmen Alexander Moor of St. Bartholomew's Parish
    in Colleton County, planter, and William Little of same,
    planter; wit. J. Hammerton, 7 Feb. 1732. MB NY

Moor, Danl (Baker), to Humphries McGreger, widow, both of
    Charleston, 4 Oct. 1794.   Trin Meth Ch

Moor, John & Justina Smith, 22 Oct. 1719.   St. And PR

Moor, Nathaniel & Sarah Grange, 13 Apr. 1720.   T & D PR

Moore, Charles & Catharine Short, 21 July 1775. St. Phil PR

Moore, David & Eliz: Searsons, widow, 9 March 1741. St. Hel PR

Moore, George & Elly Moore, Nov. 1798.   Moses Waddel

Moore, John & Elizabeth Smith, P Banns, 14 Jan. 1730. St. Phil
    PR

Moore, John & Elizabeth Moore, P Banns, 7 May 1743. St. Phil PR

Moore, Joseph & Ann Taylor, widow, 1 Jan. 1778. St. Phil PR

Moore, Michael & Martha Currant, P Licence, 6 June 1731. St.
    Phil PR

Moore, Patrick & Elizabeth Smilie, 12 Jan. 1774. St. Phil PR

Moore, Robert & Elizabeth Drew, widow, 19 Jan. 1780. St. Phil
    PR

Moore, Roger & Catherine Rhett, 10 Oct. 1721. St. Phil PR

Moorer, Peter Jun. & Margaret Larry [1740's]. Hist Oburg

Morachty, Timothy & Margret Botilou, 10 Feb. 1793.   Trin Meth
    Ch

Mordecai, Samuel of Charles Town & Catharine Andres, sister in
    law of Myer Moses, 14 Jan. 1779; Myer Moses, trustee; John
    Barrell, John Dodd, wit. Misc. Rec. SS: 399-401

More, David & Elizabeth Season, widow of Thomas Season, 9 March
    1741.   St. Hel PR

Morey, Garner, House carpenter, & Mary Beckmuss, widow, 30 Nov.
    1794.   Trin Meth Ch

Morff, Jacob & Christina Hessy, 5 June 1750.   Hist Oburg

More, Michael & Rebekah Brown, 20 June 1797.   Circ Cong

More, Phlp & Besheba Hariet Hanlins, 16 Apr. 1797.   Circ Cong

More, Stephen & Mary Sweeny, 24 Dec. 1778.   St. Phil PR

More, William of Charleston, cooper & Sarah Mackie, widow of
    James Mackie, 17 Aug. 1791; Jno Gordon Junr., Eliz. Limehouse,
    wit. Mar Set 1: 633-634

Morgan, Edward B. & Martha Rambert, 6 May 1798.   Circ Cong

Morgan, Jno & ____, 24 Apr. 1769.   Pugh diary

Morgan, Joseph & Anne Watkins, P Banns, 15 Sept. 1721.   St. Phil PR

Morgan, Joshua & Magdalen Albergotti [no date].   St. Hel PR

Morgan, Joshua & Anne Capers, (no date).   St. Hel PR

Morgan, William & Elizabeth Smith, P Licence, 14 Mar. 1730. St. Phil PR

Morgan, William & Alice Smith, per Licence, 14 May 1746. St. Phil PR

Morgan, William & Sarah Thomas, widow, 16 Nov. 1770. St. Phil PR

Morgan, William, practitioner of Physic, & Elizabeth Stewart, of St. George Dorchester, spinster, 6 Nov. 1798; James R. Stewart, planter, trustee; Jno Stewart, James Stewart, wit. Mar Set 3: 299-303

MorganDollar, John & Elizabeth Strobler, 19 July 1774. St. Phil PR

Morquereau, And. D., & J Sarah Anderson, 6 May 1770. T & D PR

Morraine, Edward & Sarah Bennett, 14 Sept. 1749. Ch Ch PR

Morray, Saml & Anne Fitzgerald, 2 Jan. 1736 [1736/7]. St. And PR

Morrell, Francis & Honora Feltham, widow, 17 Oct. 1772. St. Phil PR

Morrick (?), John & Elizbth. Lock, 23 Aug. 1740. St. And PR

Morril, Green & Mary Burney, P Licence, 19 Feb. 1750. St. Phil PR

Morris, Edward & Sarah Delabare, both of St. Helena Parish, 21 Sept. 1745.   Stoney Creek Pres Ch

Morris, Edward & Sarah Delebere, (no date, before 1753). St. Hel PR

Morris, George & Martha Singletary, 28 Oct. 1790. St. Phil PR

Morris, James & Martha Murphy, 17 Apr. 1792. St. Phil PR

Morris, Mark & ___ Wainwright, widow, 1 Jan. 1761. St. Phil PR

Morris, Owen & Mary Allen, 16 May 1764. St. Phil PR

Morris, Robert, bachelor, & Elizabeth Jenner, spinster, in the house of James Halsey, 27 June 1765; James Halsey, Francis Halsey, wit. St. Jas PR

Morris, Thomas & Mary Gadsden, 26 July 1787. St. Phil PR

Morrison, Robert of Parish of St. Thomas, bachelor, & Rebecca
    Spencer, spinster, 25 June 1767; Jos: Spencer, Lydia Perdriau,
    wit. St. Jas PR

Morrison, Rodrick & Jane Gorden, P Licence, 28 March 1745. St.
    Phil PR

Mortimore, Benjamin & Trudce. Nadswoke(?), 27 Nov. 1711. SPG

Morton, Joseph & Martha McKensey, free blacks, 31 Jan. 1793.
    Trin Meth Ch

Moses, Barnard, & Esther Delyon, (married 24 Sept. 1777), 5
    March 1792; Isaac DaCosta, & Abraham Delyon, trustees; James
    Milligan, Lyon Moses, wit. Mar Set 1: 626-633

Moses, William & Elizth Bland, of St. Helena Parish, 3 May 1750.
    Stoney Creek Pres Ch

Moses, William & Elizabeth Bland, 3 May 1750. St. Hel PR

Mosse, George & Elizabeth Martin, 30 Oct. 1767. T & D PR

Motte, Abraham of South Carolina, & Susanna Quince, 3 June
    1795; Gen Benjamin Smith of Belvidere in North Carolina,
    trustee; A. B. Darby, Danl Jas Ravenel, wit. Mar Set 2: 418-
    422

Motte, Charles & Hannah Diall, widow, 31 May 1761. St. Phil PR

Motte, Chrisn. & Ann Conrade, 18 Jan. 1766. OJ 1764-1771

Motte, Isaac & Ann Smith, 15 Dec. 1763. St. Phil PR

Motte, Isaac & Ann, daughter of Benjamin Smith, & sister of
    Thomas Loughton Smith, (already married), 5 July 1766; Thos
    Smith, Edm M. Hyrne, wit. Mar Set 1: 131-134

Motte, Isaac of Charlestown, & Mary Broughton of Parish of St.
    Johns Berkley, 18 Dec. 1777; Alexander Broughton & John
    Deas, trustees; Rachel Caw, Keatg. Simons, wit. Mar Set 1:
    165-168

Motte, Jacob & Elizabeth Martin, 1 Jan. 1725/6. St. Phil PR

Motte, Jacob Junr. & Rebecca Brewton, 11 June 1758. St. Phil PR

Mouat, William & Anne Smith, P Licence, 15 Jan. 1742. St. Phil
    PR

Mouatt, John & Mary Ash, 20 Jan. 1778. St. Phil PR

Moultrie, James & Catharine Moultrie, 4 Oct. 1790. St. Phil PR

Moultrie, John & Lucrecia Cooper, 22 Apr. 1728. St. Phil PR

Moultrie, John & Elizabeth Mathews, widow, P Licence by the
    Revd. Mr. Alexr. Garden, 29 June 1748. St. Phil PR

Moultrie, John of St. James Goose Creek Parish, & Eleanor Austin,
    spinster, 4 Jan. 1762; Thomas Lynch, trustee; Lynch Roberts,
    Jas Moultrie, wit. Mar Set 3: 355-358

Moultrie, John Junr. of Charles Town, Doctor of Physick, & Dorothy Morton, widow, of John Morton, late of St. James Goose Creek, decd., 28 Apr. 1753; William Middleton, of St. James Goose Creek, and William Dry of Cape Fear, N.C., trustees; Thomas Smith Junr., George Waring, wit. Mar Set 3: 352-355

Moultrie, William & Elizabeth Damaris De St Julian, P Licence, 10 Dec. 1749.   St. Phil PR

Moultrie, William the younger, son of Col. William Moultrie, & Hannah Ainslie, of Charleston, only daughter of John Ainslie & wife Mary, who was a daughter of Benjamin Child, 10 Jan. 1776; Thomas Ferguson, & John Parker, trustees; William W. Burrows, William Rea, wit. Mar Set 1: 115-118

Moultrie, William & Hannah Lynch, widow, 10 Oct. 1779. St. Phil PR

Mouncey, John & Jane Boyland, widow, 8 Aug. 1758. St. Phil PR

Mountjoy, Thomas & Hester Conyers, 23 Oct. 1726. St. Phil PR

Mouzon, Lewis Jr. & Mrs. Duberdeaux, 17 Oct. 1731. T & D PR

Mouzon, Lewis, Jr. & Elizabeth Bochett, 13 June 1750. T & D PR

Mouzon, Samuel of Parish of Christ Church, bachelor, & Anne Maynard, of Parish of Christ Church, spinster, at the plantation of Maj. George Paddon Bond, 17 May 1770; Chas Maynard, Elias Lewis, wit. St. Jas PR

Mowbray, Arthur & Mary Stanyarn, P Licence, 8 Nov. 1741. St. Phil PR

Mowbray, William & Martha Darby, widow, 8 Apr. 1788. St. Phil PR

Muckenfuss, Henry & Mrs. T. Postlethewaite, 26 Apr. 1797. Trin Meth Ch

Muckenfuss, Michael & Mary Catharine Nuffer, widow of Herman Nuffer, late of Charles Town, 26 Apr. 1777; Christian Gruber, Robert Johnston, wit. Misc. Rec. SS: 60-63

Muckinfuss, Michael & Mary Nuffer, widow, 27 Apr. 1777. St. Phil PR

Mullens, John of Parish of St. Bartholomew & Elizabeth Cockran, widow, 4 Oct. 1755; license to Rev. Lewis Jones; Daniel Faissoux, baker, of Charles Town, bondsman. MB Chas

Mullens, John & Elizabeth Cockran, widow, 16 Oct. 1744. St. Hel PR

Mullet, Nicholas & Mary Brown, P Licence by Mr. Leslie, 24 Oct. 1735. St. Phil PR

Mullins, George & Sarah Cattell, 17 June 1773. St. And PR

Mullrein, John & Clodia Cattell, 23 Oct. 1735. St. And PR

Münch, Johanna Adam & Anna Barbarra Heyle, 27 May 1776. St. John Luth Ch

Muncreet, John & Mary Fley, 4 Oct. 1766. St. Phil PR

Muncreef, Richard & Susannah Cray, spinster, P Licence, by the
    Revd. Mr. Robert Betham, 28 Feb. 1746. St. Phil PR

Muncrief, Richard & Elizabeth Young, 17 Dec. 1778. St. Phil PR

Muncreff, John of Charles Town, blacksmith, & Elenor Elders,
    spinster, 4 Aug. 1744; license to Rev. Alexander Garden;
    Thomas Lea of Charles Town, carpenter, bondsman. MB Chas

Munro, Barnabas, & Amelia Chappell, 2 Apr. 1776. T & D PR

Munro, John of Charleston, watchmaker, & Margaret Russell,
    spinster, daughter of Alexander Russell, ship carpenter, decd.,
    6 Dec. 1786; Charles Morgan, & Hugh Paterson, trustees; James
    Muirhead, Charles Ferguson, wit. Mar set 1: 278-280

Munroe, John & Susanna Stewart, P Licence, 9 Apr. 1733. St.
    Phil PR

Münz, Johann Capser, shoemaker, & Catharina Adein, 15 June 1777.
    St. John Luth Ch

Murchey, William of St. Matthews Parish, Orangeburgh Dist.,
    & Barbara Dantzler, widow of Jacob Dantzler, 28 Nov. 1791;
    John Shuler, Jacob Dantzler, Jr., wit. Mar Set 1: 608-609

Murer, Peter Junr. & Magdalene Horguer, 2 Apr. 1751. Hist Oburg

Murfee, Malachi & Jane Night, 11 Aug. 1775. Pugh diary

Murphey, Daniel & Jane Wilson, P Licence, 22 Feb. 1731. St.
    Phil PR

Murphy, Moses, & Lucia Troublefield, 9 Oct. 1743. Pr Fred PR

Murphy, Richard & Hanah Anderson, 21 Feb. 1727. St. Phil PR

Murphy, Roger & Minta Starnes, widow, 7 Oct. 1791. St. Phil PR

Murphy, Timothy & Jane Martin, widow, 3 Feb. 1760. St. Phil PR

Murray, Daniel & Elizabeth Frigay, 20 July 1797. St. Phil PR

Murray, Francis & Sarah Robinson, both of this parish, 23 Dec.
    1754. Stoney Creek Pres Ch

Murray, Gilbert & Elizabeth Griffin, widow of Isaac Griffin,
    11 Feb. 1742. St. Hel PR

Murray, John & Lucy Smith, P Licence, 14 Jan. 1739. St. Phil
    PR

Murray, Patrick & Margery Gorbett Oats, 22 Sept. 1774. St. Phil
    PR

Murray, Samuel & Catharine Tora Ruger, 21 Oct. 1777. St. Phil
    PR

Murray, Thomas & Grace Gibens, 4 Apr. 1741. Ch Ch PR

Murray, William of Parish of Prince George, bachelor, &
    Elizabeth Bossard, of the Parish of Prince George, spinster,

in the house of Mr. Thos. Hennings, 17 March 1785; Isaac Deliesseline, John Bossard, wit. St. Jas PR

Murrel, Jonathan & Eliza. Vardell, 11 May 1726. St. Phil PR

Murrel, Robert & Martha Combe, 2 Apr. 1749. T & D PR

Murrel, Robert & Jemima Cromwell, 3 Nov. 1763. T & D PR

Murrell, Paul of Parish of Christ Church, widower, & Anna Edwards, of Charleston, spinster, in the house of James Anderson, 29 March 1787; James Anderson, Elizabeth Barton, wit. St. Jas PR

Murriel, Francis & Elizabeth Price, P Licence, 16 Apr. 1732. St. Phil PR

Murry, John of Parish of Prince Frederick, bachelor, & Margaret Hughes of Parish of Prince Frederick, spinster, at the house of Mr. Henry Hughes, 28 Nov. 1782; Henry Hughes, Randolph Threes(?), wit. St. Jas PR

Musgrove, John & Mary King, 24 Feb. 1729. T & D PR

Muslow, Jno & Eliza Ellyott, 13 Sept. 1711. SPG

Myars, John and Ann Bruce, 15 May 1741. Pr Fred PR

Myer, Hans Jacob & Ann Buser, 1 Jan. 1740. Hist Oburg

Myers, John & Mary Marquess, 1 Aug. 1752. St. Hel PR

Myers, Matthias and Mary Abner, 24 Jan. 1736. Pr Fred PR

Myers, Michael & Mary Ann Field, sister of William Augustus Field, 26 Jan. 1792; Mary Ann Heape, Wm Elms, wit. Mar Set 1: 622-623

Myllur, John Ulrick & Anne Stopfar, P Licence, 3 Feb. 1734. St. Phil PR

Myot, John & Frances Harden, 17 Nov. 1771. St. Phil PR

Nailor, William Rigby, & Margaret Cardy, 3 March 1768. St. Phil PR

Napier, Robert & Elizabeth Clark, 26 Oct. 1781. St. Phil PR

Naser, Henry & Mary Wersching, 9 Feb. 1786. St. John Luth Ch

Nash, Arthur & Mary Coleman, P Licence, 25 Oct. 1740. St. Phil PR

Nauman, Carl & Mary Elizabeth Roby, 19 Feb. 1786. St. John Luth Ch

Naylor, John & Mary Poitevin, 30 Nov. 1742. T & D PR

Neal, William, bachelor, & Mary Joule, 8 Apr. 1788; Daniel Joulee, S. Warren, wit. St. Jas PR

Neale, Archibld. & Mary Wilkins, widow, 19 Jan. 1733/4. St. And PR

Neale, Jacob & Elizth Elliott, of the Parish of St. Helena,
22 Jan. 1747/8.   Stoney Creek Pres Ch

Nedarman, John and Sarah Dodd, 26 Sept. 1792.   Cane Creek MM

Neel, Lewis & Rachel Mason, 24 Apr. 1787.   Pugh diary

Neilson, Francis & Elizabeth Barthe, widow, 10 July 1791.
St. Phil PR

Neilson, John & Susannah Edgar, P Licence, 9 Nov. 1731.   St.
Phil PR

Nell, Jesse & Ursella Brown, 18 July 1795.   Trin Meth Ch

Nellum, Wm. & Sarah Williamson, 1 July 1759.   St. Phil PR

Nelme, John & Elenor Whitte, P Licence by Mr. Garden, 27 Oct.
1736.   St. Phil PR

Nelme, John & Elinor Watts, widow, 27 Oct. 1736.   Ch Ch PR

Nelson, James & Ann Easton, widow, 7 Apr. 1756.   St. Phil PR

Nelson, John & Sarah Warmingham, spinster, per Licence, by the
Revd. Mr. Alexr. Garden, 7 Apr. 1747.   St. Phil PR

Nelson, Thomas, overseer, & Sarah Williams, 22 Dec. 1754.
St. Hel PR

Nesbit, Robert & Mary Hepworth, P Licence by Mr. Varnon,
February 1730.   St. Phil PR

Nesbitt, Robert, Doctor of Physick, & Miss Elizabeth Pawley of
Waccamaw, 20 Dec. 1797; Benjamin Allston the younger, of the
dist. of George Town, trustee; Frans. Marshall, wit.   Mar
Set 3: 208-211

Nettles, Robt. & Ann Whitworth, 16 Nov. 1797.   Pugh diary

Neufville, Isaac & Ann Simons, 5 Apr. 1794.   T & D PR

Neufville, John & Elizabeth Moore, spinster, P Licence by Mr.
Garden Rector, 1 March 1749/50.   St. Phil PR

Neufville, William & Ann Simons, widow, 1 Dec. 1789.   St. Phil
PR

Neville, Joshua, Cabinet Maker, & Eliza Marrett, 10 Mar. 1792.
Trin Meth Ch

Newcombe, George & Hannah Skinner, P Licence, 9 Sept. 1740.
St. Phil PR

Newell, Clemmen & Elizb: Craklin, 4 May 1763.   St. Hel PR

Newell, Thomas, widower, & Lovinia Lavis, widow of William
Lavis, 3 Feb. 1733.   St. Hel PR

Newlin, Nicholas & Mary Roberts, 28 May 1723.   St. Phil PR

Newman, William & Elizabeth Harrison, widow, 3 June 1766.
St. Phil PR

SOUTH CAROLINA MARRIAGES 1688-1799

Newton, Andrew & Martha Ladson, P Licence by the Revd. Mr.
Alexr. Garden, 9 Feb. 1747.   St. Phil PR

Newton, Thomas & Sarah Hawks, per Licence, 24 Feb. 1744. St.
Phil PR

Newton, William & Mary Morton, widow, 8 Feb. 1796. St. Phil PR

Newton, William & Elizabeth Minot, 28 Jan. 1797.   Circ Cong

Neyle, Philip of Charleston, Doctor of Physic, & Elizabeth Nash
Ford, of Charleston, 17 July 1797; Mary Ford, Hannah Ford,
& Thomas William Price, trustees Isc. Ford, John Glen, wit.
Mar Set 3: 137-141

Neyle, Sampson, Merchant of Charles Town, & Martha Garden,
spinster, daughter of the Revd. Mr. Alexander Garden Rector
of the Parish of St. Philips Charles Town, by the Revd. Mr.
Garden, 14 Feb. 1750.   St. Phil PR

Neyle, William & Harriet Villepontoux, spinster; 9 Jan. 1794,
Sampson Neyle, Jane Villepontoux, trustees; Wm. Payne,
Alex Inglis, wit. Mar Set 2: 200-202

Neyle, William & Harriett Villepontoux, 11 Jan. 1794. St. Phil
PR

Nichelson, Francis & Mary Willis, 25 Dec. 1757. St. Phil PR

Nicholas, William & Mary Beech, 21 May 1713. T & D PR

Nicholls, Samuel & Jane Jarvis, 24 July 1727. St. Hel PR

Nichols, John & Catherine Thomas, widow, 6 Apr. 1735. St. Hel
PR

Nicoll, Stewart & Elizabeth Friets, 31 Oct. 1772. St. Phil PR

Nicoll, William & Dorothea Howser, 3 Aug. 1777. St. Phil PR

Nicolls, Thomas & Sarah Yarnold, 2 Dec. 1789. St. Phil PR

Nichols, George of Charleston, grocer, & Margaret Rivell, 27
May 1797.   St. Phil PR

Nietheimer, Georg, butcher, & Maria Catharine Birckmayer(in),
15 Dec. 1776. St. John Luth Ch

Night, Thos. & Faney Newnam, 10 July 1777.   Pugh diary

Nightingale, Thomas & Sarah Elder, P Licence, 30 Nov. 1749.
St. Phil PR

Nisbett, William & Jane Scott, 30 Apr. 1778. St. Phil PR

Nixon, John Bently & Ann Mondoza, 17 May 1763. St. Phil PR

Noble, Ezekiel & Mary Markley, 2 Sept. 1798.   St. Phil PR

Noland, George & Rebeccah Ellans, 31 Dec. 1737. Pr Fred PR

Nolte(?), John, from London(?), & Maria Young, from Boston,
27 Apr. 1768.   St. John Luth Ch

Norcliff, William & Ann Little, widow, 27 May 1770. St. Phil PR

Norman, James & Frances Vernoid, 27 Feb. 1738. St. Hel PR

Norman, John & Elizabeth Bealer, 25 Feb. 1763. Ch Ch PR

Norman, Joseph & Margaret Webster, 24 Jan. 1733/34. St. And PR

Norris, Daniel & Mary Ross, 27 Oct. 1783. St. John Luth Ch

Norris, James of Parish of St. Helena, Beaufort Dist., &
    Hannah Pawley, of All Saints, George town Dist., 29 Oct.
    1787; George Pawley Senr., trustee; John Withers Junr.,
    George Pawley Jur., wit. Mar Set 1: 346-348

Norris, Patrick & Mary McGilvray, __ Oct. 1736. St. And PR

Norris, William & Ruth Brown, widow, 1 May 1764. St. Phil PR

North, Benj. & Sarah Smith of this parish, 29 Sept. 1747.
    Stoney Creek Pres Ch

North, Thomas of Parish of Prince Frederick, bachelor, & Rose
    McIver of Parish of Prince Frederick, spinster, at the house
    of Joseph Willingham, 4 March 1770; Michael Boineau, Ann
    Varnor, wit. St. Jas PR

Norton, George & Elizabeth Conway, 24 Oct. 1720. St. And PR

Norton, Gideon & Anne Thomas, P Licence, 29 July 1735. St. Phil
    PR

Norton, Gideon & Anne Proscer, P Licence, 8 July 1741. St.
    Phil PR

Norton, John & Martha Phebe Perry, 30 Sept. 1767. St. Hel PR

Norton, John, carpenter, & Ann Humphreys, 26 July 1792. Trin
    Meth Ch

Norton, Jonathan & Mary Ann Chaplin, 16 May 1732. St. Hel PR

Norton, Joseph & Maryann Archibald, P Licence, 22 July 1739.
    St. Phil PR

Norton, William & Catharine Dixon, 26 Jan. 1762. St. Phil PR

Noufuille, John & Elizabeth Marston, 8 Dec. 1726. St. Phil PR

Noulson, Charles & Sarah Lowary, __ Jan. 1763. St. Hel PR

Nowell, Edward Brown of Charleston & Margaret Chalmers,
    spinster, 2 May 1796; Gen. Isaac Huger & Daniel L. Huger,
    Esqr., trustees; Ann B. Kennedy, Mary Huger, wit. Mar Set
    2: 496-499

Nowell, Edward Broun & Margaret Chalmers, 2 May 1796. St. Phil
    PR

Nowell, John & Mary Lord, 28 Nov. 1797. St. Phil PR

Nubie, John & Matty Miller, 21 March 1793. Trin Meth Ch

186

Nugint, Jacobus, son of Mr. Jacobus Nugint from London, & Maria
 Victorin, orphaned daughter of Mr. Conrad Victor, former
 inhabitant of Coos Creeq [Goose Creek], 5 March 1775.
 St. John Luth Ch

Oates, Edward & Elizabeth Walker, 15 Mar. 1767.   St. Phil PR

Oats, Charles & Mary Middleton, 8 Sept. 1788.   St. Phil PR

O'Brian, Michael & Mary Grayson, 25 March 1790. St. Hel PR

OBrien, Michael & Mary Grayson, 23 March 1790; John Grayson,
 trustee; John Mark Verdier, wit. Mar Set 1: 509-510

Obroley, William & Rachel Robinson, P Banns, 12 Jan. 1721.
 St. Phil PR

Obryan, Kenedy & Mary Wigg, P Licence, 16 Nov. 1738. St. Phil
 PR

Obryen, Timothy & Anne Thompson, widow, 24 Jan. 1742/3. Pr Fred
 PR

Odingsells, Chars. & Sarah Levingston, 7 March 1766. OJ 1764-
 1771

Ofill, John & Elizabeth Rice, both of the Saltketchers in
 Colleton County, 29 Dec. 1755. Hist Oburg

Ogelbee, James & Mary-Anne Beaver, 11 July 1737. St. And PR

Ogilvie, Henry & Hannah Simmons, widow, 18 May 1773. St. Phil
 PR

Ogle, Robert & Catharine Christian, of this parish, 5 Apr.
 1748.   Stoney Creek Pres Ch

O'Hara, Charles & Mary Ann Rose, spinster, ___ 1798; James
 McCall Ward, trustee; John McCrady, Henry O'hara, wit.
 Mar Set 3: 267-270

O'Hear, James, merchant & Sarah Fabian, daughter of Joseph
 Fabian, late of St. Paul's Parish, decd., 12 Apr. 1781;
 sd. Sarah is under 21 years of age; Alexr Macullagh, John
 Parker, wit. Misc Rec SS: 479-482

O'Kane, Henry & Margaret Seagrove, widow, 4 Dec. 1792. St. Phil
 PR

Oliphant, Alexander & Elizabeth Ham, 7 Dec. 1781. St. Phil PR

Oliphant, David & Hannah Freeman, P Licence, 1 July 1749.
 St. Phil PR

Oliver, George & Mary Sims, 25 Nov. 1731.   Ch Ch PR

Oliver, James Brush & Sarah McKay, 2 May 1789. St. Phil PR

Oliver, John & Sarah Russell, P Licence, 23 Dec. 1738. St.
 Phil PR

Oliver, Mark & Mary Magdalen Evans, 19 Jan. 1744/5. Ch Ch PR

Oliver, Peter & Margaret Duval, P Licence, 16 Oct. 1729. St. Phil PR

Oliver, Peter & Martha Thushee, 10 Apr. 1757. St. Phil PR

Oliver, Richd. & Clementine Butler, widow, 8 Dec. 1763. St. Hel PR

Oliver, Thomas & Ann Vanvelsen, P Licence, 29 Apr. 1740. St. Phil PR

Oliver, Thomas & Elizabeth Sistrunck, 10 Apr. 1774. St. Phil PR

Ollier, Pons & Jane Satur, P Licence, 16 May 1731. St. Phil PR

O'Neall, Abijah, son of William & Mary, and Ann Kelly, 9 Dec. 1784. Bush R QM

O'Neall, Henry, son of William decd., and Mary Miles, 6 Dec. 1797. Bush R QM

O'Neall, Hugh, son of William decd., and Ann Kelly, 10 Nov. 1791. Bush R QM

O'Neall, John, son of William decd., and Hepzibah Gilbert, 29 Nov. 1792. Bush R QM

Oram, Joseph & Frances Wainwright, spinster, per Licence, by the Revd. Mr. Robt. Betham, 17 Jan. 1746. St. Phil PR

O'Reilly, John & Elizabeth McMillor, 19 Sept. 1778. St. Phil PR

Ormond, Captn. & Miss An Fash, 5 May 1796. Trin Meth Ch

Orr, Henry & Mary Daly, 13 June 1738. St. Hel PR

Orr, James & Eliz: Dicks, 18 Sept. 1753. St. Hel PR

Orr, Robart, & Sarah Cowen, 8 July 1764. St. Hel PR

Orr, Robart & Susanah Dicks, 15 Apr. 177__. St. Hel PR

Orr, William & Isabella Scott, P Licence, 17 Apr. 1738. St. Phil PR

Orrett, Peter & Mary Levrick, 30 July 1763. St. Phil PR

Orrick, Thomas & Eliz: Smith, 27 June 1727. St. Hel PR

Osborn, Benjamin & Mary Brown, P Licence, 27 Juen 1735. St. Phil PR

Osborn, William & Hellena Mackie, 1728. St. Phil PR

Osmond, James & Mary Hall, 13 Apr. 1732. St. And PR

Ot, John Frederick & Magdalene Wechter, late wife of George Wechter, decd., in Amelia Township, 24 June 1750. Hist Oburg

Oth, Caspar & Mary Stehely, all of Orangeburg Township, Dec. 1752. Hist Oburg

Ott, Jacob & Margaret Fichtner, both of Orangeburgh Township, 3 Dec. 1754. Hist Oburg

Ott, Melchior & Mrs. Anna Barbara Zangerin, 19 Feb. 1746/7; Peter Maurer Sr. & Henry & Jacob Friger, Hans Huber, Henr. & Jacob Straumann, wit. Hist Oburg

Outerbridge, White & Ann Clemens Watson, P Licence, 19 Nov. 1749. St. Phil PR

Owen, John & Ann Scull, widow, P Licence by Endorsmt on the Same to the Revd. Mr. Durant, 10 Aug. 1746. St. Phil PR

Owmen, Andrew & Elizabeth Prang, 11 Feb. 1798. Trin Meth Ch

Packrow, John, of Charles Town, Cabinet Maker, & Sophia Harvey, widow, 8 Feb. 1766; Thos Stone, Thos Savage, trustees; William Ellitt Junr., Richd Chittch, wit. Misc. Rec. MM. 671-673

Packnow, John & Sopha. Harvey, widow, 12 Feb. 1766. OJ 1764-1771

Packrow, Jno & Sopha. Harvey, widow, 15 Feb. 1766. OJ 1764-1771

Padget, Francis & Anne Pointset, P Licence, 31 Aug. 1731. St. Phil PR

Pafford, John & Hannah Marshall, 5 June 1777. St. Phil PR

Page, George & Catherine Clements, P Licence, 12 Nov. 1740. St. Phil PR

Page, George & Sarah Eady, widow, 28 July 1766. OJ 1764-1771

Page, George & Sarah Eady, widow, 7 Aug. 1766. St. Phil PR

Page, John & Sarah Battoon, widow, 9 Feb. 1742 [1742/3]. St. And PR

Page, John & Mary Powers, widow, 29 March 1767. St. Phil PR

Page, Joseph of St. Bartholomews Parish & Elizabeth Battoon, 21 March 1744 [1744/5]. St. And PR

Page, Thomas, widower, & Eleanor Holden, of St. Bartholomews Parish, 25 Sept. 1749. Stoney Creek Pres Ch

Page, William of Colleton County, Victular, & Susannah McPherson, of same, widow, 1 May 1750; Burrel M. Hyrne, Adam Culliatt, wit. Misc. Rec. HH: 318-319

Pagett, Henry & Elizabeth Nichols of Colleton Co., spinster, 21 May 1766; Ebenezer Simmons, William Sams, trustees; Saml Hart, Henry Levingston, wit. Misc. Rec. NN: 20-26.

Pagett, Henry & Eliza. Nichols, Spinr., 30 April 1766. OJ 1764-1771

Pagett, Thomas & Eliza Gibson, 5 Apr. 1792. St. Phil PR

Paggett, Thomas & Pegg Folker, 21 Aug. 1788. St. Phil PR

Pain, James & Mary Bellamy, 21 Sept. 1726. St. Phil PR

Paisley, John & Mary Atchison Goddard of Black mingo, widow;
____ 1790; Nathan Shackelford, Thomas Humphries, William
Raudon, wit. Mar Set 5: 221-225

Palmer, Job & Esther Miller, 27 March 1798. Circ Cong

Palmer, John & Ann Sams, 15 Sept. 1785. St. Hel PR

Palmer, John & Frances Mead, 25 Aug. 1791. Circ Cong

Palmer, John Junr. of St. Stephens Parish, & Mary Ann Jerman,
of St. James' Parish, 5 May 1795; Thomas S. Jerman &
Samuel Warren of St. James Parish, trustee; O Neal G.
Stevens, Joseph Palmer Junr., wit. Mar Set 2: 397-399

Palmer, Joseph of Parish of St. Stephens, widower, & Catherine
Thomas, spinster, in the house of Isaac Rembert Senr., 8
Nov. 1759, by Alexr. Keith, rector of St. Stephens; John
Barnett, Judith Rembert, wit. St. Jas PR

Palmerin, Samuel & Jane Glover, widow, 1 May 1754. St. Phil PR

Palmster, Thomas & Ann Duval, 2 July 1728. St. Phil PR

Palock, Solomon & Jane Nesbitt, widow, 15 Dec. 1783. St. John
Luth Ch

Paltiser, Joachim of St. James' Santee, Craven Co., Bricklayer,
& Elizabeth Mathias, widow, of St. Thomas Parish, 23 May
1753; Robert Quash, trustee; David Anderson, Francis Dallas,
wit. Misc. Rec. II: 575-576

Panton, Joseph & Mary Howard, 2 June 1735. St. Phil PR

Paris, James & Sarah Benison, 29 June 1742. Ch Ch PR

Parison, Philip & Jane Williams, 13 March 1796. Trin Meth Ch

Parker, Daniel, & Martha Davidson, widow, 30 Aug. 1752. St.
Hel PR

Parker, Daniel, widower, & Elizabeth McQuinn, 24 Feb. 1754.
St. Hel PR

Parker, Ferguson & Jane Carroline Gough, daughter of John Gough,
of St. Pauls Parish, planter, decd; 22 Mar. 1796; Lambert
Lance, Peter M. Parker, Sarah Lance, wit. Mar Set 2: 472-474

Parker, George & Ann Peronneau, 13 May 1764. St. Phil PR

Parker, George & Elizabeth Waring, 19 Nov. 1793. Circ Cong

Parker, George & Elizabeth Russ, 17 Apr. 1794. Circ Cong

Parker, John of Charleston, butcher, & Martha Moore, widow,
____ 1786; James Millgan, inn holder, trustee; James Mylne,
wit. Mar Set 1: 332-335

Parker, Joseph & Florida Rombert, 14 Aug. 1788. St. Phil PR

SOUTH CAROLINA MARRIAGES 1688-1799

Parker, Saml. & Elizabeth Lacy, 18 Apr. 1741.   St. Hel PR

Parker, Thomas & Mary Drayton, daughter of Hon. Wm. Henry
   Drayton, decd., 25 Oct. 1791; John Drayton, trustee; Wm.
   McKenzie Parker, Ferguson Parker, wit. Mar Set 1: 600-601

Parker, Thomas & Mary Drayton, 25 Oct. 1791. St. Phil PR

Parker, William & Sarah Lesesne, 26 Dec. 1760.   T & D PR

Parkinson, John of Winton County, planter, & Sarah Crossle of
   same, widow, 17 Nov. 1796; James Harkness & Samuel Dunbar of
   same, gentlemen, trustees; Thos P. Nash, Matthew McDonald,
   wit. Misc. Rec. A: 286-289

Parks, John of Charleston, Cordwainer & Elizabeth Carson, widow,
   15 Sept. 1791; Robt Knox, trustee; Mary Simpson, Palk. Daugherty, wit. Mar Set 1: 596-599

Parks, John & Elizth. Carson, 18 Sept. 1791.   Circ Cong

Parks, Nathan of Parish of Prince George, bachelor & Anne
   Waller, of Parish of Prince George, spinster, 8 Nov. 1778;
   Simon Fortines, Samuel Warren, wit. St. Jas PR

Parmenter, Jno Junr., & Susannah Savage, 16 Sept. 1764. St.
   Hel PR

Parmenter, Joseph & Jane Wright, widow, 18 Sept. 1733. St.
   Hel PR

Parmenter, Joseph & Catherine Parmenter [no date]. St. Hel PR

Parmenter, Josp: & Martha Rich, [no date]. St. Hel PR

Parris, Alexander, widower, & Mary Cahill, 15 June 1741. St.
   Hel PR

Parris, John & Elizabeth Collins, 25 Jan. 1750. Ch Ch PR

Parrott, Benjamin & Ann Rivers, 7 Aug. 1746. St. And PR

Parrott, Benjamin & Hannah Witter, widow, 27 May 1756. St.
   And PR

Partridge, Nathaniel of the Parish of St. Marks, Craven Co., &
   Mary Tomlinson, widow of Arthur Tomlinson, 23 Nov. 1767;
   John Witherspoon, wit. Misc. Rec. NN: 45

Passwater, William & Hannah Pezaza, P Licence, 15 Jan. 1739.
   St. Phil PR

Patchelbel, Charles Theodore & Hannah Poitevin, P Licence, 16
   Feb. 1737.   St. Phil PR

Paterson, John & Mary Jenkins, 13 Sept. 1781. St. Phil PR

Patrick, Casimer & Ann Cobia, 21 Aug. 1773.   St. Phil PR

Patterson, William, of St. Paul's Parish, & Susanna Youin, of
   St. Bartholomew's Parish; 21 July 1791; James & Susanna Dyzill,
   of St. Bartholomew's Parish, trustees; Thos Richmond Collins,
   minister; John Leason, wit. Mar Set 2: 176-178

191

Patterson, William of St. Bartholomew's Parish, Shop keeper &
Freelove Elliott, widow, 24 Nov. 1797; Thomas Patterson,
trustee; George Lancaster, Esther Graves, wit. Mar Set 3:
203-204

Pattigrew, Ebenr. and Sarah Stedman, widow, both of 96 Dist.,
30 July 1782, Rev. John Harris. Surity, John Pettigrew.
Ninety Six Dist. OJ

Patton, Andrew & Katharine Tom, 8 March 1779. St. Phil PR

Patty, Charles & Mary Jay, 11 March 1773. Bush R QM

Patureau, William & Anne Grimbal, widow, 23 Oct. 1760. St. Phil
PR

Paulling, William & Mary Dunlop, 29 Dec. 1761. Pr Fred PR

Pawley, George & Anne Ellery, 26 Jan. 1748-9. T & D PR

Pawley, George & Mary Miller, 2 May 1755. Misc. Rec. KK: 346-
348

Pawley, George & Mary Miller, 22 May 1755. T & D PR

Pawley, George Junr. of P G. P. & Anne Dupre of this Parish,
23 Dec. 1746. Pr Fred PR

Pawley, Percival and Anne King, spinster; minister Thomas
Morritt; bondsmen Percival Pawley and William Poole of Prince
Georges Parish, and Joseph Massey of Charles Town, gunsmith;
wit. James Michie, 2 March 1732. MB NY

Paxton, Mr. & Miss Macquan, 13 July 1799. Trin Meth Ch

Payne, James of Charlestown & Eleanor Greaves, 17 Feb. 1768;
John Nevin, trustee; Felix Long, Martin Clime, wit. Misc.
Rec. NN: 198-203

Payne, James & Eleanor Graves, widow, 17 Feb. 1768. St. Phil PR

Payne, John, serjeant, & Elizabeth Ruple, 23 June 1797; William
Payne, trustee; J. J. Gilbert, wit. Mar Set 3: 134-137

Payne, Joseph & Eliz: Bacalesk, 17 May 1733. St. And PR

Payne, Nathaniel & Elizbh. Worral, 18 Apr. 1734. St. And PR

Payne, William & Anne Clifford, P Licence, 18 Dec. 1740. St.
Phil PR

Payne, William of Charleston, & Maria Margaret Torrens, spinster,
10 Feb. 1791; Alexander Rose, Plowden Weston, trustees.
Robt Torrans, Christ. Knight, wit. Mar Set 1: 544-546

Payne, Wm. & Maria Torrens, 10 Feb. 1791. Circ Cong

Peace, Joseph & Mary Rudhall, 5 July 1796. Circ Cong

Peacock, Hewark & Sarah Smith, P Licence, 27 April 1733. St.
Phil PR

Peacock, Newart, & Sarah Smith, widow; minister Alexander
Garden; bondsmen Newart Peacock, mariner and Aaron

Cheeseburgh (Cheesbrough) of Charles Town, watchmaker; wit. James Michie, 27 April 1733. MB NY

Peacock, Thomas & Mrs. Anna Room, 24 Feb. 1718-9. T & D PR

Peak, John & Elizabeth Harvey, 19 Apr. 1778. St. Phil PR

Peak, Stephen of P. G. Parish & Abigaill Brunston of Prince Frederick, 5 May 1746. Pr Fred PR

Peak, Stephen & Mary Ann Irvine, 9 May 1763. St. Phil PR

Pearse, Robert & Rebecca Minskey, 1 June 1793. Trin Meth Ch

Pease, Samuel & Ann Frogatte, 8 March 1792. Circ Cong

Pearson, Benjamin, son of Samuel decd., and Esther Furnam, 29 April 1790. Bush R QM

Pearson, Enoch, son of Thomas, and Ann Evins, 21 Dec. 1784. Bush R QM

Pearson, Enoch, son of Samuel, and Phebe Demans, 10 Nov. 1774. Bush R QM

Pearson, John & Mary Raiford, 25 Apr. 1742. Hist Oburg

Pearson, Samuel, son of Enoch, and Mary Steddom, 1 Oct. 1772. Bush R QM

Pearson, Samuel, son of Enoch, decd., and Ann Jay, 7 March 1799. Bush R QM

Pearson, Samuel, son of Samuel dec., and Mary Coat, 9 Sept. 1790. Bush R QM

Pearson, Thomas and Mary Cambell, 8 July 1775. Bush R QM

Pearson, William, son of Samuel, and Ann Stidham, 31 Aug. 1775. Bush R QM

Peck, Daniel & Mary Pierson, widow, 3 July 1793. St. Phil PR

Peekham, Ebenezer & Lydia Adams, P Banns, 29 June 1720. St. Phil PR

Peet, James & Debarah Robinson, 4 July 1765. St. Phil PR

Pegues, Claudius of George Town, merchant, & Henriette Butler, spinster, 26 Mar. 1749; Samuel Butler, trustee; Richd Walker Junr., Saml Rolins, wit. Misc. Rec. HH: 72-74

Penciel, Emanuel & Jeanne Messan Penciel, (already married) 21 Sept. 1793; Jas Custer, Henry Martin, Pn. Boissures, wit. Mar Set 2: 463

Pendarvis, Brand & Ursetta Jennings [1740's]. Hist Oburg

Pendarvis, James & Catherine Rumph, 3 Sept. 1741; John Hearn, John Pearson, John Hammelton, John Diedricks, John Danners, Robert Whitefords, wit. Hist Oburg

Pendarvis, John & Hannah Keys, 1721. St. Phil PR

Pendergrass, Darby of Charles Town, Taylor & Sarah Moore, widow of John Moore, 7 June 1758; John Thomas of same, Schoolmaster, trustee; Isabella Chambers, Jane Massey, wit. Misc. Rec. LL: 140-142

Pendergrass, Darvey & Sarah More, widow, 2 June 1758. St. Phil PR

Penkins, Christopher & Mary Weatherly, 16 Dec. 1761. St. Phil PR

Pepoon, Benjamin & Lucy Nott, 5 Jan. 1792. St. Phil PR

Pepper, Gilbert & Jane Verdier, 23 Apr. 1755. St. Hel PR

Perdriau, Benjamin & Mary Barton, P Licence by the Revd. Mr. Alexr. Garden, 17 Nov. 1747. St. Phil PR

Perdriau, James & Jane Brown, 9 Sept. 1771. St. Phil PR

Perdriau, John & Jane Laurans, 21 Feb. 1721. St. Phil PR

Perdriau, John of Parish of St. James Santee, & Esther Guerry, spinster, 21 May 1744; license to Rev. Thomas Hasell; Peter Laurens of Charles Town, bondsman. MB Chas

Perdriau, John of Parish of St. Stephen, bachelor, & Anne Dupont, of Parish of Prince-Frederick, spinster, in the house of Anne LeNud, 2 June 1772; Jonah Robert, A. Caleb Guerry, wit. St. Jas PR

Perdue, John & Christiana Rosina Gegerin, per Publication of Banns by the Revd. Mr. Richard Clarke Rector, 12 Sept. 1758. St. Phil PR

Perenneau, Arthur & Mary Hudson, 10 June 1762. St. Phil PR

Perkins, John & Mary Graceberry, 4 Sept. 1742. Pr Fred PR

Perkins, Samuel & Sarah Cartwright, P Licence, 16 April 1743. St. Phil PR

Peroneau, Alexander & Margeret Hext, 24 Dec. 1744. St. Phil PR

Peroneau, Samuel & Sarah Tattnall, 19 Jan. 1758. St. Hel PR

Peronneau, Alexander & Mary Pollock, 7 June 1733. Circ Cong

Peronneau, Henry, jun. & Anne Motte, spinster, P Licence, 14 May 1752. St. Phil PR

Peronneau, Wm. & Mary Lightwood, 3 Feb. 1791. Circ Cong

Perret, Abraham of Parish of Prince Frederick, widower, & Margaret Fendin, of Parish of Prince Frederick, spinster, 15 March 1787; William ___, ___, wit. St. Jas PR

Perret, Francis of Parish of Prince Frederick, bachelor & Martha Murrel, of Parish of Prince Frederick, spinster, in the house of William Murrel, 19 Jan. 1785; John Lequeux, William Murrell Junr., wit. St. Jas PR

Perret, John & Julian Newman, widow, 3 Oct. 1749. Pr Fred PR

Perriman, John & Mary Snypes, 23 Jan. 1723.   St. Phil PR

Perriman, John of St. Bartholomews Parish, & Patience Jones,
    spinster, 12 June 1744; license to Rev. William Orr; Benj.
    Perry of St. Pauls Parish, bondsman.   MB Chas

Perroneau, Richard & Ann Ball, 5 July 1767.   T & D PR

Perronneau, Samuel & Elizabeth Daniel, P Licence, 30 June 1743.
    St. Phil PR

Perry, Benjan. & Susana Rawlings, 27 June 1742.   St. And PR

Perry, Benjamin & Frances Elliott, 8 July 1764.   St. And PR

Perry, Edward the younger son of Edward Perry the elder of
    St. Pauls Parish, a minor under 21, & Ann Drayton, minor
    about 18 years old, daughter of Rebecca Drayton of Charleston,
    widow of Hon. John Drayton; Jas Postell, Jas Postell Junr.,
    wit., 9 Dec. 1793.   Mar Set 2: 210-215

Perry, Edward Junr. & Ann Drayton, 10 Dec. 1793.   St. Phil PR

Perry, Francis & Jane Mouncey, widow, 17 Sept. 1763.   St. Phil
    PR

Perry, James & Frances Hunt, 18 Dec. 1777.   St. Phil PR

Perry, John & Sarah Clift, 8 July 1719.   St. And PR

Perry, John & Mary Wood, widow, 7 July 1760.   St. And PR

Perry, Peter & Elizabeth Ladson, 24 Apr. 1753.   St. Hel PR

Perry, Samuel, soldier of the 5th Regt., with the permission of
    his captain, & Maria Yungin, 16 Dec. 1776.   St. John Luth Ch

Perryclear, Adam & Eleanor Greene, (no date).   St. Hel PR

Perryclear, Michael, widower, & Margaret ___, 14 March 1760.
    St. Hel PR

Petermann, Ludwig, & Johanna ___, 23 Apr. 1771.   St. John Luth
    Ch

Peterson, George & Sarah Milton, 26 March 1782.   St. Phil PR

Petrie, Alexander & Elizabeth Holland, P Licence by the Revd.
    Mr. Alexr. Garden, 2 Feb. 1747.   St. Phil PR

Petrie, Alexander & Mary Evans, both of Charleston, 29 Oct. 1796;
    Thomas Tudor Tucker, Practitioner of Physick, trustee;
    Susanna Mason, Elizabeth Sanders, wit.   Mar Set 3: 8-12

Petrie, Edmund & Ann Peronneau, 22 Aug. 1779.   St. Phil PR

Petrie, Edmund & Mary Bridie, 13 Jan. 1791; Adam Tunno, trustee;
    Willm Lennox, John Wagner, wit.   Mar Set 1: 537-544

Petrie, George & Mary Simmons Swinton, 11 Sept. 1794.   Circ Cong

Petrie, Ninian & Catharine Campbell, 20 Dec. 1781.   St. Phil PR

Petty, Richard & Sarah Rose, 13 Dec. 1734.   St. Hel PR

195

SOUTH CAROLINA MARRIAGES 1688-1799

Peyrand, Gabriel & Magdalen Rant, P Licence, 17 Oct. 1729.
   St. Phil PR

Peyre, Rene & Hannah Hasell, 9 Dec. 1753.   T & D PR

Peyre, Rene & Catharine Cleave, 18 July 1765.   T & D PR

Peyton, Richard Henry & Ann Smith Stobo, 27 May 1795.   Circ Cong

Philips, Benjamin & Sarah Mathews, 12 May 1757.   St. Phil PR

Philips, Elias & Marta Millener, 13 Nov. 1786.   St. John Luth
   Ch

Philipps, Francis, Englishman, & Cornelia Roberts, widow, 10
   Apr. 1768.   St. John Luth Ch

Philipps, Johann, & Regina Brumin, 9 Feb. 1773.   St. John Luth
   Ch

Phillips, Thomas & Elizabeth Gough, 21 July 1750.   Ch Ch PR

Phillips, William & Elizabeth Herbert, P Licence by the Revd.
   Mr. Alexander Garden Rector, 13 Sept. 1749.   St. Phil PR

Philp, Robert & Mary Hartley, 10 Apr. 1758.   St. Phil PR

Philsbee, Richard of Parish of St. Thomas, bachelor & Sarah
   Bennett, spinster, 30 Oct. 1783; Peter Guerry, Samuel Warren,
   wit. St. Jas PR

Piat, Claude & Anna Write, widow, 27 Feb. 1780.   St. John Luth
   Ch

Piat, Johannes, widower, & blacksmith, & Rohdy Irons(in), 15
   July 1777. St. John Luth Ch

Pichard, Charles Jacob (Son of Alexander & Anna Catharine Pichard,
   both Burgesses of the City of Yverdon in Switzerland), &
   Susannah Bourget, P Licence by A. Garden, Rector of St. Philips Chas. Town, 4 May 1747.   St. Phil PR

Pickering, Joseph & Ann Lebrasseur, P Licence, 10 Jan. 1750.
   St. Phil PR

Pickering, Samuel & Mary Maxey, 20 June 1763. St. Phil PR

Pickings, Samuel & N. Patton [1740's]. Hist Oburg

Pied, Edward & Mary Pounds, P Banns, 29 May 1720. St. Phil PR

Pierce, Thos., mariner, & Lettitia Conner, widow, 28 Nov. 1792.
   Trin Meth Ch

Piercey, John of St. James Santee, & Elizabeth Gaillard, widow,
   4 March 1786; Benjamin Webb, & Sarah Hannah Webb, trustees;
   Chas Fyffe, Jas Anderson, wit. Mar Set 1: 211-213

Piercy, Thomas & Mary Lewis, 7 Sept. 1749. Ch Ch PR

Piercy, William & Catharine Elliott, 18 May 1776. St. Phil PR

Pierre, George Dela & Elizabeth Loyd, P Licence by Mr. Garden,
   30 Jan. 1736.   St. Phil PR

196

Piggott, John Butler & Sarah Clifford, 23 July 1761. St. Phil
    PR

Pike, Thomas & Mary Inman, 11 June 1774. St. Phil PR

Pilsbury, Saml. & Miss Ahatable Emerson Stephens, 8 March 1796.
    Trin Meth Ch

Pimell, Abel & Mary Tutton, 11 July 1728.   St. Phil PR

Pinckney, Charles Esqr., & Elizabeth Lucas, spinster, 25 May
    1744; license to Rev. William Guy. MB Chas

Pinckney, Charles & Elizabeth Lucas, 27 May 1744. St. And PR

Pinckney, Charles, the younger, & Frances Brewton, P Licence by
    the Revd. Alexr. Garden, 2 Jan. 1753. St. Phil PR

Pinckney, Charles & Mary Eleanor Laurens, 27 Apr. 1788. St.
    Phil PR

Pinckney, Charles Cotesworth & Mary Stead, daughter of Benjamin
    Stead, 17 July 1786; Ralph Izard, Ralph Izard Jr., trustees;
    John Ward, Jno Drayton, wit. Mar Set 1: 245-246

Pinckney, Hopson & Eliza Quash, 19 Nov. 1772.   T & D PR

Pinckney, Hopson & Elizabeth Cannon, 21 Jan. 1777. St. Phil PR

Pinckney, Roger of Charleston & Frances Susannah Hume, widow,
    25 March 1769; Robert Wuash the younger, Josiah Bonneau of
    Berkly Co., trustees; Mary Bonneau, Elizabeth Quash, wit.
    Misc. Rec SS: 129-133

Pinckney, Roger & Mrs. Susannah Quash Hume, 26 Mar. 1769.
    T & D PR

Pinckney, Roger & Susannah Shubrick, 8 Nov. 1792. St. Phil PR

Pinckney, Thomas & Grace Beadon, spinster, 19 Sept. 1692;
    Christopher Linkely, William Smith, vintner, bondsmen. Sec
    Prov 1675-95, p. 484

Pinckney, Thomas & Elizabeth Motte, 22 July 1779. St. Phil PR

Pinckney, Thomas & Frances Middleton, 18 Oct. 1797; Rebecca
    Motte, Charles Cotesworth Pinckney, Wm Alston, Jacob Drayton,
    trustees; Ann Pernneau, Mary Bird, wit. Mar Set 3: 157-159

Pinckney, Thomas & Frances Middleton, widow, 19 Oct. 1797.
    St. Phil PR

Pinckney, William & Ruth Brewton, 6 Jan. 1725/6. St. Phil PR

Pinder, William & Rebecca Lecraft, widow, 21 Jan. 1777. St.
    Phil PR

Pingel, Philipp & Maria Küssner(in), 22 Oct. 1766. St. John
    Luth Ch

Pinyard, Phillip, of Charles Town & Anna Miller, spinster,
    8 Feb. 1743/4; license to Rev. Alex. Garden; Andrew Ruck,
    bondsman. MB Chas

Pinyard, Philip & Anne Millar, P Licence, 9 Feb. 1743. St. Phil
PR

Plair, Thomas of Christ Church Parish, & Elizabeth Wingood,
widow, 4 May 1790; Thomas Karwon, Joshua Toomer, trustees;
Sarah Hamlin, Daniel McCalla, wit. Mar Set 1: 516-518

Plaiters, William & Sarah Saller, P Licence, 23 Oct. 1744.
St. Phil PR

Player, Roger & Mary Stillery, widow, 14 Dec. 1692; Phillip
Buckely, trustee; ___ Gillchrise, Thomas ___, Atkin Williamson,
wit. Reg Prov A: 1682-90; 378

Player, Roger & Patience ___, 18 Nov. 1718. Ch Ch PR

Player, Roger & Martha ___, his second wife, 7 May 1730.
Ch Ch PR

Player, William & Ann Lewis, daughter of Daniel Lewis, decd.,
3 Apr. 1775. Ch Ch PR

Playter, William of Charles Town & Sarah Salter, spinster,
22 Oct. 1744; license to Rev. Alexander Garden; George Coker,
bondsman. MB Chas

Plowden, William & Susannah Dubois, 24 July 1777. T & D PR

Plumer, Moses & Mrs. Jean Verine, 15 Feb. 1712-3. T & D PR

Plunkett, Thomas & Elizabeth Scully, widow, 3 June 1759. St.
Phil PR

Poaug, Jacob & Charlotte Wragg, of Charleston, spinster, 1 Jan.
1763; Robert Smith, Alexr Rantoul, wit. Mar Set 1: 78-83

Poaug, John & Charlotte Wragg, 1 Jan. 1763. St. Phil PR

Poaug, John & Harriett Beresford Smith, spinster, daughter of
Thomas Luten Smith, 26 June 1794; Dr. James Clitherall,
William Smith, Joseph Allen Smith, & Alexander Inglis,
trustees; Wm. Robertson, Benjn Bayley, wit. Mar Set 2:
296-299

Poinsett, John & Mary Cattle, widow, 1 May 1756. St. Phil PR

Pollard, James & Anne Stittsm, 21 June 1735. St. Phil PR

Pollard, John & Eliza Stith, Sept. 1795. Moses Waddel

Pond, Richard & Phoebe Richardson, 26 Mar. 1762. St. Phil PR

Ponton, Archibald of Charleston, confectioner & wife Catherine,
1 Aug. 1797; Robert Brodie of same, carpenter, trustee;
Robt Anderson, Hugh Wallace, wit. Mar Set 3: 131-134

Poock, Thomas & Proscilla Dunn, P Licence, by the Revd. Mr.
Alexr. Garden, 21 June 1748. St. Phil PR

Pool, Thomas & Elizabeth Tootle, P Licence, 7 Jan. 1738. St.
Phil PR

Poole, Thomas & Jane Clifford, 17 June 1766. OJ 1764-1771

Poole, William & Hannah Warbeuf, 8 Dec. 1726. T & D PR

Pope, James & Martha Scott, widow, __ Jan. 1787. St. Hel PR

Pope, James & Susanna Wells, 28 Aug. 1755. St. Hel PR

Pope, James & Martha Scott, widow, 9 Jan. 1787. St. Hel PR

Popperwell, John & Mary Purvis, 29 Jan. 1748/9. Pr Fred PR

Porchee, Peter Philip & Mary Mazyck, 2 Dec. 1756. St. Phil PR

Porcher, Thomas & Charlotte Mazyck, 25 Oct. 1792. St. Phil PR

Porteous, Robert of Port Royal, & Ann Wigg, spinster; 4 Nov.
1771; James Cuthbert & William Hazzard Wigg, trustees;
Henry Stuart, John Cuthbert, wit. Mar Set 2: 52-56

Porteous, Robert & Ann Wigg, 6 Nov. 1771. St. Hel PR

Porter, Ebenezer & Charity Stevens, 2 Feb. 1794. Circ Cong

Porter, John, of Parish of Prince Frederick, bachelor, & Anne
Dexter of Parish of Prince Frederick, spinster, 15 April
1784; Saml. Cooper, Anthony Ford, wit. St. Jas PR

Postell, Andrew of Pirnce Williams Parish, planter, & Sarah
McPherson, widow, 18 June 1785; Martha McPherson, Sarah Massey,
wit. Mar Set 1: 175-177

Postell, James of Parish of St. Georges Dorchester, & Ann Waring,
spinster, 30 Apr. 1744; license to Rev. Thomas Thompson;
George Waring, bondsman. MB Chas

Postell, James & Catherine Douxsaint, 30 Dpc. 1764. St. Phil PR

Postell, John of Prince George's Parish, & Ann Sanders widow
of Col. William Sanders, of St. Bartholomew's Parish;
__ Oct. 1793; Major William Fishburn, trustee; Jas Perry,
John Constantine, wit. Mar Set 2: 237-239

Postell, John Junr. of Parish of St. George Dorchester, & Mary
Moore, spinster, 26 Sept. 1744; license to Rev. Thomas
Thompson; James Postell, bondsman. MB Chas

Postlethwaite, James Captn. & Miss Frances Darale, 6 Dec. 1793.
Trin Meth Ch

Potter, James & Martha Miller, widow, 4 Oct. 1760. St. Phil PR

Potter, John of Charleston, merchant, & Catherine Fuller, of
same, spinster, second daughter of Thomas Fuller Esqr., (by
his second wife), late of the Parish of St. Andrews, 10 Aug.
1791; Thomas Jones, trustee; Edward Gunter, Mary Audley
Gunter, wit. Mar Set 2: 25-27

Pottevine, Anthony & Hanah Atkins, 31 Oct. 1727. St. Phil PR

Pou, John & Elizabeth Giessendanner, both of Orangeburgh Township (no date). Hist Oburg

Powel, George & Ruth Smith, widow, 31 Oct. 1756. St. Phil PR

Powell, James Edw. & Mary Williams [no date]. St. Hel PR

Powell, John of St. Helena Parish, & Hannah Wilkinson,
    spinster; 5 Apr. 1744; license to Rev. Lewis Jones;
    Griffeth Bullard of Charles Town, bondsman. MB Chas

Powell, John & Hannah Wilkinson, 19 Apr. 1744. St. Hel PR

Powell, John, widower, & Hannah Wilkinson, 29 May 1726. St.
    Hel PR

Powell, John of Parish of St. Helena, Doctor of Physick, &
    Martha Megget, spinster, 28 Aug. 1765, William Megget,
    planter, trustee; Magdl Megget, Margaret Megget, wit. Misc.
    Rec. NN: 90-93

Powell, Joseph & Ann Young, 8 Jan. 1758. St. Phil PR

Powers, Nicholas to Sarah Gillespie, 6 Feb. 1788, Rev. Joshua
    Lewis, Marlboro Co.

Powers, Richard & Esther Morgan, P Licence, 25 Dec. 1740. St.
    Phil PR

Poyas, James & Elizabeth Portal, 7 Feb. 1755. St. Phil PR

Poyas, John Ernest & Elizabeth Grant, 20 May 1753. St. Phil PR

Poyas, John Ernest & Rachael Bourgett, 20 May 1755. St. Phil PR

Poyas, John Ernest & Magdalen Schwartskopff, widow, 24 Nov.
    1776. St. Phil PR

Poyas, John Lewis, & Mary Seabrook of St. James Parish,
    Craven Co., 29 June 1783; Isaac Deleisselin, trustee; John
    Fabre Junr., Francis G. Deleisselin, wit. Mar Set 1: 107-108

Prat, William to Mary Drennan, both of Long Cane Settlement, 28
    Jan. 1783. Revd. John Harris. William Drennan, surity.
    Ninety Six Dist. OJ

Pratt, James & Mary Marsh, 5 Feb. 1756. St. Phil PR

Preseillo, Joseph of New Windsor & Mary Raven, spinster, 27
    July 1744; license to Rev. Alex Garden; John Johnston,
    Merchant, of Charles Town, bondsman. MB Chas

Pressman, William & Ann Ferguson Cattell, 4 Nov. 1793. St. Phil
    PR

Price, Charles & Obedience Hanson, 29 Aug. 1799. Circ Cong

Price, Hopkin & Martha Steil, widow, P Licence by the Revd. Mr.
    Alexr. Garden, 23 June 1748. St. Phil PR

Price, Thomas Revd. & Eliza Caroline Holmes, 13 Dec. 1798.
    Circ Cong

Price, Thomas H. Revd., of James Island, St. Andrews Par., &
    Elizabeth Caroline Holmes, 12 Dec. 1798; David Cruger,
    trustee; Josiah Rivers, Daniel Holmes, wit. Mar Set 3:
    319-323

Price, Thomas William of Charleston & Charlotte, daughter of
Philip Smith of St. Bartholomew's parish, and granddaughter
of James Skirving; 5 March 1794; William Price, Nathaniel
Russell, John Blake, trustees; John Mauger, Julius Smith,
wit. Mar Set 2:292-296

Price, William of Charleston & Rebecca Chiffelle, widow, daughter
of Thomas Hutchinson, decd., 9 Feb. 1791; Mary Taggart, Archd
T. Taylor, Wm. Skirving Junr., wit. Mar Set 1: 587-588

Prichard, James & Eleanor Bulloch, 9 Sept. 1756. St. Phil PR

Prince, Charles & Ann Lempirier, 17 Nov. 1763. Ch Ch PR

Prince, Charles & Sarah Dearle, 9 Aug. 1789. St. Phil PR

Prince, Clement & Mary Morgan, 21 Dec. 1792. St. Phil PR

Prince, Joseph & Jemima Webb, P Licence, 22 Apr. 1729. St.
Phil PR

Prince, Thomas William of St. Pauls Parish, & wife Charlotte,
daughter of Philip Smith of St. Bartholomews Parish, decd.,
9 Nov. 1796; Benjamin Postell, William Prince, Nathaniel
Russell, John Blake, Esqr., trustees. Mar Set 3: 114-127

Pring, William & Elizabeth Jennings, 2 Sept. 1747. T & D PR

Pringell, Godfrey & Mary Tweed, 17 Apr. 1778. St. John Luth Ch

Pringle, Robert & Jane Allen, P Licence, 18 July 1734. St. Phil
PR

Pringle, Robert & Judity Bull, P Licence, 16 Apr. 1751. St.
Phil PR

Pringle, Thomas & Barbara Miller, 28 Apr. 1785. St. Hel PR

Prioleau, John & Jane Broadbelt, 27 Jan. 1774. St. Phil PR

Prioleau, John Cordes, & Mariane Cordes, 29 Nov. 1796;
Thomas Cordes the younger, trustee; Philip Orcher, Jr.,
Francis Cordes, wit. Mar Set 3: 26-27

Prioleau, Philip & Anne Etheridge, P Licence, 8 Jan. 1738.
St. Phil PR

Prioleau, Samuel & Providence Hext, P Licence, 14 Oct. 1739.
St. Phil PR

Prioleau, Samuel, the younger of Charlestown, Gent., &
Catherine Cordes, spinster; 9 Oct. 1766; Thos. Savage,
Edwd Lightwood, Junr., wit. Mar Set 2: 140-143

Pritchard, Paul & Ann Conner, widow, 17 Feb. 1765. St. Phil PR

Pritchard, Paul of Charleston, ship-wright & Mary Geyer, 12
March 1797. St. Phil PR

Pritchard, Thomas & Susannah Elliott, widow, 2 Sept. 1729. St.
And PR

Pritchard, Thos & Sarah Hutchins, 30 July 1741. St. And PR

Pritchard, William & Elizabeth Hamilton, __ Nov. 1792. St.
   Phil PR

Probe(?), Johann & Maria Freis(in), 7 Feb. 1765. St. John
   Luth Ch

Procktor, Richard & Elinor Griffin, 4 Nov. 1762. St. Hel PR

Procter, William & Margaret Dyar, 11 Oct. 1747. Pr Fred PR

Proctor, Richard & Mary Ann Vinson, 18 Oct. 1772. St. Phil PR

Proctor, William & Catharine Alexander, 28 June 1760. St. Phil
   PR

Prosser, John & Anne Harris, P Licence, 27 June 1738. St. Phil
   PR

Prue, John of Charlestown, carpenter, & Frances Dandridge, 24
   March 1743/4; license to Rev. William Orr; George Dandridge,
   bondsman. MB Chas

Pruncen, Jacob & Miss Barbara Fusters, daughter of Johannes
   Fusters, 26 Jan. 1738. Hist Oburg

Pryn, William & Widow Anderson, 27 Dec. 1744. Ch Ch PR

Puckridge, Thomas & Catherina Pfund [1740's]. Hist Oburg

Pugh, Azariah, son of Azariah & Hannah, and Sophia Wright, 2
   Dec. 1790. Bush R QM

Pugh, David, son of Azariah & Hannah and Rachel Wright, 26 Jan.
   1782. Bush R QM

Pugh, Evan & Miss Pattey Magee, 1 May 1770. Pugh diary

Pugh, Thomas & Deborah Johnston, 19 May 1774. St. Phil PR

Pugh, William, son of Azariah decd., and Joanna Pearson, 31
   Jan. 1799. Bush R QM

Purcell, Henry & Sarah Blake, 1 March 1794. St. Phil PR

Purcell, John & Margaret Meredith, widow, 7 June 1769. St.
   Phil PR

Purcell, Joseph of Charleston, & Ann Bonsall, of same, widow;
   __ Sept. 1792; Thomas Smith, trustee; Harriet Coachman,
   Saml Bonsall, wit. Mar Set 2: 27-29

Purcell, Jsoeph & Ann Bonsall, widow, 20 Sept. 1792. St.
   Phil PR

Purdy, Charles & Mary Greene, 30 Aug. 1726. St. Hel PR

Purkis, George & Mary Jones, widow, 30 Oct. 1758. St. And PR

Purkis, John & Elizabeth Ayers, widow, 4 Feb. 1732/3. St.
   And PR

Purry, Charles & Sarah Garvey, 19 Apr. 1744. St. Hel PR

Purry, Francis & Mrs. Freelove Sallens, 9 May 1728. T & D PR

Purvis, John and Sarah Johnson, 2 Apr. 1746. Pr Fred PR

Purvis, John & Eliza Ann Richard, 26 Jan. 1775. St. Phil PR

Pyat, John of this Parish & Hannah Labruce of Prince George Parish, 28 March 1744. Pr Fred PR

Pyatt, John of Craven Co., Parish of Prince Frederick, & Hannah LaBruce, spinster; 23 Feb. 1743/4; license to Rev. John Fordice; John Laurens of Charles Town, bondsman. MB Chas

Pyatt, John of Waccamaw & Elizabeth Labruce, of same, 29 Dec. 1780; Joseph Alston, Thomas Butler, trustees; David Graham, Edwd Drake, wit. Mar Set 6: 166-169

Pye, Peter & Mary Gaskins, 16 Apr. 1775. Pugh diary

Quash, Robert & Constantia Hasell, 17 May 1772. T & D PR

Quay, Alexr. & Catherine Lesley, both of this city, 18 Dec. 1794. Trin Meth Ch

Quelch, Andrew & Elizabeth Hall (Hale?), 2 July 1728. Ch Ch PR

Quelch, Andrew & Sarah Fyfe, widow, 22 Apr. 1779. St. Phil PR

Quin, James & Mary Fitzgerald, 5 Apr. 1790. St. Phil PR

Quinby, Henry & Mary Darby, 13 Jan. 1791. St. Phil PR

Quinby, Henry & Elizabeth Buluck, 20 July 1793. St. Phil PR

Quinby, Joseph & Rebecca Hannah Binnie, widow, 19 Aug. 1787. St. Phil PR

Quinby, Joseph & Elizth Speissegger, 2 Jan. 1794. Circ Cong

Quincey, Samuel & Elizabeth Hill, widow, P Licence by the Revd. Mr. Alexr. Garden, 23 April 1747. St. Phil PR

Racine, Thomas, storekeeper, & Mary Harris, 22 Feb. 1799. St. Phil PR

Radcliff, Thomas, freeholder of Charlestown, & Miss Lucretia Hust, legitimate daughter of Harmon Hust, also of Charlestown, 4 Dec. 1777, by Peter Levrier, Rector in the Church of England & Minister of the French Church in Charlestown, John Farquharson, wit. (Marriage certificate.). Misc. Rec. VV: 60-1

Radcliff, Thomas & Elizabeth Warren, 13 Sept. 1740. St. And PR

Rader, Georg & Elizabeth Rife, 8 June 1784. St. John Luth Ch

Ragg, John & Ann Clarke, widow, 27 Jan. 1759. St. Phil PR

Ragnous, John & Mary Davis, P Licence, 25 Oct. 1748. St. Phil PR

Raguley, Clodius & Rachel Braley, 3 Nov. 1725. St. Phil PR

Railey, Barnaby of Parish of St. Pauls Colleton Co., & Mary
Spry, spinster, 22 Oct. 1744; Meller St. John, Gent.,
bondsman. MB Chas

Rains, William of the Parish of All Saints, bachelor & Rhebe
Rishea of Parish of Prince George, spinster, 18 Nov. 1779;
Peter DesChampes, Caleb Lepear, wit. St. Jas PR

Ralton, Richd. & Hepziba Bedel, 22 Feb. 1721. St. And PR

Ramaje, Charles & Frances Swallow, 28 June 1774. St. Phil PR

Ramsay, Ephraim Esqr. & Mary Ann Walker, 22 Feb. 1790. Circ
Cong

Ramsay, John of Charleston, Physician, & Maria Deas of same,
widow, 21 March 1797; William Smith, David Campbell,
James Cletherall, trustees; Thos Fraser, Alexr Inglis, wit.
Mar Set 3: 87-91

Ramsey, James & Sarah Jean, P Licence, 28 Apr. 1743. St. Phil
PR

Ran, William & Ann Spencer, 23 Jan. 1759. St. Phil PR

Rand, Cornelius & Hester Orems, P Banns, 24 July 1739. St.
Phil PR

Randall, John & Susannah Bond, 25 Apr. 1751. Ch Ch PR

Randall, Robert & Anne Mathews, 10 May 1728. St. Phil PR

Randall, William & Mary Muncreef, 21 Feb. 1727. St. Phil PR

Raney, Lazarus, bachelor & Rebecca Whitfield, spinster, 3 June
1787; Hannah Bonham, Jos. Logan, wit. St. Jas PR

Range, Jeremiah & Ann Adams, 19 Feb. 1711/2. SPG

Raper, William & Elizabeth Marchand, 15 Feb. 1763. St. Phil PR

Raper, William & Sarah Kane, 1 Nov. 1781. St. Phil PR

Ratcliffe, James & Prudence Daniel, widow, 7 Jan. 1772. St.
Phil PR

Ratford, Joseph & Eugenia Carse, in Amelia Township, 1740.
Hist Oburg

Ratteray, John & Helen Govan, 2 June 1742. Ch Ch PR

Rattery, Alexander & Hannah Shell, P Licence, 19 Feb. 1738.
St. Phil PR

Rattery, Alexander & Abigail Bailey, 25 Aug. 1781. St. Phil PR

Raven, John & Sarah Holmes, spinster, P Licence by the Revd. Mr.
Alexr. Keith, 6 Nov. 1750. St. Phil PR

Raven, William & Henrietta Smith, 7 June 1761. St. Phil PR

Ravenel, Daniel & Charlotte Mazyck, 11 Feb. 1759. St. Phil PR

Ravenel, Henry of Parish of St. Johns Berkley, & wife Mary, daughter of Paul De St. Julien, decd., 2 March 1753; Isaack Mazyck, Mary Monk, trustees; Benjamin Mazyck, William Moultrie, Daniel Ravenel Sr., wit. Mar Set 1: 38-44

Rawling, Robert & Elizabeth Cole, P Licence, 24 Jan. 1733. St. Phil PR

Rawlings, James & Eliza Hyett, 20 Dec. 1711. SPC

Rawlings, Robert & Lydia Vouloux, P Licence, 23 June 1749. St. Phil PR

Rawlins, Edward & Mary Miles, 24 Apr. 1719. St. And PR

Ray, Peter Junr. & Sarah Burdell, widow of St. Johns Parish, 8 Feb. 1794; James Brickell, trustee; Peter Ray, wit. Mar Set 2: 253-256

Raynels, Christefer & Sarah Webb, 7 Dec. 1786. Pugh diary

Rayner, David & Mary Slowman, 18 July 1788. St. Phil PR

Read, Charles & Deborah Honor Petty, P Banns, 29 July 1731. St. Phil PR

Read, James & Rebecca Bond, 16 Dec. 1750. Ch Ch PR

Read, James & Elizabeth Bland, ___ 1771. St. Hel PR

Read, James Bond of Charleston Dist., & Anna Louisa Young, daughter of Benjamin Young, decd; Thomas Young, Maurice Simons, trustees; George Hall, Peter Simons, wit. 6 Dec. 1797. Mar Set 3: 215-216

Read, James Bond & Louisa Young, 7 Dec. 1797. St. Phil PR

Reardon, Timothy & Margaret McDugall, 8 March 1762. St. Phil PR

Rease, Martin & Martha Morgan, P Licence, 2 July 1733. St. Phil PR

Redford, Francis of Parish of Prince Frederick, bachelor, & Elizabeth Smith, of the Parish of Prince Frederick, spinster, in the house of Mrs. Ann Le Nud, 5 May 1771; John Leger, Joseph Gregory, wit. St. Jas PR

Redlich, Willm & Eliza Starne, 19 Oct. 1794. Circ Cong

Reed, George & Jail Leger, 23 Dec. 1735. Circ Cong

Rees, Thomas of Parish of Prince George, bachelor, & Elizabeth Brumley, of Parish of Prince George, spinster, 25 Nov. 1784; Rob. Grant, William Burnett, wit. St. Jas PR

Reeve, Ambrose & Ann Stanyarne, widow, 16 Dec. 1733. St. Hel PR

Reeves, Henry & Charlotte Elliott, 8 Sept. 1763. St. Phil PR

Reeves, Robt & Ann Due, 1 Feb. 1797. Pugh diary

Reeves, Thomas & Elizabeth Sarjeant, widow, 11 Dec. 1739.
St. Hel PR

Reichart, Christian & Catharine Peterman, both of Amelia Township, 10 March 1754. Hist Oburg

Reid, Charles & Mary Cannon, p Licence, 16 May 1738. St. Phil
PR

Reid, David & Margaret Gray, 26 Feb. 1759. St. Phil PR

Reid, John of Charleston, tin plate worker, & Mary Brindley,
widow, 11 Oct. 1799. St. Phil PR

Reid, Patrick & Elizabeth Cossens, widow, P Licence by Mr.
Keith, 16 Apr. 1753. St. Phil PR

Reid, Robert of Prince Williams Parish, Granville Co., planter,
& Martha Shaw, widow, of same, 12 Oct. 1776; John McTeer,
planter, & Jean Melville of same, trustees; Edwd Mood, Jno
Cox, Spencer Cox, wit. Misc. Rec. SS: 386-388

Reid, William & Catherine Bullen, P Licence, 20 Nov. 1743.
St. Phil PR

Reily, Charles & Elizabeth Russel, 9 May 1762. St. Phil PR

Rembert, Elias of Parish of Prince George, bachelor & Mary
Cook, of parish of Prince George, spinster, 15 Sept. 1785;
George Durant, Joseph Tomkins Cook, wit. St. Jas PR

Rembert, Isaac of Parish of Prince Frederick, widower, &
Elizabeth Varner, of Parish of Prince Frederick, widow, at
the house of Jacob Jeanneret, 24 May 1770; Jacob Jeanneret,
Wm. Walker, wit. St. Jas PR

Rembert, Isaac Jr., of Parish of Prince George, bachelor, &
Margaret Jeanneret, spinster, at the house of Capt. Jacob
Jeanneret, 13 May 1773; Wm. Thomas, Joseph Logan, wit.
St. Jas PR

Rembert, Joachim, of Parish of Prince George, bahcelor &
Obedience Cook of Parish of Prince George, spinster, 11 June
1783; Jacob Jeanneret, Mary Rembert wit. St. Jas PR

Rembert, John of St. James Santee & Martha Prichard, spinster,
2 June 1744; license to Rev. Thomas Hasell; Isaac Rembert,
bondsman. MB Chas

Rembert, Michael of Parish of Prince George, widower, & Mary
Bochet, of Parish of Prince George, spinster, 29 May 1783;
Nicholas Boshat, Samuel Warren, wit. St. Jas PR

Rembert, Peter of Parish of Prince George, widower, & Cecelia
Dexter, of Parish of Prince Frederick, widow, 25 Jan. 1782;
Jacob Jeanneret, Magdalen Jeanneret, wit. St. Jas PR

Remele, Christian & Katharina Klein(in), widow, 17 Apr. 1764.
St. John Luth Ch

Remington, Abraham & Anne Cattell, 26 Jan. 1759. St. And PR

Remington, John & Sarah Donovan, 7 Apr. 1774. St. Phil PR

Remington, John Junr. & Jane Willkins, 23 March 1758. St. Phil PR

Remington, John Junr., & Jane Dalton, 10 June 1759. St. Phil PR

Reppen(?), Alan & Maria Wrade, 28 July 1769. St. John Luth Ch

Reya, Richard & Mary Burges, daughter of Samuel Burges, 21 Nov. 1776. Ch Ch PR

Reynerson, George & Jane Caruthers, widow, 15 July 1773. St. Phil PR

Reynolds, Charles of Charleston, shoemaker, & Mary Huggins, widow of Luke Huggins, late of Christ Church Parish, 28 Jan. 1799; Susannah Talbert, planter, trustee; J. M. Frazer, Mary Walker, wit. Mar Set 3: 311-314

Reynolds, Charles & Mary Huggins, 28 Jan. 1799. Circ Cong

Reynolds, George & Mary Long, widow, 4 Dec. 1785. St. John Luth Ch

Reynolds, James & Elenor Stevens [before 1739]. St. Hel PR

Reynolds, James & Sarah Saxby [no date]. St. Hel PR

Reynolds, James & Elizabeth Myers, 14 July 1795. St. Phil PR

Reynolds, James & Mary Johnston, widow, 25 Nov. 1797; Charles Banks, trustee; Barnard Adams, William Adams, Elizabeth Adams, wit. Mar Set 3: 245-246

Reynolds, John & Penelope Stollard, P Licence, 10 Apr. 1729. St. Phil PR

Reynolds, John & Elizabeth Conyers, 3 Aug. 1755. St. Hel PR

Reynolds, Richard & Sarah Thomas, 8 July 1752. St. Hel PR

Reynolds, William & Eliz: Trueheart, widow, 8 May 1744. St. Hel PR

Reynolds, William, widower, & Jane Reynolds, 11 Aug. 1748. St. Hel PR

Rhind, David & Elizabeth Cleland, 22 Dec. 1774. St. Phil PR

Rhodes, John & Mary Talbot, 11 June 1774. St. Hel PR

Rhodes, Joseph & Sarah Pittman, 24 Sept. 1778. St. Phil PR

Rhodes, Thomas & Mary Blair, P Licence, 12 Nov. 1741. St. Phil PR

Rhodes, Thomas & Elizath. Atmore, 14 Feb. 1790. Circ Cong

Rhodes, Thomas & Mary Wright, daughter of John Wright, decd., 9 June 1795; Keating Simons, trustee, Elizabeth Wright, Edward Simons, wit. Mar Set 2: 424-427

Rhodes, Thomas & Mary Wright, 10 July 1795. St. Phil PR

Rhodes, Thomas & Sarah Grant, widow, 26 May 1795. St. Phil PR

Rice, Thomas & Elizabeth Bond, P Licence, 30 Jan. 1744/5. St. Phil PR

Rich, William & Martha Meredith, 19 Nov. 1739. St. Hel PR

Richard, Caspar & Barbara Grossmann, 6 June 1786. St. John Luth Ch

Richard, Clements & Miss Jones, 20 July 1799. Trin Meth Ch

Richard, Francis Joseph, a citizen of South Carolina, but late of St. Domingo, West Indies, & wife Genevieve, 28 July 1796; Jacob Deveaux, Jr. & Peter Reigne, trustees; Barnwell Deveaux, Israel D. Deveaux, wit. Mar Set 2: 523-526

Richards, John & Mary Thomlinson, P Licence, 23 Feb. 1734. St. Phil PR

Richards, William & Mary Ralph, 29 Apr. 1787. St. Phil PR

Richardson, Edward of Charles Town, & Elizabeth Fly, widow, of Samuel Fly, ___ Oct. 1752; Edward Vaughan, wit. Misc. Rec. KK: 271

Richardson, Edward & Elizabeth Fl'y, P Licence, 31 Oct. 1742. St. Phil PR

Richardson, Henry & Elizabeth Moore, P Licence, 22 Nov. 1748. St. Phil PR

Richardson, Henry, Physician, & Sarah Durand, daughter of Levi Durant, decd., 2 May 1795; Samuel McCormick, Peter Gaillard, trustees; Jas Lee, Thomas Cooper, wit. Mar Set 2: 389-391

Richardson, Isaac & Charlotte Bond, 26 Sept. 1796. Trin Meth Ch

Richardson, James & Elizabeth Paget of Colleton Co., widow of Henry Paget, 20 Oct. 1768; Josiah Perry, Isaac McPherson, trustee; Ulysses McPherson, Zac. Ladson, wit. Misc. Rec. OO: 585-587

Richardson, John & Barbary Bratcher, 18 Jan. 1756. Stoney Creek Pres Ch

Richardson, John & Prudence Fisher, 17 Feb. 1756. St. Hel PR

Richardson, Richard and Mary Canty, 11 Oct. 1736. Pr Fred PR

Richardson, William Guignard, & Harriet Eveleigh, daughter of Ann Eveleigh, granddaughter of Jane Simmons, 24 Feb. 1798; Cleland Kinloch & Wm Simmons, trustees; Saml Fley, James Exum, wit. Misc Rec A: 335-338

Richbourg, Nathaniel of Santee, planter, & Hester Cantey, of St. Mark's Parish, spinster, daughter of Josiah Cantey, decd. 20 Oct. 1775; Henry Richbourgh & Marta Richbourgh, trustees; Christr. Gayle, James Baggs, wit. Misc. Rec. TT: 385-388

Richey, John of Charleston, Artillerist, & Louisa Birkett of Doopland [Duplin] Co., East River, N. C., 7 May 1799. St. Phil PR

Richmond, Henry & Elizabeth Manning, 3 Dec. 1741. St. And PR

Rickam, Andreas & Anna Henas(in), 5 July 1772. St. John Luth Ch

Rickenbacker, Henry & Anna Diel, 1740. Hist Oburg

Rickets, Richard, widower, & Elizabeth Bland, 26 Sept. 1737. St. Hel PR

Riddall, Thomas & Margaret Onsilt of Parish of St. James Goose Creek, 20 Apr. 1789; John Onsilt & Christian Onsilt, trustees; Frane. Cobia, Sarah Ringer, wit. Mar Set 1: 510-513

Rideout, Richard & Ann Thomson, 9 May 1762. St. Phil PR

Rigby, Jo. & Rachel Fenton, by permission of Maj. Traile, 21 Sept. 1782. St. John Luth Ch

Righton, McCully & Florence Cooke, widow, 30 Dec. 1794; Joseph Righton & Abraham Williamson, trustees; Alexander Henry, Jno S. Rushton, wit. Mar Set 2: 348-354

Riley, Miles & Elizabeth Weekly, widow of Thomas Weekly, of Amelia Township, 22 Sept. 1750. Hist Oburg

Ringland, George & Isabella Carmichael, 30 May 1793. Trin Meth Ch

Ripault, James, of Berkly County, Chirugeon, & Elizabeth, daughter of Maj. Charles Colleton, decd., 9 March 1729/30; George Colleton, trustee; Danl Dwight, Tho Broughton, Robt Broughton, wit. Misc. Rec H, pp. 191-192

Ripfield, Eberhard, & Catharine Stein(in), 14 Dec. 1777. St. John Luth Ch

Riply, Paul & Elizabeth Veasey, 21 July 1783. St. John Luth Ch

Rippon, Isaac & Joanna Sealy, widow, 3 June 1766. OJ 1764-1771

Rippon, Isaac of St. Johns, Colleton Co., Wadmelaw Island & Ann Delebare, of Parish Island, St. Helenas Parish, 24 May 1791; John Rhodes, trustee; Wm. Skrymshire, wit. Mar Set 1: 565-567

Risby, William & Mary Sams, P Licence, 29 Feb. 1733. St. Phil PR

Ritter, Lewis & Ann Mary Lang, 4 Jan. 1785. St. John Luth Ch

Rivers, Francis & Frances Darrell, 12 May 1797. Circ Cong

Rivers, Isaac & Mary Gracia, 6 Sept. 1755. St. Phil PR

Rivers, James & Frances Pitt, widow, 5 Oct. 1791. St. Phil PR

Rivers, John & Eliza. Godfrey, 26 Dec. 1738. St. And PR

Rivers, John & Hannah Tathom, P Banns, 6 Jan. 1737. St. Phil PR

Rivers, Jonathan & Frances Stone, 6 Dec. 1757. St. And PR

Rivers, Morrice & Margaret Savige, 9 Aug. 1722. T & D PR

Rivers, Nehemiah & Beaulah Laws, 30 Nov. 1768. St. Phil PR

Rivers, Robert Collo. & Elizabeth Ston, widow, 14 Sept. 1758. St. And PR

Rivers, Robert Junr. & Anne Parrott, 23 Oct. 1733. St. And PR

Rivers, Thomas & Sarah Atkinson, 27 Nov. 1745. St. And PR

Rivers, Thomas & Ann Spencer, 7 March 1770. St. Phil PR

Rivers, Thomas & Elizabeth Cromwell, 7 May 1798; Oliver Cromwell, trustee; John S. Dart, Wm. P Johnson, wit. Mar Set 3: 246-249

Rivers, Thomas & Elizabeth Cromwell, 8 May 1798. Circ Cong

Rivers, William, son of Capt. Robert Rivers, & Susannah Frances Maverick, 6 Nov. 1740, James Island. St. And PR

Rivers, William & Mary Dill, 2 Aug. 1747. St. And PR

Roach, Francis of Parish of St. Thomas, bachelor, & Mary Jennens, spinster, 17 Apr. 1768; Aaron Littell, Samuel Littell, wit. St. Jas PR

Roach, John of Parish of St. James Santee, bachelor, & Deborah Howard, of Parish of Prince George, widow, in the house of Thomas Martin Sanders, 21 July 1785 Jot. Logan, Christopher Willingham, wit. St. Jas PR

Roach, William & Mary Campbell, 19 Apr. 1778. St. Phil PR

Roan, John & Mary Evans, 8 Jan. 1778. Pugh diary

Rob, Michael & Mary Sawyer, 16 Jan. 1792. Circ Cong

Robards, Thomas, son of Walter & Rebecah decd., and Ann Whitson, 6 Sept. 1780. Bush R QM

Roberds, Jonathan, son of Walter & Rebekah dec., and Mary Whitson, 30 Dec. 1789. Cane Creek MM

Roberds, Thomas, son of John, and Hannah Randel, 2 June 1790. Cane Creek MM

Roberson, John & Ann Boddicott, P Licence, 5 Jan. 1748. St. Phil PR

Roberts, Benjamin & Mary Holton, P Licence, 12 Jan. 1737. St. Phil PR

Roberts, David, widower, & Magdalene Vernoid, widow, 1 June 1737. St. Hel PR

Roberts, Hezekiah of St. Peters Parish, Granville Co., & Agness Buche of same, widow, 14 July 1796; Philip Givens of Port Royal Island, St. Helenas Parish, planter, trustee; Revd. Henry Holcombe, wit. Mar Set 3: 127-129

Roberts, John & Ann Johnson, 9 Nov. 1793. St. Phil PR

Roberts, Jonah, bachelor, & Mary Guerry, widow, 3 May 1774;
Henry Bochet, Ann Sanders, wit. St. Jas PR

Roberts, Owen & Anne Cattle, widow, 2 July 1755. St. Phil PR

Roberts, William & Elizabeth Lynn, 16 May 1790. Circ Cong

Roberts, William John, mariner, & Sarah Philips, widow, 17 Apr.
1797. St. Phil PR

Robertson, James & Helen Innis, P Licence, 2 Oct. 1748. St.
Phil PR

Robertson, James & Mary Godfrey, widow, 10 May 1766. OJ 1764-
1771

Robertson, James & Mary Godfrey, widow, 10 May 1766. St. Phil
PR

Robertson, Joseph & Anne Neves, P Licence, 8 July 1734. St.
Phil PR

Robins, Joseph, widower, & Mary Ratsford, widow, 19 May 1754.
St. Hel PR

Robins, Thomas & Francis Lowrie, P Licence, 28 Oct. 1729.
St. Phil PR

Robinson, David & Elizabeth Bruer, P Licence, 9 May 1732.
St. Phil PR

Robinson, Edmond & Anne Butler, 22 April 1721. St. Phil PR

Robinson, John & Anne Jones, P Licence, 19 March 1740. St.
Phil PR

Robinson, John & Isbell Butcher [1740's]. Hist Oburg

Robinson, Joseph & Jone Merideth, 4 Feb. 1741/2. St. And PR

Robinson, Thomas & Mary Rybolt, 11 Nov. 1759. St. Phil PR

Robinson, William & Sarah Baker, widow, 24 March 1757. St.
Phil PR

Robinson, William & Mary Abernethie, 24 Dec. 1795; John Munro
& John Holmes Smith, trustees; Alexr. Tweed, Francis
Robertson, Jas Runciman, wit. Mar Set 2: 456-463

Robinson, William & Mrs. Mary Abernathy, 28 Dec. 1795. Trin
Meth Ch

Robison, William & Elizabeth Filput, widow, 5 Aug. 1763. St.
Phil PR

Roche, Dominick & Mary Watkins, P Licence, 18 Sept. 1749.
St. Phil PR

Roche, Francis & Anne Simmons, spinster, by the Revd. Josiah
Smith, presbyter Ministr According to the form of their
profession, 12 Aug. 1746. St. Phil PR

Roche, John & Jane Romage, P Licence by Mr. Garden, 23 Apr.
1737. St. Phil PR

Roche, Jordan & Rebecca Brewton, P Licence, 16 Feb. 1733. St.
   Phil PR

Roche, Michael & Anne Glazebrook, P Licence, 31 Aug. 1745. St.
   Phil PR

Rochford, James & Anne Cuming, 5 Dec. 1751. T & D PR

Rocrmond, John, taylor, & Rachel trone, widow, 19 Feb. 1785.
   St. John Luth Ch

Rodda, Ralph & Anne Pawley by Mr. Garden, 22 July 1726. St.
   Phil PR

Rodda, Ralph & Dorothy Evans, P Licence, 7 Aug. 1738. St. Phil
   PR

Rodgers, Charles & Isabel McKenzie, P Licence, 12 Dec. 1752.
   St. Phil PR

Rodgers, Christopher & Elizabeth Cornish, P Licence by the Revd.
   A. G., 5 May 1753.   St. Phil PR

Rodgers, Samuel of Charle-ton & Susanna Baker, of same, spinster; 3 July 1794; Thomas Anthony Somarsall, trustee;
   Saml Legare, Edward W. North, wit. Mar Set 2: 270-275

Rodoman, John & Rachel Croan, 16 Feb. 1785; John Hart, Richd.
   Ham, wit. Mar Set 1: 101-102

Rodrigues, Abram & Rebecca, daughter of Abraham Sasportas, 8
   Feb. 1797; James Lynah, Physician & Florian Charles Mey,
   Merchant, trustees; Geo Rout, Isaac DaCosta, wit. Mar Set
   3: 23-25

Rogers, James of Queensborough Township, & Ann Edwards,
   spinster, 31 May 1744; license to Rev. Alex Garden; John
   Ray of St. Phillips Charles Town bondsman. MB Chas

Rogers, James & Anne Edwards, P Licence, 4 June 1744. St.
   Phil PR

Rogers, John to Mary Griffin, 8 Mar. 1797. Rev. Joshua
   Lewis. Marlboro Co.

Roland, Malachi & Martha Benet, widow, 23 July 1779. St. Phil
   PR

Rolang, Abraham & Marian Guerin, 6 Dec. 1733. T & D PR

Rolins, Thomas & Ann Green, 17 Aug. 1779. St. Phil PR

Rome, Samuel & Christian Mason, widow, 4 Apr. 1735. St. And PR

Romsey, Benjamin & Martha Crook, P License by Mr. Garden,
   15 May 1725. St. Phil PR

Roper, Jeremiah & Mary Warnock, 8 Dec. 1711. T & D PR

Roper, John & Ann Burnham, 13 July 1769. St. Phil PR

Roper, William and Mary Willson, spinster; minister Alexander
Garden, bondsmen William Roper and William Powell of Charles
Town, wit. James Michie, 22 March 1732. MB NY

Roper, William & Mary Wilson, P Licence, 29 March 1733. St.
Phil PR

Roper, William & Grace Hext, P Licence, 5 Sept. 1745. St. Phil
PR

Roper, William & Hannah Dart, 5 May 1771. St. Phil PR

Rose, Frances & Elizabeth Ann Lining, 2 July 1767. St. And PR

Rose, Frances & Sarah Backer, 18 Apr. 1771. St. And PR

Rose, Francis of St. Andrews Parish, Berkley Co., & Mary Ann
Elliott, spinster, 23 Feb. 1743/4; license to Rev. William
Guy; John Champneys, bondsman. MB Chas

Rose, Frances & Mary-Anne Elliott, 23 Feb. 1743 [1743/4]. St.
And PR

Rose, Francis & Sarah Balentine, 23 Feb. 1759. St. And PR

Rose, Hezekiah & Eliz. Bromate, 2 March 1752. St. Hel PR

Rose, John & Hester Bond, 10 Oct. 1754. T & D PR

Rose, John & Susannah, I'On, 14 Apr. 1778. T & D PR

Rose, Robert & Rebeca Rivers, 3 May 1770. St. And PR

Rose, Thomas & Beuler Elliott, P Licence, 12 June 1733. St.
Phil PR

Rose, Thomas & Mary Sanders, 20 May 1770. St. And PR

Rose, Thomas & Mary Blake, 13 Oct. 1774. St. And PR

Rose, Thomas & Rebekah Wilkins, 29 June 1794. Circ Cong

Rose, William of St. Bartholomew, & Lucy Bellinger, widow,
10 Dec. 1743; license to Rev. Thomas Thompson; Samuel Hurst
of Charles Town, bondsman. MB Chas

Rosetter, Thomas & Joanna Cotter, 24 May 1762. St. Phil PR

Ross, James & Elizabeth Kerr, 3 Dec. 1774. St. Phil PR

Ross, William & Ann Fuller, spinster, 9 Dec. 1743, license
to Rev. Mr. William Guy; John Mackenzie of Charles Town,
merchant, bondsman. MB Chas

Ross, William & Anne-Booth Fuller, 10 Dec. 1743. St. And PR

Roth, Jacob & Catharine Ygly, widow [1740's]. Hist Oburg

Roth, Johann Wilhelm, & Catharina Walschsinn, widow, 17 Sept.
1771. St. John Luth Ch

Roth, Peter & Agnes, widow of George Giessendanner, 2 Feb.
1752. Hist Oburg

Rothfield, Christoph, butcher, & Sara Attinger, widow, from the
city, 11 March 1787.   St. John Luth Ch

Rothmahler, Job & Anne Dubose, 9 Dec. 1722.   St. Phil PR

Rothmayer, Martin, shoemaker, son of Mr. Georg Rothmayer, &
Salome, widow of Mr. Philip Weis, 18 June 1775.   St. John
Luth Ch

Rothmeyer, John Ehrhard & Ursula Bartholomew, 11 Nov. 1766.
St. John Luth Ch

Roulain, Abraham & Mary Hutchins, P Licence, 25 Dec. 1749.
St. Phil PR

Roulain, Daniel & Catherine McLaughling, spinster, P Licence by
the Revd. Mr. Robt. Betham, 19 Feb. 1746.   St. Phil PR

Roulain, Robert & Hannah Givingston, 7 Nov. 1799.   St. Phil PR

Roulang, James & Catherine Boyden, 15 Dec. 1741.   St. And PR

Roundtree, Jethro & Jane Duthey, widow, 12 May 1768.   St. Phil
PR

Rouser, William & Mary Hartman, 31 May 1756.   T & D PR

Rousham, James of St. Georges Dorchester, & Cahterine Vanvelsin,
spinster, 30 June 1744; license to Rev. Francis Thompson;
Thomas Oliver, merchant, of Charles Town, bondsman.   MB Chas

Rout, George & Mary Nicholson, widow, 24 Nov. 1776.   St. Phil
PR

Rout, George & Ann Parker, widow, 14 May 1778.

Route, George & Catharine Houston, 27 March 1788.   St. Phil PR

Roux, Albert & Elizabeth Trapier, widow, of Georgetown, 24 Nov.
1784; Edward Martin & Thomas Waties, trustees; S. Wragg, Mary
Dick, wit.   Mar Set 1: 134-135

Roux, Albert of Parish of Prince George, bachelor & Elizabeth
Trapier, of Parish of Prince George, widow, 25 Nov. 1784;
Lewis Roux, Mary Dick, wit.   St. Jas PR

Roux, Lewis, merchant & Ann Buckle, of Charleston, widow; 22
Aug. 1796; Thomas Bass, pump maker, trustee; Mary Eliza
Boylston, wit.   Mar Set 2: 538-544

Roux, Lewis & Ann Buckle, widow, 15 Sept. 1796.   St. Phil PR

Row, Michel Christopher & Margaret Hesy, P Banns, 21 Dec.
1737.   St. Phil PR

Rowand, Robert of Charlestown, mercht., & Mary McKewn of
Charlestown, widow of Robert McKewn, late of St. Pauls
Parish, decd., & daughter of Thomas Elliott Senr., decd., 12
Sept. 1765; Benjamin Singleton & Charles Elliot, trustees;
Mary Haly, John Singleton, James Parsons, wit.   Misc. Rec.
RR: 523-533

Rowe, Christopher Col. & Mrs. Ann Chevelette, widow of John
Chevellette, of St. Mathews Parish, 7 June 1711; John Henry

Perger, William Totewine, wit. Misc. Rec. OO: p. 396

Rowel, Tom & _____, 6 Aug. 1797. Pugh diary

Rowell, Wm. & ___, 21 Apr. 1791. Pugh diary

Rowett, John of Charles Town & Mary Hall, spinster, 6 June
1744; license to Rev. Alex. Garden; William Glen, bondsman.
MB Chas

Rowl, William & Ann Sprunton, 20 July 1761. St. Phil PR

Rows, James & Mrs. Sabina Codner, 25 May 1724. T & D PR

Rowse, Edward & Hannah Gidens, 6 Sept. 1747. Pr Fred PR

Rowser, William bachelor & Elizabeth Deschamps, spinster, in
the house of Mr. Peter Deschamps, 30 June 1785; Martha Greenland, George Simmons, wit. St. Jas PR

Ruck, Andrew & Judith Miller, P Licence, 18 June 1741. St.
Phil PR

Rudd, Walter & Sarah Campbell, 6 June 1793. Trin Meth Ch

Rudhall, William & Mary Miller Meyer, 25 March 1777. St. Phil
PR

Rudley, Michael & Elizabeth Sheers, 15 Oct. 1777. St. Phil PR

Ruffin, John & Maria Barbara Wilt, widow, 28 Feb. 1779. St.
John Luth Ch

Rugeley, Lt. Henry to Elizabeth Cook, late of Camden Dist.,
28 Nov. 1782 by William Duncan, Chapn. 2d Batt. 84th Regt.
Wit: John Adamson, Wm. Rugeley, Charles-Town, Camden Dist.
WB, p. 134

Rumph, Jacob & Ann Dattwyler, 19 March 1748. Hist Oburg

Rumph, Peter of Horse Savannah, Cordwainter, & Catherine Knore
of St. James Parish, Goose Creek, widow, 4 Apr. 1746; David
Rumph of St. Pauls Parish, trustee; John Stanyarne, John
Remington, wit. Misc. Rec. FF: 415-418

Rush, ___ & Miss Ann Fair, 2 Apr. 1795. Trin Meth Ch

Rush, Joseph, Doctor of Medicine & Catharine Massey of John's
Island, spinster; Isaac Holmes & John Bee Holmes, trustees;
12 Feb. 1790; Benj. Mathewes, wit. Mar Set 1: 501-502

Russ, Abijah & Rachel Moore, P Licence, 24 Nov. 1737. St. Phil
PR

Russ, Abijah & Elizabeth Canty, 6 Apr. 1758. T & D PR

Russ, Benjamin & Elizabeth Parker, P Licence, 6 May 1740.
St. Phil PR

Russ, David & Catharine ___, 2 Nov. 1722. T & D PR

Russ, David & Mary Sheppard, 10 July 1751; William Coon,
carpenter, John Bulline Senr., trustees; Nathl. Bradwell
Junr., Thomas Bulline, wit. Misc. Rec. KK: 341-343

Russ, Hezekiah & Kathern. Douglas, 14 May 1726. St. Phil PR

Russ, Jacob & Mary Ann Nichols, 28 Jan. 1759. St. Phil PR

Russ, Jonathan & ___ Littlewere, 26 Feb. 1721-2. T & D PR

Russel, Andrew & Mary Mason, widow, 1 June 1778. St. Phil PR

Russel, Benjamin & Elisabeth Taylor, 12 Dec. 1773. St. John Luth Ch

Russel, Charles Capt. & Mrs. Grace Howell, widow, 13 March 1760; Thomas Lennon, Richard Davis, Charles Collins, wit. Misc. Rec. LL: 490-492

Russel, George & Mary Wigg, 13 March 1764. St. Phil PR

Russel, Joseph & Mrs. Margaret (Price) Russel, 24 Oct. 1737. Hist Oburg

Russel, Sol(?) & Martha Brown, 21 Feb. 1765. Pugh diary

Russell, Charles & Ann Dargan, both of Amelia Township, 22 Aug. 1754. Hist Oburg

Russell, George & Sarah Morris, 20 Sept. 1754. St. Hel PR

Russell, George & Mary Wigg, widow, 13 March 1764. St. Phil PR

Russell, Nathaniel & Sarah Hopton of Charleston, spinster, 10 June 1788; Samuel Legare, trustee; Mary C. Hopton, Joshua Ward, wit. Mar Set 1: 402-408

Russell, Nathaniel & Sarah Hopton, 19 June 1788. St. Phil PR

Russell, Samuel, son of Samuel dec., and Elizabeth Jenkins, 9 May 1799. Bush R QM

Russill, Joseph & Mary Raven, P Licence, 27 July 1744. St. Phil PR

Rust, Thomas & Susannah Honour, 27 March 1791.

Rutland, James of Mill Creek, Craven County, S. C. & Sarah Duggans, daughter of William Duggans, of Jacksons Creek, Craven Co., 10 Aug. 1773; Robert Philips, James Major, wit. Misc. Rec. PP: 603-605

Rutledge, Andrew & Rebecca Bennitt, widow, 17 Jan. 1759. St. Phil PR

Rutledge, Andrew & Elizabeth Gadsden, 29 Sept. 1767. St. Phil PR

Rutledge, Edward & Jane Harleston, daughter of John Harleston, 5 Sept. 1793; Wm. Edward & Nicholas Harleston, of St. Johns Parish, trustees; D. DeSaussure, Alexander Edwards, wit. Mar Set 2: 242-250

Rutledge, Edward & Jane Smith Harleston, 14 Jan. 1794. St. Phil PR

Rutledge, Frederick of Charleston, Esq., & Harriott Pinckney Horry of same, spinster, 11 Oct. 1797; Gen Charles Cotesworth

Pinckney, Maj. Thomas Pinckney, Charles Lucas Pinckney Horry, trustees; Henry Laurens, David Deas, wit. Mar Set 3: 162-165

Rutledge, Frederick & Harriott Pinckney Horry, 11 Oct. 1797. St. Phil PR

Rutledge, Henry M. Major & Septima Santa Middleton, 15 Oct. 1799 St. Phil PR

Rutledge, Hugh & Mary Golightly Huger, daughter of Benjamin Huger, decd., 4 Oct. 1788; John Huger, Francis Kinloch & Benjamin Huger, Esqr., trustees; J. Rutledge, wit. Mar Set 1: 400-401

Rutledge, Hugh & Mary Huger, 4 Oct. 1788. St. Phil PR

Rutledge, John Doctor & Sarah Hext, 25 Dec. 1738. Ch Ch PR

Rutledge, John Junr., & Sarah Motte Smith, 26 Dec. 1791. St. Phil PR

Rutledge, William of Charleston & Anna Grimke Coslet, daughter of Ann Coslet, widow, 11 Sept. 1797; Ann Coslet, John Faucheraud Grimke, Edward Rutledge, trustees; Roger Smith, Robert Smith, wit. Mar Set 3: 145-152

Rutledge, William & Ann Cosslet, 12 Sept. 1797. St. Phil PR

Rutlidge, William and Jenet Knox, 23 Apr. 1741. Pr Fred PR

Rybold, Thomas & Mary Thornton, P Licence, 11 Sept. 1741. St. Phil PR

Ryea, Peter & Rebecca Spencer, 11 Nov. 1738. Ch Ch PR

Sabarton, Stephen & Aylsey Robertson, 26 Sept. 1774. Pugh diary

Sadler, James & Mary How, widow, P Licence, 10 Dec. 1724. St. Phil PR

Sadler, Jeremiah to Mary Timms, daughter of Hollis Timms, 21 Feb. 1793. Chest Co. Ches Ct Min B

Sallens, John & Jane Morgan, P Licence, 9 July 1740. St. Phil PR

Sally, Henry Junr., & Magdalena Huber [1740's]. Hist Oburg

Salter, Richard & Anne Sullivan, 24 Dec. 1727. St. Phil PR

Saltridge, William & Lidia Ellis, widow, 14 Oct. 1766. St. Phil PR

Saltridge, William & Mary Bull, 22 Jan. 1778. St. Phil PR

Sampson, & Reb[?], free Negroes, 3 Sept. 1738. St. And PR

Sams, James & Catherine B. Deveaux, daughter of Jacob Deveaux, 8 Apr. 1795; Wm. Sams Jr., & Jacob Deveaux Junr., trustees; Barnwell Deveaux, Charles Henry Deveaux, wit. Mar Set 2: 387-389

Sams, John & Ann Norton, 13 June 1761.   St. Phil PR

Samways, James & Elizabeth Rose, 7 June 1720.   St. And PR

Samways, John & Mary Holditch, 5 June 1756.   St. Phil PR

Samways, Samuel & Ann Tinnable, 18 June 1766.   St. Phil PR

Sanders, John of Parish of St. Thomas & Mary Oliver, spinster,
    6 March 1743/4; license to Rev. Levi Durand; Joseph Sanders,
    bondsman. MB Chas

Sanders, John & Mary McDaniel, widow, 1 Feb. 1759; Florance
    Dunavan, trustee; Margret Brown, Mathew Whitefield, wit.
    Misc. Rec. LL: 146-148

Sanders, John & Mary Hamlin, 19 June 1792.   Circ Cong

Sanders, Nathl & Mary Mikall, 21 Sept. 1770.   Pugh diary

Sanders, Peter & Elizabeth Fishburn, P Licence, 19 June 1743.
    St. Phil PR

Sanders, Roger & Elizabeth Garrett, 27 June 1782. St. Phil PR

Sanders, Roger Parker & Amarinthia Lowndes, 23 Sept. 1776.
    St. Phil PR

Sanders, Thomas Martin of Parish of Prince Frederick, widower,
    & Ann Butler, of parish of Prince George, widow, in the
    house of Mr. Le Grand Guerry, 25 Aug. 1785; Joseph Hoole,
    Thomas Ballow Junr., wit. St. Jas PR

Sanders, William & Mary Ouarterman, widow, 1 Feb. 1774. St.
    And PR

Sandiford, Saml & Mary Jones, 20 Dec. 1736. St. And PR

Sands, Alexander & Mary Wells, P Licence, 28 July 1738. St.
    Phil PR

Sands, James & Hannah Dewick, 29 Nov. 1767. St. Phil PR

Sandwell, Azariah & Elinor Linthwaite, P Licence, 8 Dec. 1739.
    St. Phil PR

Sanger, Simon & Miss Barbara Strowmann, 3 Nov. 1737. Hist Oburg

Sansum, John & Mary Stoll, 6 Apr. 1777. St. Phil PR

Sanways, Samuel & Ann Tinnable, 17 June 1766. OJ 1764-1771

Sarazin, Jonathan & Charlotte Banbury, 28 July 1757. T & D PR

Sarrasen, Jonathan & Sarah Prioleau, widow, 22 July 1770. St.
    Phil PR

Sarrazin, Jonathan & Lucia Lance, 29 Sept. 1763. St. Phil PR

Sarsfield, Will'm & Jane Taylor, 27 Jan. 1740. St. Hel PR

Sarzedas, Moses of Charleston & Bell Myers, 17 Dec. 1790;
    Jacob Cohen, vendue master, Gershon Cohen, Jacob Jacobs,
    trustees; David Sarzedas, Abraham Myers, wit. Mar Set 1: 534-
    535

Sastry, Christian Wilhelm, & Catharina Merz(in), 19 Oct. 1766.
St. John Luth Ch

Satur, Jacob & Mary DuRofe, 30 Jan. 1709/10. Reg Prov 1711-15,
p. 449(41)

Sauer, Friedrich Balthasar, shoemaker, son of Mr. Matthias
Sauer, inhabitant, citizen and shoemaker in Baden Dutlach,
& Anna Maria, daughter of the late Mr. Daniel Henrich Neucko-
mender, who was from Germany and who died here, 18 Apr. 1775.
St. John Luth Ch

Saunders, John & Mary St. Martin, 9 May 1727. T & D PR

Saunders, John & Mary Oliver, 15 March 1744. Ch Ch PR

Saunders, John of Charles Town & Martha Hunt, widow of Joseph
Hunt, 9 July 1777; John McQueen, William Gray, trustees;
John Lahiffe, wit. Mar Set 1: 108-109

Saunders, John & Martha Hunt, widow, 9 July 1777. St. Phil PR

Saunders, Thomas Martin & Mary Ann Mouzon, 16 May 1764. T & D
PR

Saunders, Thomas Martin, & Elizabeth Thomas, 8 Jan. 1767.
T & D PR

Saunders, William of this parish, and Sarah Franks of Prince
George Parish, 20 May 1745. Pr Fred PR

Saussure, Jno Danl Hector, & Mary McPherson, 27 March 1760.
St. Hel PR

Savage, Benjamin & Martha Pickering, P Licence, 16 Jan. 1737.
St. Phil PR

Savage, Benjm. & Elizabeth Smith, widdow, 19 Aug. 1731. St.
And PR

Savage, Daniel & Mary Wells, 14 Sept. 1736. St. Hel PR

Savage, Dan'l., & Jane McKee, 2 July 1754. St. Hel PR

Savage, Jeremiah & Sarah Brown, widow, 5 July 1755. St. And PR

Savage, John & Ann Allen, P Licence, 18 Apr. 1749. St. Phil
PR

Savage, Richard & Mary Clifford, 26 Nov. 1775. St. Phil PR

Savage, William & Martha Holmes, 1 May 1760. St. Phil PR

Savy, John & Elizabeth Green, P Licence, 2 Feb. 1729. St. Phil
PR

Sawyer, Elisha & Ann Blake, 13 Feb. 1777. St. Phil PR

Saxby, George & Elizabeth Seabrook, P Licence, 13 Dec. 1741.
St. Phil PR

Saxby, William & Sarah Hales, P Licence, 30 Sept. 1742.
St. Phil PR

Sayler, John & Jacobina Catharine Stoll, widow, 6 Oct. 1770.
St. Phil PR

Scanlan, David & Susannah Wells, widow, both of St. Helena
Parish, 17 Nov. 1751. Stoney Creek Pres Ch

Scanlan, James of St. Helena Parish, & Margaret Cook, spinstress;
27 Apr. 1785; John Rose, Elizabeth Powell, trustees, of Beaufort Dist., Wm. Boon, Sarah De Traville, Ann Hogg, wit.
Mar Set 1: 301-304

Scantlin, James & Margaret Cooke, 7 Apr. 1764. St. Hel PR

Schad, Abraham & Mariam Aikler, 1 Jan. 1763. St. Phil PR

Schannen, Richard & Nancy Franck(in), 4 Oct. 1768. St. John
Luth Ch

Schein, Jacob, drayman, & Maria Margaretha Brandt(in), 31 Oct.
1772. St. John Luth Ch

Schepeler, Lewis Charles Andrew & Guderot Elizabeth Nahemann,
18 Nov. 1794; J. B. Vallaneux, J. S. Burkman, wit. Mar Set
4: 398-400

Schepelere, George & Sarah Clarke Clement, 18 Apr. 1793. St.
Phil PR

Schermerhoorne, Arenout & Eddy Hildreth, widow, P Licence by
Mr. Garden Rector, 20 Jan. 1749/50. St. Phil PR

Schermerhorn, Arnott & Mary Mackey, 23 Feb. 1769. St. Phil PR

Schero, John & Rosanna Hawkins, widow, 8 Jan. 1774. St. Phil
PR

Schikard, Abraham & Barbara Speidel(in), 19 May 1765. St. John
Luth Ch

Schikerd, Peter & Elisabeth Eggert(in), 1 Jan. 1766. St. John
Luth Ch

Schmeisser, Paul & Johanna Ell___, 6 June 1773. St. John Luth
Ch

Schmetzer, Matthaus, & Margaretha Bohn(in), 6 Apr. 1773. St.
John Luth Ch

Schmidt, Johann Herman & Anna Katharine Hutter(in), widow, 18
Apr. 1765. St. John Luth Ch

Schmidt, Johann Jacob, shoemaker, & Anne Marie Wirth(in), 29
May 1764. St. John Luth Ch

Schmitt, Georg & Barbara Werndek(in), widow, 26 Apr. 1766.
St. John Luth Ch

Schneider, Willhelm & Catharine Gregori(in), 13 June 1773.
St. John Luth Ch

Schnell, Bernhard & N. Shuler [1740's]. Hist Oburg

Schnell, Elias, son of Henry Schenll, & Anna Barbara Meyer,
daughter of John Meyer, ___ 1738. Hist Oburg

220

Schnell, Elias & M. Fritchman [1740's]. Hist Oburg

Schnell, Hans Adam & Margaret Yootzy [1740's]. Hist Oburg

Schooler, John & Ann Chapman, 26 Jan. 1786. St. John Luth Ch

Schooler, John & Elizabeth Yeates, 21 Nov. 1781. St. John
   Luth Ch

Schreiber, Jacob, gent., & Mary Ann Hall, of Charleston,
   widow, 13 Jan. 1787; Ephraim Mitchell, trustee; Charles
   Harrison, J. Mitchell, Field Farror, wit. Mar Set 1: 280-287

Schermerhorn, Cornelius & Carolina Snyder, 20 Aug. 1778. St.
   John Luth Ch

Schultz, Daniel & Mary Coddon, 2 Dec. 1784. St. John Luth Ch

Schulz, Heinrich Ephraim, baker, & Waldburga Nuffer(in), 15
   May 1777. St. John Luth Ch

Schum, Conrad, baker & Catharine Elisabetha Heinrich(in), 14
   Oct. 1777. St. John Luth Ch

Schum, Conrad & Maria Schmidt(in), 23 March 1786. St. John Luth
   Ch

Schutt, Caspar Christian & Maria Margaretha Reimers, both from
   Hamburg, merchants, in the city, 3 Dec. 1786. 24 Dec. 1786.

Schutt, Joachim Godfried, merchant & Miss Mary Dorothy Kelly,
   8 Jan. 1784. St. John Luth Ch

Schwardtfeger, Joh: Abraham & Elizabeth Souderecker, widow,
   27 Dec. 1745. Hist Oburg

Schwartz, Christ., & Elizabeth Fuster, widow, 19 Nov. 1741,
   Kilian Abecklin, John Fuster, wit. Hist Oburg

Schwerdt, Joseph Abraham & Mrs. Elizabeth Souderecker, 13 Nov.
   1745; George sen, & Jacob Giessendanner, wit. Hist Oburg

Scoles, Edward & Mary Thorp, 13 Sept. 1731. Ch Ch PR

Scot, James of Charleston, merchant & Elizabeth Porcher, of
   St. Stephens Parish, Santee, widow; 5 March 1796; Peter
   Gaillard & Samuel Porcher of St. Stephens Parish, Santee,
   trustees; Fras. Thomas, Ann Vernon, wit. Mar Set 2: 490-492

Scott, Archibald & Mary Rivers, 3 Feb. 1774. St. And PR

Scott, David & Mary Ann Fendin, 28 May 1770. St. Hel PR

Scott, David & Elizabeth Man, 10 Feb. 1774. St. And PR

Scott, David & Sarah Cattell, 3 July 1788. St. Phil PR

Scott, Edward & Mary Hopkins, 23 Jan. 1723. St. Phil PR

Scott, Gavin & Mary Sandford, widow, 21 Oct. 1797. Trin Meth
   Ch

Scott, the Honorable Henry, Esqr., & Elizabeth Fenw, 11 Aug.
   1734. St. Phil PR

Scott, James, widower, & Elizabeth Drake, 15 June 1738. St. Hel PR

Scott, John & Hannah Fogartie, P Licence, 20 May 1729. St. Phil PR

Scott, John & Mary Cray, P Licénce, 9 Dec. 1734. St. Phil PR

Scott, John & Darkes Heskett, spinster, by Banns, by the Revd. Mr. Josiah Smith, Presbyter Minister, 17 Feb. 1745. St. Phil PR

Scott, John & Eliza Coleman, 1 May 1795. Moses Waddel

Scott, Joseph & Elizabeth Lesesne, 14 June 1761. T & D PR

Scott, Joseph & Elizabeth Oswald, 18 Dec. 1786. St. Hel PR

Scott, Richard & Grace Walker, 11 Aug. 1726. St. Phil PR

Scott, Richard of St. Andrews Parish, Gent., & Harriet Smith of St. George Parish, spinster, 3 Sept. 1789; Thomas Smith & Benjamin Smith, Esqrs., exors of the L. W. & T. of Henry Smith & Ann Waring, admx. of John Earnest Poyas, admr. of Elizabeth Smith, decd., trustees. Mar Set 1: 448-450

Scott, Robert & Catharine Wallace, 14 Jan. 1772. St. Phil PR

Scott, Thomas & Mary Whitter, 11 Feb. 1756. St. And PR

Scott, Thomas & Ann Wetherston, 16 June 1763. St. Phil PR

Scott, William & Sarah Brailsford, 17 Oct. 1765. St. Phil PR

Scott, William & Frances Daniel, daughter of Adam Daniell & wife Frances, decd., 18 Nov. 1784; William Moultrie Jr., John Parker Jr., & Thomas Parker, trustees; Edward Lightwood, Chs Danl Parker, wit. Mar Set 1: 19-31

Scott, William Jun. & Elisabeth Rivers, at James Island, 22 Dec. 1778. St. John Luth Ch

Scott, William Doctr. & Elizabeth Clark, 24 Nov. 1753. St. And PR

Scott, Wm. & Jane Parker, 30 Dec. 1790. Circ Cong

Scott, William & Harriet Coachman, of St. Lukes Parish, spinster; 21 Feb. 1793 George Hip, trustee; B. B. Bellinger, Chas Glover, wit. Mar Set 2: 147-151

Screven, Robert & Martha Haddrell, 12 July 1739. Ch Ch PR

Screven, Robert & Elizabeth Cooke, 29 Nov. 1753. St. Phil PR

Screven, William & Sarah Stoll, spinster, P Licence by the Revd. Mr. Alexr. Garden, 16 June 1748. St. Phil PR

Screven, William & Catherine Stull, P Licence, 22 Aug. 1749. St. Phil PR

Scriven, Benjamin of Parish of Prince Frederick, bachelor, & Margaret Brockinton, of Parish of Prince Frederick, spinster, in the house of Capt. John Brockinton, 22 Nov. 1771; Wm.

Davidson, William Snow, wit.   St. Jas PR

Scriven, Saville & Martha Bremar, 29 Apr. 1718.   T & D PR

Scrivin, Robt & Hannah Fry, __ Jan. 1709/10.   Reg Prov 1711-15,
  p. 449(41)

Scully, Michael & Elizabeth Sergeant, by Mr. Garden, 8 Sept.
  1736. St. Phil PR

Seabrook, Benja. & Mary Bonneau, 7 Apr. 1737.   St. And PR

Seabrook, John Jr. of City of Charleston & Elizabeth Bailey
  Jenkins, widow & admx. of Joseph Jenkins, late of Edisto
  Island, granddaughter of Mrs. Ann Townsend; 20 June 1793;
  James Murray of Edisto Island, trustee; William Mills,
  Mary Mouatt, Ann Milner, wit. Mar Set 2: 117-119

Seabrook, Thomas Wilks, of St. Peters Parish, Beaufort District
  & Mary Elizabeth Partridge of St. Lukes Parish, same dist.,
  14 March 1799; Christopher Edward Leacraft of St. Lukes
  Parish, trustee; Andrew McCully, Thomas G. Houseal, Henry B.
  Seabrook, wit. Mar Set 5: 305-307

Sealy, John & Susanna Sealy, 24 Sept. 1754. St. Hel PR

Sealy, Joseph & Joanna Staples, 17 June 1754. St. Hel PR

Seaman, George, merchant of Charles Town, & Mary Allen, widow,
  P Licence by the Revd. Mr. Alexander Garden, Rector of St.
  Philips Chas Town, 2 May 1751. St. Phil PR

Seamans, Samuel & Mary Nutton, P Banns, 15 Feb. 1723. St. Phil
  PR

Searles, James & Christian Scott, 4 Aug. 1722. St. Phil PR

Sears, Jeremiah & Elizabeth Green, 20 Nov. 1770. St. Hel PR

Searson, Thomas & Elizabeth Moor, 25 Aug. 1734. St. Hel PR

Searson, Thos. & Margt Wineman, 21 June 1759. St. Hel PR

Secare, Peter and Mary Rea, 3 June 1742. Pr Fred PR

Segwalt, Christian & Mary Keller, widow, 6 June 1772. St. Phil
  PR

Seifen, Johann, widower, & Maria Franck(in), 12 Dec. 1780. St.
  John Luth Ch

Seixas, Abraham Mendex, late of New York, now of Charleston,
  Merchant, & Ritcey Hart, daughter of Joshua Hart, 11 Nov.
  1777; Levi Sheftall, Israel Joseph, wit. Mar Set 1: 53-55

Self, Samuel of Parish of Prince George, bachelor & Anne
  Morrison, at the plantation of Mr. Robert Daniel, 22 July
  1784; Mark Huggins Junr., Elias Huggins, wit. St. Jas PR

Self, Samuel Coffin & Mary Lefoy, widow, 6 Dec. 1794. St. Phil
  PR

Sellers, James & Eleoner Hill, widow, 1 Nov. 1795.   Trin Meth
  Ch

Semple, Rattrey, bachelor & Mary Boineau, spinster, at the house
of Michael Boineau, 7 Sept. 1784; Michael Boineau, William
Semple, wit. St. Jas PR

Senior, Samuel & Mary Scriber, 23 Nov. 1761. St. Phil PR

Sergeant, John & Elizabeth Johnson, 9 July 1727. St. Phil PR

Severance, John & Anne Barton, 10 June 1735. Ch Ch PR

Severance, Joseph & Ann Watson, 30 March 1732. Ch Ch PR

Seymour, Peter & Eleanor Levimore, 21 Jan. 1768. St. Phil PR

Shackelford, James of Parish of Prince George, Craven Co.,
Blacksmith & Sarah Bossard, spinster, 12 Dec. 1785; Thomas
Fleming, planter, trustee; John Stewart, Willm Murray, wit.
Mar Set 1: 204-205

Shackelford, William of George Town, merchant & Sarah Withers,
of Charles Town, spinster, 16 Oct. 1766; Richard Withers,
William Withers, trustees; Edmond Henning, Josh. Hartee,
wit. Misc. Rec. RR: 242-244

Shackelford, William Cartwright & Sarah Collins Vanderhorst,
widow, 1 June 1790; James Anderson, wit. Mar Set 1: 527-529

Shaddock, John & Ann Thompson, widow, 27 Nov. 1777. St. Phil
PR

Shannon, John & Elizabeth Simpson, 30 July 1769. St. Phil PR

Sharp, Collin & Sarah Devall, P Licence, 17 Oct. 1732. St. Phil
PR

Sharp, Captn. John, widower, & Deborah Gough, spinster, P
Licence, of His Excelcy. the Governor, by Mr. Garden, 31 Jan.
1724/5. St. Phil PR

Sharp, Joseph & Jane Baldwin, widow, 2 Nov. 1779. St. Phil
PR

Sharp, Thomas & Sarah Corke, 18 Jan. 1726. St. Phil PR

Shaumlöffel, John & Anna Maria, widow of Nicholas Dirr, 24 Feb.
1738. Hist Oburg

Sharp, Alex'r. & Mary Kayler, 11 Feb. 1776. T & D PR

Sharples, John & Ann Sleigh, 17 July 1766; Mary Liddle,
Mary Caveneau, James Caveneau, wit. Misc. Rec. MM: 675-677

Sharples, John & Ann Sleigh, widow, 3 July 1766. OJ 1764-1771

Shaw, Amos & Persis Avant, 25 Mar. 1746. Pr Fred PR

Shaw, Peter & Martha Blundall, widow, P Licence, 9 Sept. 1739.
St. Phil PR

Shaw, Robert & Eleanor Mills, P Licence, 1 Jan. 1731. St. Phil
PR

Shedtland, Nicholas & Anne Pockington, widow, 8 June 1755.
St. Hel PR

Sheed, George & Eleanor Wilkins, P Licence, 23 May 1750. St. Phil PR

Shepard, John of Parish of Prince George, widower, & Martha Loftus, of Parish of Prince George, widow, 6 Sept. 1771; Edmund Carr, John Simmons, wit. St. Jas PR

Shepheard, Peter & Elizabeth Hitchcock, 21 Oct. 1727. St. Phil PR

Shepheard, Thomas Radcliffe & Sophia Frances Perry, 10 Apr. 1798. St. Phil PR

Shepherd, John & Eliza. Wickham, 13 Mar. 1736 [1736/7]. St. And PR

Sheppard, Charles & Elizabeth Radcliff, 18 Feb. 1768. St. Phil PR

Sheppard, Charles & Elizabeth Gibbes, 27 Aug. 1775. St. Phil PR

Shevrie, Leonard & Sarah Delgrass, widow, P Licence by the Revd. Mr. Alexr. Garden, 4 July 1748. St. Phil PR

Shields, Lambert & Ann Moore, 1 Apr. 1758. St. Phil PR

Shilling, John Henry & Ann Margaret McLenne, both of Orange-burgh Township, 6 Aug. 1754. Hist Oburg

Shlappy, Hans George & Magdalene Huber [1740's]. Hisb Oburg

Shoke, John, bahcelor & Elizabeth Rich, spinster, 9 Sept. 1787; John Alexander, S. Warren, wit. St. Jas PR

Schoolbred, James, Esqr., & Mary Middleton, daughter of Thomas Middleton, decd.; 13 May 1793; John Gibbes & Robert Rene Gibbes Jr., trustees; Edwd Jenkins, Thos Gibbes, Alexr. Garden, wit. Mar Set 2: 156-160

Shoolbred, James of Charleston & wife, Mary (married May 1793), 19 June 1797; John Gibbes, John Reeves Gibbes, trustees; Alexr. Shives, Tim Ford, wit. Mar Set 3: 99-112

Shrewsberry, Stephen, and Elizabeth Bernardo, widow, minister Alexander Garden; bondsmen Steven Shrewsberry (Shrewsbury) of Charles Town, carpenter, and Robert Raper of Charles Town, 11 Apr. 1733. MB NY

Shrewsbury, Stephen & Catharine Driskill, P Licence, 10 June 1734. St. Phil PR

Shrewsberry, Stephen & Mary Ann Talbert, widow, 9 Aug. 1764. St. Phil PR

Shrewsbury, Stephen & Elizabeth Mitchell Dickinson, 22 May 1798; Francis Dickinson, trustee; A. Moore, Henry Bailey, wit. Mar Set 3: 257-264

Shrewsbury, Stephen & Elizabeth Dickinson, 23 May 1798. Circ Cong

Shubrick, Richard & Elizabeth Viccaridge, P Licence, 15 Oct. 1740. St. Phil PR

Shubrick, Richard & Susannah Bulline, 1 Oct. 1772. St. Phil PR

Shubrick, Thomas & Sarah Motte, P Licence by Mr. Garden, 8 May 1746. St. Phil PR

Shubrick, Thomas Jr. & Mary Branford, 9 Apr. 1778. St. Phil PR

Shud, William & Eleanor Elliott, 29 March 1773. St. Phil PR

Shulds, Daniel & Eliz. Sumner, 6 Feb. 1764. St. Phil PR

Shuler, John Nicolas & Verena Hoggin, 26 Sept. 1752. Hist Oburg

Shute, Joseph P., son of Thomas & Elizabeth, and Anna Arnott, 7 Sept. 1731. Charleston, MM

Shyder, Daniel & Elizabeth Richard [1740's]. Hist Oburg

Shyrer, Jo. & Elizabeth Stoll, 29 May 1785. St. John Luth Ch

Sifle(?), Ludwig, a baker & Susanna Geliff, 11 Feb. 1787. St. John Luth Ch

Simcock, Joseph & Hannah Moll, 4 June 1739. St. And PR

Simmons, Ebenezer & Eliza. Jones, 20 Dec. 1722. St. Phil PR

Simmons, Ebenezer & Jane Stanyarne, 12 Dec. 1754. St. Phil PR

Simmons, George, bachelor & Martha Allston, of Parish of Prince George, spinster, in the house of Mrs. Esther Allston, 14 June 1787; Benja Allston, Saml DuPre, wit. St. Jas PR

Simmons, James & Ann Holmes, 22 Apr. 1759. St. Phil PR

Simmons, John & Catherina Zorn, widow, [1740's]. Hist Oburg

Simmons, John & Theodora Frampton, 5 Apr. 1764. St. Phil PR

Simmons, Peter, widower, & Mary Greenland, spinster, at the plantation of George Simmons, 30 Dec. 1770; Paul Douxsaint, John Drake, wit. St. Jas PR

Simmons, Thomas of Johns Island, & Sarah Hayne, daughter of Isaac Hayne, Esqr., decd., 1 Jan. 1787; Thomas Hutson, Isaac Hayne, trustees; Richard Hutson, wit. Mar Set 1: 468-470

Simmons, William & ___, 9 March 1794. Trin Meth Ch

Simons, Anthony & Hannah Brown, 16 Sept. 1775. T & D PR

Simons, Ben of Sewee, & Ann Gray, 4 Sept. 1766. T & D PR

Simons, Benjamin & Ann Dewitt, 13 March 1755. T & D PR

Simons, Benjn. Jr. & Elizabeth Alston, 3 Dec. 1761. T & D PR

Simons, Benjn. Jr. & Catharine Chicken, 27 Sept. 1764. T & D PR

Simons, Edward & Lydia Ball, 17 Sept. 1771. St. Phil PR

Simons, Francis & Elizabeth McGrigory, 29 May 1750. T & D PR

Simons, Francis & Elizabeth Motte, 30 Apr. 1767. T & D PR

Simons, Francis & Sarah Ruth Rawlins Lowndes, youngest daughter
   of Rawlins Lowndes, Esqr., 15 Nov. 1796 Amarinthea Saunders,
   Thomas Lowndes & James Lowndes, trustees; Wm. Lowndes, wit.
   Mar Set 3: 35-37

Simons, Francis & Ruth Lowndes, 15 Nov. 1796. St. Phil PR

Simons, Henry & Elizabeth Duke, 28 Jan. 1766. T & D PR

Simons, James Esqr. & Sarah Hyrne, daughter of Henry Hyrne,
   decd., 8 Sept. 1788; John Drayton, William Peronneau,
   trustees; William Godber, Peter Lesesne, wit. Mar Set 1:
   377-379

Simons, Keating, factor & Mrs. Eleanor Wilson, of St. John's
   Parish, widow of John Wilson Esqr., decd; 26 Sept. 1793;
   John Ball of St. John's Parish, trustee; Eliza Smith,
   Benjamin Slade, wit. Mar Set 2: 160-167

Simons, Keating & Eleanor Wilson, widow, 29 Sept. 1793. St.
   Phil PR

Simons, Maurice & Elizabeth Simons, 6 Jan. 1789. St. Phil PR

Simons, Robert of Parish of Prince George, bachelor, & Mary
   White of Parish of Prince Frederick, spinster, in the
   house of Mr. Stephen Ford, 18 March 1784; Stephn. Ford Junr.,
   William Barton, wit. St. Jas PR

Simons, Robert & Mary Horlbeck, spinster, daughter of Peter
   Horlbeck, decd., 15 Nov. 1797; John Horlbeck & Henry Horlbeck,
   trustees; Jacob Sass, Thomas Baas, Elizabeth Horlbeck, wit.
   Mar Set 3: 212-215

Simons, Samuel & Elizabeth Bonneau, 4 Dec. 1724. T & D PR

Simony, George & Ann Hutchins, 19 June 1739. St. And PR

Simpson, Andrew & Ann Barlow, 13 Dec. 1772. St. Phil PR

Simpson, Archibald & Ann Arnon, 14 Aug. 1774. St. Phil PR

Simpson, Edward & Sarah Cheatham, widow, 6 Aug. 1732. St. And
   PR

Simpson, Francis & Keziah Bregard, 19 March 1776. St. Phil PR

Simpson, Green & Elizabeth Mary Greves, 9 June 1785. St. Hel
   PR

Simpson, James of Charles Town, Cordwainer, & Mary Frederick,
   of same, widow, 7 Oct. 1769; Thomas Turner, mariner,
   trustee; Jacob Remington, Elizabeth Frost, wit. Misc. Rec.
   PP: 116-120

Simpson, James & Mary Frederick, widow, 7 Oct. 1769. St. Phil
   PR

SOUTH CAROLINA MARRIAGES 1688-1799

Simpson, James Gilchrist & Sarah Eady, 3 Jan. 1763. St. Phil
PR

Simpson, Thomas James & Martha Collson, 29 Feb. 1747/8. Pr
Fred PR

Simpson, Thomas & Elizabeth Jenkins, widow, 13 Sept. 1757.
St. Hel PR

Simpson, William & Elizabeth Bull, 12 Apr. 1756. St. Phil PR

Sims, Patrick & Catharine Duncan, 18 Apr. 1791. St. Phil PR

Simson, William Doctr. & Martha Rivers, widow, 12 Feb. 1739.
St. And PR

Simson, William Esqr. & Elizabeth Bull, 12 Apr. 1756. St.
And PR

Sinckler, John & Martha Bretton, 15 Mar. 1738. Pr Fred PR

Sinclair, Daniel, Mariner of Charles Town & Mary Stephens, P
Licence, by the Revd. Mr. A. Garden, 22 March 1753. St.
Phil PR

Sinclair, John, Merchant & Sarah Cartwright, spinster, P
Licence, by the Revd. Mr. Garden, 24 June 1749. St. Phil
PR

Sinclare, Archibald & Isabel Ma___, __ July 1734. St. Phil PR

Singelton, Thomas of Charleston & Mary Strother, widow, 24 Aug.
1774; William Strother, trustee; John Hatfield, Thos
Phepoe, wit. Misc. Rec SS: 6-7

Singletarry, Braton, & Deborah Fewelling, 15 Dec. 1711. T & D
PR

Singletarry, Thomas & Elizabeth Guerin, 22 Feb. 1759. T & D
PR

Singletary, James & Lydia Ann Pedrio, 2 Aug. 1792. St. Phil
PR

Singletary, Joseph & Hannah Dunham, 30 March 1745. St. Phil PR

Singleton, Daniel of St. Bartholomews parish, Colleton Co., &
Jane Mackey, spinster, 2 Nov. 1744; license to Rev. William
Orr; Roger Saunders, bondsman. MB Chas

Singleton, John the younger & Dorothy Johnston, 2 Dec. 1779;
Benjamin Coachman of St. George Parish, trustee; Offspring
Pearce, Humphry Sommers, Mercy Sommers, wit. Mar Set 1:
576-579

Singleton, Thomas & Mary Strother, widow, 25 Aug. 1774. St.
Phil PR

Sinkler, Daniel, bachelor & Ann Dupre, widow, in the dwelling
house of Ann Dupre, widow, 20 Aug. 1769; Samuel Mouzon,
Richard Blake Junr., wit. St. Jas PR

Sinnixann, Brewer, & Anne Dewit, widow, 27 Dec. 1748. Pr Fred
PR

228

Sissons, Thomas & Mary Storey, widow, 3 Oct. 1733. St. And PR

Sitton, Philip of Charleston, mariner & Elizabeth Davis, 26
    Apr. 1797.   St. Phil PR

Skarp, Alexander & Ann Maxey, 23 July 1768. St. Phil PR

Skene, John & Hanah Palmer, 7 May 1728.   St. Phil PR

Skerving, Jas Junr. & Sara. Wilson, 10 Jan. 1766.   OJ 1764-1771

Skinner, David & Hannah Clifford, P Licence by Mr. Garden,
    25 Dec. 1736. St. Phil PR

Skinner, Joseph & Catharine ___, 28 Jan. 1741. T & D PR

Skinner, Samuel & Catherine Reid, widow, 4 Feb. 1758. St. Phil
    PR

Skirving, James & Charlotte Mathews, widow, 16 Mar 1769. St.
    Phil PR

Skirving, Wm. & Mary Sacheveral, 29 March 1766.   OJ 1764-1771

Skot, John & Rebeccah Evans, 8 Aug. 1773.   Pugh diary

Skotowe, Thomas Esqr., & Lucia Bellinger, 23 Dec. 1766. St.
    And PR

Skrine, Jonathan & Eliz: Gaillard, widow, 26 March 1718/19. St.
    And PR

Skrine, William & Susnnah Dill, 3 July 1781. St. Phil PR

Slan, Thomas & Mary Cattell, widow, 30 Apr. 1761. St. And PR

Slater, Andw & Miss Mary Ann Steward, 27 June 1797. Trin Meth
    Ch

Slatter, John & Frances Mordah, 27 Dec. 1792. St. Phil PR

Sleigh, Samle. & Mary Oldfield, 21 Aug. 1722

Sline, Bartholemew & Hannah Bregar, 19 March 1776. St. Phil PR

Sloper, William and Susannah Coshet, 20 June 1739. Pr Fred PR

Smallwood, Matthew & Judith Grace, 25 Jan. 1762. St. And PR

Smalwood, James & Charlotte Hutchinson, P Licence, 9 July 1734.
    St. Phil PR

Smart, Samuel & Katherine Johnson, widow, by Licence by the
    Revd. Mr.Garden, 9 April 1747. St. Phil PR

Smellie, William & Mary Lowrey, 13 March 1783; Joseph Stanyarne,
    H. Wilson, wit. Mar Set 1: 207-208

Smilie, William & Susanna Hayne, of St. Pauls Parish, widow,
    2 Apr. 1789; William Branford, trustee; Rebecca Peter,
    Mary B. Branford, wit. Mar Set 1: 435-437

Smith, ___ & Mrs. Vleux, 10 Sept. 1795.   Trin Meth Ch

Smith, Andreas Godfried, & Maria Margarethe Hildenbrandt(in), 8 Apr. 1783. St. John Luth Ch

Smith, Andrew & Mary Place, 20 Apr. 1778. St. John Luth Ch

Smith, Andrew & Margret Grenier, widow, 27 Nov.1780. St. John Luth Ch

Smith, Anthony & Anne Middleton, P Licence, 20 Nov. 1742. St. Phil PR

Smith, Archibald & Margaret Joyner, 11 June 1789. St. Hel PR

Smith, Benjamin & Mary Wragg, 2 Oct. 1760. St. Phil PR

Smith, Benjamin & Sarah Dry, 18 Nov. 1777. St. Phil PR

Smith, Benjamin & Rebeccah Coachman, 25 Jan. 1787; Richard Singellton, Benjamin Singellton, Esqrs., trustees; Margaret Singellton, Thos Singellton, wit. Mar Set 1: 316-318

Smith, Christian & Mary Jenkins, widow, 13 Feb. 1773. St. Phil PR

Smith, Christopher & Dorathy Blackwell, spinster of London; John Ashby, John West, Jos. Russel, John Eld(?), wit. (no date, prov. 10 Sept. 1708). Sec Prov 1704-1709: 307-308

Smith, Christopher & Susannah Huddleston, P Licence, 20 July 1737. St. Phil PR

Smith, Daniel & Ruth Goodin, P Licence by Mr. Garden, 29 Oct. 1736. St. Phil PR

Smith, Emanuel & Anne Jones, 9 Dec. 1720. St. And PR

Smith, Emanuel & Margaret Elmes, __ Dec. ___. St. And PR

Smith, George, son of Landgrave Thos Smith & Rebecca Black, widow, ___ 1716; Walter Izard, trustee; Will Livingston, Rebeckah Axtell, Ann Livingston, wit. Sec Prov 1714-1717; 537-540

Smith, George & Elizabeth Allen, 18 Dec. 1722. St. Phil PR

Smith, George & Elizabeth Jones, 20 Sept. 1762. St. Phil PR

Smith, George & Barba. VeRostick, 26 April 1766. OJ 1764-1771

Smith, George of Charles Town, merchant & Sarah Scriven of same, widow, ___ 1733; John Sandiford, of James Island, hat-maker, Francis Gracia of Charles Town, joiner; Wm Scriven, Eleanor Scriven, Mary Gratia, wit. Misc. Rec. KK: 135-139

Smith, George & Elizabeth King of St. Bartholomew's Parish, 22 June 1792; George Thompson & wife Jane, trustees; Henry Hamilton, Alexr. Miles, wit. Mar Set 2: 8-9

Smith, Henry & Mary Rambert, 4 Feb. 1794. St. Phil PR

Smith, James & Mary Cockran, of St. Paul's Parish, 27 Apr. 1729. St. And PR

Smith, James & Rachel Hardihorn, widow, 25 Feb. 1737 [1737/8].
St. And PR

Smith, James & Elizabeth Harris, P Licence, 1 Dec. 1739. St.
Phil PR

Smith, James & Sarah Ladson, 27 Nov. 1755. St. And PR

Smith, James & Ann Thomas, 18 March 1773. St. Phil PR

Smith, James & Elisabetha Betz, 9 June 1782. St. John Luth Ch

Smith, James & Hannah Wittaker, 27 Jan. 1796. Circ Cong

Smith, James & Henerietta Knight, 28 Dec. 1797. Trin Meth Ch

Smith, John & Anne Odingsells, P Licence, 9 March 1723. St.
Phil PR

Smith, John and Abigail Commander, 4 Oct. 1737. Pr Fred PR

Smith, John and Jane Ford, 10 Sept. 1742. Pr Fred PR

Smith, John of St. Andrews Parish, & Mary Deloney, widow, 24
Jan. 1743/4; license to Rev. William Guy; Henry Wood, bondsman. MB Chas

Smith, John & Mary Delony, 28 Jan. 1743 [1743/4]. St. And PR

Smith, John & Sarah Rice, P Licence, 1 May 1739. St. Phil PR

Smith, John of wt. Bartholomews Parish, & Elizabeth Arnold,
widow, 7 July 1744; license to Rev. William Orr; Joseph
Taylor of Charles Town, bondsman. MB Chas

Smith, John & Elizabeth Williamson, 11 June 1749. St. Hel PR

Smith, John & Elizabeth Palthezar, 12 Jan. 1760. T & D PR

Smith, John of Parish of Prince George, bachelor &
Elizabeth Bacot, of Prince George Parish, spinster, in the
house of Elias Foissin, 11 Feb. 1768; Elias Foissin, Saml
Bacot, wit. St. Jas PR

Smith, John & Mary Holdridge, widow, 15 Sept. 1771. St. Phil
PR

Smith, John & Elizabeth Kencler, 11 May 1772. St. Michael Luth

Smith, John & Dorothea Mensinger, 1 Nov. 1773. St. Phil PR

Smith, John & Margaret Brisbane, 18 Aug. 1781. St. Phil PR

Smith, John, widower, & Mary Long of Parish of St. Thomas,
widow, 19 Sept. 1782; John Connors, Lydia Perdrieau, wit.
St. Jas PR

Smith, John & Elizabeth Camrow, 2 Oct. 1794. St. Phil PR

Smith, John & Mary Smith, 6 July 1796. Circ Cong

Smith, John of Charleston & Susannah Ladson, only daughter of
William Ladson of St. Pauls Parish, decd., 20 May 1799;
Charles Freer, Joseph Farr, William Robertson, trustees;

D. O. Murray, Benj. Burgh Smith, wit. Mar Set 3: 342-347

Smith, John, of Charleston, upholster, & Elizabeth Norris, widow, 2 Sept. 1799. St. Phil PR

Smith, John Christian & Mary Dorothy Smith (already married), 2 Jan. 1787; Albert Auny Muller, trustee; Patrick Byrne, Richard Wrainch, wit. Mar Set 1: 311-313

Smith, John Press, Doctor of Medicine, & Elizabeth Clifford, widow, of Charles Clifford, 14 Sept. 1791; James Perry, doctor of Medicine, Benjamin Perry, & Isaac Perry, trustees; Jno Rutledge Stobo, Charles Greene, wit. Mar Set 1: 594-596

Smith, John Press & Elizabeth Clifford, widow, 15 Sept. 1791. St. Phil PR

Smith, John Rutledge, of Charleston, gentleman, & Susanna Elizabeth Ladson, 22 May 1799. St. Phil PR

Smith, Joseph & Elizabeth Culbreath, 1797. Moses Waddel

Smith, Josiah of Charleston, merchant & wife Mary, only daughter of Dr. Samuel Stevens, 25 July 1789; William Smith Stevens of Charleston physician, brother of sd. Mary, trustee; John Collins, George Smith, wit. Mar Set 1: 446-447

Smith, Melchior & Margaret Luft, widow, 27 July 1773. St. Phil PR

Smith, Nicholas & Margaret Finley, 2 Jan. 1762. St. Phil PR

Smith, Nicholas & Mary Abel Allen Crips, widow, 8 Aug. 1778. St. Phil PR

Smith, Peter & Mary Middleton, 19 Nov. 1776. St. Phil PR

Smith, Philip & Mary Snipes of St. Pauls, 7 July 1753. St. And PR

Smith, Philip & Eliza. Stobo, 7 April 1766. OJ 1764-1771

Smith, Press, & Elizabeth Miles, 19 Sept. 1776. St. Phil PR

Smith, Richard & Eliza Simmons, 10 Feb. 1794. Circ Cong

Smith, Robert & Isabell Taylor, 18 Apr. 1770. St. Phil PR

Smith, Robert of George Town, Esqr., & Ann Waties, of same, widow, 30 Oct. 1798; Joseph Wragg, Erasmus Rothmahler, trustee; R. Shackelford, Benjn. Smith, wit. Mar Set 3: 303-306

Smith, Robert of Charleston, marriner & Janet Royall, widow of William Royall, of James Island, decd., 10 Feb. 1781; John McCall, Barbara McCall, Ann Keir, wit. Mar Set 1: 7-8

Smith, Robert & Sarah Gilbrath, 16 Dec. 1798. Trin Meth Ch

Smith, Robert Revd. & Elizabeth Pagett, 9 July 1758. St. Phil PR

Smith, Robert Revd. & Sarah Shubrick, 17 Feb. 1774. St. Phil
   PR

Smith, Roger & Mary Rutledge, 7 Apr. 1768. St. Phil PR

Smith, Roger Moore & Ann Downes, daughter of Richard Downes,
   Esqr., decd., 1 March 1796; Rev. Thomas Frost, Thomas Rhett
   Smith, Esqr., trustee; Keatg. Lewis Simons, Benj. Smith, wit.
   Mar Set 2: 517-521

Smith, Roger Moore & Ann Downes, 1 March 1796. St. Phil PR

Smith, Samuel, of Charleston, & Catherine Caroline Tennant,
   daughter of Susannah Tennent; 31 Dec. 1792; Wit. Jos H.
   Ramsey. Mar Set 2: 67-69

Smith, Samuel, Junior & Elizabeth Dill, P Licence, 2 July
   1741. St. Phil PR

Smith, Saml & Christiana Marsh, 12 Feb. 1797. Circ Cong

Smith, Samuel & Jehosubeth Morris, P Licence, 7 May 1738.
   St. Phil PR

Smith, Savage & Margaret Dill, 7 Nov. 1793. Circ Cong

Smith, Stephen & Ann Clarke, 24 May 1757. St. Phil PR

Smith, Thomas & Jennet Field, 31 March 1736. St. Hel PR

Smith, Thomas & Mary Chick, P Licence, 13 Jan. 1742. St. Phil
   PR

Smith, Thomas & Mary Daniell, P Licence by the Revd. Mr. Alexr.
   Garden, 10 April 1748. St. Phil PR

Smith, Thomas & Elizabeth Holmes, widow, 8 May 1757. St. And
   PR

Smith, Thomas & Margaret Oliver, 8 Jan. 1767. St. Phil PR

Smith, Thomas & Susannah Tipper, 28 Apr. 1773. St. Phil PR

Smith, Thomas & Jane Young, 4 Nov. 1777. St. Phil PR

Smith, Thomas Esqr. & Sabina de Vignon, 20 March 1687/8,
   license directed to Mr. William Dunlopp, married 22 March
   1687/8, wit. Bernard Schenkingh. Sec Prov. 1675-95, p. 298

Smith, Thomas, Senr. & Ann Oliver, widow, P Licence by the
   Revd. Mr. Robt. Betham, 14 Feb. 1746. St. Phil PR

Smith, Thomas Rigdon & Ann Mashow, spinster, daughter of
   Abraham Mashow, decd., 30 Aug. 1749; Henry Mashow, brother
   of Ann & Elizabeth Snipes, formerly Elizabeth Mashow, mother
   of sd. Ann, trustees; Thomas Snipes, William Hull, Joseph
   Hull, wit. Mar Set 1: 421-425

Smith, William & Abigail Shannon, 1741; Richard Hasford, Thos
   Morys, James Merrimans, John Jennings, wit. Hist Oburg

Smith, William and Eleonar James, 13 Aug. 1742. Pr Fred PR

SOUTH CAROLINA MARRIAGES 1688-1799

Smith, William of the Parish of Prince William, Beaufort District, & Mary M. Branford, widow of Barnaby Branford, of same; Wm. Taylor & Frederick Fraser, trustees; John Ivey, G. Taylor Junr., Sarah S. Smith, wit. Mar Set 2: 266-270

Smith, William & Elizabeth Smith, P Licence by Mr. Garden, 19 April 1737. St. Phil PR

Smith, William and Sarah Bennet, 22 March 1738. Pr Fred PR

Smith, William & Anne Linter, P Licence, 13 Feb. 1739. St. Phil PR

Smith, William & Mary Denistone, P Licence, 27 Aug. 1743. St. Phil PR

Smith, William & Griszel Agneau, 13 Jan. 1746 [1746/7]. St. And PR

Smith, William & Elizabeth Clarke, 1 Nov. 1779. St. Phil PR

Smith, William & Mary Burow, 13 March 1796. Circ Cong

Smith, William of Charleston, merchant, & Catharine McCredy, 29 Sept. 1796. St. Phil PR

Smith, William Stevens, of Charleston, Attorney at Law, & Juliette Lee Waring, of same, daughter of Thomas Waring, Esqr.; Dr. Thomas Waring, Morton Waring, Esqr., trustees; Edward D. Smith, Edmund Tho. Waring, wit. 23 Mar. 1796. Mar Set 2: 481-484

Smith, Willm Stevens & Juliet Lee Waring, 24 Mar 1796. Circ Cong

Smithers, Gabriel of the Town of Ninety Six, house carpenter, & Mary Saunders of Ninety Six Dist., widow of Thomas Saunders, 1 March 1786; Julius Nichols, William Moor, trustees; Andrew Hamilton, John McCord, & Joseph Sanders, wit. Mar Set 1: 287-292

Smonin [sic], George & Martha Hull, widow, 12 June 1734. St. And PR

Smyser, Paul of Charleston & Hannah Elmes, widow, 1 June 1773; Hugh Allison of Berkley Co., trustee; Richard Hurlston, Elias Evans, Peter Smith, wit. Misc. Rec. PP: 586-589

Smyth, Bartlee of Charleston & Caroline Neyle, spinster, 5 Apr. 1792; William Marshall, William Neyle, trustee; John Hartley Harris, wit. Mar Set 1: 635-640

Smyth, James of Willtown, planter, & wife Mary, formerly Mary Cochran, daughter of Hugh Cochran, 16 Feb. 1731/32; Richard Wilkins, John Brown, Richd. Stricklin, wit. Sec Prov I: 1731-1732: 261-264

Smyth, John & Susannah Richardson, 25 Apr. 1772. St. Phil PR

Smyth, Robert & Mary Scott, __ Nov. 1761. St. Phil PR

Snead, Thomas & Blanch Turier, 17 Dec. 1771; Denham Fearis, Thos Stuart, Robt Sneed, wit. Misc. Rec. PP: 90

234

Snellgrove, Freeman & Ann Jenkins, widow, 26 Sept. 1751.
Hist Oburg

Snelling, John & Mary Jones, P Licence, 5 Feb. 1752. St. Phil
PR

Snelling, John & Elizabeth Fitzgerald Phipps, 19 Feb. 1793.
St. Phil PR

Snipes, Benjn. & Eliz Toomer, 8 May 1791. Circ Cong

Snipes, Thomas & Mary Rummock(?), widow, 19 Feb. 1727; John
Tucker, bondsman, license directed to Mr. David Standish.
Pvt Papers

Snipes, Thomas, of Parish of St. Paul, Berkley County, bricklayer, & Elizabeth Mashew, of Stono, widow of Abraham Meshew,
8 May 1736; Thomas Elliott & Royal Spray, trustees; North
Cott Webber, Thos Ellery, wit. Misc. Rec. HH: 27-31

Snow, John & Susannah Poitevin, 4 Oct. 1720. T & D PR

Snow, John & Susannah Poitevin, 16 Feb. 1762. T & D PR

Snow, Nathaniel & Hester Poitevin, 5 Aug. 1750. T & D PR

Snow, Thomas & Elizabeth Cartwright, P Licence, July 1731.
St. Phil PR

Snow, William of Goosecreek & Sarah Herbert, 30 Oct. 1729.
St. And PR

Snowden, Joshua & Elizabeth Evans, widow, 20 Sept. 1729. St.
And PR

Snowden, Joshua & Mary Blain, 7 Nov. 1762. St. Phil PR

Snyder, Paul & Ann Harvey, 2 Oct. 1790. St. Phil PR

Solan, Timothy & Margaret Eagan Ryan of St. John's Parish, widow,
1 Feb. 1796; Susanna Eagan McDonnald & Jane E. McKewn, trustees; John Manson, wit. Mar Set 2: 474-477

Sollee, John Stephen Leger, of Island of St. Domingo, now of
New Port & Elizabeth Neyle of Charleston; 9 Oct. 1793;
Wm. Neyle, Sampson Neyle, trustees; Harriet Lowndes Brown,
D. Lyman, wit. Mar Set 2: 228-230

Solom, Cornelius & Anne Barnes, P Banns, 20 Dec. 1742. St.
Phil PR

Solvey, Jakob, cabinetmaker, & Barbara Schmidt(in), widow,
20 Jan. 1767. St. John Luth Ch

Somarsall, Thomas Anthony & Maria Willard Stevens; 27 May 1794;
Daniel Stevens, trustee; Willm. Turpin, Saml Maverick, wit.
Mar Set 2: 282-284

Somerral, Thomas & Maria Stevens, 27 May 1794. Circ Cong

Somerville, Tweedie & Elizabeth Cawood, 8 Aug. 1727. St. Phil
PR

Somerville, Tweedie & Sarah Wigg, P Licence, 14 Dec. 1733.
St. Phil PR

Sommers, Joseph & Lovinia Newill, widow of Thomas Newill, 18
May 1739. St. Hel PR

Sonare, Daniel & Elizabeth Stanway, 6 Jan. 1726/7. Ch Ch PR

Songster, Andrew & Mrs. Anna Mills, 21 Oct. 1721. T & D PR

Soulegre, John Jas. & Anne Blake, 29 June 1749. T & D PR

Sparks, Thomas of Charleston, Harness maker, & Rachel Kilmelgo,
widow, 23 Aug. 1797. St. Phil PR

Speaks, William & Sarah Philips, 15 June 1759. St. Phil PR

Spedle, John George of Charleston, house carpenter, &
Caroline Ann Askew, 7 May 1799. St. Phil PR

Speidel, J. Georg. & Maria Eberl(in), 29 Apr. 1766. St. John
Luth Ch

Speindle(?), Johanes & Sophia Wildes(in), 9 Apr. 1766. St.
John Luth Ch

Speisseger, John Junr. & Sarah Phoebe Ladson, 8 July 1792. St.
Phil PR

Spence, Peter & Fanny Browne, 7 Apr. 1771. St. Phil PR

Spencer, Calvin, of Parish of Prince George, bachelor, &
Rebecca Ford, of Parish of Prince George, spinster, at the
plantation of Mrs. Bonneau, 22 Aug. 1783; Stepn. Ford Jun.,
Alexr. Petrie, wit. St. Jas PR

Spencer, Francis & Mary Richards, P Licence, 23 Feb. 1747. St.
Phil PR

Spencer, George & Catherine Rowland, per Licence by the Revd.
Mr. Robt. Betham, 27 July 1746. St. Phil PR

Spencer, Jacobus & Elisabetha Weiss, both of the city, 19 Nov.
1786. St. John Luth Ch

Spencer, John & Dorothy McGregory, P Licence, 14 Jan. 1731.
St. Phil PR

Spencer, Joseph & Keziah Rivers, 15 Mar. 1738 [1738/9]. St.
And PR

Spencer, Joseph & Ann Rodgers, 1 June 1739. Ch Ch PR

Spencer, Sebastian, shoemaker of Charleston, & Elizabeth
Spidell, of same, widow, 11 Dec. 1783; William Doughty,
John Webb, trustees; Mary Edwards, Susannah Doughty, wit.
Mar Set 1: 3-6

Spencer, Thomas, bachelor & Susannah Money, of Parish of Prince
George, spinster, in the house of James Anderson, 8 Oct.
1761; Daniel McGregory, Stephen Sullivan, wit. St. Jas PR

Spencer, Thomas of Parish of Prince George, widower, & Mary
Griggs, of Parish of Prince George, spinster, married at

the plantation of George Saxty, Esq., 31 Oct. 1771; Jehu Postell, Arthur Delony, wit. St. Jas PR

Spencer, William, planter & Catherine Bowman, both of St. Andrews Parish, 28 Aug. 1794. Trin Meth Ch

Spentzer, Sebastian & Elizabeth Spidel, widow, 14 Dec. 1783. St. John Luth Ch

Spessiger, John Junr., of Charleston, Musical Instrument Maker & Sarah Phebe Ladson of St. Helena's Parish spinster; William Chaplin & James Ladson, trustees; 7 July 1792; Basile Lanneau, James Paterson, wit. Mar Set 2: 12-15

Spidle, Adam & Rachell Copio, widow, 7 Dec. 1762. St. Phil PR

Spierin, Thomas Percy of Charleston, merchant & Elizabeth Lahaff, of same, widow, 6 Jan. 1797; Thomas Philips, trustee; P. Duncan, Isaac Griggs, wit. Mar Set 3: 152-154

Spights, John & ___, 3 March 1794. Pugh diary

Spikes, William of Charles Town, cordwainter, & Sarah Philipps, of same, widow & shopkeeper, 15 June 1759; Edward Cavenagh, cordwainter, trustee; James Robertson, Thomas Plunkett, wit. Misc. Rec. LL: 199-202

Spinzer, George Sebastian & Barbara Wirth(in), 8 March 1767. St. John Luth Ch

Splatt, Edward & Esther Dean, spinster, 17 July 1766. OJ 1764-1771

Spring, Robert & Elizabeth Perkins, both of Prince Fredericks Parish, 15 Dec. 1768; James Perkins, Samuel Perkins, trustees; Gill McKeithen, Abraham Brown, wit. Misc. Rec. NN: 431-435

Spry, Josep, & Catherine Tookerman, 13 May 1766. OJ 1764-1771

Spurlock, Benjamin & Mary Elizabeth Smitzer, both of Amelia Township, 12 May 1754. Hist Oburg

Spurr, Benjamin & Sarah Crawford, 30 May 1793. St. Phil PR

Squire, Thomas & Mary Sanders, P Licence 6 Dec. 1729. St. Phil PR

St. John, James & Eliz. Boomer, 12 Apr. 1770. St. Phil PR

St. John, John of Parish of St. Bartholomew, Colleton Co., & Elizabeth Reid, spinster, 22 Dec. 1743; license to Rev. Thomas Thompson; Thomas Jones, bondsman. MB Chas

St. Julien, Peter & Sarah Godin by Revd. Mr. Garden, 1 June 1727. St. Phil PR

St. Leger, John & Justina Dales, 5 Sept. 1767. St. Phil PR

St. Martin, Henry & Philipine Henning, P Licence, 10 Jan. 1741. St. Phil PR

St. Sellerie, Peter & Maria Addison (mulattoes), 8 Dec. 1797. Trin Meth Ch

Stack, John & Elizabeth Parmenter, widow, 15 Nov. 1741. St. Hel PR

Stafford, Elijah & Elizabeth Oliver, 4 Oct. 1779. St. Phil PR

Stanbrough, Hobart & Marget Millent, P Licence, 13 Jan. 1732. St. Phil PR

Stanbrough, Hobart & Margaret H, 29 July 1734. St. Phil PR

Stanley, Peter & Elizabeth Ward, P Licence by Mr. Garden, 10 June 1736. St. Phil PR

Stantin, Robert & Eliza. Nash, P Banns, 17 July 1722. St. Phil PR

Stall, Jacob, shoemaker, & Elisabetha Hinckel(in), of Johns Island, 4 May 1777. St. Johns Luth Ch

Stallings, Elias & Hannah Vaughan, 26 Nov. 1749. Pr Fred PR

Stanyarn, John & Sarah Harvey, widow, 18 Aug. 1740. St. And PR

Stanyarn, Thomas & Anne Barnwell, 19 March 1726. St. Hel PR

Starling, Nathaniel & Anne Ayers, 11 Dec. 1729. St. And PR

Stauber, Jacob & Miss ___, 17 June 1750. Hist Oburg

Stead, Benjamin & Mary Johnson, spinster, P Licence by the Revd. Mr. A. G., 15 Nov. 1748. St. Phil PR

Stead, Charles & Mary York, of St. Johns [Parish], 4 May 1797. Circ Cong

Stead, Charles & Harriet Stanyarne, 8 Nov. 1798. Circ Cong

Stead, Wm. & Grace Lindsey, spinr., 7 May 1766. OJ 1764-1771

Steadman, Charles & Anne Simpson, P Licence, 23 Feb. 1742. St. Phil PR

Steadman, James & Elizabeth Kelsey, 18 Dec. 1771. St. Phil PR

Steal, Peter & Sarah, widow, of Charles Chorwin, 2 Feb. 1792; James Jaundon of Santee, trustee; Vinct. Guerin, Joseph Singletary, wit. Mar Set 2: 2-3

Stede, Robert & Martha Watkins, P Licence, 31 Jan. 1738. St. Phil PR

Stedman, James & Sarah McLean, 30 Dec. 1779. St. Phil PR

Steel, Aaron & Elizabeth Cozby, both of Long Cane Settlement, 15 Nov. 1782. Revd. John Harris, Robt. Bond, security, Ninety Six Dist OJ

Steel, John & Catherine Roche, widow, 17 July 1743. Ch Ch PR

Steel, John & Lydia Guerry, 12 July 1746. Ch Ch PR

Steel, John, bachelor, & Dorothy Chicken, spinster, at the
    plantation of William Chicken, 30 March 1773; Jonah Robert,
    Lewis Miles, wit. St. Jas PR

Steel, Peter of Parish of Prince Frederick, bachelor, & Anne
    Varnor, of Parish of Prince Frederick, spinster, 15 Aug.
    1773; James Sinkler, John Jaudon, wit. St. Jas PR

Steel, Peter & Sarah Chovin, widow, 17 Nov. 1791. St. Phil PR

Steele, James Dr. & Anne Bowry, (no date). St. Hel PR

Stehely, Christopher & Elizabeth, widow of Christian Schwartz,
    23 Feb. 1752. Hist Oburg

Sten, David & Winnefred Knight, widow, 23 June 1785. St. Hel
    PR

Stent, Samuel & Mary Colle Ward, 24 Dec. 1780. St. John Luth
    Ch

Stephens, George Captain, & Peggy Sample, both of New England,
    29 July 1794. Trin Meth Ch

Stephenson, James & Elizabeth Scott, daughter of James Scott,
    decd., 26 Dec. 1787; Aaron Loocock, William Clarkson,
    trustee; Richd Lord, Edward Nowell, wit. Mar Set 1: 336-339

Stephenson, John of Parish of St. Michael, Charleston bachelor,
    & Mary Pacy, spinster, at the house of Mrs. Lewis, 15 Oct.
    1782; Elizabeth Barton, Sarah Piercey, wit. St. Jas PR

Sterland, William & Elizabeth Camplin, 26 Nov. 1749. St. And
    PR

Sterling, Nathanel, & Margaret Gibbons, widow, 5 March 1737
    [1737/8]. St. And PR

Sterns, Daniel, carpenter & Christina Ehny, of the city, 22
    Apr. 1787. St. John Luth Ch

Steuart, Henry & Katherine Kline, 17 Oct. 1797. Circ Cong

Stevens, David & Elizabeth Liverooke, 19 Dec. 1756. St. Phil
    PR

Stevens, David & Susannah Timmons, widow of Thomas Timmons,
    late of St. Bartholomews Parish, decd., 11 Apr. 1775;
    David Ferguson, trustee; Joseph Stevens, Joseph Edmunson,
    wit. Misc. Rec. RR: 334-336

Stevens, Jacob of St. Paul's Parish, Gent., & Ann Miles,
    spinster, daughter of Silas Miles of same, decd., 23 Aug.
    1770; Isaac McPherson, Job McPherson, uncles of sd. Ann,
    trustees; Jas Miles, Joanna Miles, wit. Misc. Rec. PP:
    200-203

Stevens, Jacob Junr., of St. Bartholomews Parish, & Mary Gough,
    spinster, 2 July 1766; Mary Jones, trustee, Iam Hext,
    Sarah Lowndes, Chas. Jones, wit. Misc. Rec. MM: 460-463

Stevens, Jacob Junr., & Mary Goff, 26 June 1766. OJ 1764-1771

Stevens, James & Judith Cowen, 4 Feb. 1741. St Hel PR

Stevens, John of St. George Parish, & Mary Oswill, widow, 19
Feb. 1749. Misc. Rec HH: 176-178

Stevens, Joseph of St. Bartholomews Parish, & Ann Nicholls,
widow of James or Samuel Nicholls, 2 Feb. 1777; Edward
Ferguson of sd. parish, & William Ferguson of Prince
Williams Parish, trustees; James Wilson, Thos Jennings, wit.
Mar Set 1: 459-461

Stevens, Nicholas & Elizabeth Garnet, 26 Jan. 1721. St. Phil
PR

Stevens, Richard, Lieut., & Margt: Whirmarsh, widow [no date,
before 1747]. St. Hel PR

Stevens, Richard & Mary Wigg, 27 Aug. 1755. St. Hel PR

Stevens, Richd. & Mary Smith, 13 Dec. 1765. OJ 1764-1771

Stevens, Samuel & Sarah Reynolds [no date]. St. Hel PR

Stevens, William Smith, & Elizabeth Legare, daughter of
Joseph Legare, 16 Nov. 1791; Joseph Legare trustee; Sarah
McCalla, Thomas H. McCalla, wit. Mar Set 1: 621-622

Stevenson, Charles & Mary Benoist, P Licence by the Revd. Mr.
Alexr. Garden, 19 May 1748. St. Phil PR

Stevenson, John & Mary Allen, P Banns, 29 Sept. 1720. St.
Phil PR

Stevenson, Peter & Mary Jones Snelling, 7 Jan. 1773. St. Phil
PR

Steward, Alexander & Mary Sinclair, 1 March 1791. Trin Meth Ch

Steward, William, mariner, & Mary Ann Wells, 2 June 1795. Trin
Meth Ch

Stewart, Charles & Esther Brindley, 16 June 1794. T & D PR

Stewart, Charles Augustus, & Sarah Stewart of Fairy Hill,
Cheraw Dist., 25 May 1785; Thomas Gadsden, & Philip Gadsden,
trustees; Charles Cotesworth Pinckney, John Ward, wit. Mar
Set 1: 57-63

Stewart, Isaac and Elizabeth Dingle, widow; minister William
Guy; bondsmen Isaac Stewart and Samuel Stock of St. Andrews
parish, planter, 11 Apr. 1733, parties live in St. Bartholomews Parish. MB NY

Stewart, Isaac & Elizabeth Dingle, widow, of St. Bartholomews,
12 Apr. 1733. St. And PR

Stewart, James & Amelia Perdriau, 14 Apr. 1766. OJ 1764-1771

Stewart, James & Ann Middleton, daughter of Thomas Middleton,
Esqr., 17 May 1785; Stephen Bull, trustee; Robt Barnwell,
Ralph E. Elliott, wit. Mar Set 1: 128

Stewart, John of Charleston, Vandue Master, and Elizabeth Wish,
of same, 22 Dec. 1799. St. Phil PR

Stewart, Robert & Elizabeth Clifford, P Licence, 7 Apr. 1743.
St. Phil PR

Stewart, Thomas of Charles Town, & Mary Forehand of same,
widow, 2 Sept. 1768; Andrew Risk, John Graham, wit. Misc.
Rec. OO: 40-41

Stewart, Thomas & Mary Watt, 16 Apr. 1777. St. Phil PR

Stewart, William & Anne Hall, P Licence, 17 Apr. 1740. St.
Phil PR

Stiddom, Henry, son of John decd., & Mary (now Pearson), and
Martha Pearson, 1 Aug. 1776. Bush R QM

Stiles, Benjamin & Sarah Staples, 13 Sept. 1759. St. Phil PR

Stiles, Copeland of Kingston, Island of Jamaica, merchant &
Ann Garden, of Charleston, spinster, 9 Sept. 1758; Benjamin
Garden, planter & Sampson Neyle & Francis Bremar, merchants,
trustees; John Neyle, John Rattray, wit. Misc. Rec. LL:
69-73

Stiles, Copeland & Ann Garden, 10 Sept. 1758. St. Phil PR

Stiles, David & Ann Reid, 6 May 1742. St. And PR

Still, James & Mary Wigmore, 9 Feb. 1725/6. St. Phil PR

Sting, Frederick & Susannah Annisiede(?), 11 Nov. 1779. St.
John Luth Ch

Stinson, Thomas of St. Thomas Parish, practitioner of Physick
& Esther Bourdeaux, spinster, 19 May 1767; Alexr Garden,
Elizth. Savineau, wit. Misc. Rec. NN: 340-343

Stinson, Thomas & Esther Bourdeaux, 19 May 1768. T & D PR

Stirling, James, widower, & Jane Wood, widow, 6 Nov. 1747.
St. Hel PR

Stoar, Benjamin and Mary Shields, 19 July 1742. Pr Fred PR

Stobo, Archibald & Mary Chapman, 24 March 1762. St. Phil PR

Stobo, Richard-Park, & Mary Harvey, 24 Nov. 1757. St. And PR

Stobo, Richard Park, & Mary Harvey, 24 Nov. 1757. St. Phil PR

Stock, Samuel & Hannah Haydon, 4 Apr. 1739. St. And PR

Stocker, Charles Stephen & Mary Bedon, 16 Apr. 1763. St. Phil
PR

Stocks, John & Margaret Young, 10 Nov. 1778. St. Phil PR

Stocks, Jonathan & Elianer Page, 24 Dec. 1723. Ch Ch PR

Stocks, Samuel & Eliz. Sanways, widow, 3 July 1729. St. And PR

Stocks, Thomas & Rachel Howman, P Licence, 19 May 1731. St.
Phil PR

Stocks, Thos & Rachel Holman, 20 May 1731. St. And PR

Stocks, William & Rachel Ladson, 9 Dec. 1731. St. And. PR

Stoll, Jacob & Elizabeth Henry, 16 Sept. 1781. St. Phil PR

Stoll, Justinus of Charleston, brick-layer, & Elizabeth Douglas, 30 Dec. 1797. St. Phil PR

Stoll, Thomas & Sarah Mary Rose at Dorchester, 26 Jan. 1797. Circ Cong

Stone, Benjamin & Ruth Rivers, 22 May 1760. St. And PR

Stone, Charles & Sarah Tucker, of Charleston, spinster, 20 Oct. 1797; Charles Snitter, trustee; M. Harrison, Jamy Fraser, George Buckle, wit. Mar Set 3: 180-183

Stone, David & Margaret Bowman, 31 Aug. 1751. St. Hel PR

Stone, James of the Parish of Prince William, & Mrs. Elizabeth Bellenger Hornby, widow, 13 June 1793; Philip Givens, Mary Dicks, wit. Mar Set 2: 205-206

Stone, John & Susanna Marshe, P Licence, 14 Nov. 1729. St. Phil PR

Stone, John & Margaret Benoist, 20 Dec. 1757. St. Phil PR

Stone, Joseph & Mary ___, 18 Apr. 1723. T & D PR

Stone, Thomas & Elizabeth Fryer, 10 Feb. 1725/6. St. Phil PR

Stone, Thomas & Anne Ferguson, [no date, before 1738]. St. Hel PR

Stone, Thomas & Martha McLane, 2 Aug. 1752. St. Hel PR

Stone, Thomas & Frances Guerin, 3 May 1759. St. Phil PR

Stone, Thomas Junior & Frances Guerin [no date, late 1758 or early 1759]. St. Phil PR

Stone, William & Mary Sayer, 20 May 1760. St. Phil PR

Storr, Antony, hatmaker, & Maria Scherten(in), widow, 21 May 1777. St. John Luth Ch

Story, Abril & Mary Pierfore, widow, 28 Aug. 1793. St. Phil PR

Story, Charles & Hannah Wannell of this parish, 17 Jan. 1754. Stoney Creek Pres Ch

Story, Ellicott & Sarah Williamson, widow, 27 Sept. 1753. St. Hel PR

Story, John & Eliz: Mikell, 23 Nov. 1753. St. Hel PR

Story, Rowland & Elliza. Ellicott, 8 Feb. 1709/10. Reg Prov. 1711-15, p. 449(41)

Stot, Hugh & Elizabeth Williams, 13 Feb. 1721. St. Phil PR

Stoutenbourgh, Luke & Sarah Mackenzie, P Licence, 29 Oct. 1741. St. Phil PR

Stoutenburgh, Luke & Susannah McKenzie, P Licence, 10 Jan. 1744/
   5. St. Phil PR

Stoutenmyer, John to Jennett Carr, 17 Sept. 1799 by Rev. J. P.
   Franklow, Orangeburg Dist. St. Mat Ch Rec

Stowe, Richard Robinson & Elizabeth Darrell, 16 Jan. 1798.
   Circ Cong

Strauman, Henry & Cahtarine Horger, 1 Apr. 1740. Hist Oburg

Straumann, John Jacob & Anna Morgaretta Schaumlöffel, 18 July
   1742; Henry Wurtz, Henry Straumann, Peter Hurger, & Hans ___,
   wit. Hist Oburg

Strickland, James & Elizabeth Hennington, 30 Aug. 1772. St.
   Phil PR

Strickland, James & Mary Wallace, 11 Aug. 1776. St. Phil PR

Strober, Joseph, widower, & Elizth. Harris, of the Parish of
   St. Helena, 28 March 1748. Stoney Creek Pres Ch

Stroboll, John & Mary Shram, widow, 12 Aug. 1761. St. Phil PR

Stroter, Jacobus, mason & Maria Fullmer, widow, both of St.
   James Parish, Goose Creek, 21 Nov. 1786. St. John Luth Ch

Strother, Charles to Elizabeth Pledger, 8 Feb. 1797, Rev. Joshua
   Lewis. Marlboro Co.

Strother, James, bricklayer, & Mary Fulmer, 21 Nov. 1786; Daniel
   Cobia, Nicholas Cobia, Jas McBride, trustees; Charles
   Skirving, John Hughes, wit. Mar Set 1: 293-297

Strubel, Daniel, widower, butcher, & Maria Elisabetha Martin(in),
   10 Dec. 1765. St. John Luth Ch

Stuart, Daniel & Anne Forguson, 26 Apr. 1764. St. Hel PR

Stuart, Francis & Anne Reeve, 28 Dec. 1752. St. Hel PR

Stuart, James & Ann Middleton, 18 May 1785. St. Hel PR

Stuart, James & Mary Martha Campbell, 17 June 1790. St. Hel
   PR

Stuart, William and Agness Spence, both of this County, 25 Dec.
   1799, York Co. York Pro 66/3119

Stuart, William of Georgetown, Hair Dresser, & Mary Fornea,
   widow of Thomas Burnham; John Hardwick, trustee; 26 March
   1793; Chs. B. Hamilton, Conrad Shum, wit. Mar Set 2: 284-286

Stull, David of Charleston, Blacksmith, & Rebecca Race, widow
   of Benjamin Race, 7 Oct. 1757; William Brisbane, William
   Scriven, trustees; Thomas Rivers, Ann Stephens, wit. Mar
   Set 1: 477-479

Sturgeon, John & Ann Duncan, widow, 20 July 1761. St. Phil PR

Styles, Benjamin of Parish of St. Pauls Colleton Co., & Sarah
   Maxwell Waight of Wadmelaw Island, St. John's Parish,
   Colleton Co., widow; Hugh Wilson, trustee; Susanna Freeman,

Eliz. Muncreef, wit. Mar Set 2: 220-222

Styles, Samuel and Rebecca Simons, widow; minister Andrew Lesly;
    bondsmen Samuel Styles (Stiles) and Richard Bedon, Esq.;
    wit. James Michie, 17 Apr. 1733. MB NY

Sucker, Richard & Charlotte Gaspel, 5 June 1777. St. Phil PR

Sullivan, Cornelius & Abigail Sprowl, 21 Sept. 1779. St. Phil
    PR

Sullivan, James & Elinaor Queen, 7 Aug. 1758. St. Phil PR

Sullivan, John & N. Snellgrove [1740's]. Hist Oburg

Sullivan, Philip & Susanna Shackleford, 9 July 1778. St. Phil
    PR

Sullivan, Stephen, bachelor, Elizabeth M'Gregor, spinster,
    23 Dec. 1762; Michael Cockran, Barthw. Gaillard, wit. St.
    Jas PR

Sullivant, John & Hesther Nelson, P Licence, 23 Sept. 1731.
    St. Phil PR

Sullivant, Stephen, widower, & Esther Axson, widow, at the
    plantation of Paul Douxsaint, Esq., 11 Oct. 1770; Francs.
    D. Champs, Jon. Barnett, wit. St. Jas PR

Sum, William & Jane Negus, P Licence, 16 Jan. 1740. St. Phil PR

Summers, James & Mary Lang, P Licence, 22 March 1744/5. St.
    Phil PR

Summers, James & Anne Morritt, daughter of the Rev. Mr.
    Thomas Morrit and wife Margaret, 1 Feb. 1745/6. Pr Fred PR

Summers, Joseph & Elizabeth Roll, P Licence, 7 Sept. 1729.
    St. Phil PR

Summers, Josp. & Mary Wilson, 21 March 1740. St. Hel PR

Summers, Samuel & Anne Snow, P Licence, 31 Jan. 1731. St.
    Phil PR

Summersett, Edmund & Catherine Shroseberry, P Licence, 9 Feb.
    1745. St. Phil PR

Sumpter, William, carpenter, & Catharine Brown, widow, 20 Apr.
    1784. St. John Luth Ch

Sunborn, Ebenezer of Charleston, mariner, & Ann Thomas, widow,
    9 Oct. 1798. St. Phil PR

Sureau, Francis & Mary Mackpherson, P Licence, 18 Oct. 1730.
    St. Phil PR

Surrey, Hugh & Hanah Smith, P Licence, 25 Aug. 1740. St. Phil
    PR

Surtell, Thomas of Charleston, & Martah Stukes, widow of William
    Stukes, 26 Feb. 1784; William Cunnington, merchant, trustee;
    William Print, Ann Wagner, wit. Mar Set 1: 69-71

Sutcliffe, John & Elizabeth Gowdey, both of Christ Church Parish, 9 June 1788; William Gowdey, Edward Trescott, trustees; Phil Prioleau, A. E. Prioleau, wit. Mar Set 1: 384-387

Sutcliffe, John & Elizabeth Gowdy, 12 June 1788. St. Phil PR

Sutherland, James & Mary Herbert, 21 June 1724. Ch Ch PR

Suthey, John & Mary Grant, P Licence by the Revd. Mr. Alexr. Garden, 10 Feb. 1747. St. Phil PR

Sutton, James, and Mary Hutching, widow; minister Alexander Garden; bondsmen James Sutton, mariner, and Abraham Mason of Charles Town, shopkeeper; wit. James Michie, 12 Apr. 1733. MB NY

Sutton, James & Mary Hutchins, P Licence, 12 Apr. 1733. St. Phil PR

Sutter, John & Susannah Tippin, 11 Sept. 1779. St. Phil PR

Sutton, Thomas & Mary Neal, widow, 17 June 1786. St. Hel PR

Swain, John & Elizabeth, widow of John Conyers, 20 Apr. 1756. St. Hel PR

Swain, Luke & Rebecca Peaton, 4 Sept. 1774. St. Phil PR

Swallow, Newman & Frances Blake, 31 March 1761. St. Phil PR

Swallow, William of Charlestown, & Sarah Prince, niece of John Prince, 1 Aug. 1771; John Prince, Barnard Elliott, trustees; Thomas Shirley, William Price, wit. Misc. Rec. PP. 490-491

Swallow, William & Sarah Prince, 26 Oct. 1771. St. Phil PR

Swann, Edward & Rachel Robinson, P Licence, 20 January 1742. St. Phil PR

Swanson, David & Mary Smilie, 31 May 1768. St. Phil PR

Sweet, James & Mary Boden, 11 Apr. 1794. Circ Cong

Sweetman, Michael Copinger & Winefred Wilson, widow of Prince George Parish, 12 Aug. 1794; Wm. Prestman, trustee; Dougald McKinley, A. Miller, wit. Mar Set 2: 304-317

Swindershore, Andrew & Sarah Bowler, widow, 6 Aug. 1789. St. Phil PR

Swinton, David and Hannah Clyatt, widow, 1 Aug. 1739. Pr Fred PR

Swinton, Hugh of Prince Fredericks Parish, & Mary Thomson Johnson, 1 May 1790; William Thomson Senr., William Potts, trustees; Tho Potts, Stephen Miller, wit. Mar Set 1: 513-516

Swinton, William & Sarah Baron, 6 June 1766. OJ 1764-1771

Sym, Hugh & Sarah Clark, 8 March 1766. OJ 1764-1771

Syme, John & Margaret Ashby, 19 Aug. 1759. T & D PR

Syme, John, Store Keeper, & Kitsey Dannel, widow, 31 May 1792. Trin Meth Ch

Symmonds, Thomas & Ann Watson, 24 March 1711/2. SPG

Taffe, Aaron & Margaret Bury, 5 Apr. 1779. St. Phil PR

Taggart, William & Mary Haly, widow, 3 Feb. 1778. St. Phil PR

Tailer, Thomas & Mary Devant, 26 Apr. 1764. St. Hel PR

Tait, Henry, of Georgetown, in the Dist., of Georgetown, & Hannah Norris of same Dist., widow, 27 May 1793; John Labruce, of same Dist., Esqr., trustee; Francis Marshall, William Brazer, wit. Mar Set 2: 101-105

Tait, Henry & Hannah Norris, widow, 7 May 1793; John Labruce, trustee; (already married by 6 July 1796); Elizabeth Graham, Jno Keith, wit. Mar Set 3: 193-195

Talbert, James & Mary Jolly, P Banns, 1 Nov. 1727. St. Phil PR

Talbert, James & Ann Herberson, 28 Aug. 1756. St. Phil PR

Talbert, James & Susanna Frizer, widow & relict of Joseph Frizer the younger late of Christ Church Parish; 13 May 1793; John Hartman, trustee; Elizabeth Frizer, Richard Hartman, wit. Mar Set 2: 133-136

Talbird, Henry of St. Helena Parish, Beaufort Dist., & Catharine Bowman, widow of same, 23 Nov. 1778; Robert Proteous & Daniel John Green, both of same, trustees; W. Hazzard, Chas Givens, wit. Mar Set 2: 215-218

Talbird, Thomas & Christiana Crawford, 29 June 1780. St. Hel PR

Tallman, John Richard & Elizabeth Snell, widow, 15 Dec. 1776. St. Phil PR

Tamplet, John & Sarah Jeuning, 2 Jan. 1758. St. Phil PR

Tampleroy, John & Veronica Wedgworth, P Licence, Sept. 1733. St. Phil PR

Tamplet, Peter of Parish of St. James Goose Creek & Mary Wood, widow, 2 July 1767; James Sheater, William Withers, trustee; John Starling, Wm. Woods, wit. Misc. Rec. NN: 46-47

Tanner, John & Barbara Rumph, P Licence by Mr. Orr, 7 May 1737. St. Phil PR

Tapp, John Julius, son of Christian Tapp, & Anna B. Hergersperger, widow, maiden name Kesebirnger, 3 Feb. 1740. Hist Oburg

Tarbet, James & Frances Chalcroft, ___ 1725. St. Phil PR

Tarbox, William of Parish of Prince George, bachelor & Sabina Rembert of Parish of Prince George, spinster, 29 May 1783; Nicholas Boshat, Samuel Warren, wit. St. Jas PR

Tarriane, Stephen & Mary Newton, 9 June 1728. Ch Ch PR

Tart, Nathan & Sarah Sanders, 7 May 1747.   T & D PR

Tart, Nathan & Priscilla Hall, 3 Dec. 1758.   T & D PR

Tart, Nathan & Elizabeth Garden, 31 Mar 1771.   T & D PR

Tatnel, Thomas & Mary Ward, P Licence, 4 Feb. 1732.   St. Phil PR

Tatnell, Thomas & Eliz: Barnwell, [no date].   St. And PR

Tattnell, Josiah & Mary Mullryne, 21 May 1768.   St. Hel PR

Tattnall, Josiah, of the State of Georgia, & Harriet Fenwick,
    married on or about 16 Jan. 1786; agreement 26 Sept. 1789;
    Harriet, youngest daughter of Edward Fenwick, Esqr., decd;
    Thomas Gadsden & Andrew Turnbull, trustees; E. H. Bay, wit.
    Mar Set 2:40-45

Taveroon, Stephen & Sarah Turner, 4 Nov. 1725.   St. Phil PR

Taylor, Alexander Capt. of Charleston, mariner & Sarah Grissel,
    widow, 15 May 1798.   St. Phil PR

Taylor, Archibald of Georgetown, merchant, & Mary Man, of same,
    21 Apr. 1785; Robert Collins, merchant, and John Pyatt, of
    All Saints Parish, trustees; Thomas Waties, Alexander
    Campbell, wit.   Mar Set 1: 37-38

Taylor, Barnard & Susannah Bonneau, P Licence by the Revd. Mr.
    Alexr. Garden, 14 Oct. 1747.   St. Phil PR

Taylor, Christopher & Ann Newcombe, 7 Dec. 1770.   St. Phil PR

Taylor, David & Jane Baynes Guy, spinster, 6 Aug. 1752;
    Christopher Guy, planter, trustee; John Rowan, William
    Godfrey, Thomas Godfrey, wit.   Misc. Rec. KK: 388-391

Taylor, David & Jane Kelsey, 6 May 1775.   St. Phil PR

Taylor, George & Elizabeth Minors, 9 Aug. 1765.   St. Phil PR

Taylor, George & Sarah Hartley Bay, 11 March 1797; Samuel Hay,
    John Goodwin, wit.   Mar Set 3: 91-94

Taylor, James & Hester Wood, 23 Oct. 1729.   St. And PR

Taylor, James & Elizabeth, widow of William Barrie, 20 Aug.
    1754, both of Orangeburgh Township.   Hist Oburg

Taylor, John & Sarah Russell, 22 May 1766.   OJ 1764-1771

Taylor, John & Sarah Rusel, 29 May 1766.   St. And PR

Taylor, Joseph Capt., mariner, & Serezel Agnes Hamilton, 25
    July 1799.   St. Phil PR

Taylor, Oliver & Ann Knight, widow, 14 Apr. 1789; Gideon
    Dupon, trustee; Saml Adams, Patrick Murry, wit.   Mar Set 1:
    421-422

Taylor, Paul & Martha Miller, 25 Jan. 1778.   St. Phil PR

Taylor, Richard, son of Jonathan, and Mary Gilbreath, 5 Feb.
    1778.   Bush R QM

Taylor, Ruffin, of Parish of Prince Frederick, bachelor &
    Anne Heughes [sic] of Parish of Prince Frederick, widow,
    4 Apr. 1783; Geo Ford, William Barton, wit. St. Jas PR

Taylor, William & Mary Bochett, 14 Nov. 1776. T & D PR

Taylor, William, son of Jonathan & Mary, and Mary Pearson,
    29 Oct. 1773. Bush R QM

Taylor, William of Savannah, merchant, & Mary Clayton Miller,
    daughter of Andrew Miller, decd., 6 May 1799; Richard Miller
    & William Scarborough Junior, of Savannah trustees; Wm.
    Adamson, Saml Mathis, wit. Misc Rec. A: 361-363

Tebout, Tunis & Sarah Darling, 1 Jan. 1765. St. Phil PR

Tellar, William and Ann Evans, 8 Dec. 1740. Pr Fred PR

Templeroy, John and Veronica Wegworth, spinster, minister
    Alexander Garden; bondsmen John Templeroy (Jean Tamplerau)
    of Charles Town, baker, and John Riviere of Charles Town,
    15 Sept. 1733. MB NY

Terence, Robert & Sarah Yeulin, 14 Feb. 1795. St. Phil PR

Tew, Charles & Mary Morgan, 20 Dec. 1796. Circ Cong

Tew, George & Mary Lambright, 23 Sept. 1760. St. And PR

Tew, Thomas and Mary You, spinster, minister William Guy;
    bondsmen Thomas Tew of St. Andrews Parish, tailor, and
    George Young of Charles Town, tailor, 11 July 1733. MB NY

Tew, Thomas & Joan Robinson, per Licence, 11 Feb. 1745. St.
    Phil PR

Thackam, Thomas & Judith Gready, widow, 1 May 1791. St. Phil
    PR

Tharin, Dnaiel & Susanna Witten, of St. Johns Parish, widow,
    21 June 1788; Ephraim Mitchell, trustee; Margaret Martin,
    John Burdell, wit. Mar Set 1: 368-374

Theis, Jeremiah & Cathrine Elizabeth Shaumlefall, P Licence,
    13 Jan. 1741. St. Phil PR

Theus, Christian & N. N. [1740's]. Hist Oburg

Theus, Simon & Elizabeth Mackey of Amelia Township, at the
    house of Simon Theus, commonly called Monk's Corner, in
    St. John's Parish, 12 Feb. 1754. Hist Oburg

Thirsting, Thomas of Parish of Prince George, bachelor & Jean
    Hinds, of Parish of Prince George, widow, 11 Apr. 1782;
    Isaac Delisseline, Mary McCollough, wit. St. Jas PR

Thomas, Edward, son of Isaac & Mary, and Mary Wright, 12 June
    1783. Bush R QM

Thomas, Edward & Elizabeth Burrington, 11 Dec. 1787. St. Phil
    PR

Thomas, Johannes, wigmaker, & Maria Monck, both of the city,
    25 March 1787. St. John Luth Ch

Thomas, John & Alice Sidney, P Licence by the Revd. Mr. Alexr. Garden, 28 Apr. 1748. St. Phil PR

Thomas, John & Deborah Scott, P Licence, 16 Oct. 1748. St. Phil PR

Thomas, John, son of Isaac & Mary, and Ann Pemberton, 1 June 1786. Bush R QM

Thomas, Noah, bachelor, & Catherine Chicken, spinster, 5 Aug. 1762; Peter Guerry, Elizabeth Dupont, wit. St. Jas PR

Thomas, Samuel & Ann Hasell, 24 July 1757. St. Phil PR

Thomas, Samuel & Jane Douxsaint, 30 Oct. 1768. St. Phil PR

Thomas, Sam'l Rev., & Elizabeth Ashby, 26 Nov. 1747. T & D PR

Thompson, Archebald, & Mary Hackness, 30 Oct. 1756. St. Phil PR

Thompson, Edward & Ann Gibbes, 27 Sept. 1767. St. Phil PR

Thompson, Frances & Martha Simpson, widow, 21 July 1744. St. And PR

Thompson, Francis of Parish of St. Helena & Martha Simpson, widow, 20 July 1744; license to Rev. William Guy; Isaac Weatherly, bondsman. MB Chas

Thompson, James of Cape Fear & Margaret Mckay, spinster, 7 Nov. 1744; license to Rev. Alexander Garden; John Mackenzie of Charles Town, merchant, bondsman. MB Chas

Thompson, James Booth, of Round O, & Elizabeth Youngblood, daughter of Col. Peter Youngblood, decd., 29 Jan. 1799; Col. William Fishburne, & Thomas Tendin, trustees; R. Singellton, R. Singellton Junr., wit. Mar Set 3: 358-360

Thompson, John & Martha Duprea, 28 Apr. 1724. Ch Ch PR

Thompson, John & Cybell Dyngle, P Licence, 2 Aug. 1739. St. Phil PR

Thompson, John & Sarah Hutchins, P Licence, 20 Nov. 1749. St. Phil PR

Thompson, John & Rebecca Frear, 3 May 1787. St. Phil PR

Thompson, John, of Dist. of Georgetown, planter & Martha Forrester of the same, widow, of James Durand; 23 May 1793; Childermas Croft, Thomas Boone the elder, trustees; Ann Durand, wit. Mar Set 2: 123-127

Thompson, Joseph, and Jane Laurance, 11 Nov. 1790. Bush R QM

Thompson, Joseph & Susanna McFarson, 5 Sept. 1796. Trin Meth Ch

Thompson, Richard, son of Joseph, and Susannah Stidman, 27 July 1782. Bush R QM

Thompson, Robert & Elizabeth Marlow, 15 Aug. 1793. Trin Meth Ch

SOUTH CAROLINA MARRIAGES 1688-1799

Thompson, William and Margaret Nesmith, 27 Oct. 1737. Pr Fred
PR

Thompson, William & Eugenia Russell, both of Amelia Township,
14 Aug. 1755. Hist Oburg

Thompson, William & Mary Hester Bine, 18 May 1782. St. Phil PR

Thomson, Francis, School master, & Constantia Reynolds, [no date].
St. Hel PR

Thomson, James & Mary Jerum, 10 Feb. 1722. St. Phil PR

Thomson, James & Margaret Mckay, P Licence, 8 Nov. 1744. St.
Phil PR

Thomson, James of Charleston, an officer of the Customs for
the Dist. of Charleston, & Mary Harvey, spinster, 27 Nov.
1798; Daniel Stevens, trustee; Lucas Florin, wit. Mar
Set 3: 317-319

Thomson, John & Mary Jones, P Licence, 27 Jan. 1731. St. Phil
PR

Thomson, Michael & Ann Fisher, 27 Feb. 1759. St. Phil PR

Thomson, Robert Campbell, late of the city of Philadelphia, but
since of the Light Horse doing duty here, Quarter Master, &
Esther Irwine, widow of Joseph Irwine, vintner, 23 May 1778;
Robert Rae of Augusta, Esqr. & Robert McCorneck of Savannah,
trustees; John Tweedell, James Whitefield, J.P. Mar Set 1:
250-253

Thorne, John Gardener & Sarah Stocks, 16 Feb. 1788. St. Phil
PR

Thorney, William & Jane Kay, widow of Joseph Kay; 12 Feb. 1799;
John Cell, Robert Clark, trustees; Mary J. Dendy, Gabriel
Bailey, Gabl Clark, wit. Mar Set 4: 81-87

Thorney, Wm. & Jane Kay, 12 Feb. 1799. Circ Cong

Thornhill, ___ & Bazzel, ___, 1 Sept. 1767. Pugh diary

Thornton, Joseph & Mary Middleton, P Licence by Mr. Jon,
21 August 1735. St. Phil PR

Thornton, Samuel & Mary Rivers, widow, 18 Nov. 1759. St. Phil
PR

Threadcraft, Thomas & Magd'n Morrena, 15 July 1745. T & D PR

Threadcraft, Thomas & Sarah Dewis, 30 Aug. 1764. St. Phil PR

Thurston, Samuel Isaac of Wilmington, N.C., merchant & Jane
Futhey of Georgetown, widow, 22 June 1799; John Cogdell,
Josias Allston of Georgetown, trustee; Childermas Croft, C.
DuPre, wit. Mar Set 3: 362-364

Thwartz, Christian & Elizabeth Fuster, widow, 19 Nov. 1741.
Hist Oburg

Thwing, David & Martha Milner, 20 June 1799.   Circ Cong

Tidd, Benjamin & Elizabeth Traddell, 13 June 1799. Circ Cong

Tidyman, Philip & Hester Rose, 31 Oct. 1772. St. Phil PR

Tilly, William & Mary Gibbs, P Licence, 5 Sept. 1740. St.
    Phil PR

Timmons, Connor of Parish of Prince George, Kingstown Township,
    & Agnes Jerdon of same, 10 Apr. 1773; John Berbant, Elizabeth
    Hankin, wit. Misc. Rec. RR: 46-47

Timmons, Lewis of Charles town, constable, & Jacobina Catarina
    Sayler, of same, shopkeeper, 12 July 1773; Abraham Spidell,
    turner, trustee; George Hahnbaum, Adam Petsch, wit. Misc.
    Rec. PP: 572-575

Timmons, Lewis & Ann Legge, 31 May 1793; rec. 5 June 1793; John
    Eberly, Philip Wesner, trustees; John Hamilton, Adair
    Spidell, wit. Mar Set 2: 98-100

Timmons, Richard of St. Johns Colleton Co., & Mary Ann Holden,
    spinster, 30 March 1744; license to Rev. John Quincey;
    Mumford Milner, bondsman. MB Chas

Timrod, Henry & Mary White, widow, 13 June 1765. St. Phil PR

Timrod, Henry of Charlestown, Taylor, & Christiana Hoff, of
    same, widow, 7 Jan. 1783; Jacob Williman, Tanner, trustee;
    J. Ward, Thos Horry, wit. Misc. Rec. UU: 188-191

Timrod, Henry, Elder of the German Church & Mistress
    Christiana Hoff, widow, 19 Jan. 1783. St. John Luth Ch

Timrod, Henry & Susannah Hargan, 19 March 1785. St. John Luth
    Ch

Timothy, Peter & Ann Donavan, per Licence, 8 Dec. 1745. St.
    Phil PR

Tims, Thomas of Charleston, Gent., & Hannah Hext of same,
    spinster, 7 May 1799; John B. Hext, trustee; Daniel Bell,
    wit. Mar Set 3: 347-350

Tipper, John & Mary Parrot, P Licence, 4 Oct. 1737. St. Phil
    PR

Tipper, John & Susannah Orem, P Licence, 18 Jan. 1739. St.
    Phil PR

Tipping, Joseph & Sarah Rush, 1 Apr. 1758. St. Phil PR

Tobias, Benjamin of Granville Co., cordwainter, & Sarah
    Kennedy, widow, 31 March 1758; Archibald Wilkins, trustee;
    John Gready, Char Grimball, wit. Misc. Rec. RR: 588-595

Tobias, Benj: & Anne Floyd, widow of John Floyd, 22 June 1742.
    St. Hel PR

Tobias, Benjamin & Elizabeth Neil, 13 Apr. 1771. St. Phil PR

Tobias, Joseph & Margt McLoud, widow of John McLoud, 21
    Dec. 1743. St. Hel PR

Tobin, Michael & Mary Merchant, widow, 3 Feb. 1779. St. Phil PR

Todd, James & Anna Bell, 30 Jan. 1787. St. Phil PR

Todd, John, widower, & Agnes Ball, 16 Jan. 1787. St. Phil PR

Todenhaver, Lewis & Christiana Canton, widow, 4 Dec. 1794.
    St. Phil PR

Tolbird, Henry and Mary Hanna, both of this Parish, 4 March
    1744/5. Stoney Creek Pres Ch

Tomlinson, William, son Jesiah decd., and Marther Coppock,
    30 Dec. 1771. Bush R QM

Tomplet, Peter & Isabella Black, 17 Apr. 1732. St. And PR

Tookerman, Richard & Magdalen Elizabeth Warnock, widow, of
    Samuel Warnock, of St. Thomas Parish, Berkley Co., 5 __ 1756;
    Stephen Hartley of Christ Church Parish, Alex. Garden Junr.,
    trustees; Nathan Tart, John Fowler, wit. Misc. Rec. KK:
    327-329

Tomson, William of Georgetown dist., & Jane Snow, 26 May 1794;
    George Heriot, Patrick Donnally & Jacob William Harvey,
    trustees; James Barron, Jno Martin, wit. Mar Set 2: 264-266

Tong, James & Catharine Webb, 13 Dec. 1761. St. Phil PR

Tonge, James & Magdalen Glasie, 3 Nov. 1757. St. Phil PR

Tookerman, Richard & Elizabeth Warnock, 6 May 1756. T & D PR

Toole, John & Susannah Jones, 25 Sept. 1792. St. Phil PR

Toomer, Caleb & Sarah Scott, 5 Feb. 1763. St. Hel PR

Toomer, Henry & Mary Baker, 23 June 1719. St. And PR

Toomer, Henry & Mary West, P Licence, 8 Feb. 1721. St. Phil
    PR

Toomer, Henry & Sophia Clerk, widow of George Clerk, 5 Dec.
    1756. St. Hel PR

Toomer, Joshua & Sophia Hypworth, spinster, per Licence by the
    Revd. Mr. Robt. Betham, 19 Jan. 1746. St. Phil PR

Toomer, Joshua & Catharine Scott, 5 Feb. 1763. St. Hel PR

Toomy, Michael & Mary Ann Simmons, widow, 18 Feb. 1779. St.
    Phil PR

Torquit, James & Jane Weatherly, P Licence, 26 March 1742. St.
    Phil PR

Torrey, Anthony & Mary Fouchee, 11 March 1785. St. John Luth
    Ch

Tough, Robert & Hannah Bennet, 18 Aug. 1720. St. Phil PR

Toussiger, James & Margaret Ball, 10 Apr. 1777. St. Phil PR

Townsand, James, son of John & Elizabeth, and Mary Cook, 6
    April 1775. Bush R QM

Townsend, Doctor John & Elizabeth Pinckney Bellinger, widow,
26 Nov. 1793; Edmund Bellenger, trustee; Charl. Washington,
Mary Bellenger, George Caborne, wit. Mar Set 2: 218-220

Townsend, Joseph, of London, now of S. C. & Mary Burnham, 1 Dec.
1729; Charles Burnham, bondsman; Sabina Rowes, John Raper,
wit. Sec Prov G: 1729-31: 197

Townsend, William & Sarah Bedon, 14 March 1750. T & D PR

Townshend, John & Hannah Holland, P Licence, 12 Feb. 1739.
St. Phil PR

Townshend, John & Elizabeth Reynolds, 13 Feb. 1787. St. Hel PR

Townsend, Joseph & Mary Burnham, P Licence, 2 Dec. 1729.
St. Phil PR

Tozar, Ephraim & Hannah Walmsley, 1 Jan. 1730. St. Hel PR

Tozer, John & Mary Sparks, P Licence by Mr. Thompson, 22 Oct.
1736. St. Phil PR

Trapier, Benjamin & Hannah Thompson, P Licence by the Revd. Mr.
Alexr. Garden, 21 April 1748. St. Phil PR

Trapier, Paul & Magdalen Horrey, 22 Sept. 1743. T & D PR

Trapier, Paul Esqr. of Parish of Prince George, widower, &
Elizabeth Waties of Parish of Prince George, widow, 1 May
1767; Job Rothmahler, Jos. Dubourdieu, wit. St. Jas PR

Trapier, Paul, of the Parish of Prince George, bachelor, &
Elizabeth Foissin, of Parish of Prince George, spinster, in
the house of Elizabeth Foissin, widow, 19 Nov. 1771; Elias
Foissin, T(?) Dubourdie, wit. St. Jas PR

Tray, George & Elizabeth Baldwin, 21 Aug. 1763. St. Phil PR

Treasvant, Theodore & Elizabeth Wells, P Licence, 11 May 1749.
St. Phil PR

Treasvant, Theodore & Catherine Timothy, P Licence by the
Revd. Mr. A. G., 24 April 1753. St. Phil PR

Trescott, Edward & Catharine Boquet, 1 May 1777. St. Phil PR

Tresvan, Theodorus, & Mrs. Martha Scriven, 24 Feb. 1720-1.
T & D PR

Tresvin, William, & Mrs. ___ Daniel, 17 July 1734. T & D PR

Trezavant, Theodore & Cathn. Crouch, 19 April 1766. OJ 1764-
1771

Trezevant, Peter & Elizabeth Willoughby Trezebant (already
married), 23 Mar. 1797; Alexander Chisolm, trustee;
Ae. Burke, wit. Mar Set 3: 53-56

Trezvant, Daniel & Mary Blackledge, 29 June 1765. St. Phil PR

Triboudett, John Francois & Lucreece Musard, P Licence, 24 May
1740. St. Phil PR

Trindle, Edward & Elizabeth Hill, widow, 1 Nov. 1761. St. Phil
 PR

Triow, Heinrich, pants maker, & Elisabetha Crus, widow, 24 Mar.
 1777. St. John Luth Ch

Trish, Charles & Elizabeth Yesekus(?), 10 June 1783. St. John
 Luth Ch

Troise, Christian & Frances Smith, 4 Dec. 1763. St. Phil PR

Trott, Nicholas Esqr. & Sarah Rhett, March 4, 1727. St. Phil
 PR

Troup, James, attorney, & Elizabeth Pagett, widow, 7 Dec. 1796;
 Robert Gibson & Thomas Gibson, gentlemen, trustees; Thos
 Gordon, Seth Yates, wit. Mar Set 3: 19-21

Trueman, William & Elizabeth Gleadorse, P Licence, 16 Aug. 1739.
 St. Phil PR

Trunker, William & Sarah Wales, of Parish of St. Helena, 12
 May 1745. Stoney Creek Pres Ch

Trunker, Wm. Senr., & Mary Vinnel, 5 Apr. 1751. Stoney Creek
 Pres Ch

Trusler, William & Jane Anderson, 31 Dec. 1778. St. Phil PR

Tubbs, Griffin & Jane Middleton, 7 Sept. 1745. St. Phil PR

Tucker, Arthur & Ann Rivers, 6 Sept. 1711.   SPG

Tucker, Daniel & Mary Elizabeth Buchanan, 28 Nov. 1793. St.
 Phil PR

Tucker, Edward & Mary Hazzard, 15 Sept. 1754. St. Hel PR

Tucker, James & Jusiah Mallory, P Banns, 25 March 1737.
 St. Phil PR

Tucker, Nathaniel & Sarah Hazard of St. Helena Parish, 1 Aug.
 1749. Stoney Creek Pres Ch

Tucker, Nathaniel & Sarah Hazzard, 1 Aug. 1749. St. Hel PR

Tucker, Thomas of Hilton Head Island, Granville Co., planter,
 & wife Sarah, late Sarah Green, daughter of Samuel Green,
 of same, 26 June 1777; John Norton, William Norton, & George
 Mosse, trustees; Saml. Ladson, Wm. Chaplin, wit. Misc. Rec.
 RR: 639-641

Tucker, Thomas Tudor, & Esther Evans, 3 July 1774. St. Phil PR

Tuffs, Simon & Rebecca Lloyd, 30 Jan. 1757. St. Phil PR

Tunley, William & Elizabeth Lockyer, P Licence, 10 Feb. 1727.
 St. Phil PR

Tunno, John & Margaret Rose, 18 Oct. 1781. St. Phil PR

Turbevil, Charles and Susannah Saunders, 12 May 1744. Pr Fred
 PR

Turbevil, William & Mary Phillips, widow, 26 May 1744. Pr Fred
  PR

Turbevill, John & Philadelphia Isabell, 19 Nov. 1749. Pr Fred
  PR

Turier, Peter & Blanch Clarke, widow, 29 March 1749. Ch Ch PR

Turnbull, Robert J. & Miss Claudia Gervais, 10 Jan. 1797. Trin
  Meth Ch

Turner, John & Elizabeth Warner, 6 June 1777. St. Phil PR

Turner, Joseph & Elizabeth Boyce, 26 Dec. 1799. Circ Cong

Turner, Shadrach & Susannah Badger, 8 July 1782. St. Phil PR

Turner, Thomas & Ann Clark, widow, 16 Sept. 1772. St. Phil PR

Turpin, Willm. & Mary Savage, 31 Dec. 1793. Circ Cong

Tuson, Thomas & Mary Varien, P Licence, 1728. St. Phil PR

Tutton, William & Mary Cogswell, P License by Mr. Garden, 20
  May 1725. St. Phil PR

Tweed, Alexr. & Eliza. Gunnars, 14 Jan. 1766. OJ 1764-1771

Tweed, Alexander Captn. & Mrs. Lyons, widow, 11 Jan. 1794.
  Trin Meth Ch

U'hl, Washington & Mary Lydston, P Licence, 10 Jan. 1752. St.
  Phil PR

Ulmer, John Frederick & Mary Barbara Shuler, all of Orangeburg
  Township, ____ 1752. Hist Oburg

Umnersetter, John & Mrs. Maria Schutte, 20 Dec. 1798. Circ
  Cong

Underwood, Samuel & Margat. Mellichampe, 23 Apr. 1734. St. And
  PR

Unckles, John & Anne Drayton, 2 June 1737. St. And PR

Urquehart, Alexander & Martha Young, 25 Nov. 1755. St. Phil PR

Urquhart, David & Catharine McGehee, April 1799. Moses Waddel

Ummensetter, Gabriel & Jane Snider, widow, 1 Feb. 1794. St.
  Phil PR

Uz, Dietrich & Maria Dorothea Sampel(in), 25 Nov. 1766. St.
  John Luth Ch

Vale, John David & Elizabeth Alexander [no date, March 1788].
  St. Phil PR

Vall, John & Margaret Sanders, 24 Feb. 1778. St. Phil PR

Valton, Peter & Elizabeth Timothy, 1 Nov. 1767. St. Phil PR

Vanall, John & Elizabeth Bonneau, P Licence, 26 June 1747. St. Phil PR

VanAssendelft, William & Mary-Ann Gruenswig, 31 March 1782. St. Phil PR

Vandalus, John & Martha Wight, 10 Dec. 1760. St. Phil PR

Vanderhorst, Arnoldus, & Elizabeth Raven, daughter of William Raven, decd., 26 Feb. 1771; Elias Vanderhorst, & James Stanyarne, trustees; William Mathewes, Elizabeth Sams, Ann Simmons, wit. Misc. Rec. PP: 10-12

Vanderhorst, Arnoldus & Elizabeth Simons, 18 July 1745. T & D PR

Vanderhorst, Elias of Christ Church Parish & Sarah Collins Withers of St. James Santee, 30 Mar. 1784; James Withers, John Buchanan, trustees; Sarah Wigfall, Charlotte Withers, William Cartwright, wit. Mar Set 1: 474-477

Vanderhorst, Elias of Parish of St. Thomas, bachelor, & Sarah Withers, spinster, in the house of Capt. Richard Withers, 1 April 1784; Wm. Douxsaint, James Withers, wit. St. Jas PR

Vanderhorst, John & Mrs. Marg't Pollock, 8 Sept. 1714. T & D PR

Vanderhorst, John & Mary Elizabeth Foissin, 14 Jan. 1734. Circ Cong

Vandle, James & Elizabeth Oliphant, widow, 12 Apr. 1787. St. Phil PR

Vane, George & Sarah Tattle, P Licence by Mr. Garden, 14 July 1736. St. Phil PR

Vangelder, Cornetys, & ___ Bateman, widow, __ Apr. 1755. St. And PR

Vanhorn, Benja., and Joanna Demoss, 13 Nov. 1783. Bush R QM

Van Kerke, Fernando & Miss Margt Mather, 27 Apr. 1796 [entry stricken]. Trin Meth Ch

Van Leuwe, David & Agnes Marignac, per Banns, 13 April 1748. St. Phil PR

Van Marjenhoff, John of St. Pauls Parish, Colleton Co., & Ruth Stevens, spinster, of St. Pauls Parish, 18 March 1762; Margaret McLaren, Phebe Stevens, Jacob Stevens, wit. Misc. Rec. LL: 473-475

Van Ramst, Saml. & Mary Wagner, 1 Oct. 1798.   Trin Meth Ch

Van Schajck, Levinus & Elizabeth Clark, widow, P Licence by the Revd. Mr. A. Garden, 12 April 1747. St. Phil PR

Vantutry, John & Mary Shumlevin, P Licence, 30 Jan. 1738. St. Phil PR

Vanvellsen, Edward & Catherine Spencer, 17 Aug. 1721. St. Phil PR

Vanvelsin, Garrat & Hannah Johnson, P Licence, 1728. St. Phil
PR

Valvensin, Garrat & Rebecca Croft, widow, P Licence, 2 April
1733. St. Phil PR

Varambaut, Francis & Ann Latu, widow, 27 July 1767. St. Phil
PR

Varner, Henry of Parish of Prince Frederick, bachelor, &
Rachel Rembert of Parish of Prince Frederick, spinster, at
the house of Jacob Jeanneret, 24 May 1770; Jacob Jeanneret,
Wm. Walker, wit. St. Jas PR

Varnod, Francis, Clerk, & Mary Dodson, 4 Sept. 1733. St. And
PR

Varnor, Henry & Widow Guellard, 21 Jan. 1744/5. Ch Ch PR

Vaughan, John & Eleanor Shaw, P Licence, 9 Oct. 1732. St. Phil
PR

Venrow, Norbert & Sarah Toshea, 26 Apr. 1794. Trin Meth Ch

Vensant, Garrard & Susannah Smoke, 25 May 1760. St. Phil PR

Verdal, Thomas & Frances Rivers, widow, ___ 1764. St. And PR

Verdier, John Mark & Elizabeth Grayson, 1 Dec. 1785. St. Hel
PR

Vereen, Ebenezer & Catharine Mckiver, 8 Sept. 1784; Thomas
Maccullough, Elizabeth Maccullough, wit. Mar Set 1: 326

Vernon, Christopher, Esq., of Chesterfield Co., to Ann Mary
Bedgegood of Marlboro Co., 13 July 1791, Rev. Joshua Lewis.
Marlboro Co.

Veronee, William of Charleston, gentleman, & Elizabeth Byrd, 20
May 1796. St. Phil PR

Verplank, Willm. & Anne Lorey, 19 March 1734. St. Phil PR

Vesey, Charles Morgan, of Charleston, gentleman, and Mary Morris,
of same, 24 Dec. 1799. St. Phil PR

Vesey, Joseph & Ann Bonniett, 2 Feb. 1798. Trin Meth Ch

Vicaridge, John & Elizabeth Ashby, P Licence, 10 Feb. 1729.
St. Phil PR

Vicaridge, John & Elizabeth Ashby, ___ March 17__, T & D PR

Vickers, James & Hannah Rion, widow, 9 Feb. 1779. St. Phil PR

Vicyra, Joseph & Ann Florentine, widow, 22 Dec. 1793. St. Phil
PR

Villepontoux, Benjamin late of Charles Town, but now of St.
Stephens Parish, & Jane Dupont (already married), 4 June
1770; Cornelius Dupont, Gideon Dupont Junr., of Colleton
Co., trustees; Paul Porcher, Charles Lining, wit. Misc. Rec.
OO: 379-382

Villepontoux, Benja., & Jane Dupont, 6 March 1766. OJ 1764-1771

VillePontoux, Drake & Mary Lockwood, 27 May 1790.   Circ Cong

Villeponteaux, Paul & Mary Gantlett, per Licence by the Revd. Mr. Robt. Betham, 12 June 1746. St. Phil PR

VillePontoux, Peter & Sarah Lockwood, 27 May 1790. Circ Cong

Vincent, Henry & Martha Miles, 27 Nov. 1711.   SPG

Vincent, Thomas Hart & Mrs. Elizabeth Hann, 8 Feb. 1798.   Circ Cong

Vinson, John & Mary Vardill, 27 Aug. 1757. St. Phil PR

Visher, Nickolis & Sarah Beck, 12 Aug. 1727.   Ch Ch PR

Vivane, John of Parish of Prince George, widower, & Mary Grant, widow, in the house of William Allston, 7 June 1771; Matthew Drake, Mary Atchinson, wit. St. Jas PR

Vivian, John of George town, Craven County, Trader, & Mary Grant of same, widow, 4 June 1771; Micajah Williams of same, gent., trustee; John Thomas, John Croft, wit. Misc. Rec. PP: 237-240

Vivian, John of George Town & Mary Tacy (Tesey), widow, 10 Aug. 1779; George Stelling, Peter Lesesne, trustees; John Tarbox, wit. Misc. Rec. RR: 625-627

Vleux, Joseph Fredrick & Elizth Oldham, 16 Sept. 1795. Trin Meth Ch

von Habermann, Philipp, overseer on Mr. Gibb's plantation & Anna Maria, widow of the late Johann Burckhardt, 2 Jan. 1783. St. John Luth Ch

Von Peterson, Lewis & Mary Ann Brown, 22 March 1789. St. Phil PR

W____, Johann Ernst, taylor, & Maria Carol(in), 7 Feb. 1769. St. John Luth Ch

W____, Johann Georg, taylor, & Sophia, daughter of Martin Klei___, 5 Aug. 1770. St. John Luth Ch

Wade, Noel & Mary Hodge, 21 Dec. 1797.   Pugh diary

Wade, William, widower, & Mary Graves, 12 July 1752. St. Hel PR

Wagner, Christopher & Elizabeth Jesper, 2 June 1784. St. John Luth Ch

Wagner, John & Ann Boquette, 16 Apr. 1758. St. Phil PR

Wagner, Michael, widower, & Euphrosian Eller(in), widow, 30 Sept. 1773. St. John Luth Ch

Waight, Abraham Junr., & Ann Fitch, spinster, 26 Apr. 1744; license to Rev. Samuel Quincey; Isaac Waight of St. Johns

Parish, Colleton, bondsman. MB Chas

Waight, Isaac & Mary Jones, 13 Nov. 1719. St. And PR

Waight, Isaac & Martha Fripp, 26 Apr. 1745. St. Hel PR

Waight, Isaac of Island of St. Helena, & wife Sarah, 1 April
    1783; Barnd Elliott, & Wm. Hazd Wigg, wit. Mar Set 1: 208-
    209

Waight, Isaac & Mary Ann Guerard, 11 Oct. 1789. St. Hel PR

Waight, Jacob of St. Johns Colleton Co., & Judith Bonneau,
    spinster, 12 June 1744; license to Rev. Daniel Dwight;
    Daniel Roulain, of Charles Town, bondsman. MB Chas

Waight, Jacob & Margaret Barnwell, 28 Oct. 1762. St. Hel PR

Waight, William & Elizabeth Field (no date). St. Hel PR

Waight, William, widower, & Sebe Jenkins, 25 Jan. 1763. St. Hel
    PR

Wainwright, Benjamin & Anna Hurst, P Licence by the Revd. Mr.
    Alexr. Garden, 23 Dec. 1747. St. Phil PR

Wainwright, Richard & Mary Joice, P Licence by Mr. Garden, 22
    December 1736. St. Phil PR

Wainwright, Richard & Susannah Allen, P Licence by the Revd.
    Mr. Alexr. Garden, 3 Sept. 1747. St. Phil PR

Wainwright, Richard & Ann Dewar, 10 Dec. 1776. St. Phil PR

Wainwright, Samuel & Frances Goddard, P Licence, 3 Feb. 1742.
    St. Phil PR

Wakefield, James & Sarah Cannon, 26 Nov. 1771. St. Phil PR

Waldren, Patrick & Mary Porter of St. Georges Parish,
    Dorchester, 19 July 1764, daughter of Thomas Porter; Isaac
    Colcock & Stephen Cater of St. Georges Parish, planters,
    trustees; Newman Swallow, Hny. Saltus, Richard. Saltus, wit.
    Mar Set 2: 545-551

Walker, Gilbert Kennady, & Elizabeth Philips, widow, 26 Sept.
    1777. St. Phil PR

Walker, James & Elisabeth Palmer, 6 Nov. 1745. Pr Fred PR

Walker, James of Parish of Prince Frederick, bachelor, & Mary
    Guerry, of Parish of Prince Frederick, spinster, in the
    house of Mr. Peter Guerry, Snr./ 5 Oct. 1786; Gabriel
    Rembert, Manasseh Michau, wit. St. Jas PR

Walker, Joel & Elizabeth Byers, widow, 12 May 1778. St. Phil
    PR

Walker, John & Sarah Morren, P Banes, 1 Dec. 1744. St. Phil
    PR

Walker, John of Charleston, merchant, & Mary Ann Williamson, a
    minor daughter of Andrew Williamson, 15 Dec. 1784; David Oli-
    phent, trustee; John Maitland, Richard Lord, wit. Mar Set 1:
    155-158

Walker, John-Alleyne & Jane Oliphant, 24 Feb. 1774. St. And PR

Walker, Robert & Ann Jones, 19 Sept. 1762. St. Phil PR

Walker, William of Parish of Prince Frederick, widower, &
    Judith Rembert, spinster, in the house of Isaac Rembert,
    16 Aug. 1764; Michael Boineau, Eth. Madalen Boineau. St.
    Jas PR

Walker, William & Susannah Baris (Bans?), 25 Feb. 1787. St.
    Phil PR

Wall, Benjamin, widower, & Ann Watson, widow, 3 May 1763. St.
    Hel PR

Wall, John & Ann Rivers, 29 Oct. 1795. Circ Cong

Wall, Robert & Margaret Shepard, widow, 18 March 1759. St.
    Phil PR

Wallace, Edward & Elizabeth Shannon, widow, 21 May 1775. St.
    Phil PR

Wallace, John & Ann Bates, widow, 28 Jan. 1761. St. Phil PR

Wallace, Thomas & Elizabeth Vanderdussen, 26 Jan. 1758. St.
    Phil PR

Wallace, William & Elizabeth Crichton, 20 Aug. 1715; Thos
    Smith, Lewis Duval, Thomas Cater, wit. Sec Prov 1714-1717;
    508

Waller, Bayfield of Charleston, Gent., & Charlotte Whilden,
    widow & Extx. of Joseph Whilden, 11 Feb. 1796; James Muirhead,
    trustee; James Horne, Charles Wittich, wit. Mar Set 2: 513-
    517

Wally, or Woolly, Thomas and Jemima Troublefield, 31 May 1742.
    Pr Fred PR

Walter, Bayfield, & Charlotte Whilder, widow, 21 Feb. 1796. St.
    Phil PR

Walter, John Jr. & Jannett Stevens, 14 March 1775. St. Phil
    PR

Walter, Paul of St. Bartholomew's Parish, & Eliza Bower, of
    same, spinster; Paul Hamilton, trustee; Jacob Walter, Thos
    Martin, wit. Mar Set 2: 258-261

Walter, Thomas & Ann Lesesne, 26 March 1769. St. Phil PR

Walter, Thomas, of St. Johns Parish, planter & Dorothy Cooper,
    niece of James Sinkler, Esqr; 16 Aug. 1781; Lydia June,
    Alexr Findlay, wit. Mar Set 2: 120-121

Walter, William & Mary Cattell, 2 Sept. 1740. St. And PR

Waltz, Jacob & Catharina Maylander(in), 14 March 1786. St.
    John Luth Ch

Wannamaker, Jacob & Susan Shuler, 1740.   Hist Oburg

Wannenmacher, Jacob & Catharine Shuler [1740's]. Hisb Oburg

War, John & _____, 5 July 1798. Pugh diary

Ward, Henry of Charleston, gent., & Mary Grimke, of same,
    spinster, 3 Aug. 1799; John Faucheraud Grimke, Thomas
    Corbett, trustees; John Browne, John Cuningham, wit. Mar
    Set 3: 415-416

Ward, John & Elizabeth Cavenah, 31 Jan. 1756. St. Phil PR

Ward, John & Love Leger, 27 Dec. 1756. St. Phil PR

Ward, John & Anne Hunley, 5 Oct. 1760. St. Phil PR

Ward, John & Lucy Boone, 29 Jan. 1763; James Guthrie, John
    Glen, wit. Misc. Rec. LL: 594-594

Ward, John of City of Charleston, Attorney at Law, & Mary
    Somarsall, daughter of Wm. Somarsall, Esqr., 4 May 1793;
    Stephen Ravenel, wit. Mar Set 2: 173-176

Ward, Jno & Susana Stone, 11 May 1775. Pugh diary

Ward, William & Mary Pearse, P Licence, 29 April 1739. St.
    Phil PR

Ware, David & Bet Defer, 5 Apr. 1793. Pugh diary

Warham, Charles & Mary Gibbes, spinster, 11 June 1784; William
    Hasell Gibbes, trustee; Charles Ferguson, Dez. Barbazan, wit.
    Mar Set 1: 129-131

Waring, John & Mary Hamlin, widow of Samuel Hamlin, of St.
    Georges Parish, Dorchester, 20 Sept. 1779; John Waring,
    Thomas Waring brother of sd. Mary Hamlin, & Benjamin Waring,
    trustees; Edith Waring, Ann Waring, wit. Mar Set 1: 189-192

Waring, Richard & Ann Ball, 27 Jan. 1771. St. Phil PR

Waring, Thomas of Charles Town, mercht., & Mary, daughter of
    Benjamin Waring, 14 Aug. 1765; Wm. Sanders, Benj. Waring,
    trustees; Ann Waring, Andrew Flavell, wit. Misc. Rec. MM:
    348-350

Waring, Thomas, Doctor of Physick, & Sarah LaBruce, of Waccamaw,
    Parish of All Saints, widow, 31 Mar. 1796; William Allston &
    Benjamin Alston, of same, trustees; Eliza Allston, John
    LaBruce, wit. Mar Set 3: 467-475

Warley, Felix, Major in the late U. S. Army & Ann Turquand,
    daughter of Rev. Mr. Paul Turquand, of Orangeburgh Dist.,
    & grand daughter of Ann Breneau late of St. Matthews, Parish,
    15 Dec. 1784; John Lewis Gervais, trustee; John Owen, William
    Caldwell, wit. Mar Set 1: 95-97

Warmingham, Joseph & Sarah Lea, 30 July 1724. St. Phil PR

Warnedow, Leonhard & Sirrah Hottow [1740's]. Hist Oburg

Warner, Henry of Parish of Prince George & Jane Mitchell,
    widow, 13 Jan. 1743/4; license to Rev. John Fordyce; James
    LeSeine of Parish of St. Thomas, bondsman. MB Chas

Warner, John & Ann Elizabeth Haniel Rivers, 13 July 1784.
St. John Luth Ch

Warnock, Andrew and Mary Wells, spinster; minister Thomas Hasly;
bondsmen Andrew Warnock of St. Thomas and St. Denniss,
planter, and Joseph Moody of Charles Town, merchant, wit.
J. Hammerton, 31 March 1733. MB NY

Warnock, Charles of Craven Co., planter, & Betsey Story (father
of sd. Betsey), trustees; Andrew White, Judith Singletary,
wit. Misc. Rec. NN: 191-194

Warnock, Joseph & Ann Metheringham, 8 Sept. 1772. Ch Ch PR

Warnock, Samuel & Magdalen Elizabeth Hartley, 12 June 1755.
T & D PR

Warnock, Samuel & Elizabeth Lochon, 24 March 1774. St. Phil PR

Warren, Joseph & Elizabeth Matson, __ Dec. 1739. St. Hel PR

Warren, Richard & Frances Labri, P Licence by the Revd. Mr.
Alexr. Garden, 30 Oct. 1747. St. Phil PR

Warren, Samuel Fenner, Rector of St. James Santee, bachelor,
& Elizabeth Perdreau, spinster, in the house of Daniel Horry,
Esqr., 19 July 1759, by Alexander Keith, Rector of St.
Stephens Santee; Daniel Horry Senr., Judith Serre, wit.
St. Jas PR

Warren, Samuel Fenner, clerk of this parish, widower, & Lydia
Perdreau, spinster, 21 Nov. 1784; Esther Perdreau, Isaac
Dubose, wit. St. Jas PR

Washington, William, late of Virginia but now of S. C. & Jane
Riely Elliott, only daughter of Charles Elliott, late of
St. Paul's Parish; 17 Apr. 1782; Thomas Ferguson, John
Parker, John Ward, trustees; Ra. Izard, David Olyphant, H.
Rutledge, wit. Mar Set 2: 340-341

Waterry, Francis, Lieut. of the British Navy, & Caroline Lequet,
of Charleston, 3 Feb. 1799. St. Phil PR

Waters, Philemon & Mary Bary, 4 Apr. 1762. St. Phil PR

Waters, Philip & Ann Rougemont, 19 Aug. 1781. St. Phil PR

Waters, Richard & Margaret Sinclair, 29 Oct. 1754. St. Phil PR

Waties, Thomas & Ann Alston, 1 Sept. 1751. T & D PR

Watkins, Isa. & ____, 26 July 1798. Pugh diary

Watson, Andrew & Mary Dowdle, 21 March 1759. St. Phil PR

Watson, James & Tabitha Sealy, 14 July 1746. St. Hel PR

Watson, John & Abigail Butler, 30 Nov. 1736. St. And. PR

Watson, John & Sarah Pigot, P Licence, 23 Oct. 1738. St. Phil
PR

Watson, John & Anne Blair, per Licence, 22 Feb. 1745. St. Phil
PR

Watson, William & Sarah White, 1 Apr. 1782. St. Phil PR

Watson, William Capt. & Anne Hatcher, 6 Feb. 1754. St. Hel PR

Watt, James, widower, & Frances Cox, widow, 1 June 1734. St. Hel PR

Watts, Jacob & Elinor Stocks, widow, 19 Aug. 1735/6 [sic]. Ch Ch PR

Watts, John & Joppe Stuard, by Banes, 8 April 1745. St. Phil PR

Watts, Thomas & Susannah Taylor, 12 Oct. 1756. T & D PR

Wattson, William & Mary Kemp, Lic. by the Reverend Mr. Alexander Garden, 26 Sept. 1723. St. Phil PR

Waud, Robert & Ann Sullivan, widow, 4 Oct. 1766. St. Phil PR

Wayne, Richard of Charles Town & Elizabeth Clifford, the younger, 14 Sept. 1769; Elizabeth Clifford, Charles Clifford, trustees; Elizabeth Yon, Martha Roberts, wit. Misc. Rec. OO: 282-285

Wayne, Richard & Elizabeth Clifford, 14 Sept. 1769; Eliz. Clifford, Charles Clifford, trustees. Misc. Rec. TT: 130-132

Wayney [Waning, Venning?], Samuel & Sarah Murrell, 1 July 1773. Ch Ch PR

Wealth, Adam & Anna Maria Heeness, widow, 23 July 1772. St. Phil PR

Weanright, William & Hannah Williams, widow [1740's]. Hist Oburg

Weatherly, George & Mary Conyears, 1 Jan. 1763. St. Hel PR

Weatherly, Isaac & Martha Waight, widow, 7 Dec. 1754. St. Hel PR

Weaver, Thomas & Ruth Roberts, 14 Sept. 1726. St. Phil PR

Weaver, Thomas & Martha Shaw, per Licence, 8 Jan. 1745. St. Phil PR

Webb, Benjamin & Mary Matthyson, P Licence, 17 Aug. 1739. St. Phil PR

Webb, Benjamin, bachelor, & Sarah Hannah Webb, spinster, at the house of Mrs. Elizabeth Gaillard, 15 Feb. 1774; Elizabeth Webb, Elizabeth Gaillard, wit. St. Jas PR

Webb, Benjamin & Rebecca Pinckney, 12 May 1763. St. Phil PR

Webb, Benjamin & Rebecca Pinckney, 14 Sept. 1796; Charles Pinckney & Thomas Odingsell Elliott, trustees; Henrietta Warner, John Loveday, wit. Mar Set 2: 530-534

Webb, Benjamin & Rebecca Pinckney, 15 Sept. 1796. St. Phil PR

Webb, John and Elizth. Raynor(?), 29 Oct. 1744. Stoney Creek Pres Ch

SOUTH CAROLINA MARRIAGES 1688-1799

Webb, John & Mary Doughty, 3 Jan. 1769. St. Phil PR

Webb, John of Charleston, & Elizabeth Legare, spinster, dau-
    ghter of Nathan Legare, decd., 29 March 1786; Thomas
    Doughty, trustee; John Scott Junr., wit. Mar Set 1: 310-311

Webb, Matthew, a free negro & Susanna Cane, a free negress, 25
    Feb. 1771. St. Phil PR

Webb, Richd. & Priscilla Emanuel, widow, 13 Feb. 1731/2. St.
    And PR

Webb, Thomas & Elizabeth Murrill, 8 Aug. 1745. Ch Ch PR

Webb, Thomas of Parish of Prince George, bachelor, & Mary
    Herries, of Parish of Prince, George, widow, 31 Aug. 1770;
    Elias M'Pherson, John Curless(?), wit. St. Jas PR

Webb, William & Sarah Peronneau, P Licence, 17 July 1740.
    St. Phil PR

Webb, William & Sarah Miles, 30 Apr. 1752. St. And PR

Webb, Wm. & Deborah Jones, 6 Feb. 1720/21. St. And PR

Weber, Peter, shoemaker, & Christina Smith, 4 Aug. 1784. St.
    John Luth Ch

Wedderburn, James & Susanna Frazer, P Licence, 23 Nov. 1740.
    St. Phil PR

Weeks, Benjamin, and Abigail Coppock, 26 March 1796. Bush R QM

Weekley, William & Martha Stocks, P Licence by Mr. Garden, 22
    Feb. 1735. St. Phil PR

Weems, John & Frances Hasell, P Licence, 8 July 1742. St. Phil
    PR

Weir, James & Elizabeth Baird, widow, 14 Oct. 1776. St. Phil
    PR

Weissinger, Johann & Magdalena Chutthiar(in)?, 14 March 1786.
    St. John Luth Ch

Welch, Jno & ____, 23 May 1792. Pugh diary

Welch, William & Rebeccah Amey, P Licence by Mr. Garden, 31
    July 1751. St. Phil PR

Wellard, Charles, Doctor & Hannah Kellham, spinster, P Licence
    by the Revd. Mr. Alexr. Garden Rector, 2 Aug. 1748. St. Phil
    PR

Wells, Allen & Mary Joyce, widow, 22 July 1742. St. And PR

Wells, Edger, & Lidia Roper, 29 June 1709. T & D PR

Wells, Jeremiah & Mary Harriss, widow, 21 Jan. 1765. St. Phil
    PR

Wells, John, widower, & Susanna Cole, widow of Paul Cole, 6 Jan.
    1740. St. Hel PR

264

SOUTH CAROLINA MARRIAGES 1688-1799

Wells, John of Johns Island, surgeon, & Mary Winborn, minor
daughter of the late Thomas Winborn, decd., 3 Dec. 1772;
Thomas Hanscome, & John Holmes, trustees; John Freer, wit.
Mar Set 1: 193-198

Wells, John, bachelor & Elizabeth Mouzon, spinster, at the
house of Susanna Elizabeth Mouzon, 16 Aug. 1778; Samuel
Warren, Lewis Mouzon, wit. St. Jas PR

Wells, Joseph & Margaret Wood, 9 March 1748. St. And PR

Wells, William & Frances Dubois, 20 Oct. 1774. T & D PR

Welsch(?), George, baker, & Sarah Class(in), from Phildelphia,
no date, 1776. St. John Luth Ch

Welsh, George & Ann Bowman, widow, 2 Nov. 1745. St. And PR

Welsh, George & Margaret Ettering, 6 Aug. 1767. T & D PR

Welsh, John Lewis & Maria Cotton, widow, 15 July 1791. St. Phil
PR

Welshuysen, Daniel & Isabella Van Kinswilder, 27 Jan. 1725. St.
And PR

Werner, Jakob & Anna Braunmiller(in), widow, 9 Apr. 1765. St.
John Luth Ch

Werner, Joh. & Maria Dorothea Bachmann(in), 13 Feb. 1766. St.
John Luth Ch

Werner, Matthias & Maria Blanern(?), 1 May 1766. St. John Luth
Ch

Wernicke, Lewis & Ann Bishop, 29 Oct. 1781. St. Phil PR

Wershing, Caspar & Catharine Harvey, 22 Dec. 1784. St. John
Luth Ch

Wescoat, William, & Anne Beswicke, 5 Aug. 1759. St. Hel PR

Weslyd, Thomas & Margaret White, P License by Mr. Garden, 6
June 1725. St. Phil PR

Wessner, Heinrich Philips, merchant, & Anna Margretha Vogel-
gesang(in), 3 June 1777. St. John Luth Ch

West, Samuel & Mary Dandridge, 27 June 1734. St. And PR

West, Samuel & Mary Dalton, 18 Dec. 1757. St. Phil PR

West, Simeon & Cynthia Shearman, 25 Sept. 1797. Trin Meth Ch

West, Wm. & Eliza Fripp, 8 Apr. 1712. SPG

Westberry, Jonathan and Mary Tamplet, 24 Dec. 1741. Pr Fred PR

Westberry, William & Elizabeth Upham, P Licence, 12 June 1740.
St. Phil PR

Weston, Dr. John of Charlestown, & Mary Raven, widow of Thomas
Raven, 22 Nov. 1768; Robt Rawlins, trustee; Denham Fearis,
Benjamin Glencross, wit. Misc. Rec. NN: 428-430

265

Weston, Plowden & Alice Hollybush, 18 July 1762. St. Phil PR

Wetstine, Henry & Barbara, widow of Hans Ulrick Morff, decd.,
24 Dec. 1750. Hist Oburg

Wetzel, Nicolaus & Sarah Clark, 20 Nov. 1785. St. John Luth Ch

Weyand, Georg, a wagoner, & Elisabetha Einsidel, 12 Nov. 1786.
St. John Luth Ch

Weyman, Edward & Catharine Turpin, 6 May 1793. St. Phil PR

Whaily, Joseph & Mary Capers, of James Island, 18 Nov. 1794.
Trin Meth Ch

Whaley, Thomas of Edisto, Parish of St. John's Colleton Co., &
Mary Jenkins, widow of Christopher Jenkins, 12 Apr. 1797;
John Jenkins, trustee; Mary Whaley, John Jenkins, Thomas
Whaley, wit. Mar Set 3: 81-85

Whealer, Joel & Frances Philips, 21 June 1747. Pr Fred PR

Wheeler, John & Sarah Winn, P Licence, 24 Aug. 1742. St. Phil
PR

Wheldon, John of Parish of Christ Church & Martha King,
spinster, 14 July 1744; license to Rev. Thomas Hasell;
Nathaniel Arthur, bondsman. MB Chas

Whilden, Elias & Sarah Dorril, 6 Jan. 1791. Circ Cong

Whilden, John & Susannah Murrell, 20 Feb. 1755. T & D PR

Whilden, Jonathan & Ann King, 19 Dec. 1749. T & D PR

Whilden, Joseph & Charlotte Robinson, 24 Aug. 1788. St. Phil
PR

Whitaker, Benjamin & Sarah Godfrey, 20 May 1719. St. And PR

Whitaker, Samuel & Hannah Sinkeler, widow, 26 Feb. 1794. St.
Phil PR

White, Anthony Junr. & Mary King, widow, 12 Feb. 1744/5. Pr
Fred PR

White, Anthony Junr., of Parish of Prince Frederick, bachelor,
& Hannah Barton, of Parish of Prince George, spinster, at the
house of William Barton, 30 Aug. 1770; Joseph Dubourdieu,
William Barton, wit. St. Jas PR

White, Anthony Walton, of City of New York, & wife Margaret,
daughter of William Ellis, decd., 26 Sept. 1789; Josiah
Smith, Thos. Doughty, trustees; Lewis Morris Junr., Catherine
Futerell, Martha Laurens Ramsay, wit. Mar Set 3: 292-294

White, Blake Leay, carpenter, & Elizabeth Bourquin, spinster,
6 Apr. 1772; Theodore Trezvant, taylor, trustee; Stephen
Thomas, Edgar Wells, wit. Mar Set 1: 356-357

White, Blake Leay of Charleston, carpenter, & Elizabeth Bourquin, original agreement, 6 Apr. 1772, this dated 21 Nov.
1793; Theodore Trezevant, trustee; Thos Marshall, W. Morgan,
wit. Mar Set 2: 192-195

SOUTH CAROLINA MARRIAGES 1688-1799

White, Christopher & Mary Ranford, P Licence, 2 Nov. 1748. St. Phil PR

White, Christopher Gadsden & Martha Walter, 21 May 1795. St. Phil PR

White, Christopher Gadsden, of St. Stephens Parish, & wife Martha, daughter of Richard & Harriet Walter, 10 Feb. 1798; John White of Charleston, trustee; Sarah White Darrell, Ed. Darrell, wit. Mar Set 3: 286-288

White, Henry of Parish of Prince Frederick, bachelor, & Susanna Boone, of Parish of Prince Frederick, spinster, at the plantation of John Boone, 5 Dec. 1771; James Durand, Rebecca Knox, wit. St. Jas PR

White, Jacob & Ephe Bowen, 18 July 1763. St. Phil PR

White, James of Charles Town, Surgeon, & Sarah Sims, of Christ Church Parish, spinster, 26 Jan. 1736; Thomas Boone, Richard Capers, gent., trustees; Mary Boone, George Oliver, wit. Misc. Rec. II: 140-143

White, James & Sarah Sims, 30 Jan. 1736/7. Ch Ch PR

White, John and Mary Drower, widow, 28 Apr. 1741. Pr Fred PR

White, John of Parish of St. Thomas, bachelor, & Isabella Chappell, spinster, 8 June 1772; Anna Gaillard, James Allen Bruneau, wit. St. Jas PR

White, John & Mary Bessellew, 24 Dec. 1768. St. Phil PR

White, John & Sarah Roddam, 6 Aug. 1774. T & D PR

White, John & Jane Pogson Purcell, 15 Nov. 1796. St. Phil PR

White, Joseph & Mary Stocks, 9 June 1728. Ch Ch PR

White, Joseph & Mary Anna King, 4 Aug. 175__, Pr Fred PR

White, Joseph & Susannah Smith, widow, 15 Sept. 1744. Pr Fred PR

White, Leonard and Hannah Brown, 2 Apr. 1745. Pr Fred PR

White, Rubin & Milly Alan, 22 Feb. 1772. Pugh diary

White, Sims & Mary Wilkin, 24 June 1760. St. Phil PR

White, Thomas & Elizabeth Leevraft, widow, 15 Oct. 1758. St. Phil PR

Whitesides, Edward & Esther Rand, 29 Apr. 1778. St. Phil PR

Whitesides, John & Sarah Dashwood, 24 March 1737. Ch Ch PR

Whitesides, John & Sarah Dorrell, relict of Robert Dorrell Jr., ___ 1775. Ch Ch PR

Whitesides, Thomas & Sarah Joy, 25 Oct. 1753. Ch Ch PR

Whitesides, Thomas & Jean Joy, relict of William Joy, 23 May 1772. Ch Ch PR

Whithill, John & Sarah Shaw, 9 July 1768. St. Phil PR

Whitley, Moses & Ann Miller, 19 Nov. 1793. Trin Meth Ch

Whitmarsh, John & Maıgaret Barnwell [no date]. St. Hel PR

Whitne, Joseph & Mary Coit by Mr. Garden, 27 July 1736. St. Phil PR

Whitney, Lebbeus & Mary Ann Ham, widow, 14 Oct. 1773. St. Phil PR

Whitson, David, son of Solomon & Phebe, and Mary Milhous, 8 June 1797. Cane Creek MM

Whittesdies, John & Sarah Dashwood, P Licence by Mr. Garden, 24 March 1736. St. Phil PR

Whittington, Francis and Martha Freeman, 8 Oct. 1743. Pr Fred PR

Wickham, Nathaniel & Martha Stone, 1 April 1746. St. Phil PR

Wifer, Henry & Mary Magdalen Davie, widow, 18 Dec. 1779. St. Phil PR

Wigfall, Benjamin & Martha Dutarque, 1 Aug. 1771.   T & D PR

Wigfall, Joseph & Susannah Durand, 3 Nov. 1768.   T & D PR

Wigfall, Joseph & Sarah Shackleford, widow of William Shackel-ford, late of George Town, 7 Jan. 1779; William Lupton, Richard Withers, trustees; Saml F. Warren, John Cogdell, James Withers, wit. Mar Set 1: 44-48

Wigfall, Joseph of Parish of Christ Church, widower, & Sarah Shackelford, of Parish of Prince George, widow, 7 Jan. 1779; Jno Cogdell, James Withers, wit. St. Jas PR

Wigfall, Samuel, son of Samuel Wigfall, & Catherine Foissin, 24 Apr. 1729.   Ch Ch PR

Wigg, Edward & Mary Hazzard, 22 Feb. 1738. St. Hel PR

Wigg, Hillersdon & Elizabeth Serjeant, 30 Aug. 1740. St. Hel PR

Wigg, Hillersdone & Mary Dunlap, 16 Aug. 1771. St. Hel PR

Wigg, Richard & Sarah Mayne, P Licence by Mr. Winterly, 18 Jan. 1732. St. Phil PR

Wigg, Richard & Anne Smallwood, P Licence, 4 Feb. 1734. St. Phil PR

Wigg, Richard & Anne Smallwood, 4 Feb. 1734. St. Hel PR

Wigg, Richard & Mary Galloway, 4 July.1757. St. Hel PR

Wigg, Thomas & Mary Evans by the Revd. Mr. Garden, 16 Feb. 1726. St. Phil PR

Wigg, Thomas of Port Royal Island, & Ann Reeves, widow of
Ambrose Reeves, 6 March 1752; Nathaniel Barnwell & John
Barnwell, trustees; Sarah Williamson, Mary Grimball, wit.
Misc. Rec. II: 596-601

Wigfall, Thomas of St. Thomas Parish, & Harriett Moore, daughter
of John Moore decd., sister of John Elias Moore (trustee),
17 March 1791; Saml Wigfall, Jno Price, wit. Mar Set 1:
563-565

Wigg, Thomas Coll: & Mary Seymour, 14 Feb. 1726. St. Hel PR

Wigg, Thomas Coll., widower & Anne Reeve, widow of Ambrose
Reeve, 6 March 1752. St. Hel PR

Wigg, William Hazzard of St. Helena's Parish, Beaufort Dist.,
& Letitia Maine, of Prince William's Parish, spinster, 30
Nov. 1789; James Gourlay, clerk, & James Maine, planter,
of Prince Williams Parish, trustees; Eliza Maine, Esther Deveaux, wit. Misc. Rec. A: 145-147

Wiggins, Job & Mary Langley, P Banns, 30 Jan. 1723. St. Phil
PR

Wigginton, Mr. & ___, 6 March 1709/10. Reg Prov 1711-15,
p. 449(41)

Wilburn, Richard of Georgetown dist., & Rebecca Gillaspy, widow
of John Gillaspy; Robert Wilburn, William Buford, trustees;
3 July 1793; Peter Robert, William Lewis, wit. Mar Set 2:
151-153

Wilcocks, Joseph of Edisto Island & Edee Miller, spinster, 1
Sept. 1744; license to Rev. Alexander Garden; Daniel Gardner,
of Charles Town, bondsman. MB Chas

Wilcox, Joseph & Elioner Miller, P Licence, 1 Sept. 1744. St.
Phil PR

Wild, Peter & Barbara Eberl(in), 18 Jun. 1765. St. John Luth
Ch

Wild, Samuel and Elizabeth Jones, 26 Mar. 1744. Pr Fred PR

Wildman, Leonard & Mary Harris, widow of William Harris, 8 Jan.
1754. St. Hel PR

Wiley, Alexander, marriner, & Ann Gibbins, 13 Jan. 1764. Ch
Ch PR

Wilkie, John & Jane Hext, widow, 27 Oct. 1770. St. Phil PR

Wilkins, Jonathan of Parish of Prince William, planter, &
Martha Brown, widow, of St. Bartholomews Parish, 17 Oct.
1770; Jeremiah Miles, planter, trustee; Patrick Turnbull,
John Ladson, wit. Misc. Rec. OO: 432-433

Wilkins, Obadiah & Elizabeth Croskeys, 9 March 1735/6. Circ
Cong

Wilkins, William & Sarah Crosskeys alias Lluellin, 13 June
1728. St. Phil PR

Wilkins, William & Sarah Marshall, P Licence, 18 Dec. 1748. St.
Phil PR

Wilkins, Willm Junr. & Rebecca Massey Junr., 25 Oct. 1737.
Circ Cong

Wilkinson, Francis & Margaret Arden, 8 May 1729.   St. And PR

Wilkinson, Capt. John & Elizabeth Wanton, 7 July 1782. St.
Phil PR

Wilkinson, Robert & Mary Burton, 6 June 1757. St. Hel PR

Wilkinson, Thomas & Martha Spencer, 2 July 1758. St. Phil PR

Wilkison, John & Mary Waters, 6 Jan. 1799.   Trin Meth Ch

Wilks, Lemuel, of Parish of Prince Frederick, widower, &
Esther Michau, of Parish of Prince Frederick, widow, 8 Sept.
1785; Jas Walker, Edward Croft, wit. St. Jas PR

Will, John & Elizabeth James, 12 May 1793.   Trin Meth Ch

Willhelm, Georg & Margaretha ___, 27 Dec. 1767.   St. John Luth
Ch

Willhelm, Johann & Maria Eva ___, 5 Nov. 1772. St. John Luth Ch

Williams, Anthony and Elizabeth Canty, 24 July 1738. Pr Fred
PR

Williams, Charles & Mary Lowell, 21 June 1764. St. Hel PR

Williams, Charles & Rachel Lemming, 12 July 1792. St. Phil PR

Williams, Charles, marriner & Ann Dilsham, 1 Oct. 1797. Trin
Meth Ch

Williams, Daniel & Elizabeth Sisom, 20 Nov. 1760. St. Hel PR

Williams, David & Leah Addison, 23 March 1769. St. Phil PR

Williams, George Robert & Catharine Williams, 27 Feb. 1782.
St. Phil PR

Williams, Henry & Mary Cart, P Licence, 4 Jan. 1732. St. Phil
PR

Williams, Jacob of St. James Goose Creek, & Margaret Ayers,
1 June 1792; William Railey, Susanna Railey, John Ayers, wit.
Mar Set 1: 650

Williams, James & Jane Hislop, 29 June 1797. Circ Cong

Williams, John & Mary Baker, 16 June 1720. St. And PR

Williams, John and Mary M'Ginney, 18 Aug. 1737. Pr Fred PR

Williams, John & Elizabeth Bullard, P Licence by the Revd. Mr.
Alexr. Garden, 1 Jan. 1747.   St. Phil PR

Williams, John, bachelor, & Patience Conner, spinster, in
the house of Edward Jerman, 3 Jan. 1771; Elizth Jones,
Edwd Jerman, wit. St. Jas PR

Williams, John & Charlotte Bury, 1 July 1781. St. Phil PR

Williams, John of Parish of Allsaints, bachelor & Elizabeth-Ann Willingham, spinster, married at Echaw Chapel, 19 Feb. 1784; Christopher Willingham, Samuel Warren, wit. St. Jas PR

Williams, Jno Mortimor, & Frances Oram, widow, 17 Sept. 1768. St. Phil PR

Williams, Joseph & Ann Deloney, 13 June 1746. St. And PR

Williams, Joseph & Elizabeth Turner, 10 Jan. 1749 [1749/50]. St. And PR

Williams, Joseph & Mary Cart, 27 Nov. 1768. St. Phil PR

Williams, Mortimore, & Sarah Bullock, 2 Feb. 1782. St. Phil PR

Williams, Nicholas & Sarah Woodside, widow, 17 Sept. 1757. St. Phil PR

Williams, Philip & Mary Magdalen Benoist, widow, per Licence by the Revd. Mr. Robt. Betham, 27 Feb. 1746. St. Phil PR

Williams, Robert Junior of Charles Town, attorney at law, & Ann Roper, spinster, eldest daughter of William Roper, 6 Feb. 1771; Thomas Roper, wit. Mar Set 1: 146-147

Williams, Robt. Esqr., & Elizabeth Hext, 1 Jan. 1755. St. Phil PR

Williams, Samuel & Martha Fields, 16 Sept. 1784. St. John Luth Ch

Williams, Shepard & Elizabeth Cherry, 1 July 1798. Pugh diary

Williams, Thomas of St. Pauls Parish, & Eliza. Cooke, widow, 9 June 1744; license to Rev. William Orr; John Williams, bondsman. MB Chas

Williams, William & Mary Mackenzie, P Licence, 18 Feb. 1738. St. Phil PR

Williams, William of Parish of St. Pauls in Colleton Co., & Mary Woodbury, spinster, 19 May 1744; license to Revd. William Orr; Emanuel Smith, of Charles Town, bondsman. MB Chas

Williamson, Abm & Mary Proctor, 18 Aug. 1791. Circ Cong

Williamson, Daniel & Sidney Fortner(?), 9 Jan. 1784. St. John Luth Ch

Williamson, Henry & Margr. Rose, 17 June 1735. St. And PR

Williamson, Jesse & ____, 29 July 1783. Pugh diary

Williamson, John & Magdalene Postell, 11 Sept. 1755. St. Hel PR

Williamson, Manly & Hannah Hogg, Exiled by the Revered. Mr. Guy, P Licence, 12 April 1733. St. Phil PR

Williamson, Manley & Hannah Hogg, widow, 12 Apr. 1733. St. And PR

SOUTH CAROLINA MARRIAGES 1688-1799

William, William of St. Peters Parish, & Mary Procher, spinster,
23 Apr. 1787; Thomas Hudson, Peter Porcher, trustees;
Willm Porcher, Margaret Smith, wit. Mar Set 1: 322-323

Williamson, Willm & Sarah Stone, 27 Jan. 1752. St. Hel PR

Williman, Jacob & Mary Spidle, widow, 27 June 1772. St. Phil
PR

Willingham, Christopher, of Parish of St. James, Santee,
& Susanna White of Parish of Prince Frederick, 15 Nov. 1785;
Sarah Hamlin, John Hamlin, wit. St. Jas PR

Willingham, Thomas & Sarah Chovin, both of St. James Santee,
15 Nov. 1796; Jno Blake, Jno Anderson, wit. Mar Set 3: 113

Willke, James & Loveridge Brown, 30 Oct. 1725. St. Phil PR

Willkins, William, widower, & Margaretta Postell both of this
parish, 4 May 1751. Stoney Creek Pres Ch

Willply, Benjamine & Sarah McGaw, 30 June 1771. St. Phil PR

Wills, Edward & Susanna Hope, P Licence, 25 July 1733. St.
Phil PR

Willson, Jo Captn. & Mary Connor, widow, 6 Apr. 1785. St. John
Luth Ch

Wilson, ___ & Mary Chesholme, ___ Apr. 1759. St. Phil PR

Wilson, Algernon & Sarah Daniel, spinster, P Licence by the
Revd. Mr. Robt. Betham, 6 Feb. 1746. St. Phil PR

Wilson, Daniel & Mary Drayton, 10 Oct. 1787. St. Phil PR

Wilson, Jehu, son of John, and Sarah Hawkins, 2 Dec. 1790.
Cane Creek MM

Wilson, John & Dorothy Smallwood, 15 July 1741. St. Hel PR

Wilson, John & Alice Lupton, 21 Oct. 1755. St. Phil PR

Wilson, John, Mariner & Mary Beckett, spinster, P Banns by the
Revd. Mr. Clarke, 6 Dec. 1755. St. Phil PR

Wilson, John & Mary Bonneau, 12 Oct. 1773. St. Phil PR

Wilson, John of Charleston, merchant & Eleanor Ball, of St.
Johns Parish, spinster, 1 Jan. 1789; Robert Quash, John
Ball, John Coming Ball, trustees; J. Ball, Cath. Simons,
wit. Mar Set 1: 502-506

Wilson, John to Charlotte Hicks, 8 June 1791. Rev. Joshua
Lewis. Marlboro Co.

Wilson, Leighton & Sarah Adams of Edisto Island, spinster;
17 Dec. 1795; James Jaffrays, Daniel Jenkins, Henry
Richardson, Esqrs., trustees; Jos Lewis, John Adams, wit.
Mar Set 2: 451-454

Wilson, Samuel, Doctor of Physic, & Mary Haig, widow, 1 Oct.
1796; John Blake of Charleston & Thomas Young, of Winyaw,
trustees; Eliza Hutchinson, Sarah Haig, wit. Mar Set 3:
27-31

272

SOUTH CAROLINA MARRIAGES 1688-1799

Wilson, Samuel of Charleston & Catharine Mariane Mazyck, 26
     March 1798; Stephen Mazyck, brother of sd. Catharine Mariane,
     trustee; and John Cords of St. Stephens Santee, Trustee;
     Mary Porcher, Rene Ravenel, wit. Mar Set 3: 294-299

Wilson, William & Hannah Andrews, 25 June 1743. St. Hel PR

Wilson, Seth, son of John & Dinah, and Mary Evans, 5 Sept.
     1792. Bush R QM

Wilson, Thomas of Parish of St. Pauls & Sarah Ninion, widow,
     19 May 1744; license to Rev. William Orr; James Hilliard,
     of Charles Town, bondsman. MB Chas

Wilson, William & Janet Harrington, widow, daughter of Danll
     Shaw, 17 March 1747/8. Pr Fred PR

Winborn, Samuel & Naomi Stiles, spinster, P Licence, by the
     Revd. Mr. Alexr. Garden, 19 Dec. 1747. St. Phil PR

Winchester, Mr. & ____, 12 Feb. 1778. Pugh diary

Windham, Jno & Nancy Watkins, 2 July 1789. Pugh diary

Wing, Ed & Mary Lowry, 7 Nov. 1774. Pugh diary

Wingood, Charvil & Mary Sasseau, daughter of John Sasseau, 23
     March 1731/2. Ch Ch PR

Winn, Thomas & Mary Ann Gissendanner, 26 Dec. 1792. St. Phil
     PR

Winter, George & Barbara Howzen, P Licence, 10 Aug. 1745.
     St. Phil PR

Winthrop, Joseph of Charleston, merchant & Mary Fraser,
     spinster, second daughter of Alexander Fraser, Esqr., 25
     Oct. 1791; Frederick Fraser, brother of Mary, trustee;
     Geo Chisolm, Jam. Murphey, wit. Mar Set 1: 601-602

Wire, Hugh & Dorothy Mellichamp, 5 Nov. 1738. St. Hel PR

Wirlowbich, Andreas, printer apprentice, & Elisabetha,
     daughter of Alexander Segfrid, 24 March 1771. St. John
     Luth Ch

Wirsching, Abraham, widower, & Christina ____, 22 Jan. 1765. St.
     John Luth Ch

Wirsching, George Casper & Catharine Margaretha Kohler, Joh.
     George Kohler's orphaned spinster daughter, 31 Jan. 1768.
     St. John Luth Ch

Wisdom, James & Mary Yeates, 2 June 1779. St. John Luth Ch

Wise, John & Ann Mary Kelly, daughter of George Kelly,
     ____ 1799(?). St. Michael Luth

Wise, Samuel & Ann Beaty, widow, 29 Jan. 1778. St. Phil PR

Wish, Benjamin & Ann Thewtus Poe, 20 Nov. 1768. St. Phil PR

Wish, John & Catharine Singletary, 14 June 1792. St. Phil PR

273

Wish, William of Charleston, merchant & Anna Johnston, 24 Apr. 1797. St. Phil PR

Witham, Solomon & Francis Merryan, 29 July 1744. Hist Oburg

Withers, James & Mary Cartwright, P Licence, 22 Dec. 1727. St. Phil PR

Withers, Lawrence & Eliza. Beauchamp, P Licence, 10 Sept. 1732. St. Phil PR

Withers, Richard, & Elizabeth Paris, 10 Apr. 1755. T & D PR

Withers, Richard, widower, & Mary Arthur, of Parish of Christ Church, widow, 20 Apr. 1786; Clement Clemons Brown, Paul Murrell, wit. St. Jas PR

Withers, Thomas & Mary Carl'e Deveaux, 8 Apr. 1778. T & D PR

Withers, William & Rebecca Hattley, 27 Nov. 1755. T & D PR

Withers, William & Mary Culloway, widow, 1 Jan. 1762. St. Phil PR

Witherston, John & Martha Perroneau, P Licence, 11 Aug. 1743. St. Phil PR

Witten, Thomas & Elizabeth Stanley, 15 Aug. 1718. T & D PR

Witter, John & Anne Marriner, 3 May 1727. St. Phil PR

Witter, John & Hannah Collins, widow, 20 Dec. 1744. St. And PR

Witter, Jonathan & Elizabeth Hogg, 24 Dec. 1788. St. Hel PR

Witter, Norwood, & Loies Holmes of James Island, widow, 4 Oct. 1796; Francis Rivers the elder & Daniel Holmes, of James Island, planters, trustees; Jos Dill, Jane S. Dill, wit. Mar Set 3: 47-51

Witter, Samuel and Loveridge Wilkie, widow; minister Wm. Buy; bondsmen Samuel Witter and John Miller (Milner) of Charles Town, gunsmith, wit. James Michie, 13 March 1732. MB NY

Witter, Samuel & Loveridge Wilkie, widow, 14 March 1732/3. St. And PR

Witter, Thomas & Judith Banbury, widow, 26 Nov. 1741. St. And PR

Witter, Thomas & Elizabeth Powell, 31 July 1785. St. Hel PR

Wolf, Jacob & Appollonia Shuler [1740's]. Hist Oburg

Wolf, Jacob & Veronica Fluhbacker, widow, daughter of Hans Domin, 1740 or 1741. Hist Oburg

Wolf, Jacob & Veronica Tommen, 10 Dec. 1740. Hist Oburg

Wolfe, Mathias of Charleston, butcher, & Margaret Mattuce, of Charleston, widow, 6 June 1786; John Wagner, John Eberly, trustees; Thos Waring Senr., B. Yarnold, wit. Mar Set 1: 242-245

Wolferstone, Lawrence, widower, & Mary Christian, 11 Apr. 1744.
St. Hel PR

Wolff, Heinrich, merchant, & Sarah Stockel(in), 15 Feb. 1787.
St. John Luth Ch

Wolff, Matthias & Margaretha, widow Mattutz(in), 18 June 1786.
St. John Luth Ch

Wolf, Solomon of Charleston & Rachel Moses, widow, 15 Jan.
1789; Jacob Jacobs, trustee; Marks Lazarus, Joshua Jones,
Ayam Solomon, wit. Mar Set 1: 450-452

Wolf, Wilhelm & Catharine Cantzenstire, 27 Dec. 1785. St. John
Luth Ch

Wood, Adam & Sarah Reid, 6 July 1760.   St. Phil PR

Wood, Alexander & Mary Slokum, pr. Licence, 14 Dec. 1731. St.
Phil PR

Wood, Alexander & Anne Partridge, P Licence, 14 Sept. 1738.
St. Phil PR

Wood, Benja. & Safre Chance, 5 July 1774.   Pugh diary

Wood, George & Anne Smith, 11 Oct. 1760. St. Phil PR

Wood, Henry & Elizabeth Ellmes, widow, 13 May 1746. St. And PR

Wood, Henry & Mary Brown, 8 July 1749. St. And PR

Wood, Joseph & Mary Sullivan, 21 April 1766. OJ 1764-1771

Wood, Joseph & Jane Webb, 24 Dec. 1771. Pugh diary

Wood, John & Lucy Jones, 22 Nov. 1761. St. Phil PR

Wood, Joseph & Mary Kempland, 18 Apr. 1756. St. Phil PR

Wood, Thomas and Elizabeth Scannell, spinster; minister John
Fulton; bondsmen Thomas Wood of Christ Church Parish,
merchant, Thomas Cooper and James Osmond of Charles Town,
merchants; wit. J. Hammerton, 13 June 1733. MB NY

Wood, Thos. & ___, 21 July 1796. Pugh diary

Wood, William & Sindinah Boswood, 7 Oct. 1735. St. And PR

Wood, William of St. James Goose Creek, & Mary Hamilton, of
same, widow, 24 Sept. 1750; James Goodbe, John Young, wit.
Misc. Rec. KK: 169-171

Woodbery, John of Charlestown, bachelor, & Sarah Anderson,
spinster, married at the plantation of Jonah Collins, 21
May 1772; Jon. Horry, James Bell, wit. St. Jas PR

Woodberry, John, planter & Ann Scott, of James Island, widow of
Archibald Scott, decd., 3 Apr. 1787; Malory Rivers, Robert
Rivers, trustees; Richd Hutson, Benjn Gibbes, wit. Mar Set
1: 313-316

Woodberry, John & Ann Scott, widow, 5 Apr. 1787. St. Phil PR

Woodhouse, William of Charles Town & Elizabeth Fairchild,
spinster, 3 May 1744; license to Rev. Alex. Garden; Richard
Mason, bondsman. MB Chas

Woodhouse, William & Elizabeth Fairchild, P Licence, 18 May 1744.
St. Phil PR

Woodrop, William & Elizabeth Crokat, P Licence by Mr. Garden,
3 May 1737. St. Phil PR

Woods, James & Rebecca Beacons, 25 Dec. 1781. St. John Luth Ch

Woodward, Benj. & Margaret Wilson, widow, 26 Dec. 1733. St.
Hel PR

Woodward, Richard & Susanna Mazyck, P Licence, June 1734. St.
Phil PR

Woodward, Richard & Elizabeth Godin, P Licence by Mr. Garden,
4 Nov. 1736. St. Phil PR

Woodwards, Samuel & Eliza. Vaughan, 23 Nov. 1722. St. Phil PR

Woolcock, Philip & Jean Dewit, 12 July 1795. Circ Cong

Woolferston, Laurens of Granville Co., & Mary Christian,
spinster, 12 March 1743/4; license to Rev. Lewis Jones;
Francis Christian, bondsman. MB Chas

Woolford, Jacob & Elizabeth Tunley, 1728. St. Phil PR

Woolridge, William & Sarah Low, P Licence, 17 Feb. 1747. St.
Phil PR

Wools, Henry & Grace Poole, P Licence, 16 Feb. 1731. St.
Phil PR

Wooly or Wally, Thomas and Jemima Troublefield, 31 May 1742.
Pr Fred PR

Worley, Paul of St. Matthews Parish, Gent., & Martha Roche of
St. Johns Parish, widow of Patrick Rouche, 12 Dec. 1799;
Robert Hales, James Scott, trustees; Jo M. Caldwell, Ga.
C. Gignilliat, wit. Mar Set 3: 412-415

Worshing, George & Mary Cobias, 30 Aug. 1769. St. Phil PR

Wort, John and Martha Jenner, 23 Mar. 1739/40. Pr Fred PR

Worth, Ralph & Elizabeth Roan, widow, 10 Oct. 1739. St. Hel
PR

Wournell, William & Sarah Spencer, 26 Oct. 1751. Ch Ch PR

Wragg, Joseph of Parish of Prince George, bachelor & Eleona
Mouzon, of Parish of Prince Frederick, spinster, in the
house of Mr. Stephen Ford, 6 Nov. 1783; G. W. Ford,
Erasmus Rothmahler, wit. St. Jas PR

Wragg, Samuel & Judith Rothmahler, P Licence by the Revd.
A. G., 1 May 1753. St. Phil PR

Wragg, William Esqr. & Henrietta Wragg, 5 Feb. 1769. St. Phil
PR

276

Wrainch, Richard & Sarah McKenzie, 13 Nov. 1781. St. Phil PR

Wrand, William & Ann Spencer, daughter of Oliver Spencer, 29 Jan. 1758. Ch Ch PR

Wright, Alexander of Charlestown, & wife Elizabeth, only child of John Izard, decd., 25 Mar. 1774; Arthur Middleton & John Izard, trustees; Thos Leech, Charles Cotesworth Pinckney, wit. Misc. Rec. TT: 183-193

Wright, Benj. & Anne, daughter of Jno Gauntlet, 1 March 1739. St. Hel PR

Wright, Benjamin & Barbary Kibler, widow, 16 Feb. ___. St. Hel PR

Wright, John & Jane Keays, P Licence, ___ 1725. St. Phil PR

Wright, John, son of John & Rachel, and Jemima Haworth, 10 Oct. 1768. Bush R QM

Wright, John & ____, 8 June 1786. Pugh diary

Wright, Richard & Mary Rhett, P Licence, April 1734. St. Phil PR

Wright, Richard & Mary Butler, 25 May 1742. St. And PR

Wright, Robert & Gibbon Cawood, only daughter of John Cawood decd., 7 June 1728 (already married); Benja Whitaker, Thos. Lamboll, Robert Hume, wit. Sec Prov F 1727-29: 106-7

Wright, Robert and Mary Blamyre; minister Edward Dyson; bondsmen Robert Wright, Junr. of Dorchester Parish, Esq., and James Greene (Graeme) gent., attorney of law, 22 June 1733. MB NY

Wright, Thomas & Ann Hutchinson, P Licence by Mr. Garden, 27 Feb. 1736. St. Phil PR

Wright, Thomas & Elizabeth Bellinger, 17 July 1743. St. And PR

Wright, Thomas & Isabell Tomplet, widow, 27 Nov. 1744. Pr Fred PR

Wright, William & Sarah Howard, 19 March 1711-2. T & D PR

Wright, William & Catherine Craig, per Licence, 15 March 1745. St. Phil PR

Wright, William & Sarah Paterson, 26 Dec. 1745. Pr Fred PR

Wurdemann, John George of Charleston, & Christiana Dorothy Strohecker, spinster, 5 Dec. 1799; John Frederick Wolf, Joseph Peace, trustees; B. Casey, John Strohecker, wit. Mar Set 3: 396-398

Wyatt, Ebenez & Mary Fullard by Mr. Morritt, 21 July 1726. St. Phil PR

Wyatt, Edward & Joanna Ellis, P License by Mr. Garden, ___ 1725. St. Phil PR

Wyatt, John & Violetta Lingard, 21 Oct. 1775. St. Phil PR

Wyatt, Lemuel of Charleston, baker & Elizabeth Wood, widow,
6 Feb. 1798.   St. Phil PR

Wyatt, Richard & Elizabeth Lebby, 12 July 1787.   St. Phil PR

Wyatt, William & Rebecca Fogartie, 9 Nov. 1777.   St. Phil PR

Wymer, John Jacob & Anne Diedrick, both of Orangeburgh Township, 27 Jan. 1756.   Hist Oburg

Yarborough, James Dandridge, & Ann Miles, widow, 2 Aug. 1774.
St. Phil PR

Yarmouth, John & Sarah Bridge, P Licence, 11 Nov. 1739.   St.
Phil PR

Yarworth, John & Mary Livingston, P Licence by the Revd. Mr.
Alexr. Garden, 11 Feb. 1747.   St. Phil PR

Yates, Jeremiah & Eliza Yates, 4 Dec. 1797.   Circ Cong

Yates, Seth & Elizabeth Lemox, 12 Sept. 1776.   St. Phil PR

Yates, William of Charleston, innkeeper, & Ann Hall, 5 Feb.
1798.   St. Phil PR

Yeadon, Richard & Mary Lining, 5 Sept. 1771.   St. Phil PR

Yeadon, Richard, Gent., of Charleston, & Mary Adams, of same,
widow, 19 Jan. 1798; Joseph Lewis, merchant, trustee; Thomas
Tew, Wm. Yeadon, wit.   Mar Set 3: 216-220

Yeamans, Thomas of St. Helena Parish, Granville Co., & Dorcas
Fendin, 28 March 1765; Isaac Fendin, trustees; Robt Oswald,
Thos Hall, wit.   Misc. Rec. MM: 240-242

Yeo, William, bachelor, & Mary Smalaga, spinster, 17 June 1770;
John Drake, Benjn Perdriaux, wit.   St. Jas PR

Yerbey, Charles & Hettibel Kolb, 27 Oct. 1768.   Pugh diary

Yong, John & Ann Ervins, 10 June 1781.   St. John Luth Ch

Yonge, Francis the younger of St. Paul's Parish, planter,
& Sarah Wilkinson, minor, daughter of Christopher Wilkinson,
decd., 24 Sept. 1766; Morton Wilkinson & Peter Slann of same
planters, trustees; William Smelie, Andrew Slann, wit.   Mar
Set 2: 399-403

Yonge, Robt & Elizabeth D'Arques, widow, 19 June 1750.   St. And
PR

Yonge, Thomas & Mary Box, P Licence, 18 July 1734.   St. Phil PR

York, Christian & Miss Barbara Heym, 18 May 1742; Henry
Wurtz, Henry Straumann, Hans Roth, Peter Hurger, wit.   Hist
Oburg

Yorke, Michael & Jane Prout, 17 March 1769.   St. Phil PR

You, Charles & Mary Reed, P Licence, 11 June 1752.   St. Phil PR

Young, Archibald & Martha Simons, 22 Nov. 1726.   T & D PR

Young, Archibald & Mary Swince, widow, 22 Dec. 1776. St. Phil PR

Young, Benjamin & Martha Alston, 7 June 1761. T & D PR

Young, George & Anne Carlisle, P Licence, 17 Sept. 1730. St. Phil PR

Young, George & Ann Millen [Miller?], 20 June 1799. Circ Cong

Young, Henry of Edisto Fork & Ann Hill, of Orangeburg Township, 9 Apr. 1754. Hist Oburg

Young, Henry & ___, 10 July 1788. Pugh diary

Young, Robert & Hepsey Wood, 23 Nov. 1733. St. And PR

Young, Thomas & Margaret Marsh, widow, 11 Feb. 1758. St. Phil PR

Young, Thomas & Eliza Maria Haig, 4 Apr. 1794. St. Phil PR

Young, Thomas of All Saints Parish, & Eliza Maria Haig, daughter of Dr. George Haig decd., under age 21; Andrew Johnston, Thomas Mitchell, trustees; 2 Apr. 1794; Lewis Roux, Danl Jas Ravenel, wit. Mar Set 2: 334-336

Young, William of Edisto Fork & Mary Linder, below Orangeburgh Township, 2 July 1752. Hist Oburg

Young, William & Mary Bachler, 14 Oct. 1762. Ch Ch PR

Yutzy, Conrad & Magdalene Warner, both of Orangeburgh Township, 16 July 1754. Hist Oburg

Zahler, Jacob & Ann Cobia, 15 Jan. 1789. St. Phil PR

Zeigler, Bernard & Anne Mary Wedlin, widow, both lately come from Germany, ___ 1753. Hist Oburg

INDEX

Barry (cont.)
Martha 12
Bart, Ann 58
Catharina 118
Barth, Johannes 143
Barthe, Elizabeth 184
Bartholomew, Ursula 214
Bartin, Ann 58
Catharina 118
Barton, Anne 45, 224
Elizabeth 21, 183, 239
Hannah 266
Mary 128, 194
Sarah 39, 84
William 84, 227, 248, 266
Bary, Mary 262
Bass, Thomas 214
Basset, Anne 85
Nathan (Revd. Mr.) 57
Bateman, (?) 256
Bates, Ann 136, 260
Eliz. Richmd. 13
Sarah 170
Batsford, Bridget 98
Batterson, Eliza. 12
Battoon, Elizabeth 165, 189
Sarah 145, 189
Bauer, Maria 62
Baumann, Margaretha 63
Baumannin, Margaretha 63
Bay, E. H. 247
Elihu Hall 90
Sarah H. 101
Sarah Hartley 247
Bayley, Benjn 198
Baynard, Elizabeth 168
Beacons, Rebecca 276
Beadon, Grace 197
Beaird, Elizabeth 13
Matthew 99
Beal, Catherine 101
Beale, Hannah 31
Bealer, Elizabeth 186
Beard, Mary 12
Bearirn, Ann 42
Bearman, Anne 19
Elizabeth 170
Bearsley, Mary 99
Beatty, William 109
Beaty, Ann 138, 273
Beauchamp, Eliza. 274
Elizabeth 170
Magdalen 50, 137
Beaver, Mary-Anne 187
Beck, Sarah 258
Beckett, Mary 272
Sarah 38
Beckmuss, Mary 178
Beckworth, Eleanor 157
Beddise, Elizabeth 116
Bedel, Hepziba 204
Bedgegood, Ann Mary 257
Bedon, Henry 93, 133
John R. 93
Mary 39, 241

Bedon (cont.)
Richard 244
Sarah 253
Stephen 133
Stephen, Jr. 93
Bee, Jane 148
John 57
Joseph 15, 21
Martha 5, 47
Mary 15
Rachel 125
Rebeccah 123
Sarah 39
Thomas 73
Beech, Mary 185
Beedle, Ann 99
Beekman, Barnard 45
Charles Desel 45
Samuel 45
Beesley, Bethia 2
Beil, Mary 25
Belin, Allard 62
Jams. 27
Mary 27
Sarah 4
Bell, (?) 53
Ann 102
Anna 252
Anne 153
Benina 141
Daniel 251
Elijah 72
Eliz. (Mrs.) 21, 30
Elizabeth 104
James 19, 160, 176, 275
John 44
Joseph 15
Mary 21, 65
Mary Ann 64
Thomas 87
William 15, 102
Wm. 15, 136, 168
Bellamy, Mary 4, 190
Bellenger, Edmond 35
Edmund 253
Edmund, Jr. 35
Esther 35
Mary 253
Sarah Esther 35
Bellinger, B. B. 222
Elizabeth 60, 75, 277
Elizabeth Pinckney 253
Lucia 229
Lucy 213
Mary 75, 140, 161
Rebecca 103
Susannah 129
Benet, Martha 212
Mary 16
Susannah 150
Benion, Sarah 175
Benison, Jane 21
Mary 93
Sarah 190
Bennet, Charlotte 142

Bennet (cont.)
  Hannah 252
  Mary 30, 100, 149
  Sarah 234
Bennett, Ann 33, 170
  Elizabeth 77, 92, 93
  John 77
  Mary 16
  Nancy 170
  Sarah 179, 196
  Thomas 33, 170
Bennison, Mary 93
Bennitt, Rebecca 216
Bennoit, Mary 141
Benoist, Margaret 242
  Mary 240
  Mary Magdalen 271
  Peter 16, 17, 37
Benson, Matilda 13
Bent, Ann 121
Bentham, Jas 169
Benton, Betsy 29
  Jane (?) 27
Berbant, John 251
Berches, Ann 32
Beresford, Mary 141
Berewic, Ann Eliza 149
Berkley, Elizabeth 103
  John 103
Bernard, Esther 150
  Paul 170
  Penelope 116
Bernardo, Elizabeth 225
Bernhard, Christina Rosina 71
  John 71
Berrisford, Elizabeth 61
Berry, Hannah 120
Bertram, Mary 141
Berwick, Ann Eliza 149
Besseleu, Anthony 85
Besselleu, Susannah 95
Bessellew, Mary 267
Bessileau, Susannah 95
Bessilew, Mary 168
Best, Sarah 82
Bestat, Hannah 160
Beswicke, Anne 265
  John 119
Beter, Catharina 169
Beterin, Catharina 169
Betham, (?) (Revd. Mr.) 45, 58,
    134
  R. (Revd. Mr.) 14
  Robert (Revd.) 31, 40, 53,
    94, 112, 117, 127, 146,
    160, 161, 182
  Robt. (Revd.) 33, 48, 53, 67,
    81, 88, 135, 152, 153, 154,
    174, 188, 214, 233, 236,
    252, 258, 271, 272
Betterson, Elizabeth 80
Betz, Christian Barbara 164
  Elisabetha 231
Betzin, Christian Barbara 164
Bevel, Elizabeth 118

Bew, Charlotte 145
Biddys, M. 177
Bine, Mary Hester 250
Binnie, Rebecca Hannah 203
Bint, Anne 79
Birch, Sarah 16
Birckmayer, Maria Catharine
    185
Birckmayerin, Maria Catharine
    185
Bird, Anne 38
  Mary 197
Birkett, Louisa 208
Birmire, Mary 44
Bishop, Ann 82, 265
Bisset, Ann 85
  Mary 39
  Susannah 165
Black, Ann 25, 162, 171
  Ann Mowhinny 80
  Anne Maria 94
  Elizabeth 148
  Hannah 1
  Isabella 252
  Joseph 3
  Rebecca 230
  Susannah 66
  Wm. 36
Blackledge, Mary 253
Blacklock, William 43
Blackstock, Wm. 162
Blackwell, Dorathy 230
  Mehetabel 49
  Michal 49
  Samuel 49
Blain, Mary 235
Blair, Anne 262
  Lucia 36
  Mary 207
Blake, Agnes 161
  Ann 149, 219
  Anne 236
  Daniel 36
  Elizabeth 76
  Frances 245
  Jno 128, 272
  John 19, 22, 201, 272
  Mary 148, 213
  Richard 149
  Richard, Jr. 149, 228
  Sarah 22, 202
Blakeley, Mary 158
Blakeway, William 154
Blalock, Rachel 110
Blamyre, Mary 277
Blanchard, Elizabeth 146
  Stephen 146
  Susannah 134
Bland, Elizabeth 180, 205,
    209
  Elizth 180
Blanern, Maria 265
Blundall, Martha 224
Blunt, Jane 164
Blyth, Jo 29

Blyth (cont.)
  Joseph 45
  Thomas 19
Blythe, Joseph 126
Boast, Sarah 169
Boatright, Sarah 61
Bochet, Frances 89
  Henry 211
  Lewis 83
  Mary 206
Bochett, Ann 11
  Elizabeth 181
  Frances 105
  Henry 11
  Mary 59, 248
Bocquet, Mary 96
  Peter 25
Boddett, Elizabeth 30
Boddicott, Ann 210
Boddington, Sophia 40
Boden, Mary 245
Bodington, Elizabeth 65
  Sarah 62
Boggs, Rebekah 76
Bohler, Jacob 92
  Magdalena 92
Bohn, Margaretha 220
Bohner, Barbra 144
Bohnin, Margaretha 220
Bohun, Elizabeth 95
Boineau, Eth. Madalen 260
  Judith 20
  Magdalen 177
  Mary 71, 224
  Michael 55, 186, 224, 260
  Micheal, Sr. 20
  Michl. 71, 177
  Stephen 20
Boissard, Ann Judith 56
Boisseau, Catharine 68
  John 105
Boissures, Pn. 193
Bold, Mary 22
Bollard, Elizabeth 31
  Mary Chris'n 72
Bollen, Sara 164
Boller, Martha 134
Bomgardner, Margaret 98
Bon Jon, Jacob (Hon.) 155
  Sarah 155
Bona, Judith 132
  Priscilla 108
Bond, Catherine 38, 92
  Charlotte 208
  Elizabeth 208
  George Paddon (Maj.) 181
  Hester 213
  Rebecca 205
  Robt. 238
  Susannah 204
Bonham, Hannah 204
Bonhost Elizabeth 21, 37
  Jane 20
  Susannah 47
Bonhoste, Hester 21

Bonhoste (cont.)
  Jacob 83
  Mary 108, 131
Bonneau, (?) (Mrs.) 236
  Anthony 150
  Arnoldus 169
  Benjamin 138
  Catharine 43, 138
  Elizabeth 227, 256
  Hester 164, 169
  Josiah 197
  Judith 259
  Magdalene 105
  Margaret Henrietta 6
  Mary 6, 197, 223, 272
  Peter 126
  Rene 28
  Samuel 138
  Sarah 124
  Sarah Henrietta 96
  Susannah 25, 247
  William 97
Bonnefons, Elizabeth Sarah
  140
Bonnell, Honora 12
Bonner, Arrabella 140
Bonnetheau, Jane 10
Bonniett, Ann 257
Bonny, Ann 127
Bonsall, Ann 202
  Saml 202
Boomer, Ann 47
  Christian 44
  Dorothy 165
  Eliz. 237
Boon, Esther 156
  Wm. 220
Boone, Capers 83
  Elizabeth 54
  James 19, 21
  Jane 71
  John 22, 267
  Lucy 261
  Lydia 83
  Mary 22, 54, 71, 83, 267
  Rebecca 154
  Saml 21
  Sarah 80, 120
  Susanna 87, 89, 267
  Susannah 17, 71
  Thomas 22, 54, 71, 89,
    131, 249, 267
  Thos. 7, 54
  Thos., Jr. 89, 177
  William 21, 54, 83
  Wm., Jr. 154
Booner, John 134
Booth, Catherine 74
  Margaret 28
Boquet, Catharine 253
Boquette, Ann 258
Bordeau, Elizh. 60
Bordon, Elizabeth 6
Borland, Jannet 38
Boshat, Nicholas 206, 246

Bosher, Sarah 159, 170
Bossard, Anne 62
  Elizabeth 182
  John 62, 183
  Sarah 224
Boston, Dinah 112
Boswood, Elizabeth 37
  Mary 170
  Nancy 3
  Sindinah 275
Bothwell, Susannah 126
Botilou, Margret 178
Boucheay, Marie 166
Bouchet, Joseph 166
Bounetheau, Ann 174
Bourau, Anthoine 69
Bourdeaux, Daniel 63
  Eliza 137
  Eliz'th 60
  Esther 241
  J. 24
Bourget, Susannah 196
Bourgett, Daniel 9
  Rachael 200
Bourke, Thoms 128
Bourlay, James 23
Bourquin, Elizabeth 266
Boutwell, Joseph 20
Bowdon, Mary 34
Bowen, Ephe 267
Bower, Agnew 153
  Alexander 43
  Eliza 260
  Patrick 63
Bowler, Eliza 48
  John 127
  Martha 134
  Sarah 245
Bowman, Ann 265
  Catharine 246
  Catherine 237
  Elizbth 43
  Elizth. 162
  James 101
  Margaret 242
  Martha 95
  Mary 19, 79
  Samuel 30
  Wm. 101
Bowry, Anne 239
Box, Mary 278
Boyce, Elizabeth 255
Boyd, Ann 61, 66
  Nancy 135
  William 135
Boyden, Catherine 214
Boyer, Mary 110
Boyland, Jane 181
Boylston, Mary Eliza 214
Brabant, Jean 70
Bradford, Jas 162
Bradley, Jane 11
Bradsher, Elizabeth 131
Bradwell, Elizabeth 86
  Harriet 86

Bradwell (cont.)
  Isaac 86
  Jacob 86
  John 86
  Nathl., Jr. 215
  Sarah 86
Brailsford, Jos. 110
  Samuel 14
  Sarah 222
Braithwaite, Sarah 71
Braley, Rachel 204
Bramston, Mary 25
Brand, Mary 133
Brandford, Ann 135
  Susannah 116
Brandt, Maria Margaretha 220
Brandtin, Maria Margaretha
  220
Branford, Anne 124, 167
  Barnaby 234
  Elizabeth 122
  Martha 30
  Mary 226
  Mary B. 229
  Mary M. 234
  Molcey 73
  William 229
Brannon, James 35
Brasher, Lula 140
Bratcher, Barbary 208
Braun, Maria 1
Braunmiller, Anna 265
Braunmillerin, Anna 265
Bray, Sarah 162
Brazer, William 246
Breed, Mary 8
  Sarah 175
Bregar, Hannah 229
Bregard, Keziah 227
Bremar, Eliza Harry 90
  Elizabeth 144, 148
  Francis 241
  James 144
  Martha 150, 223
  Mary 164
  Sarah 2
Breneau, Ann 261
Brersford, Susannah 119
Breton, Mary Eyre 141
Bretten, Elizabeth 128
Bretton, Martha 228
Brevard, Joseph 69
Brewton, Eliza. 54
  Elizabeth 175
  Frances 197
  Mary 57, 135
  Rebecca 180, 212
  Ruth 197
Brian, Mary 137
Brick, Margaret 92
Brickell, James 128, 205
Brickles, Sarah 163
Bridge, Sarah 278
Bridget, Elizabeth 80
Bridie, Mary 195

Bull (cont.)
  Lucia 104
  Martha 177
  Mary 33, 217
  Stephen 31, 90, 240
  Stephen, Jr. 140
  Stephen, Sr. 140
Bullard, Elizabeth 270
  Griffeth 200
Bullein, Mary 70
Bullen, Catherine 206
Bullin, Susanna 139
Bulline, John, Sr. 215
  Nath. 21
  Susannah 226
  Thomas 215
Bulloch, Eleanor 201
Bullock, Mary 74
  Mary Ann 86
  Sarah 271
Buluck, Elizabeth 203
Bunch, Naomy 137
Bunker, Catherine 123
Burce, Mary 103
Burckhardt, Anna Maria 258
  Johann 258
Burdell, Elizabeth 12
  John 248
  Robert 26
  Sarah 176, 205
Burden, Henry 153
Burges, Mary 207
  Samuel 207
Burgin, Anna 3
Burke, Ae. 253
  Margaret 142, 143
  Raymond 142
Burkett, Mary 50
Burkhart, Katharine 131
Burkitt, Rachel 28
Burkman, J. S. 220
Burkmyer, John 104
Burley, Sarah 79
Burn, Margaret 118
  Mary 159
  Walter 32
Burnett, Mary 94
  Sarah 124
Burnham, Ann 212
  Charles 253
  Elizabeth 78
  Mary 50, 74, 253
  Thomas 243
Burnett, William 205
Burney, Mary 179
Burnly, Priscilla 164
Burns, Elizabeth 81
  Sara 171
Burow, Mary 234
Burrey, Susannah 120
Burrington, Elizabeth 248
Burrows, Catherine 9
  Sarah 144
  William W. 181
  Wm. 88

Bursote, Elizabeth 92
Burt, Elizabeth 6
  Henny 154
Burton, Margt. 122
  Mary 270
Burwick, Jno 6
Bury, Charlotte 270
  John 37
  Margaret 246
Buser, Ann 183
  Anna 171
Bush, Agnes 105
  Magdalene 110
  Mary C. 168
Buskin, Lucy 99
Bustrin, Anna 171
Butcher, Isbell 211
Butlar, Grace 81
Butler, Abigail 262
  Ann 218
  Anne 172, 211
  Clementine 188
  Elizabeth 60, 74, 101,
    119, 120
  Henriette 193
  Henry 155
  Hester 75
  Jas Heny. 10
  Judith 82
  Mary 75, 277
  Rebecca 8
  Samuel 193
  Sarah 68, 110, 155, 170
  Thomas 203
Buttler, Rebecca 8
Buy, Wm. 274
Byers, Elizabeth 259
  Robert 152
  William 34
Byrd, Elizabeth 257
Byrne, Patrick 117, 232
Byshop, Elizabeth 80
Caborne, George 253
Cadell, Ann 123
Cadman, Ann 83
Caen, Dorothy 146
Cahill, Mary 191
Cahusac, Eliza. 94
  Susanna 161
Caier, Angelica 22
Cain, Edward 104
  John 42
  John O. 21
Cains, John 118
  Mary 118
Caldwell, Jo M. 276
  William 261
Callebeuff, Rachel 78
Callibuff, Mary 148
Callyhon, Mary 44
Calvert, John 100
  John, Jr. 61
Calwel, Maria 66
Cam, Catherine 35
Cambell, Mary 43, 193, 210

INDEX

Caveneau (cont.)
  Mary 224
Caw, Rachel 180
Cawood, Elizabeth 235
  Gibbon 277
  John 277
Cayer, Catherine 168
Cellar, Sarah 5
Chalcroft, Frances 246
Chalmers, Ann Bemley 140
  Elizabeth 126
  Margaret 186
Chamberlain, Charles 38
Chambers, Isabella 10, 194
Chambless, Jeney 152
Champanare, Esther 8
Champneys, John 173, 213
Champs, Francs. D. 244
Chance, Safre 275
Chandler, Elizabeth 159, 172
  Isaac 8
Chaney, John 19
Chanler, Isaac 101
  Isaac (Rev. Mr.) 101
  Mary Susanna 165
  Susannah 101
Chaplin, Elizabeth 77
  Martha 11
  Mary Ann 186
  Phebe 132
  Sarah 80
  Sarah Toomer 63
  William 133, 237
  Wm. 254
Chapman, Ann 221
  Elizabeth 97
  Jane 106
  Jean 161
  Mary 97, 241
  Rebecca 77
  Rebeccah 77
  Robert 109
Chapmann, Elisabetha 125
Champney, Jno 14
Chapnis, Jane Lewis 84
Chappell, Amelia 182
  Elizabeth 97
  Isabella 267
Charity, Martha 87
Cheatham, Sarah 227
Chechez, Jane 168
Cheesborough, Elizabeth 119
  John 119
Cheesbrough, Aaron 193
Cheeseburgh, Aaron 192, 193
Cherry, Elizabeth 271
  Martha 56
Cheshire, Mary 98
Chesholme, Mary 272
Chevelette, Ann (Mrs.) 214
Chevellette, John 214
Cheves, Langdon 36
Chevillette, John 70
Chichet, Martha 17
Chick, Mary 233

Chicken, Catharine 226
  Catherine 249
  Dorothy 239
  William 239
Chiffelle, Rebecca 201
Child, Benjamin 181
Childs, Eliza 78, 165
  Mary 5
China, Elisabetha 7
Chisholm, Alexander, Sr.
  129
  Alexr 25
Chisolm, Alexander 253
  Geo 273
  Sarah 129
Chittch, Richd 189
Chitty, Sarah 29
Chorwin, Charles 238
  Sarah 238
Chovin, Alex. 109
  Alexander 149, 170
  Ches 131
  Elizabeth 42
  Esther 11, 15
  Sarah 239, 272
Christian, Ann Modiner 40
  Catharine 187
  David 19
  Dorothy 135
  Francis 276
  Mary 275, 276
Christie, Ann 2
  Elizabeth 111
  G. 87
Churchill, Mary Ann 32
Chutthiar, Magdalena 264
Chutthiarin, Magdalena 264
Clancy, Joanna 84
Clap, Sarah 124
Clapp, Mary 171
  Sarah 124
Clare, Jane 120
  Rachel 122
Clarivendike, Hellina 9
Clark, Ann 255
  Bailey 157
  Elisabeth 78
  Elizabeth 53, 183, 222,
    256
  Gabl 250
  Judith 66
  Katharin 44
  Robert 250
  Sarah 245, 266
Clarke, (?) (Revd.) 71, 272
  Anr 203, 233
  Blanch 255
  Elizabeth 234
  Mary 36, 166
  Richard (Revd.) 194
Clarkson, William 239
Class, Sarah 265
Classin, Sarah 265
Clay, Mary 77
Clayter, Martha 155

Commander (cont.)
  Frances 70
  Mary 177
Compton, Elizabeth 48
  Joseph 97
  Sally Nelson 173
  Samuel 48
Connelly, Elizath. 161
Connely, Judith 53
Conner, Ann 201
  Lettitia 196
  Patience 270
Connor, Mary 272
Connors, John 231
  Sarah 134
Connolly, Elizabeth 154
Conrad, Sarah 77
Conrade, Ann 180
Conroy, Mary 124
Constantine, John 199
Conway, Elizabeth 186
Conyears, Mary 263
Conyers, Elizabeth 207, 245
  Hester 181
  Isaac 59
  John 245
Cook, Amos 50
  Ann 115
  Charity 27, 50
  Dinah 140
  Elizabeth 50, 67, 215
  Hannah 65
  Isaac 49, 50
  Joseph Tomkins 206
  Margaret 5, 220
  Mary 49, 50, 127, 206, 252
  Mary Eleanor 12
  Obedience 206
  Olive 115
  Priscilla 77
  Rachel 140, 152
  Rebecca 10
  Ruth 88
  Sarah 17, 49, 92, 117
  Theodorah 59
Cooke, Eleanor 134
  Eliza 31, 271
  Elizabeth 58, 222
  Florence 209
  Margaret 220
  Panuell 50
  Sarah 17
Coomer, Mary 80
Cooms, Mary 54
Coon, William 215
Cooney, Margaret 63
Cooper, Dorothy 260
  Eliza. 30
  Elizabeth 106
  Jennet 101
  Lucrecia 180
  Lucy (Mrs.) 167
  Mary 121
  Saml. 94, 199
  Thomas 158, 208, 275

Copio, Rachell 237
Copley, Thomas 50
Coppock, Abigail 264
  Marther 252
  Susannah 74
Corbet, Joannah 14
Corbett, Hannah Margaret 130
  Thomas 2, 102, 130, 261
  Thomas, Jr. 130
  Thomas, Sr. 130
Corbin, Rebekah 54
Cordes, Catherine 201
  Eleanor 89
  Francis 201
  Hester 71
  James 89
  James, Jr. 89
  John 89
  Mariane 201
  Samuel 89
  Thomas 201
  Thomas, Jr. 165
Cordoza, Hannah 88
Cords, John 273
  Margaret 97
Corke, Sarah 224
Corker, Eleanor 86
Cormack, Alexander 66
  Mary 25, 66
Cornish, Elizabeth 212
Corsan, Robt 52
Corvasier, France 51
Coshet, Susannah 229
Coslet, Ann 217
  Anna Grimke 217
Cossens, Elizabeth 206
Cosslet, Ann 217
Cotten, Charity 147
Cotter, Joanna 213
Cotton, Maria 265
Coulet, Catharine 57
Coulin, Sarah 107
Coulliette, Lawrence 133
Coursey, Mary 112
Courtonne, Mary 15
Couturier, John 69
  Thos 161
Cowen, Judith 239
  Sarah 116, 188
Cowley, Mary 54
Cox, Ann 9, 122
  Elijah 112
  Frances 263
  James 45
  Jno 206
  Martha 7
  Mary 110
  Priscilla 77
  Sarah 77
  Spencer 206
Cozby, Elizabeth 238
Cozzins, Mary 93
Crab, Robt 95
Crabb, Sarah 106

Danford (cont.)
  Isaac 62
  Margaret 126
Daniel, (?) (Mrs.) 253
  Ann 6
  Anna 98
  Catherine 88
  Elizabeth 195
  Frances 222
  John 133
  Marg't 121
  Martha, Jr. 154
  Prudence 204
  Robert 17, 154, 223
  Sarah 272
Daniell, Adam 222
  Frances 222
  Martha, Sr. 154
  Mary 233
Dannel, Kitsey 246
Danner, Hans 129
Danners, John 193
Dantzler, Barbara 182
  Jacob 182
  Jacob, Jr. 182
Dar, Sussana 8
Darale, Frances 199
Darby, A. B. 180
  Ann 61
  Joseph 95
  Martha 181
  Mary 21, 203
Dargan, Ann 216
  Mary 1, 130
Darling, Abigail 97
  Sarah 248
D'Arques, Elizabeth 278
Darrell, C. 109
  Elizabeth 243
  Frances 209
  Sarah White 267
Dart, Ann Amelia 157
  Elizabeth 155
  Hannah 213
  John S. 210
  John Sandford 110
Dashwood, Ann 77
  Sarah 267, 268
Dattwyler, Ann 215
Daugherty, Palk. 191
Davidson, Martha 190
  Wm. 222, 223
Davie, Mary Magdalen 268
Davies, Mary 24, 158
Davis, Catherine 47
  Elizabeth 130, 136, 229
  Harry 67
  Mary 41, 203
  Richard 120, 216
  Thos. 115
  William 67
  William Ransom 161
Davison, Elisabeth 116
  Priscilla 163
Dawes, Ann 7

Dawson, Lavinia 148
  Mary 165
Day, Margaret 91
  William 32
Dean, David, Jr. 27
  Esther 237
Dearle, Sarah 201
Deas, Chas Dundas 90
  David 60, 150, 217
  Henry 172
  John 180
  Maria 204
  William Allen 60
Debesse, J. J. 90
Deceaux, William 74
Decker, Mary 23
Dees, David 61
de Farcy, Jean 69
  Susanne Marguerite 69
Defer, Bet 261
De Filleau, Mary 115
Delabare, Sarah 179
DelaChappelle, Patience 97
Delamere, Elizabeth 10
Delany, Sarah 113
Delebach, John George 142
Deleback, Mary 142
Delebare, Ann 209
Delebere, Sarah 179
Delegal, Cath. 36
Delegall, Marsell Marg't 72
Deleisselin, Francis G. 200
  Isaac 200
Delescure, Penelope 72
DeLesseline, John 42
De Lesslienne, France 89
DeLessline, Joseph 118
Delesure, Penelope 72
Delgrass, Sarah 225
Delient, Andrew 146
Deliesselin, Isaac 62
De Liesseline, Elizabeth
  Mary 70
Deliesseline, Francis G.
  159
DeLiesseline, John 47
Deliesseline, John 62, 160
Delisseline, Isaac 23, 167,
  183, 248
Delky, Katharine 25
Dellamare, Mary 9
Deloney, Ann 271
  Mary 231
Delony, Arthur 237
  Mary 231
Delworth, Godard 139
Delyon, Abn 61
  Abraham 180
  Esther 180
  Isaac 46, 62, 151
  Judith 46
Demans, Phebe 193
Demoss, Joanna 256
Dempsey, Edward 111
Dendy, Mary J. 250

Donaldson, James 25
  Mary 25
Donavan, Ann 251
Donnald, Agnes 157
Donnally, Patrick 252
Donner, Margaret 111
Donnom, James 176
  Jane P. 24
  Jo. 109
  John 176
  Sarah 97
  Susanna 73
  Susannah 24
Donolly, Catharine 26
Donovan, Sarah 206
Doorne, Hannah 154
Dormer, James (Revrd.) 97
Dorr, Katharine 25
Dorrell, Robert, Jr. 267
  Sarah 267
Dorrill, Robert, Sr. 67
  Robt., Sr. 67
  Sarah 266
Dorrin, Katharine 25
Doryherty, Ann 84
Dossette, Mary 36
Dott, Sarah 88
Doughty, Elizath. Hall 48
  Martha 90
  Mary 37, 99, 264
  Susannah 236
  Thomas 51, 135, 176, 264
  Thos. 266
  William 236
Douglas, Elizabeth 242
  Kathern. 216
  Mary 19
Douglass, Jane 121
  Mary 40
Doujon, Eleanor 34
Douxsaint, Catherine 199
  Jane 249
  Paul 226, 244
  W. 43
  Wm. 256
Dow, Elizabeth 117
Dowdle, Mary 262
Downes, Ann 233
  Elizabeth 87
  Richard 233
Downs, A. 95
Doyell, Edward 44
Doyle, Edward 44
Doyley, Anna 95
  Daniel 35, 95, 103
Dozer, Abraham 67
Drain, Sarah 113
Drake, Edwd 96, 203
  Elizabeth 75, 222
  John 102, 226, 278
  Matthew 258
Drayton, Ann 195
  Anne 255
  Jacob 197
  Jno 197

Drayton (cont.)
  John 24, 68, 191, 227
  John (Hon.) 195
  Mary 88, 191, 272
  Rebecca 24, 195
  Sarah 116
  Susanna 24
  Susannah 24
  Wm. Henry (Hon.) 191
Drennan, Mary 200
  William 200
Drew, Elizabeth 178
Dring, Elizabeth 52
Dringat, Margaret 61
Driskill, Catharine 225
Drower, Mary 267
Dry, Sarah 230
  William 181
Dubberline, Esther 166
Dubbertin, Catharina 104
Duberdeaux, (?) (Mrs.) 181
Dubois, (?) (Widow) 40
  Esther 105
DuBois, Frances 20
Dubois, Frances 265
  Hester 105
  Martha Esth'r 4
  Peter 28
  Susannah 198
Dubose, Anne 214
  Catherine 69
  Daniel 69
  Isaac 89, 262
  James 105
  Joanna 89
Dubosque, Anne 131
Dubourdie, T. 253
Dubourdieu, Jos. 114, 253
  Joseph 266
Dubusk, Susannah 152
Ducant, Lilles 51
Ducat, Robt 51
Ducket, Lillies 52
Duckett, Robt 51
Dudley, Maria Phillis 69
  Mary 139
Dudly, Maria Phillis 69
Due, Ann 205
Dueston, Stephen 150
Duff, (?) 148
Duggan, Margaret 110
Duggans, Sarah 216
  William 216
Dugle, Rachael 111
Dugue, Judith 69
Duke, Benj. 20
  Elizabeth 227
  Mary 86
  Rachel 21
  Robert 69
Dumay, Jean-Elizabeth 15,
  176
  Martha 151
  Peter 176
  Stephen 106

Dumons, Isaac 95
Dunavan, Florance 218
Dunbar, Mary 92
  Samuel 191
  Walter 119, 174
Duncan, Ann 243
  Catharine 228
  Charles 135
  Eleanor 177
  Geo. 115
  P. 237
  William 215
Duncook, Bridget 168
Dunham, Hannah 228
Dunlap, Elizabeth 15
  Mary 268
  Samuel 79
Dunlop, Mary 192
  Wm. 85
Dunlopp, William 233
Dunmere, Mary 102
Dunn, Katherine 177
  Proscilla 198
Dunnam, John 49
Dunning, Ann 72
  Catharine 6
Dunnom, Jos. 24
Dupon, Gideon 247
  Gideon Faucheraud 23
Dupont, Alexander 137
  Ann 70
  Anne 194
  Cornelius 257
  Elizabeth 249
  Gideon, Jr. 257
  Jane 257, 258
  Jane Dupree 162
  Mary 23
Dupre, Ann 89, 228
  Anne 192
DuPre, C. 250
Dupre, Daniel 149
  Josias 20
DuPre, Lewis 159
Dupre, Sam 66
DuPre, Saml 160, 226
Dupre, Samuel 89
Duprea, Martha 249
Dupree, Saml. 4
Dupuy, Ester 29
  Mary Ann 169
Durand, Ann 249
  James 36, 84, 249, 267
  Levi 120
  Levi (Rev.) 35, 37, 43,
    174, 218
  Martha 36, 84, 94
  Martha (Mrs.) 94
  Sarah 208
  Susannah 268
Durant, (?) (Rev.) 189
  Benjn 109
  George 206
  Levi 208
  Levi (Rev.) 130, 147

Durant (cont.)
  Liev (Rev.) 93
  Paul 109
Durante, Levi (Revd.) 89
DuRofe, Mary 219
Durousseau, Susannah Maria
    163
Durtatree, Susanah 7
Dutarque, Catharine 38, 69
  Esther 83
  Hester 133
  John 71
  John, Jr. 83, 124
  Martha 174, 268
  Mary 27, 28, 133
Dutart, Ann 19
  Anne 154
  John 154
Duthey, Jane 214
Dutilly, Maria 24
Duval, Ann 190
  Lewis 260
  Margaret 188
  Susannah 15
Duynmire, Albert 79
Dwight, (?) (Widow) 139
  Daniel 50
  Daniel (Rev.) 13, 16, 30,
    33, 51, 259
  Danl 209
Dwyer, Judith 37
Dyar, Margaret 202
Dyer, Joanna 55
Dymes, Anne 64
  Rob. 19
Dyngle, Cybell 249
Dyson, (?) (Revd.) 21, 155
  Edward 277
Dyzill, James 191
  Susanna 191
Eady, Sarah 189, 228
Eagle, Christian 8
Eagner, Jacob 108
Eairr, Rebecca 86
Easton, Ann 184
  Juliana 48
  Mary 28
Eaton, Catharine 79
Eberl, Barbara 269
  Maria 236
Eberlin, Barbara 269
  Maria 236
Eberly, John 137, 138, 251,
    274
Eberson, E. 16
Echardt, Elisabetha 120
Echardtin, Elisabetha 120
Eckhard, Mary 169
Eckstein, Maria 15
Ecksteinin, Maria 15
Edee, Amey 76
  William 76
Edenburgh, Rebecca 80
Edgar, Margaret 146
  Susannah 184

Finley (cont.)
  Elizabeth 104
  Margaret 232
  Mary 80
Finn, Mary 4
Fishburn, Ann 152
  Elizabeth 218
  William (Major) 199
Fishburne, William 154
  William (Col.) 249
Fisher, Ann 250
  Mary 111
  Mary Ann 32
  Prudence 208
Fitch, Ann 172, 258
  Anne 172
  Constant 34
  Elizabeth 5
  Izabellah 159
  Jonathan 172
  Mary 153
  Rachel 176
Fitchett, Elizabeth 29
Fitig, Susannah 158
Fittermus, Mary 169
Fitzgerald, Anne 179
  Edward 153
  Mary 203
FitzHarris, Mary 44
Fitzpatrick, William 80
Flagg, Magdeline 102
  Mary 62
Flavell, Andrew 261
Fleming, Margaret 109
  Martha 47
  Patrick 3
  Sarah 70
  Thomas 224
Flemming, Anne 62
  Elizabeth 118
Fletcher, Allen 56
  Elizabeth 94
Fley, Mary 182
  Saml 208
  Samuel 124
Flood, Elizabeth 141
  Sarah 85
Florentine, Ann 257
Florin, Lucas 250
Florishton, Elizabeth 54
Flot, Anna 68
Flower, Amelia 149
Floyd, Anne 251
  Elizabeth 28
  John 251
Flud, Daniel 59
Fludd, Margaret 93
Fluhbacker, Veronica 274
Fl'y, Elizabeth 208
Fly, Elizabeth 136, 208
  Samuel 208
Fogartie, Hannah 222
  Joseph 83
  Rebecca 278
  Stephen 83

Foggle, Charlotte 86
Foisin, Charlotte 128
Foissin, Catherine 268
  Elias 231, 253
  Elizabeth 253
  Mary Elizabeth 256
  Rebecca 8
Foley, Catherine 88
Folker, Pegg 190
For, Mary 24
Forbes, Elizabeth 100
  Hannah 50
  Margaret 86
Ford, Ann 77
  Ann Motte 83
  Anne 126
  Anthony 47, 199
  Eliza 63
  Elizabeth Nash 185
  G. W. 276
  Geo 84, 248
  George 126
  Hannah 185
  Isaac 84
  Isc. 185
  Jacob 80, 81
  Jane 231
  Mary 106, 185
  Rebecca 236
  Sarah 124
  Stephen 227, 276
  Stephn., Jr. 227
  Stepn., Jr. 236
  Tim 8, 225
  Tobias 16
Fordice, John (Rev.) 203
Fordyce, John (Rev.) 15, 42,
    56, 78, 114, 131, 151,
    261
Forehand, Mary 241
Forester, Catharine 134
Forget, F. 55
Forgey, Frances 61
Forguson, Anne 243
Fornea, Mary 243
Forrest, Elizabeth 102
  Thomas Hunter 177
Forrester, Alexr. 112
  B. 120
  C. C. 36
  Martha 249
Forrett, James 97
Forrister, Martha 36
  William 36
Forshaw, Sarah 82
Forster, Margaret 29
Forth, Eleanor 5
Fortines, Simon 191
Fortner, Sidney 271
Fossin, Margaret 96
Foster, Blanch 42
  Mary 96, 166
  Tho 96
Fouchee, Mary 252
Founds, Sarah 163

Gadsden (cont.)
Mary 179
Philip 240
Thomas 36, 240, 247
Thos 61
Gaillard, Anna 267
Barthw. 244
Catherine 9, 164
Chas 89
Eliz. 229
Elizabeth 164, 196, 263
Elizabeth (Mrs.) 263
John 21, 89, 102
Lydia 71
Mary 102, 131
Peter 69, 151, 174, 208,
221
Peyre 89
Samuel 9
Theodore 9
Theodore, Sr. 89, 164
Gairdner, James 90
Gale, Katharine 13
Galloway, Mary 146, 268
Thomas 90
Gallwey, Thomas 90
Gambell, Elizabeth 159
Gandy, Margaret 57
Gannaway, Mary 152
Gant, Rebecca 119
Gantlett, Mary 258
Garden, (?) 7, 12, 18, 23,
29, 32, 33, 39, 40, 43,
44, 52, 54, 62, 78, 85,
86, 87, 93, 99, 108,
110, 112, 122, 123, 126,
142, 146, 147, 151, 152,
156, 166, 167, 184, 196,
211, 212, 220, 223, 224,
226, 228, 229, 230, 234,
237, 238, 255, 256, 259,
264, 265, 268, 276, 277
(?) (Revd. Mr.) 18, 37, 40,
50, 58, 96, 115, 128,
144, 167, 170, 185, 268
A. 4, 91, 126, 129, 196
A. (Revd.) 31, 77, 121,
228, 256
Alex 74, 138
Alex., Jr. 252
Alex. (Rev.) 1, 3, 6, 30,
51, 58, 60, 91, 96, 99,
124, 156, 175, 197, 200,
212, 215
Alexander 19, 27, 32, 44,
50, 53, 69, 72, 90, 98,
133, 177, 192, 213, 225,
245, 248
Alexander (Rev.) 15, 51,
55, 82, 87, 102, 104,
108, 116, 140, 141, 142,
146, 148, 164, 165, 166,
174, 176, 182, 185, 196,
198, 223, 249, 263, 269
Alexr. 86, 225, 241

Garden (cont.)
Alexr. (Revd.) 11, 15, 27,
28, 53, 54, 62, 66, 70,
72, 73, 74, 75, 81, 87,
100, 106, 108, 117, 120,
136, 140, 141, 147, 152,
153, 156, 170, 171, 180,
184, 185, 194, 195, 197,
198, 200, 203, 222, 225,
233, 240, 245, 247, 249,
253, 259, 262, 264, 270,
273, 276, 278
Ann 241
Benjamin 241
Elizabeth 247
Marg't Ame'a 83
Martha 185
Gardenor, Margaret 5
Gardner, Daniel 269
Garman, John 70
Garnear, Thomas 97
Garner, Frances 135
Joanna 91
Melcher 91
Garnes, Hannah 145
Margaret 66
Garnet, Elizabeth 240
Garnier, Elizabeth 124
Garrett, Elizabeth 218
Gartman, Barbara 157
Garvey, James 24
Michl 24
Sarah 202
Gary, Dorothy 85
Gas, Barbary 33
Gascoign, Sarah 143
Gascoigne, Mary 64
Gaskins, Mary 203
Gaspel, Charlotte 244
Gasser, Mary 165
Gaudie, Catherine 62
Gaultier, Francis 20
Joseph 98
Mary Henriette 165
Gaunt, Maria 133
Zebulon 92
Gauntlet, Anne 277
Jno 277
Gayle, Christr. 208
Gayssoux, Daniel 174
Gearing, Frances 75
Geautier, Charlotte 48
Geddes, John 39
Gegerin, Christiana Rosina
194
Geliff, Susanna 226
Gell, John 250
Gendron, Elizabeth 107, 126
Madelaine 126
Phillipee (Sire) 126
Gendroon, Eliza 89
George, Catharine 45
Gervais, Claudia 255
John Lewis 261
Geurard, Ben. 104

INDEX

304

Godin (cont.)
  Charlotte 167
  Elizabeth 276
  Judith 150
  Martha 31
  Sarah 237
  Susannah 140
Godwin, Mary 51, 52
Goette, Anna Christiana 45, 142
  George 45
Goff, Mary 239
Goin, Ann 79
Golding, Patrick 96
Goldsmith, John 98
  Rebekah 33
Golightley, Mary 129
Golightly, Culcheth 68
  Dorothy 68
Goll, Isabell 141
Golsan, Lewis 86
Goodale, Elizabeth 51
  Thomas 98
Goodbe, Anna 175
  James 275
Goodbie, Eliz'th 115
Goodby, Sirrah 172
Goodbye, Martha 60
Goodin, Jane 18
  Ruth 230
Goodson, Margaret 135
Goodwin, John 247
  Mary 72
Goold, Mary 158
Gorden, Elander 112
  Jane 180
  John 90
  Mary 90
Gordon, Alex. (Rev.) 119
  Isabel 99
  Jane Drummond 90
  Jno, Jr. 178
  John 90
  Penelope 98
  Thos 158, 254
  Thos Knox 52
Gordyce, John (Rev.) 45
Gossmann, Maria Agnes 112
Gotsman, Mary 113
Gotzinger, Maria 151
Gotzingerin, Maria 151
Gough, Ann 153
  Deborah 224
  Elizabeth 196
  Jane Carroline 190
  John 119, 190
  Mary 239
Gould, Mary 66
Gourlay, James 269
Govan, Christian 104
  Daniel 70
  Helen 204
Gowdey, Elizabeth 245
  William 245
Gowdy, Elizabeth 245

Gowens, Massy 11
Grace, Judith 229
Graceberry, Mary 194
Gracebery, Elizabeth 57
Gracia, Anthony 13
  Francis 230
  Mary 209
Graeme, James 277
Graey, Isabel 117
Graham, Alice 87
  David 61, 203
  Elizabeth 34, 246
  Isabella 165
  John 241
  Margaret 133
  William 36
Grandon, Elizabeth 143
Grange, Hugh 100
  Sarah 178
Grant, Catherine 85
  Elizabeth 200
  Frances 108
  Margt. 161
  Mary 245, 258
  Mary Esther 161
  Rob. 205
  Sarah 208
Granttin, Kitty Ecklin 149
Granvill, James 47
Gratia, Mary 230
Grattan, Catharine Ecklin 149
  Daniel 15, 149
Graveell, Jane 62
Graves, Anne 112
  Betsy 160
  Esther 192
  Martha 141
  Mary 121, 258
Gray, Ann 226
  Jane 174
  John 63
  Margaret 57, 110, 206
  Martha 127
  Mary 7
  Rachel 87
  Sarah 147
  Sibella 146, 147
  William 57, 219
Grayson, Elizabeth 257
  John 137, 187
  Mary 187
Gready, John 251
  Judith 248
Greaves, Eleanor 192
Grege, Mary 154
Gregg, Mary 165
Gregori, Catharine 220
Gregorin, Catharine 220
Gregorius, Elisab. Marg. 168
Gregory, Joseph 205
  Susannah 120
Green, Ann 212
  Daniel John 246

Green (cont.)
  Elizabeth 161, 219, 223
  Jas 91
  Mary 45, 151, 165
  Rebecca 83
  Samuel 254
  Sarah 254
  Susanna 16
  Susannah 121
  Thomas 70
  William 97
Greene, Charles 232
  Eleanor 195
  James 277
  Margaret 24
  Mary 202
  Susannah 101, 137
Greenland, Ann 113
  Elizabeth 103
  Martha 132, 215
  Mary 226
Greensword, John 174
Greenwood, Elizabeth 98
Grenier, Margret 230
Greves, Elizabeth Mary 227
Grey, Sibella 147
Grier, James 146
  Judith 146
Griffen, Sarah 27, 48
Griffeth, Martha 73
Griffin, Ann 123
  Elinor 202
  Elizabeth 182
  Isaac 182
  Joyce 56
  Mary 212
  Patrick 145
  William 132
Griffith, Edward 91, 162
  Martha 162
Griggs, Isaac 107, 237
  Mary 236
Grim, Susannah 157
Grimbal, Anne 192
Grimball, Ann 104
  Catharine 2
  Char 251
  Charles 101
  Eliz. 13
  Mary 56, 269
  Paul 106
Grimboll, Anne 104
Grimes, Eleanor 162
Grimke, Ann 52
  John F. 145
  John Faucheraud 52, 217, 261
  John Paul 52
  Mary 261
Grindlay, James 150
Grissel, Sarah 247
Grive, Elizth. 87
Grives, John 104
Groning, John 129
Groom, Mary 151

Grossman, Barbara 208
  Sarah 2
Grove, Janna 51
  Samuel 51
Gruber, Christian 19, 70, 85, 140, 181
  John 13
  Margaret B. 70
  Maria 140
Gruenswig, Mary-Ann 256
Grunzweig, Frederick 172
Guadee, Mary 96
Guellard, (?) (Widow) 257
Guerard, Benjamin 142
  Jacob 140
  John 150
  Marianne 142
  Martha 44, 90
  Mary Ann 259
  Maryanne 142
Guerin, Elizabeth 125, 228
  Frances 242
  Hester 69
  John 108
  Judith 105
  Marian 212
  Martha 105, 131
  Mary 16
  Mathurin 105
  Vinct. 238
Guering, Francis 75
Guerry, A. C. 160
  A. Caleb 105, 194
  Ann 70
  Anne 171
  Benj. 106
  Benja 24
  Dorothy 105, 160
  Esther 194
  John 106, 160
  Legrand 106
  Le Grand 218
  Lydia 238
  Margaret 42
  Mary 211, 259
  Peter 45, 47, 60, 63, 150, 196, 249
  Peter, Sr. 171, 259
  Theod 160
Guignard, Frances 82
  Gabriel 99, 164
  Margaret 124
Guines, Elizbth. 125
Gull, Hanah 6
Gullardeau, James 146
Gunn, Eleanor 52
Gunnars, Eliza 255
Gunter, Edward 199
  Martha 5
  Mary Audley 114, 199
Guthrie, Elizabeth 168
  James 261
Gutstrings, Barbary 118
Guttry, Mark 66
Guy, (?) (Revd.) 271

Guy (cont.)
  Ann 13
  Christopher 173, 247
  Elizabeth 37, 58
  James 112
  Jane Baynes 247
  Mary 41
  Rebecca 97
  Rebeccah 97
  Sarah 172
  William 106, 248
  William, Jr. 42
  William (Rev.) 64, 84, 97,
    106, 119, 147, 197, 213,
    231, 249
  Willm, Jr. 146
  Wm. (Rev. Mr.) 133
Gyer, Ann Barbara 76
H-(?), Margaret 238
Haberman, Margeret 137
Hackell, Philip 140
Hackett, Fraces 91
Hackness, Mary 249
Hadding, Jane 3
Haddock, Ann 50
  Mary 18
Haddrell, Alice 125
  Elizabeth 93
  George 125
  Martha 222
Hagin, Ann Maria 143
Hagood, Johnson 140, 158
Hague, Elizabeth 149
Hahnbaum, Geo F. 107
  George 155, 166, 251
Haig, Eliza Maria 279
  George 128
  George (Dr.) 279
  John James 128
  Mary 272
  Sarah 272
Hails, Robert 59
Haily, Eleonora 121
Haines, Alice 62
  Deborah 17
Hains, Elizabeth 174
Haire, Mary 107
Hale, (?) (Widow) 12
  Elizabeth 108, 203
Hales, Rebecca 27
  Rhoda 31
  Robert 276
  Sarah 219
Hall, Ann 278
  Anne 241
  Collins 89
  Daniel 167
  Dom. A. 36
  Elizabeth 203
  George 205
  Grace 133
  Henrietta 122
  John 176
  Katherine 1
  Lucretia 43

Hall (cont.)
  Martha 171
  Mary 12, 141, 188, 215
  Mary Ann 221
  Priscilla 247
  Thos 278
Halliburton, (?) (Widow)
    69
Halliday, Eleanor 108
Hallmann, Maria 107
Hallmannin, Maria 107
Halsey, Francis 179
  James 179
  Jas 152
Haly, Margaret 15
  Mary 150, 246
Ham, Elizabeth 187
  Mary Ann 268
  Richd. 212
Hambleton, Mary 170
Hamean, Elizabeth 79
Hamilton, Andrew 234
  Ann David 102
  Chs. B. 243
  David 92
  Eleanor 40
  Eliz. 123
  Elizabeth 92, 160, 202
  Henry 230
  James 120
  James, Jr. 48
  John 251
  Magdalen 99
  Magdalena 99
  Margery 120
  Mary 32, 33, 275
  Paul 103, 260
  Robert 33
  Sarah 72
  Serezel Agnes 247
Hamlen, Sarah 47
Hamleton, Elizabeth 136
Hamlin, George 33
  John 272
  Martha 159
  Mary 33, 218, 261
  Samuel 261
  Sarah 159, 198, 272
Hammelton, John 137, 193
Hammer, Margaret 122
Hammerton, J. 8, 53, 100,
    105, 138, 178, 262, 275
Hammond, Rachel 43
Hampton, Wade 59
Hanbaum, Elisabetha 58
  J. Severin (Rev.) 58
Hancock, Deborah 108
  Mary 17
  Mary 74
Hand, Elizabeth 87
Handlen, Edward 118
  John 117
Handlin, Thomas 27
Handock, Mary 97
Handshy, Maria 139

Lambright, Mary 248
Lampert, Mary 136
Lancaster, George 192
  Maria 112
Lance, Lambert 9, 33, 190
  Lambert Gough 9
  Lucia 218
  Rachel 111
  Sarah 190
Lane, Catharine 5
  Elisabeth 61
Lang, Ann Mary 209
  Mary 244
Langdon, Ann 154
  Carolina 32
Langley, Jane 164
  Mary 269
Lanneau, Basile 237
Lanson, Mary 1
La Pierre, Esther 116
Larimore, Mary 122
Larkins, Margaret 77
Laroche, Christian 65
  Mary 159
  Susannah 163
Larry, Margaret 178
  Mary 94
  Michael 118
  Susannah Eliza 117
Larrywecht, Ann Catharine
  144
Lary, Susanna 26
LaSalle, Peter 124
Lasberry, Eleanor 38
Lashley, Andrew 178
  Katherine 63
Lassale, P. 20
Latham, Sarah 84
Latta, James 38
Latu, Ann 257
Laurance, Jane 249
Laurans, Jane 194
Laurence, Jona. 146
Laurens, Henry 217
  John 203
  Lydia 148
  Martha 26
  Mary Eleanor 197
  Mary (Mrs.) 20
  Peter 194
Laurense, Susannah 160
Lavis, Lovinia 184
  William 184
Law, Bulah 74
  Theodora 72
Lawrence, Henry 69
  William 38
Lawrens, Mary 95
Lawry, Sarah 85
Laws, Beaulah 210
Lawson, Ann 99
Laywood, Rachel 3
Lazarus, Aaron 46
  Leah 46
  Marks 275

Lea, Isabel 80
  Sarah 261
Leacraft, Christopher Ed-
  ward 223
Leander, Marian 47
  William 177
Leason, John 191
Leay, Mary 79
  Susannah Mary 29
Leaycroft, Ruth 52
Lebby, Elizabeth 278
Lebert, Anna Margaretha 18
Lebertin, Anna Margaretha
  18
LeBoulinger, Mary Jane 68
Lebrasseur, Ann 196
LeBruce, Mary 63
Lechmere, Catharine 6
  Catherine 6
  Nicholas 6
Lecraft, Ameliah 103
  Rebecca 197
Ledbette, Catherine 10
Lee, Ann 14
  Catharine 37
  Elizabeth 161
  James 130
  Jas 208
  Mary 49, 154
  Maurice 150
  Sarah 63
  Stephen, Jr. 152
  Susannah 71
  Wm., Jr. 152
Leech, Thos 277
Leecroft, Jane 76
Leever, Catharine 68
  Jacob 68
Leevraft, Elizabeth 267
LeFond, Susannah 99
Lefoy, Mary 223
Legare, Eleanor Sarah 21,
  102
  Elizabeth 2, 6, 240, 264
  Isaac 69
  Joseph 240
  Joseph, Jr. 149
  Katharine 139
  Nathan 6, 264
  Saml 212
  Samuel 43, 102, 216
Leger, Elizabeth Love 128
  Jail 205
  John 205
  Love 261
  Peter 128
  Wm. 149
Legg, Henry 137
Legge, Ann 251
Legrand, Isaac 106
LeGrand, Mary Ann 104
Lehre, Ann 150
  Thomas 150
  Thomas, Sr. 150
Leibert, Martha 34

Mackey (cont.)
  Mary 220
Mackgrew, Jane 55
Mackie, Hellena 188
  James 178
  Sarah 178
Mackintosh, Elizth. 128
  Mary 49
Mackmortree, Mary 167
Mackpherson, Mary 244
Macnair, John 168
Macnobney, Margaret 44
Macquan, (?) 192
Mackqueen, Jane 14
Macrea, Mary 109
Macullagh, Alexr 187
Madan, James 144, 163
Maddutz, Elizabeth 96
Magee, Pattey 202
  Rebekah 41
Maggs, Saley 49
Magill, John, Jr. 168
  William 36
Magott, Madolen 87
Mahan, Elizabeth 141
Maine, Eliza 269
  Isabella 53
  James 269
  Letitia 269
Maitland, John 65, 259
Major, James 216
Makin, Charlotte 73
Malcomson, James 109
Male, James 130
Mallery, Sarah 35
Mallory, Jusiah 254
  Rebecca 33
  Rebekah 98
Man, Elizabeth 221
  Mary 73, 247
Manduvel, Margaret 116
Manigault, Ann 172
  Gabriel 88, 119
  Gabriel (Hon.) 172
  Harriet 119
  Henrietta 119
  Joseph 119, 172
  Peter 172
  Peter (Hon.) 119
  Pierre 105
Mann, (?) (Mrs.) 119
  Henry W. 104
  Martha 59
  Ruth 103
Manning, Elizabeth 145, 209
  Rosanna 108
Mansby, Margareth 146
Manson, John 235
  Margaret 102
  Mary 7
Manuel, Eleanor 50
Manwaring, Mary 96
Manzequen, Mary 35
Marant, John 136
Marbeust, Hannah 141

Marchand, Elizabeth 204
Marckly, Ann 72
Mardoh, Vertue 10
Marignac, Agnes 256
  Jane 155
Mariner, Deborah 3
  Priscilla 54
Marion, Ann 139
  Franc. 164
  Francis 139
  John 47
  Mary 105, 138
  Mary E. 139
  Paul 153
  Peter 105
  Theodore Samuel 26
Marit, Angelica 125
Markee, Mary 14
Markley, Mary 185
Marlow, Elizabeth 249
Marquess, Mary 183
Marrett, Eliza 184
Marriner, Anne 274
  Hanah 49
Marronette, Ann 76
Mars, Mary 106
Marsh, Christiana 233
  Margaret 279
  Mary 200
Marshall, Alexr. 16
  Cornelia 89
  Francis 96, 246
  Frans. 184
  Hannah 189
  Margaret 81
  Rachel 50
  Sarah 269
  Thos 266
  W. 27
  William 234
Marshe, Susanna 242
Marsingall, Pattey 135
Marston, Anna Maria 54
  Elizabeth 186
Martin, Ann 153
  Edward 66, 214
  Eliz 139
  Elizabeth 64, 180
  Findla 54
  Hannah 71
  Henry 193
  Jacob 150, 156
  Jane 182
  Jno 252
  Johanna Magdalena Elisa-
    betha 6
  John 176
  John Christopher 29
  Katherine 57
  Margaret 248
  Maria Elisabetha 243
  Mary 17, 44, 127
  Moses 127
  Sarah 178
  Thos 260

Martineau, Pierre 166
Martinin, Johanna Magdalena
  Elisabetha 6
  Maria Elisabetha 243
Martins, William 137
Marton, Findaly 83
Mary, Joseph 132
Mashew, Elizabeth 235
Mashow, Abraham 233
  Ann 233
  Elizabeth 233
  Henry 233
Mason, Abraham 245
  Christian 212
  Mary 216
  Rachel 184
  Richard 276
  Susanna 17, 195
  Susannah 65
  William 84
Massey, Catharine 215
  Elizabeth 14
  Jane 194
  John 157
  Joseph 192
  Rebecca, Jr. 270
  Sarah 199
Massique, Isaac 124
Masson, Peter James 52
Mather, Margt 256
Mathewes, Anthony 148
  Benj. 215
  Edith 167
  Edmund 97
  George 158
  John 107
  Lois 107
  Mary 148
  Sarah 107
  William 256
Mathews, Ann 86, 99
  Anne 204
  Anthony 154
  Benj. 46
  Benjamin 86
  Charlotte 229
  Edith 167
  Edmund (Rev.) 128
  Elizabeth 180
  Elizabeth Stanyarne 82
  Esther 83
  James 142, 154, 168
  John 168
  John Raven 82
  Mary 46, 154, 167, 168
  Sarah 55, 196
  Susanna 107
  Thomas 14
  Wm. 15
Mathias, Elizabeth 190
Mathis, Saml. 69, 248
Matson, Elizabeth 262
Matthew, Margaret 59
Matthewes, Mara. 97
Matthews, Elizabeth 9

Matthews (cont.)
  F. 144
George 86
  James 135
  John 168
  Mary 46
  Raven 86
  Susanna 84
Matthyson, Mary 263
Mattrass, Jane 117
Mattuce, Margaret 274
Mattutz, (?) (Widow) 275
  Friedrich 89
Mattutzin, (?) (Widow) 275
  Christina 89
Mauger, John 201
Maume, Peter 92
Maurer, Peter, Sr. 189
Mauzet, Amelia 61
Maverick, Saml 235
  Susannah Frances 210
Maxey, Ann 229
  Mary 196
Maxwel, Eliza 10
Maxwell, Elizabeth 10
  James Rivers 129
  Jane 129
  Margaret 126
  Sarah 129
  Sarah Glaze 42
May, J. R. 24
Maybank, Esther 43, 44
  Mary Ann 37
  Peter B. 169
Maybanks, Mary 37
Mayer, Maria 153
Mayerin, Maria 153
Mayfield, Mary 20
Maylander, Catharina 260
Maylanderin, Catharina 260
Maynard, Anne 181
  Charles 133
  Chas 181
Mayne, Martha 125
  Sarah 268
Mayrant, John 124
  Judith 31
  William 124
Mazick, Ann 47
Mazyck, Benjamin 205
  Catharine Mariane 273
  Charlotte 199, 205
  Isaac 90, 124
  Isaack 205
  Mary 41, 199
  Stephen 273
  Susanna 276
McBride, James 28
  Jas 243
McCall, Barbara 232
  Hext 45
  John 232
  John, Jr. 45
  Mary 39, 64
McCalla, Daniel 198

INDEX

321

INDEX

Miles (cont.)
  Annie 5
  Catharine 172, 173
  Eliza 33
  Elizabeth 9, 88, 145, 162,
    232
  Elizth. 162
  James 110
  Jas 239
  Jeremiah 269
  Joanna 239
  Joseph 9
  Josiah 145
  Lewis 239
  Martha 258
  Mary 110, 115, 119, 188,
    205
  Moses 172
  Robert 110, 162
  Sarah 73, 264
  Silas 239
  Sophia 162
  Thos. 35
  William 116, 172, 173
  William, Sr. 173
  Wm. 145
Milhous, Ann 115
  Dinah 48
  Mary 268
  Sarah 49
Milhouse, Elizabeth 139
  Henry 173
  Jane 49
  Rebecca 173
Millar, Anne 198
Millechamp, (?) 53
Millen, Ann 279
  Elizabeth 142
Millener, Marta 196
Millent, Marget 238
Miller, A. E. 89
  Andrew 248
  Ann 150, 268, 279
  Anna 197
  Anne 144
  Barbara 201
  Catharina 18
  Cathcart 168
  Edee 269
  Eleanor 73
  Elioner 269
  Eliza 34
  Elizabeth 23, 66, 165
  Esther 190
  Jane 24
  John 28, 274
  Judith 215
  Julia 53
  Magdalen 132
  Maria 38
  Martha 14, 95, 96, 199,
    247
  Mary 22, 34, 57, 118, 192
  Mary Ann 123
  Mary Clayton 248

Miller (cont.)
  Matty 186
  Richard 248
  Sarah 135, 152
  Stephen 95, 245
  Susannah 21
Millerin, Catharina 18
  Maria 38
Millhouse, Sarah 49
Milligan, James 180, 190
  Sarah 164
Mills, Andw 13
  Anna 236
  Eleanor 224
  Elizabeth 104, 114, 131
  Jemima 131
  John 174, 175
  Sarah 75
  Thos 78
  William 223
Milner, Ann 61, 223
  Deborah 46
  Elizabeth 46
  Jeremiah 90, 156
  John 28, 274
  Martha 250
  Mumford 84, 146, 251
  Munford 89
  Sibell 41
Milton, Sarah 195
Minchin, Humpy. 130
Mindemen, Anne 123
Minick, Rebecca 175
  Johann Georg 139
  Maria Margaretha 139
  Rosannah 81
Minorr, Martha Crofts 130
Minors, Elizabeth 247
  Sarah 64
Minot, Elizabeth 185
Minott, Ann 11, 84
Minskey, Rebecca 193
Mintz, Catharine 91
Minus, Mary 55
Miot, Alex. 16, 169
  Eliza. 21
Miott, Elizabeth 30
Miscally, Daniel 95
Mitchel, Mary 3
Mitchell, Anth F. 129
  Anthy 4
  Edward 176
  Ephraim 221, 248
  Ephraim (Major) 26
  J. 221
  James 62
  Jane 261
  Jno 122
  John H. 35
  Margaret 39
  Mary 147
  Ro 90
  Sarah 1, 129
  Susannah 26
  Thomas 279

323

INDEX

326

Oneal (cont.)
Elizabeth 175
O'Neal, Patience 175
O'Neall, Mary 188
William 188
Onsilt, Christian 209
John 209
Margaret 209
O'Quin, Elizabeth 15
Oram, Elizabeth 118
Frances 271
Oran, Frances 55
Orcher, Philip, Jr. 201
Orem, Susannah 251
Orems, Hester 204
Orr, Jane 36
Janet 79
Margaret 65
William (Rev.) 11, 145,
173, 195, 202, 228, 231,
271, 273
Orval, Jeanne 96
Osborne, Martha Ann 168
Osmond, James 275
Oswald, Dorothy (Mrs.) 59
Elizabeth 222
Martha 133
Robt 278
Sarah 47
Wm 133
Oswill, Mary 240
Ott, Esther 117
Otto, Anna 103
Isaac 129
Owen, John 261
Packrow, Jane 96
Pacy, Mary 239
Thomas 152
Padgett, Constantia 21
Judith 57
Page, (?) (Widow) 18
Elianer 241
Elizabeth 162
Sarah 37, 135
Paget, Constantia 21
Elizabeth 208
Henry 208
John 21
Pagett, Ann 82
Elizabeth 232, 254
Thomas, Jr. 82
Thomas, Sr. 82
Painter, Elizabeth 150
Hannah 122
Pair, Elizabeth 29
Pallett, Mary 67
Palmer, Ann 109, 129
Elisabeth 259
Elizabeth 91
Hanah 229
Joseph, Jr. 190
Lucy 52
Patience 156
Thos. 20
Palmetor, Deborah 38

Palthezar, Elizabeth 231
Paminto, Moses 169
Paris, Elizabeth 274
Parish, Helena 128
Parker, Ann 2, 214
Chs Danl 222
Elizabeth 129, 215
Ferguson 191
Grace 175
Jane 222
John 68, 181, 187, 262
John, Jr. 142, 222
Mary 44
Peter M. 190
Thomas 58, 222
William 150
Wm. McKenzie 191
Parkins, Elizabeth 159
Jemima 159
Parks, Ann 19
Parmenter, Anne 82, 153
Benjamin 19
Catherine 191
Elizabeth 238
John, Jr. 19
Sarah 20
Parrey, Phebe 136
Parris, Anne 59
Parrot, Mary 251
Parrott, Anne 210
Catharine 34
Parry, Barbara 96
Parsons, Elizth. 161
James 214
Margarett 41
Martha 149
Parteridge, Katherine 54
Partridg, Elizabeth 106
Partridge, Anne 275
Mary Elizabeth 223
Rebecca (Mrs.) 67
Pasquereau, Lewis 141
Magdalen Eliza 130
Patchabel, Elizabeth 159
Pater, Maria Evan 76
Paterson, Hugh 182
Paterin, Maria Evan 76
Paterson, James 237
Sarah 277
Patient, John 29
Patridge, Mary Eliza 162
Patterson, Elizabeth 10
Mary T. 93
Thomas 93, 192
William 93
Patton, Jno 134
N. 196
Paty, Sarah 139
Paulling, Wm. 139
Pawley, Anne 212
Elizabeth 114, 184
Geo, Jr. 27
George (Col.) 88
George, Jr. 186
George, Sr. 186

Pawley (cont.)
  Hannah 186
  Mary 114
  Percival 100, 192
Payne, Mary 26
  William 192
  Wm. 185
Paysau, Marie 96
Peace, Joseph 277
Peacock, (?) 105
  Newart 192
Pearce, Offspring 228
  Rebecca 94
Pearcey, Elizabeth 12
Pearse, Mary 261
Pearson, Ann 129
  Enoch 193
  Hannah 139
  Joanna 202
  John 193
  Martha 241
  Mary 86, 129, 241, 248
  Rebeca 50
  Samuel 193
  Sarah 88
  Thomas 193
Peaton, Rebecca 245
Pedriau, Mary 131
Pedrio, Lydia Ann 228
Pegues, Claudius 132
Peirud, Gabriel 69
Pelleo, Elizabeth 139
Pelot, Francis 128
Peltro, Mary Magdalena 52
Pemberton, Ann 249
Penciel, Jeanne Messan 193
Pendarvis, Brand 133
  Hanah 125
  Mary 75, 100
Pendervais, Mary 153
Pendroos, Margaret Eliz. 48
Pennan, Edward 90
Peporn, Benjamin 30
Pepper, Charlotte 94
  Park 109
Perdreau, Anne 105
  Elizabeth 124, 262
  Esther 262
  Lydia 262
Perdriau, Amelia 240
  Benj. 55, 89
  Benja. 78
  Benjn. 35, 70, 131, 175
  Esther 105
  Lydia 44, 116, 169, 175, 180
  Mary 83
Perdriaux, Benjn 278
Perdrieau, Lydia 167, 174, 231
Perenneau, Ann 50
Perger, John Henry 214, 215
Perkins, Elizabeth 237
  James 237
  Lydia 174

Perkins (cont.)
  Samuel 237
Pernneau, Ann 197
Peroneau, Arthur 73
  H. 100
Peronneau, Ann 190, 195
  Arthur 81, 83
  Elizabeth 90, 122, 152, 164
  Henry 80
  Margaret 73
  Mary 80, 81
  Sarah 264
  William 227
  Wm. 80, 83, 115
Perroneau, Martha 274
Perry, Benj. 195
  Benjamin 232
  Benjn L. 128
  Edward 73
  Edwd, Jr. 24
  Elizabeth 44, 145
  Isaac 232
  James 176, 232
  Jas 199
  Joseph 172
  Josiah 208
  Kezia 172
  Martha Phebe 186
  Rachel-Dadson 145
  Rosamund 73
  Sophia Frances 225
Perryman, Elizabeth 57
  Jane 12
Pert, Sarah 103
Pestell, Mary 40
Peter, Rebecca 229
Peterman, Catharine 206
Peters, Sarah 135
Peterson, Elizabeth 47
  Sarah 129
Petrie, Alexr. 236
Petsch, Adam 29, 251
  Elizabeth 29
Petsh, Anna Maria 22
Petter, Sara. 53
Pettigrew, John 192
Petty, Deborah Honor 205
  Mary 175
Peyrad, Gabriel 69
Peyre, Ann 6
  Floride 9
Pezaza, Hannah 191
Pfund, Ann 63
  Barbara 142
  Catherina 202
Pheasant, Mary 107
Phepoe, Thos 95, 228
Philip, Catherine 153
Philipps, Sarah 237
Philips, Catherine 138
  Elizabeth 26, 126, 259
  Frances 266
  Heinrich 265
  Robert 216

INDEX

Philips (cont.)
Sarah 211, 236
Thomas 237
Phillips, Eleanor 17
Elizabeth 132
Mary 255
Wm. 26
Phipps, Elizabeth Fitzgerald 235
Phorde, Margreatt 83
Phyfer, Barbara 22
Pichard, Alexander 196
Anna Catharine 196
Pickering, Elizabeth 157
Joseph 157
Martha 219
Picking, Mary 110
Pickings, Ann 165
Martha 26
N. 82
Piemento, Leah 56
Rebecca 56
Pier, Jacob 143
Pierce, John 56
Piercey, Magdalene 110
Sarah 146, 239
Pierfore, Mary 242
Pierson, Mary 193
Pigeot de Louisbourg, Jean Baptiste 79
Pigeot de Louisburg, Sophie Jeanne Marie 78
Piggot, Sarah 53
Pight, Mary 96
Pigot, Sarah 262
Pilkington, Gabl 60
Pinckney, Anna 67
Anna Maria 135
Charles 8, 46, 75, 263
Charles Cotesworth 172, 197, 240, 277
Charles Cotesworth (Gen.) 216, 217
Eliz. 8
Elizabeth 68, 111
Elizth. 100
Harriot 124
Harriott 68
Hopson 111, 135
Mary 18, 75
Rebecca 263
Roger 111
Thomas 75
Thomas (Maj.) 217
Pipung, Catharine 140
Pitt, Fraces 209
Rowdy 134
Pittman, Sarah 207
Pitts, Elizabeth 146
Place, Mary 230
Plante, Marie 96
Player, Rebekah 72
Thomas 38
Playstowe, Dorothy 171
Pledger, Elizabeth 243

Plunkett, Thomas 237
Pockington, Anne 224
Poe, Ann Thewtus 273
Poinset, Elizabeth 82
Susanna 122
Poinsett, Mary 31
Pointset, Anne 189
Poitevin, Hannah 191
Mary 183
Susannah 235
Pollock, Marg't (Mrs.) 256
Mary 194
Ponton, Catherine 198
Poo, Mary 66
Pool, Phereby 112
Poole, Grace 276
William 192
Poor, Christopher 2
Mary 81
Pope, Joseph 81
Margaret 118
Sarah 27
Sarah (Mrs.) 27
Popenhim, Lewis 144
Porcher, Cath 4
Elizabeth 221
Mary 273
Paul 257
Peter 89, 272
Rachel 67
Saml 73
Samuel 221
Willm 272
Port, Rachel 58
Portal, Elizabeth 200
Mary Esther 92
Porter, Anzy 85
Benjamin 81
Eliza. 107
Elizabeth 150
Elizabeth Clegg 85
James 3, 176
John 85
Mary 150, 259
Thomas 150, 259
Postell, Benj. 99
Benjamin 99, 201
Catharine 154
Elizabeth 60, 91, 92
James 60, 99, 199
James, Jr. 60, 99
Jas 195
Jas, Jr. 24, 195
Jehu 45, 123, 237
John, Jr. 100
Judith 101
Magdalene 271
Margaretta 272
Mary 95
Samuel 19
Sarah 99
Susannah 91
William 91
Postlethewaite, T. (Mrs.) 181

Ramsay, Martha Laurens 266
Rand, Esther 267
Randal, Robert 148
Randel, Hannah 210
Randell, John Bond 155
Randles, Esther 121
Randolph, Esther 153
Ranford, Mary 267
Rannels, Ann 49
Rant, Magdalen 196
Rantoul, Alexr 198
Raper, John 253
  Robert 225
Ratcliffe, Judith 41
Ratford, Mary 71
Ratsford, Mary 211
Rattray, Helen 45
  John 241
Raudon, William 190
Raven, Elizabeth 133, 256
  Elizabeth Diana 100
  John 133
  Mary 200, 216, 265
  Sarah 57
  Thomas 265
  William 256
Ravenel, Daniel, Sr. 205
  Danl Jas 130, 180, 279
  Rene 273
  Stephen 165, 261
Ravenell, Ann 51
Rawlings, Susana 195
Rawlins, Catherine 113
  Ellen 54
  Robt 265
Ray, John 212
  Peter 26, 205
Raynor, Elizth. 263
Rea, Mary 223
  William 181
Read, William (Dr.) 51
Rechon, Elizth 3
Rector, A. G. 56
Reder, Catharine 16
Redford, Elizabeth 149
Redman, Joseph 148
Reed, Mary 278
  Sarah 98
Reeve, Ambrose 264
  Anne 243, 269
  Sarah 108
Reeves, Ambrose 269
  Ann 269
  Henry 57
  Laney 120
Reid, Ann 241
  Catherine 229
  Elizabeth 31, 237
  George 107
  James 16, 31
  Margaret 166
  Sarah 275
Reigne, Peter 208
Reilly, Elizabeth 98

Reimers, Maria Margaretha 221
Reinhardt, Susannah 143
Reinhardtin, Susannah 143
Rembart, Lydia 137
Rembert, Andrew 8
  Catherine 106
  Elizabeth 76
  Gabriel 259
  Isaac 60, 106, 131, 132, 177, 206, 260
  Isaac, Jr. 76
  Isaac, Sr. 106, 131, 190
  James 71
  Judith 11, 71, 190, 260
  Margaret 132
  Martha 60
  Mary 206
  Nancy 69
  Rachel 257
  Sabina 246
Remington, Ann 33, 117
  Jacob 227
  Jno 56
  John 37, 114, 215
  Wm. 37
Remy, Martha 43
Rennie, Jane 94
Reschor, Jachanan 14
Revell, Hannah 54
Reyley, Eliza. 37
Reynolds, Amey 87
  Amy 3
  Benjamin 22
  Constantia 250
  Eleanor 40
  Elizabeth 75, 109, 253
  Jane 207
  Lidia 5
  Sarah 40, 240
Rhett, Catherine 178
  Mary 277
  Mary Jane 68
  Sarah 3, 85, 254
Rhodes, John 209
Ribert, Margaretha Katharine 12
Ribertin, Margaretha Katharine 12
Rice, Eliza. 33
  Elizabeth 187
  Grace 61
  Sarah 231
Rich, Elizabeth 225
  Martha 91, 191
Richard, Eliza Ann 203
  Elizabeth 226
  Genevieve 208
  Jane 54
  Margaret 33
Richards, Mary 26, 236
Richardson, Elizabeth 114
  Frances 98
  Henry 272
  Lydia 7

INDEX

Sheftall (cont.)
 Sarah 62
Sheily, Catne 144
Shekelford, Vollentine 26
Shelkelford, Elizabeth 26
Shell, Hannah 204
Shelton, John 20
Shepard, Margaret 260
Shepherd, Mary 8
Sheppard, Catharine 55
 John 8
 Mary 114, 125, 215
Shepperd, Elizabeth 162
 Joanah 18
Sheridan, H. (Major) 35
Sherman, Mary Anne 163
Sherriffe, Isobel 148
Shields, Anne 50
 Mary 241
Shingleton, (?) (Col.) 168
 Rebecca 164
Shirer, Ann 44
Shirley, Thomas 245
Shives, Alexr. 225
Shoolbred, Mary 225
Short, Catharine 178
Shortey, Mary 97
Shortt, John 169
Shram, Mary 243
Shrewberry, Rebecca 175
 Stephen 175
Shrewsberry, Steven 225
 Mary 60
Shrewsbury, Steven 225
Shroseberry, Catherine 244
Shubrick, Elizabeth 156
 Hannah 119
 Mary 77
 Sarah 233
 Susanna 15
 Susannah 197
Shuler, Ann Elizabeth 94
 Appollonia 274
 Catharina Margaret 118
 Catharine 261
 Catharine Magdalena 118
 Eve Catherine 137
 John 182
 Margaret 107
 Margaret Barbara 125
 Mary Barbara 255
 N. 220
 Susan 260
 Susanna 102
 Susannah 144
Shum, Conrad 243
Shumlevin, Mary 256
Shute, Elizabeth 27, 38, 226
 Thomas 226
Shutte, Maria (Mrs.) 255
Sidney, Alice 249
Sigwell, Christian 77
Silberling, Veronica 143
Silberlingin, Veronica 143
Simmons, Ann 77, 172, 256

Simmons (cont.)
 Anne 211
 Ebenezer 142, 189
 Eliza. 51, 232
 Elizabeth 63
 George 6, 54, 63, 102,
  172, 215, 226
 Hannah 187
 Harriet 142
 Jane 208
 John 35, 225
 Mary 6, 54, 100, 132
 Mary Ann 47, 252
 Mary Esther 123
 Mary (Mrs.) 63
 Patience 102
 Peter 102
 Thomas 142
 Wm. 208
Simon, James 174
Simons, Alice 125
 Ann 4, 87, 184
 Anne 47, 86
 Anthony 54
 Benj. 108
 Benjamin 30, 125, 168,
  169
 Cath. 272
 Catharine 125
 Catherine (Mrs.) 168
 Edward 30, 207
 Elizabeth 60, 70, 119,
  227, 256
 Frances 69
 Hannah 113
 Hester 4
 Keatg. 158, 180
 Keatg. Lewis 233
 Keating 135, 158, 207
 Lydia 30
 M. 158
 Martha 278
 Mary 151, 168
 Mary Esther 123
 Maurice 205
 Peter 205
 Rachel 30
 Rebecca 131, 244
 Thos. 115
Simonsinn, Elisabetha 107
Simpson, Ann 43
 Anne 238
 Elizabeth 147, 224
 Judith 88
 Martha 249
 Mary 191
 Sarah 31, 92
Sims, Mary 187
 Sarah 267
Sincklar, Anne 37
Sinclair, Ann 116
 Margaret 262
 Mary 240
Singellton, Ann 27
Singellton, Benjamin 230

Smith (cont.)
  Rosalie 8
  Ruth 199
  Samuel 120
  Sarah 44, 50, 120, 161,
    186, 192
  Sarah Motte 217
  Sarah S. 234
  Susanna 74
  Susannah 29, 267
  Thomas 29, 74, 111, 124,
    145, 202, 222
  Thomas, Jr. 181
  Thomas Loughton 44, 180
  Thomas Luten 198
  Thomas Rhett 233
  Thomas Rigdon 77
  Thos 180, 260
  William 36, 74, 93, 145,
    162, 197, 198, 204
Smitzer, Mary Elizabeth 237
Smoke, Susannah 257
Smyth, Catherine 116, 123
  Mary 234
Sneed, Robt 234
Snell, Elizabeth 246
  Frances 49
Snellgrove, N. 244
Snelling, Margaret 170
  Mary Jones 240
Snetter, Charles 140
Snider, Jane 255
Snipes, Elizabeth 233
  Mary 232
  Thomas 233
  William Clay 77
  Wm. Clay 91
Snitter, Charles 242
Snow, Anne 244
  Jane 252
  William 223
Snowden, Charles 23
  William 23
Snyder, Carolina 221
Snypes, Mary 195
Sola, Mary (Mrs.) 9
Sollie, John 38
Solomon, Ayam 275
Solzer, Rebecca 166
Somarsall, Mary 261
  Thomas A. 61
  Thomas Anthony 212
  Wm. 261
Somervill, Mary 176
Sommers, Humphrey 168
  Humphry 228
  Jno 168
  Mercy 228
Sommersett, Thomas (Capt.)
  114
Sondy, Jeanne 96
Souderecker, Elizabeth 221
  Elizabeth (Mrs.) 221
  John 93
Soverince, Ann Elizabeth 23

Spagner, Geo. 108
Sparks, Mary 80, 253
Speidel, Barbara 220
  Christina 65
Speidelin, Barbara 220
Speissegger, Elizth 203
  Maria 54
Spence, Agness 243
  Jane 107
  Mary 35
Spencer, Ann 132, 204, 210,
    277
  Catherine 256
  Francis 56
  Hannah 91
  John 79
  Jos. 180
  Martha 270
  Mary 111, 158
  Oliver 277
  Rachel 37
  Rebecca 180, 217
  Sarah 77, 276
  Thos, Jr. 5
  Thos., Sr. 46
Spera, Maria Margretha 12
Spidel, Adam 49
Spidell, Abraham 251
  Adair 251
  Christiana Elizabeth 45
  Elizabeth 236, 237
Spidle, Mary 272
Spierin, Geo H. 29
Splatt, Anne 148
Springer, John Casper 119
Springin, Johannes 143
  Magdalina 143
Sprowl, Abigail 244
Sprunton, Ann 215
Spry, Mary 204
  Samuel 176
Squeal, Frances 19
Stack, Eliz. 71
Stafford, Jane 161
Standish, David 235
Stanley, Anna 138
  Elizabeth 274
Stanton, Elizabeth 81
Stanway, Elizabeth 236
Stanyard, Mary 72
Stanyarn, Mary 181
Stanyarne, Ann 205
  Harriet 238
  James 82, 256
  Jane 226
  John 215
  Joseph 229
  Mary 130
  Rebecca 131
  Thomas 14
Staples, Elizabeth 19
  Joanna 223
  Sarah 241
Starling, Ann 24
  John 246

Starne, Eliza 205
Starnes, Minta 182
Starrat, George 159
  Sarah 159
  Thomas 159
Stathams, Mary 19
Stead, Benjamin 197
  Jean 19
  Mary 197
  Susannah 174
Stean, Chris. 7
Steddom, Eunice 122
  Mary 193
Stedman, Robert 134
  Sarah 192
Steel, Anne 131
  John 137
  Wm. 131
Steele, Lydia 138
  Wm. 78
Stehely, Elizabeth 98
  Mary 188
Steidel, Katharina 104
Steidelin, Katharina 104
Steil, Martha 200
Stein, Catharine 209
Steinin, Catharine 209
Steinson, Mary 36
Steirer, Juliet 122
Stelling, George 258
Stent, Samuel 22
Stephen, Margaret 104
Stephens, Ahatable Emerson
    197
  Ann 243
  John 27
  Mary 228
  Mary Ann 93
Stephenson, Elizth 147
Sterland, Hannah 79
Sterling, Anne 148
Steuart, Arabella 95
Stevens, Ann 24
  Catherine 134
  Charity 199
  Daniel 142, 235, 250
  Elenor 207
  Eliza 103
  Elizabeth 117
  Gough Oneal 158
  Jacob 256
  Jannett 260
  John 27
  Joseph 24, 239
  Maria 235
  Maria Willard 235
  Mary 232
  Mary Ann Elizabeth 46
  O Neal G. 190
  Patsy 136
  Phebe 256
  Ruth 256
  Samuel (Dr.) 232
  Susanna 12
  William Smith 232

Stevenson, Mary 113
Steward, Mary Ann 229
Stewart, Cs. 86
  Elizabeth 33, 179
  Esther 31
  James 179
  James R. 179
  Jas 61
  Jno 179
  John 224
  Judith 13
  Kesia 149
  Margaret 26
  Marian 148
  Martha 140, 142
  Sarah 67, 240
  Susanna 182
  Susannah 177
Stewert, Ester 151
St. John, Elizabeth 9, 31
  James 9
  Mary 146
  Mary Gough 9
  Meller 204
St. Julien, Jane Mary 169
Stiddom, John 241
  Mary 241
Stidham, Ann 193
Stidman, Susannah 249
Stiles, Martha 121
  Naomi 279
  Samuel 244
Still, Mary 114
Stillery, Mary 198
Stillman, Mary 112
Sting, Frederick 13
Stinger, Thomas (Revd.) 51
Stirling, Margaret 147
Stith, Eliza 198
Stittsman, Anne 198
St. Martin, Ann 125
  Elizabeth 22
  Mary 219
Stobo, Ann 119
  Ann Smith 196
  Eliza. 232
  James 60
  Jno Rutledge 232
Stock, Ann 128
  Rachel 145
  Thomas 57, 122, 128
Stockel, Sarah 275
Stockelin, Sarah 275
Stocks, Anne 94
  Elinor 263
  Martha 264
  Mary 90, 267
Stock's, Mary 123
Stocks, Sarah 250
Stoll, Catharine 220
  David 24
  Elizabeth 226
  Mary 158, 218
  Sarah 222
Stollard, Penelope 207

Ston, Elizabeth 210
Stone, Ann 169
  Anne 49
  Frances 209
  Hannah 45
  Martha 146, 268
  Mary 95
  Sarah 272
  Susana 261
  Susanna 10
  Thos. 189
Stonestreet, Julia Felicity
  51
Stongeon, Mary 18
Stoosin, Regina 139
Stopfar, Anne 183
Storey, Elizabeth 58
  Mary 229
  Rebecca 41
Story, Betsey 262
  John 101
  Mary 30
  Sarah 59, 140
Stow, Elizabeth 44
Strahan, Margaret 154
Straumann, Henr. 189
  Henry 243, 278
  Jacob 189
Streater, Elizabeth 125
Street, Elizabeth 98
Stricklin, Richd. 234
Stricland, John 32
Stringer, Thomas (Rev.) 51
Strobel, Daniel 166
Strobler, Elizabeth 179
Strohacker, Elizabeth 137
Strohecker, Christiana
    Dorothy 277
  John 39, 277
  Maria Elizabeth 39
Stronach, Priscilla 171
Strother, Mary 228
  William 228
Strouber, Mary 159
Strowmann, Barbara 218
  Henry 129
Stuard, Joppe 263
Stuart, Ann 55
  Elizabeth 23
  Henry 199
  Mary 7
  Thos 234
Stuges, Jonath. 146
Stukes, Martah 244
  William 244
Stull, Catherine 222
Styles, Copeland 90
  Rebecca 170
  Samuel 244
Suany, Hester 9
Sulivant, Martha 157
Sullivan, Ann 263
  Anne 217
  Daniel 154
  Esther 21, 168

Sullivan (cont.)
  Hannah 21
  Joseph 168
  Mary 275
  Rebecca 46, 158
  Stephen 46, 108, 160,
    236
Sullivant, Sarah 64
Sulliven, Joseph 83
Summers, Margaret 114
Sumner, Eliz. 226
  Susanna 166
Sutcliffe, E. L. 104
  Ellis 70
  Elizth. 143
Sutherland, Mary 18
Sutter, Susannah 42
Sutton, Ann 118
  Anne 171
  Constant 171
  Hezekiah 30
  James 245
Swala, Ane 54
Swallow, Frances 204
  Newman 259
Swan, Rachael 15
Swansey, Rebecca 174
Sweeny, Mary 178
Swieger, Mary 166
Swince, Mary 279
Swindershine, Anna Christina
  77
Swinger, Mary 166
Swint, John 66
Swinton, Hugh 4
  Margaret 16
  Mary Simmons 195
  Sarah 27, 109
  Sy. 44
Switzer, John Randolph 142
Syer, Mary 73
Syfrith. Rebecca 85
Syme, John 114
Symmonds, Hannah 57
Symmons, Anne 134
  Elizabeth 122
Tacy, Mary 258
Taggart, Mary 201
Talbert, Mary Ann 225
  Susannah 207
Talbot, Mary 207
Tallman, Elizabeth 28
Tamelson, Martha 176
Tamilson, Martha 176
Tamplereau, Jean 248
Tamplet, John 148
  Mary 265
  Peter 61
Tanveir, Lewis 72
Tapp, Ann Barbara 76
  Christian 246
Tarbox, John 258
Tart, Mary 42
  Nathan 10, 252
  Sarah Amelia 10

Tash, Maria 34
Tathom, Hannah 209
Tattle, Sarah 256
Tattnall, Sarah 194
Taveroone, Sarah 108
Taylor, Alexander 96
  Ann 47, 175, 178
  Archd. T. 201
  Archibald 144
  Elizabeth 83, 216
  G., Jr. 234
  George, Jr. 142
  Hester 81, 116
  Isabell 232
  James 101
  Jane 173, 218
  Jonathan 247, 248
  Joseph 231
  Margareth 56
  Martha 134, 152
  Mary 135, 172, 248
  Mary-Anne 4
  Rhoda 11
  Sarah 114, 125
  Susannah 263
  Wm. 84, 234
Teasdale, Isaac 68
Tech, Mary 143
Templeroy, John 248
Tendin, Thomas 249
Tennant, Catherine Caroline
  233
Tennent, Susannah 233
Tesey, Mary 258
Tew, Thomas 248, 278
Tharin, Susanna 176
Theus, Ann 149
  Charlotte 169
  Simeon 152
  Simon 248
Thomas, Ann 231, 244
  Anne 186
  Catherine 34, 185, 190
  Edward 111, 168
  Eleaner 46
  Elisabetha 53
  Elizabeth 79, 219
  Fras. 221
  Isaac 248, 249
  John 194, 258
  Mary 111, 118, 248, 249
  Sarah 207
  Stephen 19, 56, 266
  Wm. 206
Thomlinson, Mary 208
Thompson, (?) 253
  (?) (Capt.) 136
  Ann 224
  Anna 95
  Anne 187
  Christian 127
  Elisabeth 141
  Esther 56
  Francis (Rev.) 214
  George 230

Thompson (cont.)
  Hannah 253
  James 112
  Jane 101, 136, 230
  John 165
  Joseph 249
  Margaret 117
  Mary 116, 134
  Sarah Wigfal 7
  Thomas (Rev.) 39, 67, 162,
    199, 213, 237
Thoms, William 42
Thomson, (?) 56
  Alice 29
  Ann 70, 209
  Anne 37
  Elizabeth 70
  Giehne 114
  Jane 12, 70, 101, 114,
    163
  John 79
  Mary 47
  Rebecca 134
  William, Sr. 245
Thornton, Anne 171
  Elizabeth 151
  Jane 30
  Mary 217
Thornwell, Elizabeth 126
Thorp, Mary 221
Thorpe, Hannah 119
Threadcraft, Bethel 33
Threadcroft, Mary 9
Threes, Randolph 183
Thurston, Saml. J. 159
Thushee, Martha 188
Tidyman, (?) (Mrs.) 13
  Hester Rose 68
  Philip 68
Times, Mary 37
Timmons, Sarah 32
  Susannah 239
  Thomas 239
Timms, Hollis 217
  Mary 217
Timothy, Elizabeth 253, 255
  Sarah 166, 167
Tinnable, Ann 218
Tipper, Elizabeth 153
  Rebekah 115
  Sarah 91
  Susannah 233
Tippin, Susannah 245
Tisseaux, James (Rev.) 132
Tobias, Eliz. 87
  Isaac 151
  Joseph 141
  Joseph, Sr. 151
  Leah 151
Todd, Eliza 19
Toes, Benjamin 46
Tom, Katharine 192
Tomlinson, Arthur 191
  Jesiah 252
  Mary 191

Walter (cont.)
  Harriet 267
  Harriot 151
  Harriott 151
  Isaac 115
  Jacob 260
  Martha 267
  Richard 151, 267
  Richd Chs 151
  Thomas 158
Walters, Ann 146
Wandissen, Margaretha 149
Wanlys, Eliza. 41
Wannel, Hannah 65, 66
  Thomas 65
Wannell, Hannah 242
Wanton, Elizabeth 270
Warbeuf, Hannah 199
Ward, D. 43
  Dan. 44
  Elizabeth 238
  Frances 14
  Frances Caroline 14
  Henrietta 107
  J. 102, 251
  James M. 61
  James McCall 14, 187
  John 35, 61, 72, 167, 197,
    240, 262
  Joshua 167, 216
  Martha 72
  Mary 33, 55, 247
  Mary Colle 239
  Peter 14
  Samuel 36
  Sarah 42
Warden, Elizabeth 40
Wardz, (?) 129
Ware, Ann 153
  James 20
Waring, Ann 91, 199, 222, 261
  Benj. 261
  Benjamin 261
  Edith 261
  Edmund Tho. 234
  Elizabeth 19, 68, 78, 190
  George 181, 199
  John 261
  Joseph 128
  Juliet Lee 234
  Juliette Lee 234
  Mary 261
  Morton 103, 234
  Thomas 234, 261
  Thomas (Dr.) 234
  Thos, Sr. 274
Warley, Melicha 86
Warmingham, Sarah 26, 184
Warner, Elizabeth 255
  Henrietta 140, 263
  Magdalene 279
  Penelope 140
Warnicke, Ann 65
Warnock, Andrew 262
  Anna 16

Warnock (cont.)
  Magdalen Elizabeth 252
  Mary 14, 58, 121, 212
  Samuel 252
Warrant, Mary 147
Warren, Eliz. 118
  Elizabeth 171, 203
  S. 14, 132, 183, 225
  S. F. 8, 69, 89
  Saml F. 268
  Saml. Fenner 89
  Samuel 5, 62, 63, 76, 149,
    151, 160, 174, 190, 191,
    196, 206, 246, 265, 271
Warrin, (?) (Rev.) 23
Washington, Charl. 253
  William 82, 157
Wasson, Elizabeth 103
Waterman, Anne 12
Waters, Elizabeth 48
  Mary 270
  Richd 177
Waties, Ann 45, 232
  Elizabeth 253
  Jnt. 4
  John 62
  John, Jr. 166
  Tho. 176
  Thomas 214, 247
  Thomas (Hon.) 139
Watkins, Ann 34, 85
  Anne 179
  Beersheba 143
  Elizabeth 122
  Joan 107
  Martha 73, 155, 238
  Mary 211
  Nancy 273
Watson, Ann 224, 246, 260
  Ann Clemens 189
  Eleanor 111
  Elizabeth 100, 148
  Hannah 48
  Isabella 116
  Izabella 63
  Jane 115
  Jean 51
  Jno 59, 115
  Katherine 44
  Martha 59
  Mary 173
  Ruth 15
  Samuel 110
  Sarah 110
Watt, Ann 156
  Anne 156
  Mary 241
  Susana 7
Watts, Elinor 184
  Elizabeth 128
  Esther 150
  Rebecca 20
Wattson, Martha 59
Way, Sarah 176
Wayne, Katherine 83

Willson (cont.)
  Mary 161, 213
  Robert 161
Wilson, Algernon 82
  Ann 67
  Dinah 273
  Eleanor 227
  Eleanor (Mrs.) 227
  Elizabeth 1, 66, 102
  Esther 88
  Gilbert 40
  H. 229
  Hannah 88
  Hugh 243
  James 240
  Jane 121, 182
  Jno 48
  John 227, 273
  Leighton 130
  Margaret 276
  Mary 39, 40, 45, 54, 114,
    213, 244
  Mary Ann 32
  Phebe 115
  Sara. 229
  Sarah 115
  Thos 8
  William 97
  Winefred 245
Wilt, Maria Barbara 215
Winborn, Mary 265
  Thomas 265
Winder, John 24
Windham, Patience 22
Wineman, Margt 223
Wingat, Sarah 130
Wingood, Elizabeth 119, 198
  John 119
  Mary 10
Wingwood, Anne 90
Winigood, Anne 90
Winigum, Amy 31
Winn, Martha 37
  Sarah 266
Winstanley, Thomas 24, 102
  Thos 100
Winter, Margaret 138
  Mary 82, 164
Winterly, (?) 268
Winton, Ann 56
Winyaw, George 69
Wippey, Rebecca Sawyer 149
Wirosdick, John 13
Wirsching, Anna 130
  George 130
Wirth, Anne Marie 220
  Barbara 237
  Susannah 112
Wirthin, Anne Marie 220
  Barbara 237
Wirtz, Catharina 144
Wirtzin, Catharina 144
Wish, Elizabeth 240
Withers, Ann 26, 153
  Charlotte 31, 256

Withers (cont.)
  Eliz. (Mrs.) 91
  Elizabeth (Mrs.) 70
  James 91, 256, 268
  John 61, 186
  Mary 69
  Mary Ann 100
  Rd. 69, 135
  Rebecca 61
  Richard 160, 224, 268
  Richard (Capt.) 146, 256
  Sarah 224, 256
  Sarah Collins 256
  Will. 70
  William 69, 224, 246
Witherspoon, John 191
  Robert 161
Wittaker, Hannah 231
Witten, Peter 26
  Susanna 248
Witter, Elizabeth 15
  Hannah 191
  Samuel 274
Wittich, Charles 260
Wittick, Charles 134
Wittimar, Sarah 96
Woerner, Jacob 143
  Maria 143
Wolf, Clary 23
  Frederick 39
  John Frederick 277
  Lucas 133
  Nessa 1
Wood, Ann 87
  Anne 159
  Benja. 23
  Elizabeth 36, 41, 278
  George 66
  Henry 231
  Hepsey 279
  Hester 247
  Jane 241
  John 3
  Margaret 265
  Martha 23, 173
  Mary 3, 49, 114, 116, 117,
    195, 246
  Nancy 23
  Olivia 63
  Rachel 3
  Sarah 121
  Susanah 32
  Susanna 155
  Susannah 17
  Thomas 275
Woodberry, Jonah 22
Woodbridge, Thos M. 177
Woodbury, Mary 271
  Sarah 123
Woodford, Elisabeth 78
Woodman, Catherine 46
Woodmason, Charles 90
Woodroope, Ann 169
Woodrow, Christian 147
Woodruffe, Mary 25

ADDITIONS